Global Competition Enforcement

New Players, New Challenges

Edited by

Paulo Burnier da Silveira
William Evan Kovacic

Wolters Kluwer

Published by:
Kluwer Law International B.V.
PO Box 316
2400 AH Alphen aan den Rijn
The Netherlands
E-mail: international-sales@wolterskluwer.com
Website: lrus.wolterskluwer.com

Sold and distributed in North, Central and South America by:
Wolters Kluwer Legal & Regulatory U.S.
7201 McKinney Circle
Frederick, MD 21704
United States of America
Email: customer.service@wolterskluwer.com

Sold and distributed in all other countries by:
Air Business Subscriptions
Rockwood House
Haywards Heath
West Sussex
RH16 3DH
United Kingdom
Email: international-customerservice@wolterskluwer.com

ISBN 978-94-035-0283-0

e-Book: ISBN 978-94-035-0212-0
web-PDF: ISBN 978-94-035-0231-1

Editors

William Evan Kovacic is currently a professor of Global Competition Law and Policy at George Washington University, where he is also director of the Competition Law Center. He is a Non-executive Director of the United Kingdom's Competition and Markets Authority. Before joining the GW Law School in 1999, he was the Commissioner of Federal Trade Commission (FTC) from January 2006 to October 2011 and served as Chairman from March 2008 until March 2009. Previously, Professor Kovacic was the FTC's General Counsel from 2001 through 2004, and he also worked for the Commission from 1979 until 1983, initially as a staff attorney in the Bureau of Competition's Planning Office and later as an attorney advisor to former Commissioner George W. Douglas. Before he became a Commissioner, Kovacic was the E.K. Gubin Professor of Government Contracts Law at George Washington University Law School, where he began teaching in 1999. He had taught at the George Mason University School of Law since 1986, after practicing antitrust and government contracts law for three years at Bryan Cave's Washington, DC, office. Earlier in his career, Prof. Kovacic spent one year on the majority staff of the US Senate Judiciary Committee's Antitrust and Monopoly Subcommittee. Since 1992, Prof. Kovacic has been an adviser on antitrust and consumer protection issues to the governments of Armenia, Benin, Egypt, El Salvador, Georgia, Guyana, Indonesia, Kazakhstan, Mongolia, Morocco, Nepal, Panama, Russia, Ukraine, Vietnam, and Zimbabwe. Kovacic received a bachelor degree from Princeton University (1974) and a law degree from Columbia University (1978).

Paulo Burnier da Silveira is a Law Professor at the University of Brasilia (UNB) where he teaches Commercial and Competition Law. He worked at the Brazilian Competition Authority (CADE) as Commissioner (2015-2019) and as Head of its International Unit (2011-2015). He holds a PhD from the University of Paris, a LL.M from the Catholic University of Lisbon and a LLB from the Catholic University of Rio de Janeiro.

Contributors

Aleine Obregón Natera. Associate at Creel, García-Cuéllar, Aiza y Enríquez, S.C. She focuses on Competition and Antitrust matters. The views hereby expressed are exclusively of the authors and do not necessarily reflect those of the organizations involved.

Alexey Ivanov leads the HSE-Skolkovo Institute for Law and Development (ILD), the research division of the leading Russian University Higher School of Economics, in its academic and strategic pursuits. ILD conducts interdisciplinary research in order to identify optimal policy strategies for the transformation of Russia's legal framework and the global institutions to which it connects. Mr Ivanov has guided the HSE-Skolkovo joint venture since its inception. As an Associate Professor at the HSE University Law School Alexey is teaching the course Antitrust in the New Economy and publishes prolifically on the subject. Alexey serves also as a Head of the BRICS Competition Law and Policy Centre, whose aim is to provide the meeting point for BRICS competition law research and to promote a distinct BRICS competition law agenda for the global economy. For many years, Prof. Ivanov has served as Director for Legal Policy and Social Development at the Skolkovo Foundation, the Russian Innovation Agency, and has contributed heavily to the adaptation of legal environment to the needs of the rapid technological development. Ivanov has graduated with honors the Russian State University for Humanities (undergraduate), the Russian Presidential School for Private Law (Master of Laws), and the Harvard Law School (Master of Laws), and is awarded by the President of Russia with the Medal of the Order "For Merit to the Fatherland"

Andrés Valdivia is a Senior Legal Analyst at INDECOPI's Tribunal for the Defense of Competition. He holds a Law degree from Pontificia Universidad Católica del Perú. The views hereby expressed are exclusively of the authors and do not necessarily reflect those of the organizations involved.

Augustine Peter was Member, Competition Commission of India, from 10 April, 2014 to 15 January, 2019. He has also been the Economic Adviser in the Commission during

2006–2009 and held the Office of the Director General of the Commission when enforcement started. He has been the spearhead of the advocacy programme of the Commission and has also been involved in the framing of the Commission's Regulations. He is a Gold Medalist in MA (Eco) and also holds MSc (Eco) (University of Bradford). He is an expert in Competition law specializing in the areas of Competition, Trade, and Investment Policy. He has authored various publications in reputed journals and books on issues related to Competition Policy and Law. He has been the Member Secretary to the Chakravarty Committee on Competition Law (1998–1999). He has participated in various meetings of the United Nations Conference on Trade and Development (UNCTAD) Inter Governmental Group of Experts on Competition Policy and Law, Geneva, and was also elected as its Vice Chairperson in 2003. During that period, he has also participated and contributed to the evolution of the UNCTAD Model Law on Competition. As an officer of the Indian Economic Services (1982), he has looked after various issues related to the WTO Working Group on the 'Interaction between Trade and Competition Policy'. He has also served as the Indian Delegate representing the India Investment Centre, at the United Nations Industrial Development Organization Investment Promotion Service Office in Paris during 1989–1993, promoting investment and technology transfer. He was the lead international consultant to the Government of Nepal and drafted the Industrial and Investment policies during 2002.

Carlos Mena Labarthe. Partner at Creel, García-Cuéllar, Aiza y Enríquez, S.C. His practice focuses on Competition and Antitrust. He was the first Chief Prosecutor at the Mexican Competition Authority among other senior positions.

Cunzhen Huang is Counsel based in the Washington DC office of Cleary Gottlieb Steen & Hamilton LLP. Her practice focuses on competition/antitrust law. Cunzhen has worked in Brussels, London, and Washington DC, focusing on antitrust review of mergers and acquisitions, antitrust investigations and enforcement matters, and antitrust litigation in the European Union, the United States, and Asia.

Deborah Healey LLM Hons (Syd), Professor, University of New South Wales Law Sydney, Australia, and Director of Herbert Smith Freehills China International Business and Economic Law Centre.

Dennis M. Davis is a Judge at the High Court of Cape Town, appointed by former South African president Nelson Mandela, as well as Judge President of the Competition Appeal Court of Cape Town, South Africa's specialized antitrust tribunal. He teaches constitutional law and tax law at the University of Cape Town and currently hosts a South African television program on current political and economic issues entitled 'Judge For Yourself.' He has been a visiting professor at the Universities of Cambridge, Florida, Toronto, Georgetown, and Harvard. Judge Davis' research interests include constitutional law, socioeconomic rights, and human rights and litigation. He served as a legal advisor on electoral law and federalism to the Constitutional Assembly during the formation of South Africa's new constitution. Judge Davis has extensively published in academic journals and co-written eight books on a number of legal subjects including *Rights and Constitutionalism* (Jutas, 1994), *Beyond Apartheid* (Ravan, 1991), and *Detention and Torture in South Africa* (St. Martin's, 1987). Judge Davis earned a BCom and LLB from the University of Cape Town and an MPhil from the University of Cambridge.

Deshmuk Kowlessur is the executive director of the Competition Commission of Mauritius (CCM). He holds a DEUG from the University of la Réunion and a Masters Grande-École from the École Supérieure de Commerce (ESC) de Rouen, France. Before joining the CCM, Mr Deshmuk Kowlessur was the chief operating officer of Elytis (DistriPC Ltd), a member of Leal Group and which is the distributor of major leading technology brands in the Indian Ocean. Prior to that, he occupied senior positions such as business analyst at KPMG, and planning and development manager in Rogers Group, among others.

Ekaterina Semenova is an Research Fellow at the BRICS Competition Law and Policy Centre at the National Research University - Higher School of Economics (Moscow, Russia). She graduated from leading Russian Universities' Law Schools, such as Lomonosov Moscow State University (LLB), Russian School of Private Law (LLM), and National Research University Higher School of Economics (LLM). In her research Ekaterina focuses on issues of law and technology intersection.

Elizabeth Servan is a Senior Economic Analyst at INDECOPI's Tribunal for the Defense of Competition. She holds a MSc. in Economics from University of Leeds, England. The views hereby expressed are exclusively of the authors and do not necessarily reflect those of the organizations involved.

Ioannis Lianos, Professor of Global Competition Law and Public Policy and Director, Centre for Law, Economics and Society, UCL Faculty of Laws; Academic Director, BRICS Competition Law and Policy Centre, HSE National Research University.

Jorge Enrique Sánchez Medina is founding partner in JSM Abogados, and a lecturer at Universidad Javeriana, Universidad de los Andes, Universidad Sergio Arboleda, and Universidad Externado, where he teaches about law, practice and policy of antitrust and consumer protection. He is a graduate of Universidad Externado de Colombia where he majored in Economic Law. He holds an Executive LLM from Northwestern University and a CBA from the Instituto de la Empresa de Madrid (IE) and specializes in economic law, as well as economic analysis of law. Early in his career he was a clerk both in the Constitutional Court and in the Supreme Court of Justice. He has also worked at the Secretaría Jurídica de la Presidencia de la República de Colombia. And most recently, he served as Deputy Superintendent for the Protection of Competition during two administrations and also as a Deputy Superintendent for Consumers Protection.

Junko Shibata is a Professor in the Faculty of Law of Kagawa University. She was the Vice-President of Kagawa University from 2015 to 2017. She was engaged in research at Max-Planck Institute in Germany by receiving scholarship from Alexander von Humboldt Foundation from 1999 to 2000. Her research interests lie in the regulations on monopoly such as private monopolization and abuse of dominance in competition law and business law.

Mario A. Umaña is a Senior Trade, Integration and Competition Specialist for the Inter-American Development Bank where he concentrates on the design of loans and technical cooperations for countries in Latin America. Prior to joining the Inter-American Development Bank, he worked as an International Consultant for the Organization for Economic Co-Operation and Development and as an International Consultant for INCAE, the Latin American Center for Competitiveness and Sustainable Development. While attending Georgetown University Law Center, Professor Umaña was a fellow for the Law Center's International Economic Law Institute.

Michel Narcia Martínez. Senior associate in the competition department of De Brauw Blackstone Westbroek N.V., where he regularly splits his time in between the Amsterdam and Brussels offices. Before joining De Brauw, Michel was an associate at Creel, García-Cuéllar, Aiza y Enríquez, S.C.

Neha Singh is a legal practitioner currently engaged as a Research Associate (legal) with the Competition Commission of India. She specializes in Competition Law, International Trade Laws, and Intellectual Property Laws. She possesses an experience of seven years in Competition Laws and two years in Customs and Trade laws. She has authored various articles on Competition Law and Intellectual Property Rights published in reputed journals and books. She is a rank holder at the University level in Bachelors of Law (LLB) and a Gold Medalist rank holder in Masters of Law (LLM) from University of Delhi. She also possesses a degree in Commerce and a diploma in Customs and Trade.

Pablo Trevisán is co-author of law 27,442. Master of Laws (LLM), London School of Economics and Political Science (LSE), United Kingdom. Visiting Research Fellow, Fordham School of Law, USA. PhD on Antitrust Damages, thesis pending, Pontificia Universidad Católica Argentina (UCA). Commissioner, Comisión Nacional de Defensa de la Competencia (CNDC), Argentina. Between 2001 and 2015, Partner of Estudio Trevisán Abogados. Member, International Advisory Board, Institute for Consumer Antitrust Studies, Loyola University Chicago, US. Author, speaker, and professor in the topics of his specialty at UCA, Torcuato Di Tella University (UTDT), ESEADE, and other institutions.

Rachel Burgess is a competition and consumer law lecturer at the University of Southern Queensland and a research fellow at the Deakin University IPA-Deakin SME Research Centre. With a broad corporate and commercial background in both the public and private sectors, Rachel has been specializing in the field of competition and consumer law for nearly twenty years. Since 2010, Rachel has worked primarily in the ASEAN region where she has completed a range of capacity building and technical assistance programmes for new competition regimes. Rachel holds an LLM from the University of London.

Ruben Lapa Maximiano is a senior competition expert in the OECD Competition Division where he is responsible for the work of the Division in the Asia Pacific Region, including the OECD/KPC Competition Programme. He is also a lecturer on EU Merger Control at Lille Catholic University. Ruben has previously worked as a Senior Competition Expert at the European and Securities and Markets Authority, as case handler at the European Commission (DG Competition, Mergers and Financial Crisis Task Force) and the Portuguese Competition Authority. Prior to that, Ruben was a lawyer at Vieira de Almeida & Associados, in Portugal, and Squire, Sanders & Dempsey in Brussels. Ruben holds an LLM from the College of Europe.

Tembinkosi Bonakele has been the Commissioner of the South African Competition Commission since 2013. Mr Bonakele joined the Commission in 2004 and occupied various positions in the Commission's core divisions. He was appointed Deputy Commissioner in 2008, and prior to that worked as head of mergers, head of compliance, and senior legal counsel respectively. Mr Bonakele's accomplishments at the Commission include establishing the Cartels division. He has worked on all of the Commission's major cases and overseen its policy evolution for more than ten years. He has been involved in negotiating most of the Commission's ground-breaking settlements and helped develop the Commission's Corporate Leniency Policy. Mr Bonakele is an admitted attorney and previously practised with Cheadle Thompson and Haysom in Johannesburg largely in the areas of labour law, regulation, and health and safety. He has also spent a year working in corporate finance and antitrust groups at Clifford Chance, New York office. He is a an adjunct visiting professor of law at Wits Law School, an adjunct professor in the Business School of Nelson Mandela University, an Associate of the European Summer School and Conference in Competition and Regulation of Athens University of Economics and Business, a Fellow of the University of Johannesburg's Centre for Competition, Regulation and Economic Development, and a Board Member of the University of Stellenbosch's Centre for Competition Law and Economics. He has published widely in academic journals and writes for newspapers and business magazines on competition matters. He has recently co-edited a book titled 'Competition Law for the New Era'. He is a PhD candidate at University College London and holds a BJuris and an LLB from the University of Fort Hare and an MBA from Gordon Institute of Business Science, University of Pretoria. Mr Bonakele currently serves as the Chairperson of the African Competition Forum, is a member of the BRICS competition forum, and a member of the International Competition Network Steering Group. He is also a member of the Johannesburg Stock Exchange's Take-Over Regulation Panel and is the Chairperson of Buffalo City Development Agency. Bonakele is an activist who has been a leader in the youth and student movement and is a former President of the Student Representative Council of the University of Fort Hare. He is a recipient of the Black Management Forum's Black Excellency Award and is a regular speaker at international competition policy conferences.

Victor Oliveira Fernandes is a Chief of Staff at a Supreme Court's Office in Brazil (Supremo Tribunal Federal – STF). He is also a former Chief of Staff at a Commissioner's Office of the Brazilian Competition Authority (CADE). He is a PhD Candidate in

Law at the University of São Paulo (USP), and he holds a LLM and a LLB Degree from the UNB. He was also Deputy Chief-Editor of CADE's Competition Journal.

Wouter Meester is a competition expert in the OECD Competition Division. At the OECD, he has focused on developing and implementing effective policy reforms to enhance competitiveness in Central Asia as well as effective competition policy reforms in the Asia Pacific. Before joining the OECD, Wouter worked as a senior economist at PwC Advisory in the Netherlands and Canada and served as merger case handler at the Netherlands Authority for Consumers and Markets. Wouter holds a MSc. in Economics (Industrial Organization) from the University of Amsterdam.

Yiming Sun is an associate in the Beijing office of Cleary Gottlieb Steen & Hamilton LLP. Her practice area is competition/antitrust law. Prior to joining the Beijing office, Yiming worked in the firm's Brussels office for two years.

Yosuke Okada is a Professor in the Graduate School of Economics at Hitotsubashi University where he has been a faculty member since 2000. He is the Dean of the Graduate School of Economics since 2019. He received a BA and a PhD in economics from the University of Tokyo. His research interests lie in the policy issues in the area of competition, regulation, and innovation. He has collaborated actively with law researchers and practitioners in anti-monopoly laws and intellectual properties laws. He has served as the Director of Competition Policy Research Center of Japan Fair Trade Commission since 2012.

Summary of Contents

Table of Contents

Foreword

Digitalization opened a new era of competition law and policy. Nowadays, more than 130 countries have adopted competition law including mechanisms to fight anticompetitive conducts and merger control in most of them. The digital economy entails new challenges to competition authorities worldwide which require greater cooperation efforts towards convergence and consistency.

In this context, this book edited by Professor William E. Kovacic and Paulo Burnier da Silveira addresses many of today's hot topics. The title 'Global Competition Enforcement: New Players, New Challenges' gives the flavour of its chapters and invites readers to a tour around the globe including views from America, Europe, Africa, Asia, and Oceania.

In the first part, Professor Ioannis Lianos presents an overview of the digital economy issues that raise challenges to competition authorities and policy makers. Then, contributions from India and Mexico enforcers illustrate with recent cases how competition authorities from these two jurisdictions have addressed these challenges.

The second part explores enforcement cases in traditional markets, regarding recent experiences in Japan and Mauritius. Professors Yosuke Okada and Junko Shibata analyse the first ruling by the Japanese Supreme Court on whether refusal to deal with competitors constitutes exclusionary practice in the telecom sector. Another contribution illustrates how the Competition Commission of Mauritius succeeded to crack more than 100 cases on resale price maintenance, thanks to an interesting immunity programme and advocacy efforts.

Furthermore, a contribution from Brazil consolidates the current state of play of its 'Car Wash' investigations that is considered the biggest on-going cartel investigation in the world. The Peruvian experience in the fight against cartels is also presented with three recent bid-rigging cases in the healthcare sector that affect a great number of consumers and public expenditure. A last contribution addresses the tissue paper cartel investigated by some Latin American countries and subject to a rich debate on the design and practice of a regional organization with competition enforcement powers: the Andean Community.

The third part highlights the topic of competition neutrality, which intends to level the playing field of private and public companies. Professor Deborah Healey presents a glance at experiences in Europe and the Asia-Pacific region. Then, Judge Dennis Davis and Tembinkosi Bonakele explore the South African experience with its State-Owned Enterprises and public interest unique clauses.

The forth part looks forward and sheds light into future perspectives. It analyses regional convergence efforts in Asia-Pacific and Latin America, including the links between regional integration and competition policy. In addition, two contributions highlight recent developments in the Chinese merger control regime and the Argentinean new competition law that adopted a pre-merger control system as well as a leniency program to tackle cartels. A last section by Professor William E. Kovacic and Paulo Burnier da Silveira concludes the book with final remarks.

It is a great set of contributions for those interested in the development of competition law and policy across the world. Besides, the book focus on emerging economies and competition authorities' experience that do not usually have the opportunity to showcase its experiences, differences, and success stories in writing. In this way, it fosters diversity and inclusiveness that are the cornerstone of the United Nations' mandate. It is very much in line with the mandate and work of UNCTAD, the focal point for Competition law and policy within the United Nations system, and the custodian of the United Nations Set on Competition Principles and Rules, the only internationally agreed instrument in this field.

I thank the editors for inviting me to write these introductory words and wish you a great reading.

Teresa Moreira
Head of Competition and Consumer
Policies Branch at UNCTAD

Part I Challenges in Digital Economy

CHAPTER 1
Digitalisation and Competition Law: New Challenges

Ioannis Lianos[*]

§1.01 INTRODUCTION

The rise of the digital economy has been the major economic transformation of our time. 'Digital platforms' relying on network effects and 'Big Data' have been the focus of competition law enforcement activity and have attracted the interest of competition scholars.

The fact that data constitutes the basic input in the digital economy is now well accepted.[1] Although data constitutes the raw material in this era of 'informational capitalism'[2] or 'digital capitalism', artificial intelligence (henceforth 'AI'), algorithms, machine learning and automation technologies, among other technologies of the 'fourth industrial revolution', constitute the real game changers as the adoption of these technologies will immensely affect international competition in all the economic sectors affected by the digital revolution.

Most competition law scholars have addressed this process of transformation by focusing on its technological dimension and its impact on business models. Their work

---

* The Chapter partly draws on previously published research, in particular that of I. Lianos, "Blockchain Competition" in *Regulating Blockchain: Political and Legal Challenges*, (edited by P. Hacker, I. Lianos, G. Dimitropoulos and S. Eich, Oxford University Press, 2019, Forthcoming) and a research paper on Digital Value Chains. The author would like to thank Meg Cochrane and Riccardo Savona-Siemens for excellent research assistance.

1. *See*, for instance, Economist, "The World's Most Valuable Resource Is No Longer Oil, But Data", (*economist.com*, 6 May 2017) https://www.economist.com/leaders/2017/05/06/the-worlds-most-valuable-resource-is-no-longer-oil-but-data.
2. *See* J. Cohen, "Property and the Construction of the Information Economy: A Neo-Polanyian Ontology" in *Handbook of Digital Media and Communication* (edited by L. Lievrouw and B. Loader, Routledge, Forthcoming).

usefully explores the ways in which the existing competition law framework may apply in order to address current technological challenges, taking into account the importance of data in the digital economy as the essential raw material. Nevertheless, there has been less work done on the input-output process that ultimately generates value in the digital economy. Indeed, value is generated through the elaborate processes of transformation and monetisation, which ultimately take place in both the product and financial markets. This process of value creation is organised along, more or less, elaborate value chains which encompass various input-output steps. These value chains compete with each other in complex ecosystems, where, for example, the firms can be competing with one another in relation to one activity along the chain while simultaneously co-operating or producing complementary products in regard to some other activity. Firms operating in each of the different individual layers of a digital value chain face an important dilemma – they want to maximise their market power, but they will suffer harm if distinct firms operating in other parts of the chain seek to and succeed in doing such as well. For firms operating in these different layers of a digital value chain, their strategy is to increase competition in other parts of the chain by promoting entry and fragmenting supply while maintaining their monopoly position in their segment of the chain and/or cooperating with other monopolised segments with the aim of sharing the profits, which arise out of the activities undertaken within the chain, among themselves.

The intricate relationships between different segments of the value chain, which in itself can be characterised as an inherently 'complex system', may give rise to issues if intervention or non-intervention is pursued in relation to one or more of its segments; the pursuit or non-pursuit of such may lead to unintended, adverse consequences in other segments of the chain. Therefore, it is necessary to internalise the complexity of the digital value chain as an integral part of the overall business models and organisational structures in the digital economy. It is also necessary to avoid any localised silo-based competition assessment of a particular segment. The important role of financial markets in the development of the digital economy, and the aforementioned monetisation process, also helps to shift attention from the traditional focus of competition law on competition within an industry, to competition between industries with capital moving from one industry to another in search of higher profits.

The rapid and revolutionary development of digital capitalism over the last three decades has led to an important 'information overload' and to social paralysis.[3] Competition authorities have reacted slowly. They have tried, unsuccessfully, to deal with the problems that have emerged by applying the framework of competition law, tailored to the era of industrial capitalism, to the 'next generation competition' of the post-industrial informational capitalism era. By applying this antiquated framework, competition authorities have failed to challenge both a considerable number of M&A transactions between emerging Internet giants and start-ups and the potential for markets to tip, while, at the same time, they have allowed incumbent firms to harvest a considerable amount of data and to develop the tools to process such data.

3. A. Toffler, *Future Shock* (Random House, 1970).

Competition authorities have failed to focus on the structural changes inherent in the shift towards digital or informational capitalism.

These structural changes, some of which pre-date to a certain extent the beginning of the 'digital revolution', can be categorised into three broad trends.

The first trend is that of *futurity*. This term, originally coined by John Commons, describes the re-orientation of economies towards the future. This is linked to the practice of treating businesses as 'going concerns' and measuring their value in terms of their anticipated future value. The most important driver of value creation is based, not on their net cash flows and expected short-term profits, but on 'pots of gold' being found far into the future. The development of blockchain technology and, in particular, the funding of blockchain projects provides an excellent illustration of futurity. Initial coin offerings ('ICOs') emerged as the main source of funding for blockchain projects with outperforming venture capital serving as the financing of cryptocurrency and blockchain start-ups since 2017. Developers are attracted to the prospect of potential future profits, which shall be generated by the appreciation in value of the native token, once the ICO has been completed. Swartz provides a good explanation of this fundamental characteristic of blockchain: 'as soon as a proposal is offered – whether as a white paper, a slide deck or a blog post – it is treated as though it already exists, ready to go. Indeed, blockchain projects exist in a particular temporality and have their own sense of the past and future, of change. It performatively leans into a future, always just around the corner, which might as well be here already'.[4]

The second trend stems from the harvesting and processing of personal data, the trend of *personalisation*. It is increasingly acknowledged that data collection is key in relation to the ability of firms to compete in the future Internet of Things ('IoT') or Internet of Services ('IoS').[5] Data analytics connected to the use of software for predictive modelling reinforce and crystallise the competitive and 'architectural' advantages of firms holding substantial portions of this data.[6] Much of the aforementioned data relates to the digital identity of the consumer and, thereby, enables companies possessing such data to draw relatively accurate preference maps for each of their clients. In this era of 'mass personalisation',[7] the focus of firms will be not only on 'attention markets',[8] but also on the development of bespoke products that suit the

4. L. Swartz, "Blockchain Dreams: Imagining Techno-Economic Alternatives After Bitcoin" in *Another Economy is Possible: Culture and Economy in a Time of Crisis* (edited by M. Castells, Polity Press, 2017), 83.
5. There is a discussion regarding the definition of 'data' – does it encompass syntactic information, semantic information, or both; and where should one draw the line in reference to protecting 'data'? *See* J. Drexl, "Designing Competitive Markets for Industrial Data – Between Propertisation and Access", (2016) Max Planck Institute for Innovation and Competition Research Paper, 12; A. Wiebe, "Protection of Industrial Data – A New Property Right for the Digital Economy?", (2017) 12 *Journal of Intellectual Property Law & Practice*, 67.
6. M. Jacobides, S. Winter and S. Kassberger, "The Dynamics of Wealth, Profit, and Sustainable Advantage", (2012) 33 *Strategic Management Journal*, 1386.
7. Deloitte, "Made to Order: The Rise of Mass Personalisation", (2015) Deloitte Consumer Review (11th ed).
8. On this concept, *see* T. Wu, "Blind Spot: The Attention Economy and the Law", (2017) *Antitrust Law Journal*; D. Evans, "The Economics of Attention Markets", (31 October 2017) https://ssrn.com/abstract=3044858.

individual preferences of each and every consumer. Once a specific amount of data is harvested about an individual, these personalised markets will likely tip, with the possible outcome being that only one firm has the capabilities to perfectly satisfy the relevant individual consumer's demand function in relation to specific products. The firm that is capable of providing such satisfaction will be able to leverage this power in the financial markets as well as convert it to power in other spheres of social activity.[9] Firms may also organise the production process within their own ecosystem become its gatekeepers by providing access to this personal consumer profile to a number of firms they control directly, or which are dependent on them to reach these 'captive' consumers.

The third trend and, arguably, most important is that of *cybernetics*. In the static model of competition applied by competition authorities, prices provide complex information in a condensed way to producers about consumer preferences, thus, enabling conventional markets to work. New data harvesting and processing techniques are revolutionary in multiple ways. First, the use of data serves to improve market matches. As customers continue to shop online, the capability of digital assistants to make ever better recommendations develops. The 'learning' process undertaken by digital assistants takes place completely or largely unassisted by humans, with data being constantly fed into machines that continuously update their algorithms. Algorithmic firms gather comprehensive personal data on their customers and in doing so they remove the need to rely on decentralised markets to acquire knowledge on the preferences of consumers. Second, these techniques may more easily discriminate between groups of consumers/users, choosing a price structure that would subsidise some while effectively 'taxing' others with higher prices. The economic literature on multi-sided markets has correctly identified this as an issue but more work needs to be done in order to understand the broader implications for competition law because the effect of such techniques in decentralised markets is that 'price' loses its central position as an indicator of consumer preferences. Consumers/buyers are not in the commanding position as they are influenced by both explicit recommendations and the ways in which options are filtered and presented, particularly as their 'trust in machines' may be higher than their trust in humans. Digital platforms may, therefore, replace markets to a certain extent, particularly in a 'winner-takes-most' world in which the presence of strong network effects means digital markets may easily 'tip'. The way these digital platforms not only regulate their ecosystems, but also more broadly demand, presents some similarities to a private version of a centrally-planned mini-economy, hence my reference to cybernetics.

These considerations lead me to put forward the following points:

- The increasing complexity of production in the digital era highlights the importance of conducting a careful analysis of the power relations along various digital value chains with the aim being to unveil *value extraction*

9. *See* for instance, P. Danziger, "Made-To-Order Clothing Is an Opportunity Tailor-Made for Amazon", (*forbes.com*, 3 May 2017) https://www.forbes.com/sites/pamdanziger/2017/05/03/made-to-order-clothing-is-an-opportunity-tailor-made-for-amazon/#2a816c336dcb.

bottlenecks affecting the distribution of the total surplus value generated by digitalisation. I consider that because of the important social implications of the transition to digital capitalism and the important tensions to social stability these may engender, as well as the limited ability of the tax system and/or regulation to deal with the social costs of this transformation, it becomes important to analyse the distributional implications of competition law enforcement. This analysis cannot always be undertaken by the traditional 'neoclassical price theory' framework, which mainly focuses on horizontal competition and its effects on consumers or total welfare (i.e., economic efficiency) and assesses the competitive interactions between firms within a specific relevant market. Competition law and policy should critically engage with the distributional implications of the transformations introduced by digital capitalism to an already complex economy and should provide a clear theoretical framework to policymakers so that they understand how important changes affecting international competition may impact upon the various stakeholders at the national, regional and global levels, and the subsequent trade-offs to be made.

- It becomes important to integrate a complex economy perspective, considering the broader array of interactions, beyond market exchanges, between the different stakeholders, as these may provide them with resources they may use in their competitive struggles in the digital economy. It is also important to integrate the most recent technological developments affecting the various resources and assets at the disposal of the actors in order to gain strategic *and* architectural competitive advantage in the digital economy. I consider that the effort of designing competition law policy institutions for the digital economy should start with a proper understanding of the value-generation and allocation processes at play in the era of digital capitalism and of the interaction of competition law with other tools and institutions (e.g., digital consumer protection, data protection, intellectual property ('IP') law etc.) in order to understand the role it plays and should play in each BRICS jurisdiction, something which has, crucially, been missing from previous analyses of these markets.
- In understanding the role of competition law in this new environment, one needs to develop a wider understanding of the function of competition law and adopt a broader reach for competition policy, in particular in relation to developing and emergent economies.[10]

In following these broader principles, competition authorities should no longer solely focus on statically-defined economic efficiency in the relevant market but should include into their considerations the value capture and value generation processes operating in the digital economy, and they should seek to draw lessons from these

10. J. Stiglitz, "Towards a Broader View of Competition Policy" in *Competition Policy for the New Era: Insights from the BRICS Countries* (edited by T. Bonakele, E. Fox and L. Mncube, Oxford University Press, 2016).

processes in order to configure the optimal design and enforcement mechanisms required by modern competition law. I consider that to the extent that promoting disruptive innovation, rather than just preserving an efficient allocation of existing resources, becomes the driving principle of modern competition law enforcement, it makes sense to focus on the way the value brought by innovation is captured, shared and generated as these three processes are intrinsically linked.

This chapter explores some of the challenges the digital revolution presents to competition law. The first section of this chapter examines the complex issue of the scope of competition law. The second emphasises the need to focus on value chains and, in particular, to map the value capture processes at play in the economy. The third calls for the expansion of the traditional competition law toolkit, which focuses on relevant market definitions, with other tools capable of helping it better analyse 'next generation competition'. The last section concludes by exploring the competition law implications of the centralisation and decentralisation trends that characterise the modern digital economy.

§1.02 DIGITAL CHALLENGES FOR THE SCOPE OF COMPETITION LAW

Competition law usually applies to entities exercising an economic activity in an independent (i.e., non-subordinate) way. This may raise difficulties in view of the changing nature of labour relationships in today's 'gig' or 'collaborative' economy and of the collapse of the traditional binary divide between employment and self-employment. The classic example is how competition law addresses the relation between Uber and Uber drivers.

Normally, competition law is seen as applying to 'undertakings' and most competition law systems exonerate themselves from interfering within the boundaries of a relevant undertaking, particularly in relation to the way in which workers and management operating within that undertaking interact with one another. Hence, when workers come together and conclude collective agreements with employers in order to fix a rate or price concerning the sale of their labour, competition law systems typically consider these practices as being distinct from the (anticompetitive) price-fixing practices in which undertakings may be engaged. In essence, collective agreements concluded by unions on behalf of their workers typically benefit from an exclusion from the scope of application of European Union (EU) competition law. Employees/workers cannot be undertakings under EU competition law – they do not exercise an autonomous economic activity, in the sense of offering goods or services on a market and bearing the financial risk attached to the performance of such activity. By the same token, a labour agreement between an employer and an employee will not fall under the scope of Article 101(1) of the Treaty on the Functioning of the European Union ('TFEU') because it is not an agreement between different undertakings.[11]

11. *See* Joined Cases 40–8/73 etc, *Coöperatieve Vereniging 'Suiker Unie' UA and Others v. Commission* [1975] ECR 1663, [539], which refers to the situation of an agent forming an integral part of the undertaking of a principal. For a discussion, *see* P. Nihoul, "Do Workers Constitute Undertakings for the Purpose of the Competition Rules?", (2000) 25 European Law Review, 408;

In *Jean Claude Becu*, the Court of Justice of the European Union ('CJEU') examined a collective labour agreement relating to dock work at the Port of Ghent, made mandatory by a Belgian Royal Decree, which allowed only duly recognised dockers to perform dock work and also made the outcome of collective bargaining between employers' and employees' representatives negotiations binding *erga omnes*. The preliminary question sent to the CJEU by the national court involved the possible application of both Articles 102 and 106(1) TFEU to the Belgian Royal Decree. The CJEU assessed if these dock workers could be considered an 'undertaking'. The CJEU held that:

> [...] the employment relationship which recognised dockers have with the undertakings for which they perform dock work is characterised by the fact that they perform the work in question for and under the direction of each of those undertakings, so they must be regarded as 'workers' within the meaning of [Article 45 TFEU], as interpreted in the case law [...].
>
> Since they are, for the duration of that relationship, incorporated into the undertakings concerned and, thus, form an economic unit with each of them, dockers do not therefore in themselves constitute undertakings.[12]

C. Townley, "The Concept of 'Undertaking': The Boundaries of the Corporation – A Discussion of Agency, Employees and Subsidiaries" in EC Competition Law: A Critical Assessment (edited by G. Amato and C.-D. Ehlermann, Hart, 2007), 3.

12. Case C-22/98, *Criminal Proceedings Against Jean Claude Becu, Annie Verweire, Smeg NV and Adia Interim NV* [1999] ECR I-5665. It is noteworthy that the situation of employees is dealt differently in the EU than in the US. In US law, all 'persons' are subject to the Sherman Act, unless they benefit from an exemption. Labour benefits from a statutory and a non-statutory exemption. The statutory labour exemption (Clayton Antitrust Act, 15 USC §§ 12–27; Norris-La Guardia Act, 29 USC §§ 101–15) enables workers to organise to eliminate competition among themselves and to pursue their legitimate labour interests, so long as they act in their self-interest and do not combine themselves with a non-labour group. Yet, the statutory labour exemption did not immunise the collective bargaining process or collective bargaining agreements from potential antitrust liability; they only covered unilateral actions undertaken by labour organisations. The US courts, thus, developed the non-statutory basis of the labour exemption in order to remove, from antitrust scrutiny restraints, trade that is the product of a collective bargaining agreement between labour and management (*see Local Union No 189, Amalgamated Meat Cutters & Butcher Workmen of N Am v. Jewel Tea Co Inc*, 381 US 676 (1965)). These (i.e., antitrust scrutiny restraints) more typically apply to agreements between employees or their unions and employers when the relevant agreements are intimately related to a mandatory subject of bargaining and do not have the 'potential for restraining competition in the business market in ways that would not follow naturally from elimination of competition over wages and working conditions': *Connell Construction Co v. Plumbers and Steamfitters Local Union No 100*, 421 US 616, 635 (1975). According to the US Supreme Court, at paragraph 622, of the aforementioned case, 'the non-statutory exemption has its source in the strong labour policy favouring the association of employees to eliminate competition over wages and working conditions. Union success in organising workers and standardising wages ultimately will affect price competition among employers but the goals of federal labour law never could be achieved if this effect on business competition were held a violation of the antitrust laws. The Court, therefore, has acknowledged that labour policy requires tolerance for the lessening of business competition based on differences in wages and working conditions'. Courts have even extended this immunity beyond the expiration of a collective bargaining agreement: *see Brown v. NFL*, 518 US 231 (1996). The non-statutory labour exemption has been frequently applied in the field of professional sports, for instance, exempting a labour agreement between the US National Football League ('NFL') or the National Basketball Association and a national union of student-athletes.

From the CJEU's reasoning it followed that workers could not be considered as an undertaking if they were acting collectively as an association of workers.

Since *Becu*, the possible application of Article 101 TFEU to collective agreements concluded between trade unions and associations of employers has led to the development of a fully-fledged exception to the application of EU competition law, for reasons of social policy. Provided two cumulative conditions are satisfied, EU competition law, as developed by the CJEU, now provides immunity to collective labour agreements concluded between associations of workers (i.e., labour unions) and employers from the application of competition law. These two cumulative conditions are that (i) the relevant collective labour agreement is entered into in the framework of collective bargaining between employers and employees, and (ii) the agreement directly contributes towards improving the employment and working conditions of workers. However, the relevant case law does not relate to the concept of 'undertaking' as such but mostly to that of the restriction of competition and is known as the *Albany* exception.

In *Albany*,[13] the CJEU took the view that it was 'beyond question that certain restrictions of competition are inherent in collective agreements between organisations representing employers and workers'. However, it was also willing to concede that 'the social policy objectives pursued by such agreements would be seriously undermined if management and labour were subject to [EU competition rules] when seeking jointly to adopt measures to improve conditions of work and employment'.[14] This concession was premised both on various treaty-based textual justifications and on the understanding that the 'nature and purpose' of the agreement was, per paragraph 63 of the judgment, that of 'improving ... working conditions, namely ... remuneration'. The CJEU found that (i) the collective agreement at issue was concluded in the form of a collective agreement and was the outcome of collective negotiations between organisations representing employers and workers, and (ii), its purpose, the establishment of a supplementary pension scheme aiming to guarantee a certain level of pension for all workers in the sector 'contributed directly to improving one of their working conditions, namely their remuneration'.[15] These two factors served to exclude this agreement from the scope of Article 101(1) TFEU.

Pursuit of a liberal profession has often been considered to constitute an 'economic activity' that falls within the scope of application of competition law if such activity is not related to employment.[16] This raises the question of whether the *Albany* exception would apply to exclude, from the scope of Article 101(1) TFEU, collective agreements concluded between members of liberal professions regarding the fixing of

13. Case C-67/96, *Albany International BV v. Stichting Bedrijfspensioenfonds Textielindustrie* [1999] ECR I-5751.
14. *Ibid.*, [59].
15. *Ibid.*, [62]–[63].
16. *See*, for instance, self-employed accountants (Case C-1/12, *Ordem dos Técnicos Oficiais de Contas*, ECLI:EU:C:2013:127), pharmacists (Case T-23/09, *CNOP & CCG v. Commission* [2010] ECR II-5291), medical doctors (Joined Cases C-180–4/98, *Pavel Pavlov and Others v. Stichting Pensioenfonds Medische Specialisten* [2000] ECR I-6451), and musicians (Case C-413/13, *FNV Kunsten Informatie en Media*, ECLI:EU:C:2014:2411).

minimum rates or other agreements restricting competition between them, to the extent that self-employed persons are considered to be undertakings?[17] The CJEU has examined the categorisation of an association acting on behalf of self-employed persons and has also explored the extension of the *Albany* exception to collective agreements concluded by unions representing both employees and self-employed persons.

Under the current approach followed by the EU courts, an association acting on behalf of self-employed persons is to be regarded as an association of undertakings under Article 101(1) TFEU.[18] It has become increasingly clear that (a) when self-employed persons seek to bargain collectively in relation to the terms and conditions of their services, or (b) where collective agreements concluded by trade unions for subordinate workers also contain minimum labour costs provision that also apply to self-employed workers, then the exclusion from competition law will not apply to such self-employed persons or workers as the competition authorities and/or courts consider them to be 'undertakings'.

More recently, in *FNV Kunsten*, the CJEU held that 'insofar as an organisation representing workers carries out negotiations acting in the name, and on behalf, of those self-employed persons who are its members, it does not act as a trade union association and therefore as a social partner, but, in reality, acts as an association of undertakings', and is therefore also exposed to the full application of EU competition law rules. An exception to these rules, the court said in *FNV Kunsten*, is only possible 'if the service providers, in the name and on behalf of whom the trade union negotiated, are in fact "false self-employed", that is to say, service providers in a situation comparable to that of employees'.[19]

Cases such as *FNV Kunsten* raise the crucial question of the scope of competition law in view of the changing nature of labour relationships in today's 'gig' or 'collaborative' economy and the collapse of the traditional binary divide between employment and self-employment.[20] They also raise important questions as to the optimal boundaries between competition law and labour law and the politically sensitive issue of a possible extension of workers' protection to these 'new jobs'.[21] It

17. *See* Joined Cases C-180–4/98, *Pavel Pavlov* (16); Commission Decision *Belgian Architects Association* (Case 2005/8/CE) [2005] OJ L 4/10.
18. Case C-309/99, *JCJ Wouters, JW Savelbergh and Price Waterhouse Belastingadviseurs BV v. Algemene Raad van de Nederlandse Orde van Advocaten*, intervener: *Raad van de Balies van de Europese Gemeenschap* [2002] ECR I-1577. In *Wouters*, the CJEU examined the compatibility, with Article 101 of the Treaty on the Functioning of the European Union ('TFEU'), of a regulation adopted by the Netherlands Bar Association prohibiting lawyers practising in the Netherlands from entering into multi-disciplinary partnerships with members of the professional category of accountants.
19. Case C-413/13, *FNV*, (16), [28] and [31].
20. For a useful discussion, from a labour law but also an economic perspective, *see* M. Freedland and N. Kountouris, The Legal Construction of Personal Work Relations (Oxford University Press, 2011); N. Kountouris, "The Concept of 'Worker' in European Labour Law: Fragmentation, Autonomy and Scope", (2017) 47 Industrial Law Journal, 192; A. Stewart and J. Stanford, "Regulating Work in the Gig Economy: What are the Options?" (2017) 28 Economic and Labour Relations Rev*iew*, 420.
21. *See*, most recently, European Parliament, "The Social Protection of Workers in the Platform Economy: Study for the EMPL Committee", (2017) Study, 11, which found that "the greater the

requires some effort to reconcile the respective domains of application of competition law and labour law, regulation in the digital economy and the possibility of generalising the labour exception beyond the strict confines of trade unions of 'workers', in order to include, for instance, those persons who are 'dependent self-employed' as well.

Determining the existence of an 'economic activity', and, thus, of an 'undertaking' is not the only challenge in the context of applying competition law rules in the digital economy. It is also important to determine the entity liable for competition law infringements. This also may, for instance, raise concerns regarding distributed ledger technology ('DLT'). Similar to the Internet, blockchain is borderless. However, the crucial factor is that it is decentralised, which makes it difficult, particularly if the relevant activity takes place in the context of public permission-less blockchains, to determine who should bear the responsibility for the social costs and private harms generated by the blockchain-related activity. A distributed ledger may need forms of 'distributed liability', that is, the notion that 'all entities in the system need to consider contingent liability risk'.[22] This raises the question of whether such liability should extend to all participants in the blockchain, irrespective of their governance roles, or only to those that exercise a significant influence on the activity that led to the specific social costs or private harm to be compensated. Furthermore, if the option of collective responsibility is selected, how would responsibility be apportioned between the various nodes, to the extent that node owners in permission-less blockchain may not even be aware of the specific conduct or the identity of the other node owners involved.

Although the concept of 'entity' is less important to determining the existence of an 'economic activity', in view of the functional approach followed by EU competition law, this concept is crucial when it comes to (i) determining, under Article 101 TFEU, the liability of two or more entities that have entered into an illegal agreement or concerted practice, (ii) attributing liability for the illegal conduct and the related issue of determining appropriate remedies/sanctions, and (iii) determining the market shares of the undertaking involved in the infringement of competition law, with this being either in the context of merger control or in the context of abuse of a dominant position, or determining the existence of a single undertaking for the application of a 'block exemption' regulation.

The concept of 'control' plays an important role in the process of defining the scope of the competition law intervention against an 'economic entity'. It determines the tangible or intangible assets that constitute the core of the 'undertaking' and defines its boundaries. Such assets are presumed to be under the authority of the undertaking's agents, who through pursuing anticompetitive strategies, may engage the liability of the undertaking liability.[23] Under the 'single entity' doctrine, several legal persons may

level of financial dependence [of the labourer] on platform work, the lower the access that workers have to social protections".

22. *See* Z. Zetzche, R. Buckley and D. Arner, "The Distributed Liability of Distributed Ledgers: Legal Risks of Blockchain", (2017) 52 *University of New South Wales Law Research Series*, 9.
23. Case 170/83, *Hydrotherm Gerätebau GmbH v. Compact del Dott. Ing. Mario Andreoli & C. Sas.* [1984] ECR 2999.

form an 'economic entity' if a control relationship exists between them; the application of the doctrine presupposes the exercise of 'control' or 'decisive influence'.[24]

Should an entity, such as a mining pool, a blockchain intermediary or an intermediary or platform off-blockchain, take control of the blockchain, and the existence of 'control' will have to be determined according to the specific consensus protocol utilised by the blockchain (and if this is based on Proof of Work, Proof of Stake or something else), then it may be considered as reasonable to hold this entity liable for anticompetitive conduct perpetrated in the context of the specific blockchain. The same deterrence reasons that have so far justified the liability of parent companies for the anticompetitive activity of their subsidiaries may also operate in this case.[25] However, this expansion of the personal scope of liability has also been criticised.[26] Discussions over the boundaries of the 'single entity' doctrine constitute a specific facet of broader debates over (i) 'enterprise' liability vs. 'business participant' liability and (ii) when the corporate veil should be pierced.[27]

Such discussions are indirectly related to the debate concerning the boundaries of the 'firm' in economics, with a number of approaches glossing over Coase's seminal, but incomplete from a descriptive perspective, distinction between 'markets' and 'hierarchies'.[28] The discussion over the boundaries of the firm has also caught the attention of blockchain experts who rightly observe that blockchain technology

24. *See, inter alia*, Case C-97/08 P, *Akzo Nobel and Others v. Commission* [2009] ECR I-8237; Joined Cases C-628/10 P and C-14/11 P *Alliance One International and Standard Commercial Tobacco v. Commission and Commission v. Alliance One International and Others*, ECLI:EU:C:2012:479, [46]–[47], with regard to the liability of a parent company for the conduct of its wholly-owned subsidiary or on which it exercises a decisive influence; Article 3(2) & 3(3) of Council Regulation (EC) No. 139/2004 on the Control of Concentrations Between Undertakings, OJ 2004 L 24/1, in the context of merger control.
25. C. Koenig, "An Economic Analysis of the Single Economic Entity Doctrine in EU Competition Law", (2017) 13 *Journal of Competition Law and Economics*, 281–327.
26. For a criticism of this case law, *see* A. Kalintiri, "Revisiting Parental Liability in EU Competition Law", (2018) *European Law Review*, 145, noting that it may deprive undertakings of the protection afforded to them by the Charter of Fundamental Rights and the general principles of EU law.
27. For a discussion, *see* E. Orts, *Business Persons – A Legal Theory of the Firm* (Oxford University Press, 2013).
28. R. Coase, "The Nature of the Firm", (1937) 4 *Economica*, 386. Williamson added 'hybrids': O. Williamson, *The Mechanisms of Governance* (Oxford University Press, 1996). Some approaches explain the emergence of firms, and their boundaries, by transaction costs economics ('TCE') and more broadly contractual theories of vertical integration (*see, inter alia*, O. Williamson, *The Economic Institutions of Capitalism* (Free Press, 1985); P. Joskow, "The New Institutional Economics: Alternative Approaches", (1995) 151 *Journal of Institutional and Theoretical Economics*, 248. Others focus on property rights by identifying the allocation of residual decision rights with the ownership of the assets of the firm (tangible and intangible): O. Hart and J. Moore, "Property Rights and the Nature of the Firm", (1990) 98 *Journal of Political Economy*, 1119. Others take an agency perspective, defining the firm as 'a nexus of agency relationships including managerial lines of authority, employment and structures of governance': Orts, (27), 13. A more dynamic perspective views the boundaries of a firm as related to its strategy to leverage its internal capabilities in related markets or to exploit its superior management capabilities and resources: B. Wernerfelt, "A Resource-Based View of the Firm", (1984) 5 *Strategic Management Journal*, 171.

contributes to the 'hollowing out' of the firm as initiated by the digital revolution.[29] It is expected that blockchain technology will challenge the 'efficiency' justification for establishing centralised islands of authority (as is put forward by proponents of the Transaction Costs Economics/contractual theory approach) while also enabling a wider distribution of entrepreneurial finance through its distinctive way of attracting finance, the ICO. 'Hollowing out' the firm does not, however, necessarily imply a corresponding growth in the sphere of activities organised through markets to the extent that the dominant strategy of blockchain developers and intermediaries may be to build 'walled gardens' and design eco-systems that could progressively lead to some form of centralisation. In this context, determining the entity that could be found liable for a competition law infringement might be an easier task.

§1.03 SHIFTING THE FOCUS FROM RELEVANT MARKETS TO VALUE CHAINS

Thirty years after the PC revolution and the constitution of the PC value chain and twenty years after the introduction and expansion of the Internet, we are now facing new developments such as the rise of smartphones as the principal medium of interaction between consumers and the World Wide Web.[30] The widespread use of smartphones and the development of tablet computers have led to the transition from browsers to apps with mobile broadband subscriptions having quadrupled in the past five years with more than 3.5 billion being recorded in 2015.[31] 'Big data' analytics and the massive collection of personal data may enable Internet service providers ('ISPs') and search engines to track with detail the behaviour of consumers (their digital identity), when navigating the Internet, thereby helping companies predict the kinds of products and services in which consumers may be interested. The transition from smartphones to the IoT, where devices such as thermostats, refrigerators, cars etc. will be directly connected to the Internet, will increase the types of devices through which companies may gain access to valuable consumer data. The importance of social media may also promote new approaches in understanding the formation of consumer preferences and, in particular, their interdependent character with the idea being that individual preferences are influenced by the preferences of other individuals, an idea that mainstream economic theory has rejected thus far.[32]

One cannot help but notice the strategic position of digital platforms. They often act as gatekeepers for the Internet as they enable direct interactions between groups of

29. C. Mulligan, "Blockchain Will Kill the Traditional Firm", (*imperial.ac.uk*, 16 October 2017), https://www.imperial.ac.uk/business-school/knowledge/finance/blockchain-will-kill-the-traditional-firm/.
30. Commission Staff Working Document, "Online Platforms", Accompanying the Document Communication on Online Platforms and the Digital Single Market, SWD/2016/0172 final, 10, noting that 'the larger proportion of the EU population now accesses the Internet via mobile phones than via laptops or other devices'.
31. *Ibid.*, 10.
32. *See*, for instance, the discussion in S. Drakopoulos, "The History of the Mainstream Rejection of Interdependent Preferences", (2012) 34 *Journal of the History of Economic Thought*, 541.

users. The significant amount of intellectual property rights ('IPRs') they hold over technology and their control over and possession of data ('big data' and 'smart data'), may enable lead companies to control global digital value chains from which they can extract an important share of the total surplus value generated. These companies benefit from 'network effects' – the value of the services they provide increases with the number of users and this, in turn, contributes significantly to digital value creation, notably through data accumulation. These multi-sided platforms rely on a great variety of business models.

Digital value chains rely on multi-sided platforms that provide a medium through which one set of platform customers delivers value to another set of platform customers. Platforms tend to develop business models that take advantage of these interdependencies of demand between distinct groups of customers.

Figure 1.1 An Example of a Digital Value Chain[33]

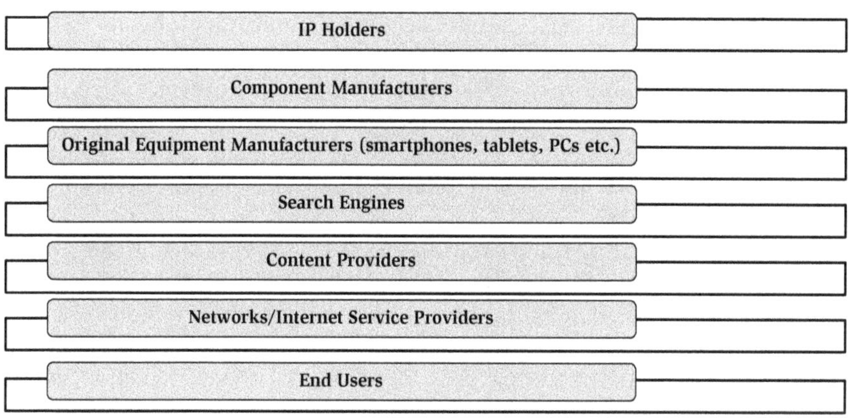

The concentration of the search engine and web directory segment of the value chain may raise some concerns in view of its gatekeeping role with regard to the access of end users to content on the Internet. Search engines have been monetising search through a variety of different revenue streams, primarily, advertising and providing search results for third party sites. The markets for search-based and online advertising have a number of specific features that set them apart from most markets. These features include network effects, double-sidedness and high levels of R&D and innovation. There are certainly some positive network effects, in view of the improvement of algorithmic results following the increase of end users' searches. It is also possible to advance the existence of indirect network effects as advertisers consider a search engine with a greater number of end users as being more valuable.

The structure of the search engine market and its pricing/quality strategies have certain distinctive features. The search engine acts as a platform intermediating

33. This depiction of the value chain is, of course, simplified for presentation purposes as many more layers can be added depending on the circumstances of the industry.

between content providers (who want users), users (who want content) and advertisers (who want users). Closely related to this interconnected structure comprising these distinct groups is the associated pricing structure in which users enjoy the search service for free while advertisers are required to pay positive prices to feature on the results provided by the search engine services (at least with regard to sponsored or paid links) and while content providers are subsidised by the search engine. Thus, prices and profits on two-sides are linked. These features of the search engine market call for the application of two-sided market models. While a positive price is only set for one of the three groups, specifically for advertisers, quality competition plays an important role with regard to the relationship between: (i) a search engine and its users and, (ii) a search engine and content providers via the intermediary of users. In relation to (ii) the higher the quality of the search engine, the more users it will attract and, thus, the more valuable it will be for content providers.

Furthermore, search engines are different from other websites because of their crucial gateway role. From the perspective of advertisers, users of search engines are more valuable than users of any other websites because they provide important information about both themselves and their intentions through their search query. Search engines act as information gatekeepers. They not only provide information on what can be found on the web (modern, online equivalent of the yellow pages) but also are an essential first-point-of-call for anyone venturing onto the Internet. Search engines retain an important amount of information about their customers and advertisers.

Utilising this information allows search engines to increase the relevance of their advertisements and this increased relevance, in turn, means increased value to those who wish to advertise. Hence, the quality of matching and the quality and the relevance of search results are valued not only by users of the search engine but also by advertisers. These arguments imply that the quality of the search itself and the relevance of the search results supplied play a crucial role for both consumers and advertisers. Entry into the search engine segment of the value chain is relatively difficult. Some authors contend that search engines present some characteristics of natural monopolies as their cost structure involves important fixed costs, such as hardware, support, updates, monitoring, but almost zero marginal costs on both the user and advertiser side of the market.[34] This reinforces the tendency of this market towards being concentrated. The search engine market is highly concentrated with the pre-eminent player, Google, which is owned by Alphabet, disposing of an important and substantial share (more than 90%) of the search/query volume. However, it is not clear if this, the search/query market, can be defined as the relevant market for competition law purposes as one may also opt for the market encompassing general Internet search or the market for search advertising, in view of the fact that search is free and that the main revenue stream is advertising, or for the market for comparison shopping services, in which case Amazon may compete with Google in the category of 'product search'.

34. R. Pollock, "Is Google the Next Microsoft? Competition, Welfare and Regulation in Online Search", (2010) 9 *Review of Network Economics*, 1.

Google has diversified its activities in search-related activities, such as digitising documentary collections of certain university libraries and private editors (Google Books), offering new specialised search engines relating to News (Google News), price comparison websites (Google Shopping), maps (Google maps), videos (YouTube), the Internet browser (Google Chrome), online applications (such as cloud computing) and other services and applications (including technologies for marketing and disseminating advertising, such as DoubleClick).

Possible strategies that might reinforce this trend towards concentration are considered to be exclusionary practices. Such practices include, but are not limited to: discrimination or refusals to deal with competitors downstream (if the search engine is vertically integrated to specialised search or other services/products), anticompetitive capacity building or passive investment in competitors' business, practices reducing multi-homing by advertisers in the form of obstacles to the simultaneous use by advertisers of several search-based ads platforms, tying and bundling, among others.

The search engine is not the only 'bottleneck' through which a digital platform may take hold in order to leverage its economic power in relation to other segments of the value chain. In theory and (based on some evidence) in practice, bottlenecks may arise at all possible points of control of the Internet.[35] App store centres constitute the first type of these new points of control, as Internet access through smartphones, rather than browsers, has gained traction thereby enabling 'the majority of Internet-mediated practice' to be undertaken 'with devices that are either narrowly customizable appliances or controlled on the app store model'.[36] The move to wireless cellular networks and cable broadband offers further possibilities in comparison to the old copper network concerning the identification of Internet users and their usage and the development of monetisation strategies in relation to Internet access, which is now controlled by a limited number of players.[37] The rise of cloud computing that emerged in order to provide co-location services for data storage and computation is controlled by a few firms with resources (including control over data) moving away from end-users and towards centralised systems that possess huge processing power and storage capacities.[38] The shift towards the IoT will further revolutionise the Internet. For the first time, it will make the 'unconscious' use of the Internet possible and will offer a new point of control to the extent that most of Internet use will occur through smart devices taking action on their own without any direct human intervention.

35. On Internet's various points of control and power, *see* J. Benkler, "Degrees of Freedom, Dimensions of Power", (2016) 145 *Daedalus*, 18.
36. *Ibid.*, 21.
37. *Ibid.*
38. P. de Filippi and S. McCarthy, "Cloud Computing: Centralization and Data Sovereignty", (2012) 3 *European Journal for Law and Technology* observes that 'cloud services, whether they are infrastructural, platform-based, or software as a service, present a fiction of decentralisation to the user in the form of network effects, while the service is increasingly operated by large companies that leverage their position to limit interoperability. Because of their dominant position, large service providers can exert a degree of subjugation never conceived of by smaller and more local services, and a degree of control that would be impossible in a peer-to-peer network'.

Indeed, those that control these devices will control Internet *use*, not just Internet access.

However, that which is most important are the strategies employed by the few players who have come to control the bottlenecks in these points within the chain and the vast amounts of information generated by Internet use.[39] There are various competition law issues that may arise concerning the control of an essential bottleneck for competition law purposes. Traditional approaches followed in competition law, for instance, market definition, may fail to adequately map and address such issues.[40] Big data may also constitute a barrier to entry that can be used strategically to exclude competitors and prevent competition in various markets for which data constitutes an essential input.[41] Although there have not been any exclusionary antitrust cases with regard to the exclusionary potential of big data-related conduct by competition authorities in Europe, this likely eventuality should not be excluded.[42]

Furthermore, it is possible that privacy breaches, discrimination and exploitative contracts may be facilitated by the control of big data with companies interchanging individualised offers on the basis of the information they acquire on individuals' willingness to pay based on their past browsing history or other personalising factors, thus, leading to different prices charged to various customers for homogeneous products (i.e., 'online personalised pricing').[43] Certain competition authorities have opened investigations into whether these practices represent an abusive imposition of unfair conditions on users.[44]

It will be crucial to consider the bottlenecks that may emerge in the future, in particular, in the IoT and/or IoS and the Cloud, which are all quite significant, especially given the importance of the transition to Industry 4.0 and the possible strategies that may be adopted by the incumbents controlling digital platforms. It would also be particularly interesting to reflect on the respective role of competition law and regulatory alternatives in this context.

39. This process and strategies are well described in T. Wu, The Master Switch: The Rise and Fall of Information Empires (First Vintage Book, 2011) and T. Wu, The Attention Merchants: The Epic Scramble to Get Inside Our Heads (Penguin, 2016).
40. I. Graef, "Market Definition and Market Power in Data: The Case of Online Platforms", (2015) 38 *World Competition*, 473.
41. D. Rubinfeld and M Gal, "Access Barriers to Big Data", (2017) 59 *Arizona Law Review*, 339.
42. Autorité de la Concurrence and Bundeskartellamt, Competition Law and Data (16 May 2016), 17–20.
43. *See Ibid.*, 21–22; A. Acquisti and H. Varian, "Conditioning Prices on Purchase History", (2005) 24 *Marketing Science*, 367; Office of Fair Trading ('OFT') "Personalised Pricing: Increasing Transparency to Improve Trust", (2013) Report 1489, also found evidence of search discrimination, targeted discounting and dynamic pricing (use fluctuations in demand to change the prices of products depending on availability); A. Ezrachi and M. Stucke, "The Rise of Behavioural Discrimination", (2016) 37 *European Competition Law Review*, 484; A. Ezrachi and M. Stucke, *Virtual Competition* (Harvard University Press, 2016), Chapter 12; M Bourreau, A. de Streel and I. Graef, "Big Data and Competition Policy: Market Power, Personalised Pricing and Advertising", (2017) CERRE Project Report.
44. The (German) Bundeskartellamt, "Bundeskartellamt Initiates Proceedings Against Facebook on Suspicion of Having Abused its Market Power by Infringing Data Protection Rules", (*bundeskartellamt.de*, 2 March 2016) www.bundeskartellamt.de/SharedDocs/Meldung/EN/Pressemitteilungen/2016/02_03_2016_Facebook.html.

§1.04 COMPETITION LAW, REGULATION AND ALTERNATIVES

Some jurisdictions have been concerned by the transformation of these digital platforms into important gatekeepers for various economic activities in the digital economy[45] and by their ability to leverage their economic power (power which results from controlling resources such as big data, advanced algorithms and AI, on which the new model of economic production depends) in various domains of activity, including the capture of an even higher percentage of the total surplus value of the respective value chain. Algorithmic firms may harvest an immense technological and, ultimately, economic power differential vis-à-vis their non-algorithmic rivals. Would domain expertise enable these firms to resist the technological prowess of digital platforms? What would be the appropriate role for competition law in this context? Should competition law be enforced when digital platforms adopt exclusionary practices that may stifle the capacity of non-algorithmic firms to innovate or to develop independent technological capabilities and, thus, limit their technological dependence on them but by doing so improve their own efficiency? Control of (personal) data by these digital platforms may also affect privacy.[46] More generally, though control of such data may also have an impact upon the democratic process,[47] thereby leading to the emergence of an entrenched dominant position or oligopolistic market structure over an essential social good, that of information, which is required for the proper functioning of democratic debate. Such control may also provide the 'Big Five' with important economic and/or political and/or cultural power.[48] Should competition law also address these concerns? Or should these concerns be resolved through the use of other tools, such as different forms of regulation on issues such as platform-to-business, net neutrality, interoperability etc.? Or should even more informal ways be employed to deal with the concentration of power held by digital platforms, such as codes of conduct and self-regulation? These questions may explain the recent focus of competition authorities in Europe on leveraging practices; they seek to ensure 'equality of

45. *See* EU Communication on Digital Platforms of 25 May 2016 (COM(2016)288 final), 12, noting that 'as online platforms play an increasing role in the economy, the terms of access to online platforms can be an important factor for online and offline companies. For SMEs and micro-enterprises, some online platforms constitute important, sometimes the main, entry points to certain markets and data'.
46. *See* European Data Protection Supervisor, 'Privacy and Competitiveness in the Age of Big Data: The Interplay Between Data Protection, Competition Law and Consumer Protection in the Digital Economy', (2014) Report; Autorité and Bundeskartellamt, (42); US Federal Trade Commission ('FTC'), "Big Data – a Tool for Inclusion or Exclusion?", (2016) Report. Some public authorities have also looked at these questions when exploring the changes brought by platform competition, *see*: European Commission, "Online Platforms and the Digital Single Market Opportunities and Challenges for Europe", (2016) Report, COM/2016/0288 final; House of Lords, "Online Platforms and the Digital Single Market", (2016) House of Lords Paper, 129; Organisation for Economic Co-operation and Development ('OECD'), "Big Data: Bringing Competition Policy to the Digital Era", (2016) Report DAF/COMP(2016)14.
47. *See*, for instance, the debate about 'fake news' being an 'antitrust problem': S. Hubbard, "Fake News Is a Real Antitrust Problem", (2017) *Competition Policy International*; S. Sacher and J. Jun, "Fake News is Not an Antitrust Problem", (2017) *Antitrust Chronicle*.
48. These are Alphabet, Amazon, Apple, Facebook and Microsoft.

opportunity' among economic operators.[49] Competition authorities have also recently focused on ideas to regulate platform-to-business relations from a fairness perspective.[50]

Regarding net neutrality, public authorities have not limited their action in the search engine segment. They have not sought to limit the action they pursue in order to protect content providers regardless of their segment being the most competitive segment of the digital value chain because of its low costs of entry and the absence of natural monopoly characteristics. Rather public authorities have sought to act in the aforementioned segment and have sought to regulate the other segment with which content providers interact, specifically the network segment, in which ISPs operate and which presents some natural, monopoly-like characteristics given the important fixed costs one needs to incur for the last mile service, plant wiring (or fiber) linking the premises with the content delivery network.

Network neutrality policy aims to (i) regulate ISPs and ensure equal treatment of data traffic being transmitted over the internet, (ii) prohibit ISPs from blocking or slowing down Internet traffic unless this is to comply with a legal order, (iii) ensure network integrity and security, and (iv) manage congestion. The policy is broadly intended to prevent network operators from gaining an advantage because of the structure of the market (i.e., their commercial bonds with downstream operators) to affect competition either in the market of reference or in related markets. The principle of net neutrality was enshrined in EU law by Regulation 2015/2120 (also called the Telecom Single Market ('TSM') Regulation). The TSM Regulation encompasses common EU rules on net neutrality.[51] According to these rules, there can be no blocking, limiting or discrimination of internet traffic by ISPs; this prohibition effectively denies ISPs the possibility of selecting who wins and who lose on the internet and/or of deciding which content and services should be made available to whom.[52] Given the inherent vagueness of the TSM Regulation, it has been argued that competition law should be used as an interpretative tool in reaching the objectives set out in the regulation.[53] Some authors argue that competition law has the right standards of analysis on how the 'non-discrimination' principle (which stands at the basis of net neutrality) should be enforced while maintaining the right level of flexibility with which *ex ante* regulation is not necessarily concerned.[54] *Ex ante* regulatory intervention would be justified if its benefits outweigh its costs. It would be important to avoid a situation in which the inability of network providers to obtain a return would reduce their incentive to invest in the network level and infrastructure. *Ex post* competition

49. *See* European Commission, Case AT 39.740 – *Google Search*, [332] and [334].
50. *See* European Commission, "Inception Impact Assessment, Fairness in Platform to Business Relation, Ares (2017) 5222469", (2017) Report.
51. Regulation (EU) 2015/2120 of the European Parliament and of the Council of 25 November 2015 Laying Down Measures Concerning Open Internet Access, [2015] OJ L310/1.
52. For more information on these rules, *see* European Commission, "Open Internet Policy", (*ec.europa.eu*, 24 July 2018) ec.europa.eu/digital-single-market/en/open-internet-net-neutrality.
53. P. Alexiadis, "EU Net Neutrality Policy and the Mobile Sector: The Need for Competition Law Standards", (2016) 3 *Concurrences Review*, 1.
54. *Ibid.*, 3.

law would, instead, allow network providers to gain returns (that can then be reinvested on infrastructure) in whatever way they seek, provided this does not distort competition dynamics. Furthermore, it is argued that *ex post* competition intervention will provide contend providers with greater flexibility to develop application-level innovation without the constraints of an *ex ante*, obstructive non-discriminatory regulation.[55] Other jurisdictions, like the US, have adopted net neutrality regulations only before subsequently abandoning them because of pressure from ISPs, allegedly, concerning the taking advantage of opportunities offered by the IoT to develop new business models, the possibility of discriminating between users and the costs required for funding the transition from 4G to 5G.[56]

Interoperability and open access policies, which may be implemented through competition law and/or sector-specific regulation, may also tame the power of digital platforms and open up bottlenecks thereby enabling the 'open innovation' process to take place. 'Interoperability is a characteristic of a product or system, whose interfaces are completely understood, to work with other products or systems, at present or future, in either implementation or access, without any restrictions'.[57] With regard to sector-specific interoperability or open access regulation, one may cite the example of financial services, where the UK Competition and Markets Authority paved the way towards 'Open Banking' by implementing a competition law remedy it had imposed in 2016, following the retail banking market investigation.[58] The Open Banking regulatory intervention requires the six largest deposit-taking financial institutions (i.e., banks) in the UK to enable personal customers and small businesses to share their data securely with other banks and third parties and to manage their accounts with multiple providers through a single 'digital app'. The regulatory intervention also provides them with more possibilities to compare financial services and products from competing providers, including account information service providers and payment initiation service providers.

The interoperability of cloud computing services and heterogeneous IoT platforms are also an important concern for competition authorities worldwide and has led

55. N. Garzaro and A. Garzaro, "EU Competition Law and the Telecoms Single Market: Network Neutrality in the Aftermath of the TSM Regulation", (2016) 23 *Lex ET Scientia International Journal*, 44.
56. This is also explained by the degree of competition in the Internet Service Provider segment of the value chain, which, it is alleged, will increase as 5G wireless will compete with cable.
57. B. Lundqvist, "Regulating Competition and Property in the Digital Economy – The Interface Between Data, Privacy, Intellectual Property, Fairness and Competition Law", (2018) Stockholm University Research Paper No. 54, 32, discusses the distinction between 'syntactic' and 'semantic' interoperability: 'beyond the ability of two or more computer systems to exchange information (i.e., syntactic interoperability), semantic interoperability is the ability to automatically interpret the information exchanged meaningfully and accurately in order to produce useful accurate and neutral results as defined by the end users of both systems. To achieve semantic interoperability, both sides must refer to a common information exchange reference model'.
58. Competition and Markets Authority ('CMA'), "Retail Banking Market Investigation", (2016) Final Report, 441–461.

some jurisdictions to consider specific interoperability and access policies in this context.[59] This, of course, also relates to the broader standardisation debate.[60]

Beyond the simple choice between competition and regulation, one may enhance the development of markets for data and a more active engagement of consumers via general,[61] or sector-specific,[62] policies of data portability. Such an institutional choice may depend on the conducting of a careful comparative institutional analysis for *each* jurisdiction which considers the capabilities of the competition authorities and/or courts in that individual jurisdiction as well as the capabilities of the institutions overseeing other legal fields that may have the potential to help in the regulation of digital platforms.

It has been argued that the return to some form of 'populist' antitrust may provide an adequate response to the current rise in the level of inequalities, particularly those generated by the prevalence of the network effects and 'winner-takes-most' dynamics of the digital economy.[63] Such an approach may be considered adequate for as long as the existence of market concentration, market power and declining labour share are among the principal causes of these inequalities. These inequalities may not necessarily be addressed through more aggressive competition law intervention in markets. Antitrust 'conservatives'[64] may find comfort with approaches that suggest the expansion of markets and the re-conceptualisation of property rights,[65] in order to deal with the 'complete markets assumption' problem that has always bedevilled equilibrium analysis in economics.[66] Equally, however, other approaches emphasising the role of

59. *See*, for instance, Deloitte, "Emerging Issues of Data Ownership, Interoperability, (Re-)Usability and Access To Data, and Liability", (2016) Study Prepared for the European Commission DG Communications Networks, Content and Technology; Deloitte, 'Industry 4.0', (2016) Study for the ITRE Committee, European Parliament.
60. *See*, European Commission, "Standardisation to Support Digitisation", (2017) Report from the Workshop; B. Lundqvist, "Standardisation for the Digital Economy – The Issue of Interoperability and Access under Competition Law", (2017) 62 *The Antitrust Bulletin*, 710; W. Kerber and H. Schweitzer, "Interoperability in the Digital Economy", (2017) 8 *Journal of Intellectual Property, Information Technology and Electronic Commerce Law*, 39.
61. In the EU, this is Article 20 of the General Data Protection Regulation (EU) 2016/679 ('GDPR').
62. *See*, for instance, the recent proposals for an EU European Commission, Staff Working Document, 'Impact Assessment', Accompanying the document Proposal for a Regulation of the European Parliament and of the Council on a Framework for the Free Flow of Non-Personal Data in the European Union, SWD/2017/0304 final – 2017/0228 (COD); European Commission, Staff Working Paper on the Free Flow of Data and Emerging Issues of the European Data Economy, COM /2017, 9 Final, cited by B. Lundqvist, (57).
63. L. Khan and S. Vaheesan, "Market Power and Inequality: The Antitrust Counterrevolution and Its Discontents", (2017) 11 *Harvard Law and Policy Review*, 235.
64. By this expression I mean those that fear more Type I Errors (over-enforcement) than Type II Errors (under-enforcement).
65. *See*, for instance, the recent book by E. Posner and E. Weyl, *Radical Markets Uprooting Capitalism and Democracy for a Just Society* (Princeton University Press, 2018), which suggests a greater use of Harberger taxes and the end of the monopoly paradigm of property rights perceived as a right to exclude.
66. The assumption that consumers may access a full set of insurance contracts and, thus, be protected against any possible idiosyncratic risk that may affect their individual consumption (e.g., loss of a job, accident, stock market boom or bust) deals with the inherent uncertainty of a market system, with contingent consumption claims being settled before uncertainty is revealed, and enables economists to assume that individual behaviour coincides with aggregate behaviour, thereby, greatly simplifying economic analysis and, consequently, the lessons that

countervailing bargaining power (specifically of final consumers and/or of other market participants) in order to neutralise economic power and its various sources have also been put forward.[67] The choice of the adequate approach will depend on the political economy of the specific jurisdiction, the comparative institutional analysis performed and the prior beliefs of policymakers. However, there is value in making these complex considerations explicit and providing some transparency as to the decision-making process so to respond to concerns expressed as to the use of competition law strategically and to the perceiving of discrimination against foreign firms.

§1.05 TAKING INTO ACCOUNT THE 'NEXT-GENERATION' COMPETITION IN THE DIGITAL ECONOMY

In addition to the necessary adjustments that need to be made in the implementation of competition law in the digital economy, some express the view that the fundamentals of the competitive game have changed with the advent of the digital economy and that we need a more serious effort to re-conceptualise competition law so that this area of law continues to be relevant from the perspectives of both technology and business.[68] Some authors have referred to the competitive game taking place in the digital economy as 'next-generation competition' or 'turbo-charged competition'.[69] Hence, the question raised is whether we do, in fact, need a 'next-generation competition law' or a 'turbo-charged competition law' to deal with competition in the

may be drawn for both individual and aggregate analysis just by studying either indifferently. For a critical discussion *see*, T. Jappelli and L. Pistaferri, "Complete Markets" in The Economics of Consumption: Theory and Evidence (edited by T. Jappelli and L. Pistaferri, Oxford University Press, 2017), 46.

67. *See*, for instance, M. Gal and N. Elkin-Koren, "Algorithmic Consumers", (2017) 30 *Harvard Journal of Law and Technology*, 309, which advances the possibility of consumers to also turn algorithmic and, thus, tame the technological power of algorithmic firms. Other suggestions, which also implement this countervailing power narrative, include the call for wider exceptions for collective bargaining of the self-employed when such persons are economically dependent on digital platforms, in particular, to protect those working in the gig economy who may not be within the protective scope of labour law (for a discussion, *see* European Parliament Report, (21), which finds that 'the greater the level of financial dependence [of the labourer] on platform work, the lower the access that workers have to social protections'). The news media industry has also invoked the countervailing power narrative in order to ask for antitrust exemptions on collective bargaining with digital platforms: The Guardian, "News Media Alliance Targets Facebook and Google in the Fight Against Fake News", (*theguardian.com*, 10 July 2017) https://www.theguardian.com/media/2017/jul/10/news-media-alliance-targets-facebook-and-google-in-fight-against-fake-news, which notes that the News Media Alliance, which represents 2000 news organisations, would need an exemption from antitrust law to be able to negotiate as a group with digital platforms, such as Google and Facebook. Another similar suggestion concerns the ability of search engines' users to resort to collective bargaining with digital platforms: *see* I. Ibarra et al., "Should We Treat Data as Labour? Moving Beyond 'Free'", (2017) 1 *American Economic Association Papers and Proceedings*.
68. *See*, for instance, I. Lianos, "Polycentric Competition Law", (2018) UCL CLES Research Paper 4/2018).
69. D. Teece, "Next-Generation Competition: New Concepts for Understanding How Innovation Shapes Competition and Policy in the Digital Economy", (2012) 9 *Journal of Law & Policy*, 105–106.

digital economy? This section shares some reflections as to what has significantly changed from the competition times of old and the possible implications for competition law and the work of competition authorities.

[A] 'Winner-Takes-Most' Competition, Value Capture and Value Chains in the Digital Economy

Strong network effects, which have led to the rise of the digital economy and the multi-sided markets strategies of digital platforms have, in turn, increased the number of instances in which distinct products or services, previously considered to form separate relevant markets, are considered to be a package of complementary products and technologies, which form a system competing with other systems (i.e., 'systems competition').[70] The value of the relevant product does not depend solely on the number of persons who adopt it but depend also on the adoption of some complementary products that are bundled/packaged with the first product. Network effects lead to collective switching costs and lock-in effects, which reduce competition and may entrench the dominant position of the winner for a significant period of time. Multi-sided effects may transform 'systems competition' to 'platform competition'.

Firms are quite imaginative in their business models, sometimes distributing the product for free to one side of the market, thereby inducing more users to join the network, which, in turn, increases the value of the product for other users situated on the paying side of the market, with the platform facilitating the interaction between two or more different groups of customers (referred to as two- or multi-sided market platforms).[71] They may also use various business practices, such as penetration pricing where they charge low prices (even less than their costs) to gain market share, or strategically bundling their products in order to gain a foothold in another market which they can then use as a basis for expanding their presence in that market. In these markets, it is possible that firms may incur losses for a significant period of time in order to invest in acquiring market share, either through natural growth or by buying out actual or potential competitors through mergers and acquisitions, or to be considered as constituting one-stop-shop solutions or essential platforms for various groups of customers.[72]

Competition between firms takes unexpected forms, such as competing for consumers' attention and then profiling these consumers and using algorithms in order to predict, and possibly manipulate, their behaviour.[73] It has been alleged that personal data harvesting techniques have enabled digital platforms to create 'digital replicas' of our personalities, that is a 'digital representation of an individual, object, or asset' that has been 'constructed based on [how] an individual, object, or asset interacts with its

70. M. Katz and C. Shapiro, "Systems Competition and Network Effects", (1994) 8 *Journal of Economic Perspectives*, 93.
71. *See* our analysis in Chapter 3.
72. For an example of this strategy *see*, L. Khan, "Amazon's Antitrust Paradox", (2017) 126 *Yale Law Journal*, 564.
73. F. Pasquale, *The Black Box Society – The Secret Algorithms That Control Money and Information* (Harvard University Press, 2015).

environment'. These platforms have access to various facets of their users' personality, for instance 'how they interact with a whole host of appliances and other objects in their homes', information that 'industrial-age firms' specialising in a specific industry were not able to, or even interested in, use when designing or marketing their product.[74] Other authors have predicted that the harvesting of users' data will be done 'during [the] earlier, consumer-oriented stages of development' in order to build AI capacity, which 'once built, this [AI capacity] can be lucratively rented out to governments and companies', thereby engendering competition in relation to the provision of AI services.[75] These developments require a renewal of the theoretical frameworks used thus far used by competition economics for traditional markets as well as a clear understanding of business strategy. The sources of wisdom for competition law need to be widened beyond neoclassical price theory economics.[76]

However, this is not the only implication of the 'winner-takes-most' dynamic of platform competition. As indicated earlier, competition among platforms mostly takes the form of 'competition for the market', as important network effects lead to 'winner-takes-most' competition, with the outcome being only one platform controlling a market or being the significant player on the relevant market (resulting in them being capable of restricting horizontal competition) or dominating the value chain (resulting in them being capable of restricting vertical competition). Thus, markets marked by platform competition are horizontally concentrated, sometimes to such an extent that the second or third player in the market may not offer a viable competitive alternative to the established platform with the result that inter-platform competition remains weak and that there is *significant inequality in the distribution of market shares* among horizontal competitors.

At the same time, the centralised platform forms a 'bottleneck' with the power to determine the allocation of the surplus generated by the value chain between the various contributors and the power to keep an overwhelming portion of this surplus, thereby, accumulating significant profits and exercising vertical economic power. In view of the anchoring and lock-in of users and the low levels of switching to competing platforms, platform operators can be confident that any reduction of vertical competition between the different segments of the value chain with regard to the allocation of the total surplus value generated by the value chain, will not lead to a significant number of applications developers deserting their platform. Hence, value chains

74. B. Iyer, M. Subramanian and U. Rangan, "The Next Battle in Antitrust Will be About Whether One Company Knows Everything About You", (2017) *Harvard Business Review*. The authors note that access to the digital replicas of consumers will lead to 'new-age' monopolies. They explain that 'such new-age monopolies may not be visible through traditional industry concentration measures but they will wield tremendous influence over consumers. Their allure will be their ability to provide unprecedented personalisation based on the information they hold. Yet with such personalisation, customers may be restricted to see only what the provider wants them to see'.

75. *See* E. Morozov, "Will Tech Giants Move on From the Internet, Now We've All Been Harvested?", (*theguardian.com*, 28 January 2018) https://www.theguardian.com/technology/2018/jan/28/morozov-artificial-intelligence-data-technology-online.

76. On the importance, for instance, of other fields than economics *see*, among others, the special issues of the (2016) 61(4) *Antitrust Bulletin on Entrepreneurship and Antitrust*; and (2014) 59(4) *Antitrust as a Multi-Disciplinary Field*.

dominated by digital platforms are also marked by a very unequal distribution of profits between the established platforms and participants in their ecosystem and the emergence of 'superstar' firms.[77]

Users are also unable to identify how much value they add to the platform's operations as one's transactional history is not public; this information is collected and stored by, and only accessible to, the relevant platform or online intermediary. This practice raises issues concerning fairness, issues which may influence the enforcement activity undertaken by some competition authorities. In this chapter, I attempt to define the various dimensions of fairness and how this may be considered in competition law enforcement, particularly within the context of the digital economy.[78]

As the focus shifts to considering the processes of value creation and value sharing, new tools need to be developed in order to map out the complex horizontal and vertical competitive interactions between firms. The value chain approach enables us to better understand the different steps of value generation and to explore whether such an approach is efficient, in the sense of promoting innovation and productivity, and whether it is fair, in the sense of rewarding economic productivity and investment.[79]

[B] The Changing Dynamics of Competition: From Competition to Co-opetition, from Competitive Advantage to Architectural Advantage

Traditional (i.e., 'old-generation') antitrust perceives competition as taking place in markets with the concept of the 'relevant market' being a hallmark of 'modern' competition law analysis. Competition can be 'in the market' or, in the context of a 'winner-takes-most' or 'winner-takes-all' scenario (like in case there is a natural monopoly), competition can be 'for the market'. The fact that the concept of 'relevant market' has been criticised in recent times by economists,[80] who favour the direct assessment of assessment market power and consumer harm, neither does bring into

77. D. Autor et al., "The Fall of the Labour Share and the Rise of Superstar Firms", (2017) NBER Working Paper No. 23396.
78. This may relate to: political fairness, vertical fairness (relating to the split of surplus between firms on the one hand – in the form of profits – and consumers on the other – in the form of consumer surplus), horizontal supply-side fairness (relating to the extent to which firms compete on a level playing field – think of interoperability and open access standards), horizontal demand-side fairness (relating to the distribution of surplus between different consumers (personalised markets) or different categories of consumers (vulnerable and old consumers) etc. For a discussion of these different dimensions of fairness, *see* M. Trebilcock and F. Ducci, "The Multi-Faceted Nature of Fairness in Competition Policy", (2017) *CPI Antitrust Chronicle October*.
79. I. Lianos, "Regulating Digital Value Chains in Europe and Competition Law", (2019) UCL CLES Research Paper 1/2019.
80. Professor Kaplow called into question the practice of 'market definition' arguing that it would be preferable to dispense with it altogether and instead try to measure firms' price-cost mark-ups directly: L. Kaplow, "On The Relevance of Market Power", (2017) *Harvard Law Review*; L. Kaplow, "Market Definition, Market Power", (2015) Harvard Law School, Discussion Paper No. 826; L. Kaplow, "Why (Ever) Define Markets?", (2010) 124 *Harvard Law Review*, 437.

question this fundamental tenet of competition law and its focus on rivalry on a marketplace nor does it bring into question the need to define a 'relevant market' for the purposes of a competition law assessment.[81] The idea is that the process of competition and free markets, whether in product or technology (in case an IP right is involved) markets, rewards people according to their individual efforts/initiatives and economic productivity.

Competition may take different forms. The most common form is the acquisition of a cost-advantage vis-à-vis other undertakings in the same relevant market. Focusing on costs makes sense if the dominant facet of competition in the relevant market concerns price, which is often the case in most traditional markets. Conversely, in the digital economy, competitive interactions are quite complex. The notion and distinction between an 'established' or 'potential' competitor becomes blurred in the context of the digital economy because economic entities are actively pursuing strategies to alter the relevant industry's structure in order to alleviate competitive pressures to its own benefit; this involves positioning the firm where competition, horizontal and/or vertical, is the weakest.[82] In traditional strategy analysis, competing entities (most often corporations) seek a competitive advantage, either by imitating successful competitors while lowering their costs or by differentiating themselves from their competitors by developing idiosyncratic resources and capabilities and designing strategies to exploit these differences.

Competition economics has largely focused on horizontal competition from established competitors producing substitute products and on the threat of entry of potential competitors. Rivalry between established competitors is often measured by reference to the market share of the largest producers in a specific market in order to determine the level of market concentration, which is often measured by a concentration ratio. In contrast, vertical competition has rarely been the focus of competition economists despite its potential to play a significant role with regard to the allocation of the total surplus value generated by a value chain. The relative bargaining power of a supplier upstream or of a customer downstream have been considered to be less important than issues arising in horizontal competition because it is assumed that, in most cases, vertical competition-related issues do not affect the overall economic efficiency of transactions. Thus, in mainstream competition economics, the objective of which is to achieve economic efficiency rather than fairness in the distribution of the total surplus value, the exercise of relative bargaining power is not considered to be problematic for competition law unless such would harm economic efficiency (e.g., the rather confined case of monopsony or buyer power). Vertical competition may, however, become an important concern, if one focuses on the productivity and ability of 'superstar' large digital platforms to pull away from competition and enjoy tremendous levels of profitability, without these accumulated profits being used for productive investments.

81. G. Werden, "Why (Ever) Define Markets? An Answer to Professor Kaplow", (2013) 78 *Antitrust Law Journal*, 729.
82. R. Grant, *Contemporary Strategy Analysis* (Wiley, 2013), 74–76.

Furthermore, to fully understand the competitive strategies pursued in the digital economy in this era of financialisation, one must consider the product and technology markets in which these strategies are employed alongside the financial markets dimension inherent in these competitive strategies. Valuation by financial markets plays a significant role in determining the competitive strategies pursued by digital platforms; the most important driver of value creation is based not on net cash flows and expected short-term profits but on there being 'pots of gold' found far into the future.[83] This section engages with the financial markets dimension more fully in order to better understand the competitive strategies of firms in the digital economy and develop operational concepts that might be useful for competition law analysis. The important role of financial markets in the development of the digital economy and the monetisation of digital inputs also shifts attention from the traditional focus of competition law on competition within an industry, to competition between industries with capital (in the sense of value-enhancing activity, which does not constitute labour) moving from one industry to another in search of higher profits.

In addition to these competitive strategies taking place in product, technology or financial markets that engage directly with the actual and potential sources of competition, a firm may also acquire a durable competitive advantage if it holds a position that enables it to reshape the 'industry architecture' to its own advantage. The concept of 'industry architecture' follows Teece's seminal contribution on who profits from innovation and how the various governance arrangements between the innovator and other vertically-related firms may influence the distribution of these innovation gains.[84] According to Jacobides et al., 'the concept of industry architecture describes how labour is typically organized and structured within an industry ("who does what") and which firms capture value and profit as a result ("who takes what")'.[85] Being in a position to influence the way in which the industry is organised/structured and the value allocation between the industry (or ecosystem) actors provides a firm with an 'architectural advantage'. Such an advantage may serve as important source of sustainable yet abnormal profits. This is most likely the reason underlying the 'architectural fights' which have characterised the development of all industries.

Industry architecture is framed by the various economic actors at the birth of a new industry. These new players define the interfaces (technological, institutional and/or social) that allow different entities to co-specialise and divide labour.[86] Competition to become the industry architect has played a crucial role in periods of profound technological transformation, such as the development of new general purpose technologies in which new technologies that confer significant advantages, such as reducing costs or increasing productivity, are progressively integrated into the

83. *See* The Economist, "Are Technology Firms Madly Overvalued?", (*economist.com*, 23 February 2017), https://www.economist.com/business/2017/02/23/are-technology-firms-madly-overvalued.
84. D. Teece, "Profiting from Technological Innovation: Implications for Integration, Collaboration, Licensing and Public Policy", (1986) 15 *Research Policy*, 285.
85. M. Jacobides, "Industry Architecture" in The Palgrave Encyclopaedia of Strategic Management (edited by M. Augier and D. Teece, Palgrave Macmillan, London, 2016).
86. *Ibid.*

production processes employed in a specific industry.[87] These technologies offer a higher rate of return on investment. Furthermore, in the context of the inter-industry competition, these technologies often attract capital from other industries, which is one of the primary characteristics of financial capitalism.[88] As the industry matures, it is possible to observe the emergence of 'winners', i.e., actors who strive to frame the industry architecture in their own advantage by developing complex strategies. The objective of these strategies is to capture a disproportionate amount of the surplus value created by the innovation. This may happen by acquiring a bottleneck and converting it to abnormal profits. However, as the focus shifts from competition concerning prices to the more complex issue of capturing value, the competitive strategies of firms may also change. Value may not only be captured from other (weaker) members of the value chain but also be created through a process of 'co-specialisation', a process which very much characterises the way in which the digital economy operates.

Focusing on the appropriation of value from other value chain participants is sensible if one conceptualises competition, whether it be horizontal or vertical, as essentially a process that occurs on product or technology markets and focuses on capturing value through the protection and/or leveraging of innovation. However, value may also be created by 'investing in assets that will appreciate'[89] and will, thus, increase the market value of the firm from the perspective of financial markets. There has been a 'subtle shift of mindset from profit (and isolating mechanisms) to wealth creation (and the potential for asset appreciation)', which explains why an industry architect may sometimes favour imitation by competitors – even if imitation reduces profitability, an industry architect may permit this provided that such increases the value of the underlying assets.[90]

In situations where a system of 'open innovation' is considered to be the most effective way to generate higher value in the relevant industry, the optimal strategy to adopt will be to opt for one that promotes 'open architecture' and seeks to nurture complementarity through an open eco-system. In other situations, firms may prefer to opt for a 'walled garden approach'; they may opt for a closed architectural system, with regard to firms with competing assets and capabilities entering the value chain, while maintaining an open one for firms with complementary assets. Finally, in other situations, firms may opt for a strategy that is wholly closed architecture-centric; that of 'vertical integration'. By pursuing a strategy of vertical integration, firms can take full control over the rents generated by the complementarities brought by the innovation and can maintain the possibility of excluding or marginalising any new entrant, for instance, by denying interoperability with regard to some indispensable technological interfaces.

87. C. Ferguson and C. Morris, "How Architecture Wins Technology Wars", (1993) 71 *Harvard Business Review*, 86.
88. *See* A. Shaikh, *Capitalism: Competition, Conflict, Crises* (Oxford University Press, 2016).
89. M. Jacobides, T. Knudsen and M. Augier, "Benefiting From Innovation: Value Creation, Value Appropriation and the Role of Industry Architectures", (2006) 35 *Research Policy*, 1201.
90. *Ibid.*, 1212.

In this 'co-opetition framework',[91] business is neither a 'winner-takes-all' game nor a 'winner-takes-most' game, as the industry architecture should be conceived by all economic actors as being 'fair' in order for them to maintain their incentives to participate in it and for the relations between the various firms forming the eco-system to maintain some form of stability.[92]

This raises interesting questions as to the space in which competitive interactions take place to capture or create value, which, in view of the complexity of the competitive strategies that I highlighted earlier, cannot be solely limited to the relevant market. It will be important to think of these other spaces of competition and consider whether competition authorities should adopt new operational concepts that are capable of accounting for these new competitive spaces.

[C] From Markets to Platforms and to Eco-systems

The Internet era gave rise to many online intermediaries and digital platforms controlling and orchestrating value-generating ecosystems that not only offer products and online services but also provide the infrastructure and tools on which other platform businesses are built. At the same time, the development of Big Data and multi-sided markets strategies have raised questions and cast doubt on the sole focus of the assessment undertaken by competition law concerning the definition of the relevant market. How could one proceed to delineate a market in a world in which the possible personalisation of production means that consumers can themselves become the designers of the individually-customised products they consume with the products being produced by 3-D printing and robots? Will firms be competing mainly on the market for personal information? What will serve as the raw material on which personalised production will be based? Competition law analysis needs to consider, when assessing competitive constraints, the type of competition taking place in the specific 'field'. Competition can be *for* the market as well as *in* the market. Platform or system competition characterises a lot of competitive interactions in the network economy. The shift from competition and value capture to mixed strategies of value capture and value creation, involving strategies of co-opetition, indicates that an additional 'field' of competition-related activity should also be added: that of the 'eco-system'.

Developed in the early 1990s,[93] the concept of an 'ecosystem' has been defined in broad terms as 'a group of interacting firms that depend on each other's activities'.[94]

91. B. Nalebuff, "Co-opetition: Competitive and Cooperative Business Strategies for the Digital Economy", (1997) 26 *Strategy and Leadership*, 28.
92. For the importance of fairness in order to keep stable a social equilibrium, *see* K. Binmore, *Natural Justice* (Oxford University Press, 2005), 3–14, which takes an 'evolutionary' approach to social contract theory, advancing that a social contract may be 'internally stable' if it combines efficiency and fairness.
93. J. Moore, "Predators and Prey: A New Ecology of Competition", (1993) 71 *Harvard Business Review*, 75.
94. M. Jacobides, C. Cennano and A. Gawer, "Towards a Theory of Ecosystems", (2018) 39 *Strategic Management Journal*, 2255.

Teece notes that a characteristic of eco-systems is their 'co-evolution' in the sense that the 'attributes of two or more organisations become more closely complementary', 'the system being typically reliant on the technological leadership of one or two firms that provide a platform around which other system members, providing inputs and complementary goods, align their investments and strategies'. Teece also notes that 'co-creation' is a characteristic of eco-systems as two or more organisations 'combine forces to pioneer new markets'.[95] Adner observes that 'the ecosystem is defined by the alignment structure of the multilateral set of partners that need to interact in order for a focal value proposition to materialise'. Adner proceeds to define this 'alignment structure' as 'the extent to which there is mutual agreement among the members regarding positions and flows'.[96] The concept of 'eco-system' has emerged as the dominant idea for depicting the competitive environment in the modern digital economy. The 'eco-system manager' determines the elements of the value chain that will need to be internalised and those which will be supported externally so as to capture value. Most studies on eco-systems focus on the role of the eco-system as a 'hub' of inter-firm relations taking place within the context of a platform, often referred to as the 'lead firm' or 'ecosystem captain', which 'defines the hierarchical differentiation of members' roles and establishes standards and interfaces, a number of formal mechanisms, such as the management of standards and interfaces, platform governance, IP rights etc. forming the "key tools that hubs use to discipline and motivate ecosystem members"'.[97] However, from a theoretical perspective, a platform eco-system has never been the only option even if, in practical terms, the platform model has become dominant - it is possible to imagine an eco-system in which power is neither concentrated in a hub nor governed by a platform but is distributed among various economic actors and stakeholders who will take decisions by consensus.

The essence of this new insight comes from the realisation that competition analysis should engage with the 'value capture' strategies put in place by economic actors competing for strategic or architectural advantage.[98] These should form the starting point of competition analysis, rather than the relevant market concept which no longer constitutes the sole reference point firms consider when devising their strategies and identifying the competitive constraints to which they are subject. Abandoning solely focusing on the relevant market concept also stems from the relatively more limited role of price competition in the digital economy. Firms often compete for customers in order to (i) enlarge their customer base, and/or (ii) take advantage of network effects and be perceived by financial markets as holding a 'bottleneck', even if such trade, from a price-cost perspective, may not be profitable. This struggle for a large customer base explains why firms continue to offer 'free goods', even if the gains in market share they obtain or their ability to harvest consumer data (personal data being the 'price' to pay for these 'free goods') may not be

95. Teece, (69), 105–106.
96. R. Adner, "Ecosystem as Structure – An Actionable Construct for Strategy", (2017) 43 *Journal of Management*, 42.
97. Jacobides et al., (94), 2258-2259 and the literature review provided.
98. D. Teece, "Business Models, Value Capture and the Digital Enterprise", (2017) 6 *Journal of Organizational Design*.

immediately monetised in data markets. However, capturing a large customer base at reduced or negative profitability is not the ultimate aim of these strategies. This strategy makes sense if, by acquiring a large customer base, firms are able to develop dynamic capabilities (e.g., the firm may use consumer data to enable it to improve its algorithms). These benefits do not only materialise in the long-term but may also be enjoyed through a higher market valuation by the financial markets in the short-term.

[D] Beyond 'Attention Markets': Towards 'Personalised' Markets?

It is increasingly acknowledged that data collection is fundamental to firms' ability to compete in the future IoT, IoS and/or Internet of Everything. The firms that have obtained access to the largest amounts of data will benefit from a competitive advantage.[99] Data analytics connected to the use of software for predictive modelling, will also reinforce the competitive advantages of such firms, with this ultimately being crystallised in architectural advantage because of their control of 'idiosyncratic rent-earning resources' (i.e., in the form of superior algorithms) or, more generally, by their development of capabilities that cannot be imitated by competitors (because of increasing returns to scale).[100] With the advancement of the IoT and IoS and the possible emergence in the near future of the Internet of Everything, the amount of data that will be collected will increase immensely, including in industries that were not previously digital.

Much of this data will relate to the digital identity of the consumer and will enable companies to draw a pretty accurate individual preferences map for each of their clients. More than just an 'attention market',[101] firms will be able to develop bespoke products that suit the individual preferences of their consumers without incurring prohibitive costs as they will be able to achieve economies of scale by developing various series of products that could satisfy the entire demand function of the specific consumer in various product categories. In this era of 'mass personalisation',[102] these new conglomerates will not just control markets in the traditional sense, but they will control the personalised markets of individual consumers on whom they hold a level of data superior to that held by other firms. This, in turn, will permit them to cater for the entirety of demands and needs of that individual, for instance, in consumer goods or entertainment.[103] Once a specific amount of data is harvested, these personalised markets will tip with the result that only one firm will have the capabilities to perfectly satisfy the individual consumer's demand in an array of products. Indeed, consumers will economise their time if they rely on the personalised made-to-order and customised-to-their-preferences offer of one digital platform or reseller that has been able to harvest their personal data and, from that, gain a greater understanding of their

---

99. There is a discussion regarding the definition of 'data': does it encompass syntactic information, semantic information, or both; and where should one draw the line in reference to protecting 'data'? *See* Drexl, (5); Wiebe, (5).
100. Jacobides et al, (6), 1386.
101. On this concept, *see* Wu, (8); Evans (8).
102. Deloitte, (7).
103. *See*, for instance, Danziger, (9).

individual preferences map. Firms may then be able to organise the production process within their ecosystem. They may do this by limiting access to an individual consumer's profile to a number of firms that they control, either directly or indirectly, and such access will be dependent on this latter firm ensures their products fit the relevant consumer's specific preferences. Even assuming that consumer preferences may evolve and that the process of their formation is complex, and that some degree of competition may still be possible, it is clear that mass personalisation will increase demand stickiness and the ability of firms to exploit consumers while simultaneously reducing consumer surplus, product variety and consumer choice.

Some of these 'personalised markets' may well appear in the pharmaceutical industry through the development of personalised healthcare, precision medicine and smart healthcare. Changes brought about by developments in digital technology will transform the pharmaceutical and the medical services industries. Data and algorithms are important game-changers as they will enable the development of new 'beyond-the-pills' solutions. Firms will be able to combine drugs, sensors collecting information on the patient's condition and different sorts of data (early R&D data, digital medical records, including diagnostic results, medication history, genomic or gene-expression data, lifestyle data) to develop such solutions. Future medical service providers may be able to 'personalise' patient care, better identify optimal therapies, better predict the patient's response to treatment, as well as engage more fully with physicians, in particular, enabling them to draw from superior insights when making decisions.

The digital revolution will likely transform the pharmaceutical and health service industries beyond recognition in the same way the media, retail, transport and banking industries have been reshaped in recent years. The role of 'personal data', in particular 'genetic data' (such as gene expression data) and 'lifestyle data', in the delivery of personalised medical services and personalised medicine will change the current paradigm, which is very much based on the development of therapies that target an entire population. New digital and/or data-based business models will certainly develop on the basis of competitive advantage in accessing this pool of personal data. This, in turn, will enable the development of health and medical solutions tailored to the characteristics of a specific individual. Hence, it might be expected that the main industrial actors in this area in the future will be not only the pharmaceutical industry and biotechnology companies but also digital intermediaries, which may rely on their superior technological (e.g., algorithms, specialised human resources etc.) and data-gathering capabilities in order to move to the centre of this new emerging health services ecosystem. This move may be based on their own initiative or be done in combination with other firms benefitting from expertise in a specific domain.[104]

In view of the 'intermediary power' some digital platforms may enjoy, to the extent that intermediaries dispose of privileged access to consumer data and/or of 'a significant ability' to steer consumers,[105] such platforms may acquire a unique level of

104. Jacobides et al., (89), 1200.
105. H. Schweitzer et al., "Modernising the Law on Abuse of Market Power", (2017) Report for the (German) Federal Ministry for Economic Affairs and Energy. For example, the German Competition Act was amended in 2017; it states that "access to relevant data is a potential

access to and control over personalised data. This raises concerns over them being the sole source and controller of it in relation to further processes of data monetisation and commercialisation; or of multiple firms being the individual controllers over different sources of data, thus constituting 'data thickets'. The right of access to the data (i.e., through a request to the manufacturer, maker or generator of the data) will certainly constitute an important element in devising the public policy aim that should frame the principles that would apply in each regulatory framework. However, conceiving access to data as a right that any actual (and/or potential) business participant may stumble across raises considerable theoretical and practical difficulties, such as the issues of:

- ownership of this data (i.e., if data may be 'owned'),
- the business practices of firms holding the data limiting or conditioning access to it (i.e., hold-up situations in cases of split ownership),
- this information being subject to moral rights,
- this information being subject to rules concerning inalienability,
- regulatory prohibitions or limits to the sharing of personal data,[106] and
- the technical means and way in which access to the specific data will be implemented and the transaction costs inherent in such (these costs are likely to be considerable).

source of market power". *See also* W. Kerber, "Digital Markets, Data, and Privacy: Competition Law, Consumer Law and Data Protection", (2016) *Gewerblicher Rechtsschutz und Urheberrecht Internationaler Teil*, 639–647. There are several authors who purport that holding big data does not equate to market power: G. Colangelo and M. Maggiolino, "Big Data as Misleading Facilities", (2017) Bocconi Legal Studies Research Paper No. 2978465. Generally, they argue that big data does not create a significant barrier to entry and they base their claims, *inter alia*, on the non-exclusive and non-rivalrous nature of data and a claimed ease of collecting it, while disregarding many potential entry barriers. Other scholars argue that the harm created by big data pertains mainly to privacy. Yet, these conclusions are based on the limited existing economic studies on big data, which often focus on one specific market (most commonly on search engines or personal data markets). *See*, for example, Rubinfeld and Gal, (41), 339; D. Tucker and H. Wellford, "Big Mistakes Regarding Big Data", (2014) 6 *Antitrust Source*, 10; M. Ohlhausen and A. Okuliar, "Competition, Consumer Protection, And the Right [Approach] To Privacy", (2015) 80 *Antitrust Law Journal*, 121; J. Cooper, "Privacy and Antitrust: Underpants Gnomes, the First Amendment and Subjectivity", (2013) 20 *George Mason Law Review*, 1129.

106. This is particularly the case for 'genetic data', which forms a 'special category' under Article 9 of the GDPR. According to Recital 34 of the GDPR, 'genetic data should be defined as personal data relating to the inherited or acquired genetic characteristics of a natural person which result from the analysis of a biological sample from the natural person in question, in particular chromosomal, deoxyribonucleic acid (DNA) or ribonucleic acid (RNA) analysis, or from the analysis of another element enabling equivalent information to be obtained'. However, this is not the only type of personal data of interest. There is also ample discussion on the issue of the ownership of databases containing such type of data, in particular if this is generated by sensors or machines/algorithms for the purposes of the 'Database Directive' 96/9/EC (i.e., Directive 96/9/EC of the European Parliament and of the Council of 11 March 1996 on the legal protection of databases, [1996] OJ L 77/20) in view of Article 1(3) of the Directive, which provides that 'protection under this Directive shall not apply to computer programs used in the making or operation of databases accessible by electronic means'. For a discussion, *see* Joint Institute for Innovation Policy and Technopolis Group, 'Study in Support of the Evaluation of Directive 96/9/EC on the Legal Protection of Databases', (2018) Study for the European Commission DG Communications Networks, Content and Technology.

One should expect that many of the actors operating in the digital pharmaceutical and health services industry will engage in extensive long-term collaborations in reference to the creation, the exchange and trade of data. These collaborations will likely be based on the high level of transaction costs and specificity of data and technological capabilities required by this industry in order for it to flourish. It should also be expected that various industry players will seek to control bottlenecks and, thus, preserve their ability to gain abnormal profits, even after the superior technological capabilities of which they currently dispose have dissipated in view of the diffusion of any necessary and relevant technologies among all players in this new ecosystem.

Indeed, pharmaceutical firms, especially the so-called 'Big Pharma' ones, have traditionally focused on 'taking drugs to the market' while having, as the basis for their business model, a large patent portfolio consisting of substance and/or process patents. They have traditionally been at the forefront of controlling and driving the (downstream) procedure of obtaining marketing authorisations while also managing the (upstream) R&D procedure by purchasing or licensing-in potential successful R&D results from often smaller R&D firms. Now health data and the control of health data will challenge that traditional value chain of taking drugs to the market.

Effectively, the digital transformation has caused both a need and opportunity for pharmaceutical firms to explore new business models, that is, the logic or framework they use to create and capture value.[107] Business model innovation can be particularly challenging in the context of disruptive change especially when there is a lack of clarity as to what the new business model would or should look like,[108] and its organisational structure.[109] Moreover, the complexity involved in emerging technologies, in terms of both potential problems and solutions, gives rise to a need to connect disciplines and organisations. This will likely lead to there being more open business models[110] that focus on joint value creation with complementary partners operating within larger ecosystems.[111]

Future product markets will likely face a paradigm shift when data becomes the starting point of the value chain as pharmaceutical products and medical services will likely be framed according to the genetic and lifestyle data of an individual patient.[112] The vast amounts of collected data will also enable producers to understand what consumers and/or patients value in the pharmaceutical products and medical services they purchase. This will influence the way in which products are designed and developed thereby increasing product quality, which, in turn, should help generate products that, in accordance with preferences revealed by their data, match the relevant buyer's expectations. This could fundamentally alter 'old economy' markets.

107. A. Afuah, Business Model Innovation: Concepts, Analysis and Cases (Routledge, 2014).
108. H. Chesbrough, "Business Model Innovation: Opportunities and Barriers", (2010) 43 *Long Range Planning*, 354–363.
109. K. Sund et al., "Managing Tensions Between New and Existing Business Models", (2016) 57 *MIT Sloan Management Review*, 8–10.
110. H. Chesbrough and M. Bogers, "Explicating Open Innovation: Clarifying an Emerging Paradigm for Understanding Innovation" in *New Frontiers in Open Innovation* (edited by H. Chesbrough, W. Vanhaverbeke and J. West, Oxford University Press, 2014), 3–28.
111. Adner, (96), 39-58.
112. *See* OECD, (46); Autorité de la Concurrence and Bundeskartellamt, (42), 7, 10 ff.

They would no longer be solely focused on marginal cost and price. Instead, firms would compete on a wider range of variables. The knock-on effect of the possible personalisation of offers and the dependency of patients on one specific firm may provide said firm with further sources of monopolistic rents thereby reducing the percentage of the surplus going to consumers.

Health data could, for example, enable the creation of new human health services solutions. The organisation of health services and the production of pharmaceutical products within the same digital eco-system would allow for feedback loops feeding health information back to pharmaceutical companies. These companies would then be able to develop business processes that could respond in real-time in order to improve the effectiveness of the relevant drugs or medicinal products. Such improvements would be done not on the general level of populations but on the specific level of individual patients. Patients would also be given the possibility of becoming more engaged with their health through an array of digital tools that provide them with the possibility of being better informed about their health and making lifestyle changes accordingly and of monitoring their own health and constantly sharing this information with medical experts. Data would become part of a 'digital ecosystem that constantly monitors a patient's condition and provides feedback to the patient and other stakeholders',[113] and tailors any treatment or therapy required to the patient's clinical and lifestyle needs.

In the health sector, several firms (claimed 'proprietors') hold different types of data. For example, we have clinical (i.e., patient) data, which is normally held by physicians, and we have clinical trial data held by pharmaceutical firms. Pharmaceutical firms also hold early R&D data. We have public health authorities, insurance firms and specific health data firms (e.g., IMS Health), which hold data regarding the cost and consumption of pharmaceuticals. Further, Internet firms like Google, or specific vertical medical search engines, may hold much data about patients' behaviour, their fears and conduct. If the data collected by these bodies could be anonymised, pooled and combined, that might prove very useful in the fight against all kind of diseases. It may substantially decrease the time currently required for identifying outbreaks of diseases, for developing new drugs or health solutions, for understanding the impact of new drugs, side-effects etc.[114] Personal health solutions can thus be developed. Indeed, data pools may be very successful in the human medical products and healthcare industry.

Generally, the current situation on data-driven markets is that there are a number of de facto data holders, each with a limited set of data. This situation has the potential to lead to market failure because to achieve the best results from any analysis undertaken, either all the relevant firms would need access to all this data or there would need to be one sole firm/provider that would be responsible for such. This is where the need for a federated 'data commons' becomes clear; it is necessary to enable

113. D. Champagne, A. Hung and O. Leclerc, *The Road to Digital Success in Pharma* (McKinsey & Co, 2015).

114. *See*, for example, P. Groves et al., "The 'Big Data' Revolution in Healthcare", (2013) McKinsey & Company Report for the Centre for US Health System Reform Business Technology Office.

interoperability between the various systems put in place by the participants in this ecosystem so that they provide an effective solution for patients. Borrowing the concept of 'integrated care' from health law,[115] the importance of ensuring that data is shared and relied upon so that care becomes responsive to the specific person's needs and genetic characteristics is crucial. Investigations should be undertaken to see whether dynamic efficiencies of 'data aggregation' exist in specific sectors and whether the market is capable of dealing with such. Investigations should also be undertaken to consider whether a federated data commons may be organised in the context of 'data pooling' or organised and closely-supervised in the context of markets for 'data trading'.[116]

A federated data commons provides a discrete possibility, which for reasons related to the efforts of limiting the diffusion of personal data, a policy aim for data protection legislation (which creates an artificial scarcity), and for reasons related to the important economic value of this data (may be as a consequence of this scarcity) may not provide an adequate governance regime for 'genetic data' or lifestyle data. Hence, the need to establish a form of conditional or permissioned access to this data, the condition being that the harvesting and the sharing of this data complies with the letter and spirit of the constitutional protections of privacy and data protection legislation. This conditional or permissioned access could be organised in the context of a federated data commons. Such could be organised, either on the supply side, with a number of industry players forming a data consortium or a data pool sharing access, or on the demand side, with a number of users' based data commons, societies and/or trusts providing a conditioned access to this data and managing the data commons. The likelihood of practically achieving these various options requires an in-depth analysis of their adequacy with regard to the specific nature of the data to be pooled and of the legal implications of each federated data commons design with regard to the various areas of law that regulate these economic activities.

For instance, there are various benefits to data pools. However, it is important to remember, as discussed in the following texts, that there are also competition law concerns linked to such practices. Data pooling may create barriers to entry and could also facilitate collusion between competitors. Why and how would this anticompetitive behaviour occur? The firms agreeing to pool data must agree on the method for gaining access to get access, the technology to be used for the collection, the processes concerning the storing and exchange of data, the type of data to which access will be provided etc. It is possible that the pool may exclude non-participating firms from access to the data; such a practice would raise concerns about anticompetitive foreclosure. Furthermore, the sharing of information in the context of this pool may also facilitate collusion or the pool may serve as a support-mechanism for a pre-existing

115. UK Government, "Complying with Monitor's Integrated Care Requirements", (*gov.uk*, 27 March 2015) https://www.gov.uk/government/publications/integrated-care-how-to-comply-with-monitors-requirements/complying-with-monitors-integrated-care-requirements.

116. *See* D. Burk, "Patents as Data Aggregators in Personalised Medicine", (2015) 21 *Boston University Journal of Science and Technology Law*, 233–255; N. Duch-Brown, B. Martens and F. Mueller-Langer, "The Economics of Ownership, Access and Trade in Digital Data", (2017) 1 JRC Digital Economy Working Paper.

cartel. Equally, the large amount of data in a pool connected to smart pricing algorithms may render it difficult to judge innovative pricing schemes. Firms connected to the pool may seek to unilaterally employ discriminatory pricing algorithms that enable them to charge each customer the maximum price; firms would be exploiting patients. The counter-argument would be that if you have all data about certain customers, you would seek to tailor and personalise the price in reference to each and every one of them. However, these exemplary anticompetitive disadvantages of federated data commons can be offset by the benefits a federated data commons brings with regard to access to data.

§1.06 CONCLUSION

The Internet era gave rise to many online intermediaries and digital platforms controlling and orchestrating value-generating ecosystems that not only offer products and online services but also provide the infrastructure and tools on which other platform businesses can be built. The developments of the last decade and the more recent rise of the cloud computing model indicate a growing trend towards centralisation, which, in conjunction with the development of Big Data, behavioural profiling and online manipulation, let us contemplate a future where a small number of digital platforms will hold immense power in all sectors of the digital economy. The threat of these digital platforms holding power in both the digital economy and beyond, specifically in the political and cultural spheres of society, have led some legal scholars to plead for specific regulation and law for the platform economy, to plead for the introduction of some form of democratic control and accountability.[117]

This rather gloomy prediction for our shared Internet future may not become reality if blockchain or DLT delivers on its promises. Blockchain is set to become the 'Internet of value',[118] that will complement the current Internet architecture, albeit on very different principles. Blockchain constitutes a technology that facilitates the exchange of value in a secure and decentralised manner without the need for an intermediary. Its main components are a distributed ledger that records all transactions or assets that are part of its domain, an encryption that protects this ledger from tampering and a distributed storage of all data through the sharing of excess drive and network capacity on PCs and in data-centres. While in the 'digital platform' model only the centralised online platform collects information about past transactions, blockchain offers a distributed decentralised ledger, which keeps a complete record of all past transactions on the network. This enables all participants to have access to information about past transactions and, thereby, ensures that no single participant on the network enjoys a position of superior bargaining power due to informational asymmetries. This equality is furthered by the transparency of the process – each new transaction is broadcast to the entire network and each participant has the power to determine its authenticity. This breaks with the centralised data silos model of the

117. J. Cohen, "Law for the Platform Economy", (2017) 51 *UC Davis Law Review*, 133.
118. *See*, https://www.mckinsey.com/industries/high-tech/our-insights/getting-serious-about-blockchain.

platform economy in which only some actors have access to this information as all interactions between the network participants happen through them, thereby, enabling them to accumulate data, which, in turn, can help them to increase their bargaining power and to erect barriers to entry. Of course, blockchain is not a monolith. There exist various types of blockchain, some of which are closer to the centralised ledger model of digital platforms. It is customary to distinguish 'private' or 'federated' blockchains from 'public' blockchains.

However, the essence of the 'blockchain dream' is that the decentralisation and disintermediation it enables will challenge the current centralised architecture of the Internet and will accomplish the expectations of the original Internet dream for a borderless and radically democratic space. Blockchain technology sets out numerous challenges to competition authorities and brings forward the need to implement conceptual innovations in the way competition law enforcement is envisioned in this area (this is examined in-depth in a separate paper).[119] However, more importantly, at the symbolic level, blockchain is often opposed to the centralised paradigm of digital platforms that dominate different segments of the digital economy and often reduce consumer choice and privacy. The entities controlling these digital platforms now constitute the largest companies in the world.[120] An essential component of the blockchain dream is that it would finally fulfil the aspiration of a competitive space for the Internet, where peer-to-peer exchange without intermediaries would provide immense opportunities to establish alternative communities of economic, social and political exchange while also resolving the difficulty of combining this with the respect of privacy and digital autonomy. But is this more than just a 'dream'? Does blockchain lead to disintermediation of trust, or is it merely the development of new forms of intermediaries and intermediation?[121]

In the upcoming IoT paradigm, firms, at least small- and medium-sized enterprises ('SMEs'), will likely use e-platforms for e-retail services and marketing while simultaneously storing their data in the cloud and purchasing cloud services and storage from the large e-platform providers doubling as cloud providers. However, often the contracts linking these cloud platforms with third party sellers may oblige them to agree to not assert any of their IPRs vis-à-vis the provider or the provider's network.[122] Moreover, the providers may, under certain circumstances, seek to access and make use of the users' data created on the platforms or in the cloud in order to give themselves a competitive advantage vis-à-vis third party sellers since providers will have access to far greater levels of data; they may even have access to data originating from the third party sellers' competitors, suppliers, customers and so on.[123] Providers

119. I. Lianos, "Blockchain Competition – Gaining Competitive Advantage in the Digital Economy and Competition Law Implications", (2018) UCL CLES Research Paper 3/2018.
120. The five largest companies in the world are tech platforms, *see* A. Wilhelm, "Big Tech Goes Five for Five" (*techcrunch.com*, October 2017) https://techcrunch.com/2017/11/06/big-tech-goes-five-for-five/.
121. Lianos, (119).
122. B. Lundqvist, "Data Collaboration, Pooling and Hoarding Under Competition Law", (2018) Stockholm University Research Paper No. 61.
123. See the recent investigation into Amazon Marketplace initiated by the European Commission and the German Bundeskartellamt, *see*: S. Rolland, "After Attacking Google, Vestager Now

will be able to use all the data available to them to obtain fuller picture of whole industries and they may use their advantage in terms of data as leverage for them to enter into specific customer markets. Indeed, they may use said data to pursue data-driven business strategies that enable them to enter the core market of the firms that provided them with the relevant data in the first place.

A further example of decentralisation that could be of relevance for the IoT, is the possible shift from 'cloud computing' to 'fog computing'. The concept of 'cloud computing' comprises a group of computers and servers that are connected together over the Internet to form a network. Today, as many enterprises and large organisations are beginning to adopt the IoT, the need for large amounts of data to be accessed more quickly and locally is growing exponentially. The concept of 'fog computing' may bring a decentralised infrastructure to power the IoT which may change the traditional centralisation dynamics. The concept of 'fog computing', or 'fogging', is defined as a distributed infrastructure in which certain application processes or services are managed at the edge of the network by a smart device while other processes or services remain managed in the cloud. In essence, it is a middle layer between the cloud and the hardware in order to enable more efficient data processing, analysis and storage by reducing the amount of data that needs to be transported to the cloud. This may also add to the decentralisation dynamic brought about by blockchain technology.

One of the possible uses of blockchain technology and associated cryptocurrencies will be to become the backbone of the machine-payable web, i.e., machines communicating, sharing processing power and exchanging value with each other and serving as the base layer connecting the different industries. IOTA[124] is the first cryptocurrency designed to power the IoT revolution. It enables the secure sharing of resources between smart devices with zero transaction fees. IOTA has also been used as the underlying ledger for transferring information during the production process, while also leading to a tamper-proof audit trail.

It is important to closely engage with these technological developments and to invite industry actors to provide their take on the centralisation and decentralisation dynamics of the digital economy and on the competitive strategies employed by various economic players in the different business eco-systems. Competition authorities should be open to new sources of learning. Their reaction should depend on the meta-regulatory paradigms that influence their approach to market intervention: (i) an 'imperfect competition' one, which expresses concern over the increasing trend towards concentration observed in these markets and the fact that solid quasi-monopoly positions are generated and entrenched by 'network effects', which last for a considerable period of time, absent 'disruptive innovation', and (ii) a 'Schumpeterian' conception of the role of state authorities in nurturing and/or facilitating the innovation process in these industries, which is perceived as being accomplished by

Turns to Amazon", (*euractiv.com*, 5 October 2018), https://www.euractiv.com/section/competition/news/apres-google-vestager-attaque-amazon/; Bundeskartellamt, "Bundeskartellamt Initiates Abuse Proceeding Against Amazon", (*bundeskartellamt.de*, 29 November 2018) https://www.bundeskartellamt.de/SharedDocs/Publikation/EN/Pressemitteilungen/2018/29_11_2018_Verfahrenseinleitung_Amazon.pdf?__blob=publicationFile&v=2.

124. S. Popov, "The Tangle", (2018) White Paper.

the development of large technology firms that dispose of the necessary dynamic capabilities to generate and introduce innovations. Resorting to these prior beliefs becomes necessary in the absence of incontestable empirical evidence as to the role of competition for innovation, the debate among economists still going on.[125]

The tension between these paradigms of intervention (or non-intervention) is particularly intense in periods of technological change when regulators have to make clear choices about either taking a hands-on or hands-off approach. In relation to the hands-on (and possibly prophylactic) approach, regulators would need to address all the possible social costs following the implementation of this technology, even if these have not yet materialised. They would need to implement the principle of precaution but would need to do so in a way that limits the risk of stifling innovation. Conversely, regulators could adopt a hands-off approach, an approach of 'permission-less innovation', in which they would effectively accept that the 'public good' may be better pursued if entrepreneurs are left undisturbed in their effort to develop new business models and to explore new ways of implementing general purpose technologies. One may also advance a third approach, which would offer the possibility of a compromise that would both permit the continuance of regulating as usual while also allowing for there to be open spaces for monitored experimentation that, if they are proven to be successful, may be generalised and lead to structured regulatory change. These meta-principles of regulatory action form the broader institutional context that economic actors riding the wave of new technology consider when they shape their strategies in order to gain architectural advantage, although it is still unclear, from an empirical perspective, how these may impact upon improving economic performance and/or upon increasing the equality of opportunities in the digital economy.

125. The Schumpeterian view alleges that large firms and monopolists may be more innovative than firms in competitive markets in view of their head start and them having a dominant position on a market and the resources to fund large research and development ('R&D'). In contrast, economist K. Arrow has challenged the incentives of a monopolist to invest in R&D in view of the fact that the new products may displace, partially or totally, the monopolist's products from the market, thereby, leading the monopolist to competing with himself. Recent empirical economic studies have examined these claims attempting to link market concentration in an industry (on the basis of the Lerner index, thought of as a proxy for product market competition) to R&D expenditures in the same industry. They found the existence of an 'inverted-U' relationship – the level of innovation rises in industries with oligopolistic market structures whereas it is more modest in industries having a more competitive market structure and in industries dominated by monopolists. *See* P. Aghion et al., "Competition and Innovation: An Inverted U Relationship", (2005) *Quarterly Journal of Economics*, 701. However, some other economists find these studies unconvincing. *See* the discussion in J. Baker, "Beyond Schumpeter vs. Arrow: How Antitrust Fosters Innovation", (2007) 74 *Antitrust Law Journal*, 584–587, which suggests some alternative measures of innovative activity.

CHAPTER 2

Online Vertical Restraints and Abuse of Dominant Position: The Emerging Indian Perspective

Augustine Peter & Neha Singh[*]

§2.01 INTRODUCTION

The way business is done in India is fast changing. The change is characterised by the adoption of new technology and innovation in almost all sectors of the economy. E-commerce has transformed the way business has been conducted traditionally in a market place.[1] Not only does e-commerce lower entry barriers for new entrants, lower prices for consumers and reduce information asymmetry, but the e-commerce market is also marked by high rates of innovation, increasing returns to scale, network effects and negligible marginal cost.[2]

Over the years, technology has been the backbone of e-commerce. E-commerce has been disruptive to the traditional way of doing business, i.e., disruptive to the bricks and mortar retailers. It has led to unearthing of massive economic potential generally absent in the bricks and mortar sector. Network effects resulting from disruptive innovation is something that cannot be ignored. Network effects are seen to

* The authors can be reached at apeter1900@gmail.com and advocate.nehasingh@gmail.com. Views are strictly personal and not to be construed in any manner as the views of the Competition Commission of India.

1. Directorate for Financial and Enterprise Affairs Competition Committee, *Implications of E-commerce for Competition Policy – Note by India* (6 June 2018), DAF/COMP/WD (2018) 52, accessed from https://one.oecd.org/document/DAF/COMP/WD(2018)52/en/pdf, accessed on 26 December 2018.
2. Directorate for Financial and Enterprise Affairs Competition Committee, *Implications of E-commerce for Competition Policy – Note by India* (6 June 2018), DAF/COMP/WD (2018) 52, accessed from https://one.oecd.org/document/DAF/COMP/WD(2018)52/en/pdf, accessed on 26 December 2018.

be particularly important in two/multi-sided markets where users on each side of the market derive positive effect from the expansion of users on the other side. Such disruptive way of doing business in e-commerce not just introduces new propositions and business models, but also transforms the rules of the game of competition. While the fact remains that e-commerce has a number of procompetitive effects on the market, it also tends to pose a host of challenges to the regulatory landscape and competition law enforcement all over the world. Naturally, the e-commerce sector is increasingly catching the attention and indulgence of the competition authorities all over the world.

Given the splurge of e-commerce, online vertical agreements are increasingly noticed on an online platform taking forms such as Most Favoured Nation (MFN) clauses, online Resale Price Maintenance (RPM), selective Distribution etc. Such agreements in antitrust are generally evaluated following the rule of reason approach. Online vertical restraints are also seen as posing multiple challenges to a competition authority when it comes to enforcement as they primarily make the new entrants face entry barriers. In addition, platform technologies may create vertical restraints by indulging in market foreclosure and distorting level playing fields. Due to online market being resistant to the Small but Significant Not Transitory Increase in Prices (SSNIP), the definition of relevant market warrants needs extra care in its delineation and the traditional techniques, modes and analysis of defining the same may require modifications when it comes to defining online markets.

Competition law jurisprudence in India is evolving. During the last less than a decade, the Indian competition authority, the Competition Commission of India (the Commission) has had the occasion to deal with some of the challenges thrown up by e-commerce in the form of online vertical restraints. In this chapter, we discuss the provisions of the Act with respect to vertical restraints and check if the same are adequate to address cases of online vertical restraints. The recent cases of *Jasper Kaff*[3] and *Google*[4] pronounced by the Commission are pointers to the fact that Competition Law of India has been drafted in a manner so as to bring to books the infringements of the law taking place due to technological changes in the economy. Besides, enforcement provisions of the Competition Act, 2002 (the Act) as well as definitions under section 2 are extensive enough to be applicable to online cases of vertical restraints.

Several issues pertaining to online vertical restraints which are likely to come up before the Commission as a result of the surge of e-commerce transactions in India are also discussed.

§2.02 IMPORTANCE OF E-COMMERCE IN INDIA

E-commerce, deals with the buying and selling of goods and services, or the transmitting of funds or data, over an electronic platform, mainly the internet, with transactions categorised into either business-to-business (B2B), business-to-consumer (B2C),

3. Case No. 61 of 2014, Competition Commission of India.
4. Case Nos 07 & 30 of 2012, Competition Commission of India.

consumer-to-consumer, consumer-to-business or the recently evolved business-to-business-to-consumer (B2B2C).[5] The growth of e-commerce is facilitated by devices such as laptops, smartphones, tablets which, on one hand, accelerates the pace of online sales manifold and on the other puts continuous competitive pressure on the traditional channels and models of distribution.

With the recent disruptive policies including demonetisation[6] and the thrust on digitisation in India, the share of e-commerce has suddenly shot up. Foreign direct investment (FDI) guidelines issued by the government in March 2016[7] and December 2018[8] turned the spotlight on pricing practices of e-commerce firms. It has been clarified that the automatic route of foreign investment would be available only to those e-commerce market places that refrained from influencing sale prices and helped maintain a level playing field.[9] With e-commerce expected to grow at a massive Compound Annual Growth Rate of 44.77% from 2016 and expected to touch USD 63.7 billion by 2020,[10] India is all set to become one of the fastest growing retail markets along with Indonesia, Mexico and China. Online retail sales in India are expected to grow by 31% and are expected to have touched USD 32.70 billion in 2018, led by Flipkart, Amazon India and Paytm Mall.[11] Most of the growth witnessed has been triggered by the fast pace in the internet and smartphone penetration. While e-commerce helps lower prices and foster better choices for the consumers, it also significantly widens the geographic market, tends to strengthen competition, remove

5. Bijlani, J and Singh, S, *E-Commerce in India Accelerating Growth* (February 2015), PricewaterhouseCooper (PwC), PD- 325, accessed from https://www.pwc.in/assets/pdfs/publications/2015/ecommerce-in-india-accelerating-growth.pdf, accessed on 28 May 2018.
6. On 8 November 2016, the Government of India announced the demonetisation of all INR 500 and INR 1000 banknotes of the Mahatma Gandhi Series. It also announced the issuance of new INR 500 and INR 2000 banknotes in exchange for the demonetised banknotes. For demonetisation, also *see* https://en.wikipedia.org/wiki/2016_Indian_banknote_demonetisation.
7. *Guidelines for Foreign Direct Investment (FDI) on E-commerce*, Press Note No. 3, 2016 Series (2016), Ministry of Commerce and Industry, Department of Industrial Policy and Promotion (FC Series), Government of India, available at https://dipp.gov.in/sites/default/files/pn3_2016_0.pdf, accessed on 31 December 2018.
8. *Review of policy on Foreign Direct Investment (FDI) in E-commerce* (26 December 2018), Press Information Bureau, Ministry of Commerce & Industry, Government of India, available at http://pib.nic.in/newsite/PrintRelease.aspx?relid=186804, accessed on 31 December 2018.
9. Press Note No. 3, 2016 Series (2016) issued by the Department of Industrial Policy and Promotion on 29 March 2016 allowed 100% FDI in the marketplace model of e-commerce under the automatic route, subject to specified conditions. The 'marketplace based model' is defined to any information technology platform created on an electronic network that allows an e-commerce firm to act as a facilitator between buyers and sellers. *See Guidelines for Foreign Direct Investment (FDI) on E-commerce*, Press Note No. 3, 2016 Series (2016), Ministry of Commerce and Industry, Department of Industrial Policy and Promotion (FC Series), Government of India, available at https://dipp.gov.in/sites/default/files/pn3_2016_0.pdf, accessed on 31 December 2018.
10. *E-commerce* (July 2017), India Brand Equity Foundation, available at https://www.ibef.org/download/Ecommerce-July-2017.pdf, accessed on 28 May 2018.
11. *E-commerce* (October 2018), India Brand Equity Foundation, October 2018, available at https://www.ibef.org/industry/ecommerce.aspx, accessed on 04 January 2019.

information asymmetries and make distribution system more efficient. On the flip side, e-commerce may turn out to be a fertile ground for collusion and price obfuscation.[12]

In a recent case, *Jasper Kaff*,[13] where the Commission had the occasion to deal in depth with the issues pertaining to the online world, the importance of e-commerce was captured as:

> Capitalizing on the advantages of internet penetration, these online market platforms synthesize the advantages of traditional commerce and ecommerce and reduce their administrative and transaction costs. In many ways these online portals act as a parallel distribution chain along with the offline distribution channels. The customer/buyer also, when purchasing the products online, perceives the online portal as a valuable link between such customer and the seller.
>
> ... E-commerce platforms help users of different sides of the market (sellers, buyers, social media users, advertisers, software developers, etc.) to find what they are looking for. The quantum of users attracted to the platform depends upon how efficient the platform is in matching users with their desired product/service. Online platforms do not only provide a (virtual) location for market exchanges, contrary to conventional (offline) markets they also actively collect information on suppliers' products and consumers' preferences and use matching algorithms to match these in an efficient way in order to reduce search costs.

While growth in e-commerce exposes Indian enterprises/manufacturers/retailers to overseas competition, it may also pose challenges such as exclusive distribution arrangements, online RPM and MFN clauses, requiring the competition regulator to be on constant watch out for infringement, if any, of competition law. Such specific forms of online vertical restraints when coupled with network effects can cause foreclosures in the relevant market. A few of such challenges have been touched upon in the next section of this chapter.

§2.03 VERTICAL AGREEMENTS/RESTRAINTS AND THEIR PROS AND CONS

Vertical agreements are agreements between enterprises at different levels of the supply chain. Vertically positioned enterprises deal in complementary products. In sharp contrast to horizontal agreements, they are typically imposed through a sophisticated contractual relationship incorporating complex clauses imbibing several obligations imposed on the contracting parties.

Vertical agreements, when they turn into restraints, manifest themselves in numerous forms, ranging from a requirement that dealers operate in designated territories, to exclusive dealing agreements[14] and to RPM.[15] While exclusive dealing

12. Singham, G. and Tan, M., *Singapore: The Benefits and Harms of Ecommerce on Competition Law* (2017), available at http://www.mondaq.com/x/585566/Trade+Regulation+Practices/The+Benefits+And+Harms+Of+eCommerce+On+Competition+Law, accessed on 26 December 2018.
13. Case No. 61 of 2014, Competition Commission of India.
14. *See* Bernheim, B.D. and Whinston, M.D., *Exclusive Dealing* (1998), Journal of Political Economy, Volume 106, No. 1, February, 64–103.

arrangements are contracts mandating a seller to sell all or a substantial portion of its products or services to a particular buyer, or requiring a buyer to purchase all or a portion of its requirements of a product or service from a particular seller, RPM agreements typically set the minimum price below which the dealers are not allowed to charge for the manufacturer's product.

The restrictions generally included in vertical agreements are of the following nature: (1) the seller usually accepts not to supply goods to anybody else than the buyer within a territory; (2) the purchaser agrees not to buy goods from other providers; (3) in some cases, the conditions under which the products can be resold can be determined in the agreements, particularly as regards price, location or consumers.[16]

Vertical restraints by their very nature impose restraints down the supply chain. Such restraints may have certain beneficial effects on competition. They are seen to ameliorate the conditions of the consumers by encouraging the creation and development of efficient streams of product distribution from manufacturer or distributor to the consumer. The intricate nature of vertical restraints has been captured by the US Supreme Court in *Continental T.V. Inc. v. GTE Sylvania. Inc*,[17] as:

> The market impact of vertical restrictions is complex because of their potential for a simultaneous reduction of intrabrand competition and stimulation of interbrand competition.

The implications of vertical restraints has also been explained by the Competition regulator of India in its most recent order of *Jasper Kaff*[18] wherein it was observed:

> Though restraints like minimum RPM may affect price competition amongst retailers/distributors, in situations where intra-brand price competition among retailers/distributors is likely to create an incentive to free ride in the short run and under-provisioning or complete eradication of such useful services in the long run, imposition of such vertical restraint may not only be desirable from the manufacturer-retailers' point of view but also from the point of view of consumers.

The likelihood of positive effects of vertical agreements outweighing the negative effects, in fact, is the reason for them being tested on the touchstone of *rule of reason*[19] in multiple jurisdictions, including India (discussed later in the chapter). Briefly, we describe the desirable effects of vertical restraints as: First, it may lead to a situation of

---

15. Directorate for Financial and Enterprise Affairs Competition Committee, Competition Law and Policy, OECD, *Roundtable on Resale Price Maintenance* (10 September 2009), DAF/COMP (2008) 37, available at https://www.oecd.org/daf/competition/43835526.pdf, accessed on 08 February 2019.
16. Kerber, W. and Vezzo, S., *EU Competition Policy, Vertical Restraints, and Innovations: An Analysis from an Evolutionary Perspective* (May 2004), Working Paper presented in 10th International Joseph A Schumpeter Society Conference (ISS) (Milan, 2004). Also *see* Hughes, M., Foss, C. and Ross, K., *The Economic Assessment of Vertical Restraints Under UK and EC Competition Law* (2001) European Competition Law Review P. 424. Also *see* Colino, S.M., *Vertical Agreements and Competition Law: A Comparative Study of the EU and US Regimes* (2009), Hart.
17. 433 U.S. 36 (1977).
18. Case No. 61 of 2014, Competition Commission of India.
19. *See* Peritz, R.J., *The Rule of Reason in Antitrust Law: Property Logic in Restraint of Competition* (1989), Hastings Law Journal, Volume 40, pp. 285–342.

increased social welfare[20] whereby the settlement of a maximum RPM can reduce double[21] mark-ups or double marginalisation, promoting a higher surplus to suppliers and consumers by reducing the distributor's surplus. The issue behind double marginalisation[22] is that if both producers and distributors add mark-up over their costs, the resulting double mark-up leads to excessive prices.[23] This is of particular concern if both, the manufacturers and the retailers, have market power since each will set price above marginal cost.[24] Such double mark-ups are kept under check by RPM. Second, Manufacturers who invest in improving retail outlets, promoting retail products, or training outlet managers might worry that dealers will free ride on those investments[25] making the manufacturers impose vertical restriction on the dealers. Not only do dealers have incentives to free ride on the value of the brand putting in little effort by themselves, by means of a vertical externality, they may also exhibit incentives to free ride on services offered by other dealers, commonly known as a horizontal externality.[26] Minimum price restraints[27] could solve both of these free-riding problems by preventing retailers from competing on price and making them compete instead on quality or customer service.[28] Third, Vertical restraints can also increase sales and create brand image by imposing certain standards of quality on the distributors. In such cases, exclusive or selective distribution can be justified when introducing a new

20. Florencio, P.A.L. and Prof. Englander, E., *Vertical Restraints: A Historical Comparative Perspective Between Brazil and the United States of America* (2002), Institute of Brazilian Business and Public Management, Minerva Program, Issues 15, available at https://pdfs.semanticscholar.org/3cb9/65e8b11323e3974e9bca6837b31d4e19ef89.pdf, accessed on 27 December 2018.
21. Directorate for Financial and Enterprise Affairs Competition Committee, *Roundtable on Vertical Restraints for Online Sales -Note by the United States* (25 February 2013), DAF/COMP/WD (2013) 15.
22. *See* Motta, M., *Competition Policy: Theory and Practice* (2004), Cambridge University Press. The best-known example of externalities affecting vertically separated firms is given by the double marginalisation problem, first identified by Spengler (1950). *See* Spengler, J.J., *Vertical Integration and Antitrust Policy* (1950), Journal of Political Economy, Volume 58, pp. 347–352.
23. *See* Hilderbrand, D., *Economic Analyses of Vertical Agreements: A Self-Assessment* (2005), Kluwer Law International, International Competition Law Series, Volume 17.
24. Lever, J. and Neubauer, S., *Vertical Restraints and their Motivation and Justification* (2000) European Competition Law Review, Volume 21, p. 10. Also *see* Hilderbrand, D., *Economic Analyses of Vertical Agreements: A Self-Assessment* (2005), Kluwer Law International, International Competition Law Series, Volume 17.
25. Slade, M.E., *The Effects of Vertical Restraints: An Evidence Based Approach in The Pros and Cons of Vertical Restraints* (2008), Konkurrensverket Swedish Competition Authority, available at http://www.konkurrensverket.se/globalassets/english/research/report-the-pros-and-cons-of-vertical-restraints-18mb.pdf, accessed on 14 May 2018.
26. Slade, M.E., *The Effects of Vertical Restraints: An Evidence Based Approach in The Pros and Cons of Vertical Restraints* (2008), Konkurrensverket Swedish Competition Authority, available at http://www.konkurrensverket.se/globalassets/english/research/report-the-pros-and-cons-of-vertical-restraints-18mb.pdf, accessed on 14 May 2018.
27. *See* Bergh, R.V., and Camesasca, P.D., *European Competition Law and Economics: A Comparative Perspective* (2006), Sweet and Maxwell, 2nd edition.
28. Telser, L.G., *Why Should Manufacturers Want Fair Trade?* (1960) Journal of Law and Economics, Volume 3, No. 1, pp. 86–105.

product into the market for a limited period of time.[29] Fourth, it also leads to economies of scale and removal of downstream pricing distortions by standardising downstream facilities. Fifth, they can be employed to reduce transaction costs or to achieve other efficiencies.[30]

On the undesirable side, vertical restraints may also often provide a veil under the garb of which multiple anticompetitive conducts may flourish. For example, they may foreclose[31] entry by competitors at some level of the vertical chain.[32] Foreclosure is the strategic behaviour of one or a group of undertakings to restrict the entry of the competitors to downstream or upstream markets. Alternatively, vertical restraints can also facilitate collusion among manufacturers.[33] For example, exclusive dealing ties each seller to a manufacturer and eliminates the manufacturer's temptation to grant secret price cuts in order to steal rival customers and increase market shares.[34] It may also lead to reduction in *inter* brand and *intra* brand competition and create obstacles to market integration.[35] The Commission in *Jasper Kaff*[36] held:

> that the vertical agreements (including minimum RPM) may lead to anti-competitive outcomes—when they have a horizontal dimension to it i.e. when the restraint, though imposed vertically, has the ability to restrict competition at the horizontal level in either of the markets—upstream level (inter-brand) or down-stream level (intra-brand).

Thus, for reasons that vertical restraints are endowed with both positive and negative effects, the antitrust authorities the world over, instead of condemning vertical restraints outright, follow an approach of weighing the *pros* and *cons* to come to the ultimate conclusion of anticompetitive conduct or otherwise of the impugned vertical restraints. In India, such vertical agreements need to be scanned by the test of

---

29. Hildebrand, D., *Economic Analyses of Vertical Restraints – A Self-Assessment*, European Economic & Marketing Consultants – EE&MC GmbH, available at https://www.ee-mc.com/fileadmin/user_upload/ccr_en/Economic_Analysis_Vertical_Agreements_Part_1.pdf, accessed on 27 December 2018.
30. *See* Hilderbrand, D., *Economic Analyses of Vertical Agreements: A Self-Assessment* (2005), Kluwer Law International, International Competition Law Series, Volume 17.
31. Also *see* Fox, E., & Crane, D., *Global Issues in Antitrust and Competition Law* (2010), American Case Book Series, West Academic Publishing, 1st edition.
32. Slade, M.E., *The Effects of Vertical Restraints: An Evidence Based Approach in The Pros and Cons of Vertical Restraints* (2008), Konkurrensverket Swedish Competition Authority, available at http://www.konkurrensverket.se/globalassets/english/research/report-the-pros-and-cons-of-vertical-restraints-18mb.pdf, accessed on 14 May 2018.
33. Slade, M.E., *The Effects of Vertical Restraints: An Evidence Based Approach in The Pros and Cons of Vertical Restraints* (2008), Konkurrensverket Swedish Competition Authority, available at http://www.konkurrensverket.se/globalassets/english/research/report-the-pros-and-cons-of-vertical-restraints-18mb.pdf, accessed on 14 May 2018.
34. Slade, M.E., *The Effects of Vertical Restraints: An Evidence Based Approach in The Pros and Cons of Vertical Restraints* (2008), Konkurrensverket Swedish Competition Authority, available at http://www.konkurrensverket.se/globalassets/english/research/report-the-pros-and-cons-of-vertical-restraints-18mb.pdf, accessed on 14 May 2018.
35. Hughes, M., Foss, C. and Ross, K., *The Economic Assessment of Vertical Restraints Under UK and EC Competition Law* (2001) European Competition Law Review p. 424. Also *see* Hilderbrand, D., *Economic Analyses of Vertical Agreements: A Self-Assessment* (2005), Kluwer Law International, International Competition Law Series, Volume 17.
36. Case No. 61 of 2014, Competition Commission of India.

anticompetitiveness (the test of appreciable adverse effect under section 19(3) under the Indian law discussed later in the chapter in order for them to be termed as violative of competition law. It is to be noted that there is no presumption of anticompetitiveness in such cases.

§2.04 CHALLENGES POSED BY ONLINE VERTICAL RESTRAINTS

Vertical restraints in the context of an online platform are called online vertical restraints. Online markets, like mobile networks, exhibit strong network effects in the sense that the value of the product or service concerned increases with each added user. Network effect reduces the variable cost to almost zero benefitting large players having billions of users, such as Google or Facebook. In addition, online platforms facilitate information flows by collating and presenting before the users the relevant information. This is done by bringing together information from different suppliers and product offerings facilitating the customers to quickly and efficiently access and process information. The entire process reduces search cost. Posing multiple challenges to a competition authority when it comes to enforcement (as compared to the traditional offline markets), online vertical restraints make the new entrants face entry barriers, predominantly due to large networks of incumbent players created due to their first mover advantage. In addition, platform technologies may create vertical restraints by practising discrimination, indulging in market foreclosure and distorting level playing fields.

On the whole, the competitive harm posed as well as the possible beneficial effects of online vertical restraints are similar to those of offline vertical restraints. However, on account of the unique competition concerns posed by online vertical restraints, the customary approach of a competition authority in dealing with offline cases may require modification when it comes to online vertical restraint. We, briefly, discuss the reasons as: first, the traditional markets are comparatively slower in growth as compared to the online markets which are, generally speaking, faster paced and hectic; Second, while dealing with business models concerning online markets a full-fledged relevant analysis of efficiency enhanced and harmful effects posed by the online vertical restraints is sought to be undertaken. This may require a clear and full understanding of the business models besides appreciating the incentives and strategies involved in online markets. Needless to say that business models, incentives and strategies are distinct in online markets as compared with the traditional ones. Whether or not they are wholly different or difference arises superficially is a matter to be established on a case to case basis. Third, online market being 'resistant to the SSNIP' the definition of relevant market needs extra care in its delineation. The techniques, modes and analysis used in defining relevant market in traditional offline cases may prove futile when it comes to defining online markets, posing a significant challenge to the competition authorities. Fourth, online markets being double-sided or multi-sided, balancing the benefits or harm on one side of market *vis-à-vis* the benefits or harm, actual or potential, on the other side, is practically problematic. Fifth, online markets may involve multi-jurisdictional investigations, posing problems related to difference in laws and regulations in respect of proceedings and investigations.

We shall look at the specific challenges posed by various online vertical agreements before moving forward to the Indian scenario on vertical and online vertical restraints. Such challenges may range from MFN Clauses to online RPM and from Internet Minimum Advertised Price (IMAP) to cases of dual pricing.

Briefly, we discuss the aforesaid issues:

(a) MFN – MFN clauses,[37] which have their source in international investment and trade law have sound business reasons to exist in contractual relationships, denote that an investor/exporter or its investment would necessarily be treated 'no less favourably' than the most favoured investor/exporter.[38] In the context of vertical agreements they consist essentially of arrangements between suppliers and distributors whereby the supplier grants the distributor a price that will not be less favourable than the prices granted to its other customers.[39] MFN clauses when reversed into *'most favoured supplier'* clauses, results in buyer guarantees to the suppliers that the commercial terms are better than, or at least as good as, those agreed with another supplier.[40] The overall purpose of the MFN clause is to control, and in some cases reduce, input prices.[41]

MFN clauses are noticed to result in or generate conditions conducive for a number of anticompetitive conducts by enterprises: *First*, they enhance the risk of perpetrating 'the supreme evil of antitrust'[42] by facilitating collusion between competitors. *Second*, they can be used to reinforce vertical price fixing. *Third*, MFN Clauses have been criticised for having many of the same effects as RPM even though the two may possess noticeable differences in the sense that RPM is usually initiated by the supplier and MFN by the buyer. There are commentators who claim that the similarities between the two are so striking that MFN should be treated as strictly as RPM.[43] *Fourth*, the typical restrictive effect of MFN clauses is foreclosure of new entrants and raising barriers to entry even though such a strategy will not be successful if the existing retailers benefit from MFN clauses from the same supplier.

37. MFN clauses are also referred as 'price parity clauses,' 'most-favoured customer clauses,' 'meeting competition clauses,' 'price parity clauses,' 'prudent buyer clause' and 'non-discrimination clause'.
38. Directorate for Financial and Enterprise Affairs, *Most-Favoured-National Treatment in International Investment Law* (2004), OECD Working Papers on International Investment, 2004/02. Available at: http://www.oecd.org/daf/inv/investment-policy/WP2004_2.pdf, accessed on 01 December 2019.
39. European Commission Press Releases IP/11/257 and IP/05/710, available at available at http://europa.eu/rapid/latest-press-releases.htm, accessed on 07 December 2019.
40. Universal Music Group/ EMI Music, Case COMP/M.6458.
41. Vandenborre, I. and Frese, M.J., *Most Favoured Nation Clauses Revisited* (2014), European Competition Law Review, No. 12, p. 588.
42. *Verizon Communications v. Law Offices of Curtis V. Trinko*, LLP, 540 U.S. 398 (2004).
43. *See* Fletcher, C.F. and Hviid, M., *Retail Price MFNs: Are They RPM at Its Worst?*, CCP Working Paper 14-5, 2015.

Though MFN clauses are increasingly being scrutinised by competition authorities, they are not regarded as anticompetitive in themselves because of the likelihood of their engendering benefits, especially because they act in many cases as a bulwark against likely price increases by suppliers. Such clauses, in fact, help buyers reduce costs both in terms of price negotiations and in terms of research as regards the best price available in the market. They also incentivise further investments by buyers while protecting investments already made by them on the request of the seller, because of the assurance that costs could be recouped over time.[44]

(b) RPM – In the United States, RPM in respect of light bulbs became a major issue in *United States v. General Electric, Westinghouse and Ors.*[45] RPM may arise in an overt or covert manner. It is overt when a supplier imposes, directly, a resale price on its buyers. It may take the form of being covert, when a supplier recommends a resale price but ensures its observance through incentives or threats to terminate the contract.[46] While the law generally permits suppliers to impose maximum or recommended resale prices, fixed or minimum resale prices are frowned upon on the ground that they stifle retail level competition. The competition law perspective on online RPMs is that as in the case of offline businesses, online business should be free to determine their online sales prices in order to compete and attract customers who use the internet to shop around for the best deals.[47]

Online RPM is seen to increase the chances of collusion both at the manufacturer's level[48] and at the retailer's level. It can soften competition between retailers and also between the suppliers. While online RPM tend to make prices more transparent, facilitating upstream collusion,[49] it also offers a focal point for retailers to increase their ability to coordinate higher retail prices. In addition, they can result in softening of competition between the products of two manufacturers besides serving as an entry deterrent.

44. Plankensteiner, M. and Créquer, E., *Most Favoured Nation Clauses* (24 March 2016), available at https://gettingthedealthrough.com/area/41/article/28952/vertical-agreements-favoured-nation-clauses/, accessed on 19 June 2018.
45. *United States v. General Electric Co.*, 272 U.S. 476 (1926). Also *see* Kleit, A.N. (ed), *Antitrust and Competition Policy* (2005), Edward Elgar Publishing Limited.
46. Petit, N. and Henry, D., *Vertical Restraints under EU Competition Law: Conceptual Foundations And Practical Framework* (13 December 2010), available at SSRN: http://ssrn.com/abstract=1724891, accessed on 19 May 2018.
47. Clarke, O., *Competition and Markets Authority Alleges Online Resale Price Maintenance* (17 March, 2016), accessed from http://marketinglaw.osborneclarke.com/advertising-regulation/competition-and-markets-authority-alleges-online-resale-price-maintenance/, accessed on 19 May 2018.
48. *See* Telser, L.G., *Why Should Manufacturers Want Fair Trade?* (1960), Journal of Law and Economics: Volume 3, No. 1, pp. 86–105. Also *See* Shaffer, G., *Slotting Allowances and Resale Price Maintenance: A Comparison of Facilitating Practices* (1991), RAND Journal of Economics, Volume 22, No. 1, pp. 120–135.
49. *See* Jullien, B. and Rey P., *Resale Price Maintenance and Collusion* (2007), RAND Journal of Economics, Volume 38, No. 4, pp. 983–1001. Also *see* Akman, P. and Sokol, D.D., *Online RPM and MFN under Antitrust Law and Economics* (2017), Review of Industrial Organization (Springer), Volume 50, No. 2, pp. 133–151.

(c) IMAP – IMAP Policy, a control on the advertised price in contrast to the actual price of the product, is a contractual arrangement that requires a retailer to display a minimum advertised price even in the presence of the actual selling price. With the US case of *Leegin Creative Leather Products, Inc. v. PSKS, Inc*[50] holding that IMAPs actually promote competition, the supporters of IMAP, advocate that they regulate only advertised price and not actual prices.

IMAP policies, which technically speaking, are unilateral, are set by manufacturers or suppliers for the retailers or resellers informing the latter that the manufacturer will not work with companies that advertise below a manufacturer selected minimum price and thereby prohibiting the retailers from advertising their products online below a fixed price.[51] Unlike RPM, an IMAP does not impose any restriction on the sales price at which a product can be sold. However they are likely to soften intra-brand competition and result in higher prices for consumers. While IMAP policies are typically analysed under the RPM framework the legality of which has always been a contentious issue in antitrust regulation, they may not fit ostensibly into the category of RPM due to they being only a regulation on the advertised pricing rather than on the actual selling prices.

(d) Dual Pricing – Dual pricing systems can be another price-related restriction directed specifically against online sales. In a system of dual pricing, a retailer is granted different purchase prices, depending on whether he or she intends to sell the product online or over-the-counter.[52] A general presumption of procompetitive or anticompetitive effects is difficult to be drawn in the case of dual pricing. The best way is to approach on a case to case basis.

(e) Selective Distribution and Storage – Selective distribution limits the number of authorised distributors and restricts resale.[53] Generally speaking, the aim of such an agreement is to eliminate or impede price competition.[54] A supplier can distribute its products in many ways. To name a few, a supplier may make use of controlled subsidiaries, licensees, agents, franchise systems, independent distributors, etc. While a selective distribution renders benefits such as protection of brand image, it is also viewed as a protection from the free rider problem. However, it can serve as a threat to efficient *intra* brand competition as well as it can result in foreclosure on the distribution market. There is a risk that such systems lead to competition being softened and collusion between

50. 551 U.S. 877 (2007).
51. Rosch, T, *Current Issues in Competition and Consumer Protection Enforcement in the Retail Sector* (2010), Remarks at the Retail Industry Leaders Association's Retail Law Conference, Tampa, Florida (10 November, 2010). Also *see* Albert, J.B., *Adding Uncertainty to the Virtual Shopping Cart: Antitrust Regulation of Internet Minimum Advertised Price Policies* (2012), Fordham Law Review, Volume 80, No. 4.
52. Kaiser-Friedrich-Straße, *Vertical Restraints in the Internet Economy* (10 October 2013), Meeting of the Working Group on Competition Law, Background Paper.
53. Gunther (Dr.) et al., *Competition Law: European Community Practice and Procedures* (2008), Sweet and Maxwell.
54. Gunther (Dr.) et al., *Competition Law: European Community Practice and Procedures* (2008), Sweet and Maxwell.

suppliers being facilitated, especially where there is a cumulative effect of several selective distribution systems. Selective distribution can also increase the likelihood of anticompetitive behaviour among suppliers.[55]

In *Coty*,[56] the Court of Justice of the European Union has recently ruled that, in the context of a selective distribution network for luxury goods, suppliers can contractually prohibit their distributors from selling the goods on third-party internet platforms visible to the public. The court found that such a restriction is justified to preserve the luxury image and aura of the goods.

§2.05 ENFORCEMENT BY THE COMPETITION COMMISSION OF INDIA AGAINST ANTICOMPETITIVE VERTICAL RESTRAINTS, INCLUDING ONLINE VERTICAL RESTRAINTS

Part A of this section outlines the law relating to vertical restraints as covered under section 3(4) of the Act. Part B deals with the law relating to the conduct of the dominant party in imposing a vertical restraint as a result of abuse of dominant position under section 4. Part C deals with the discussion of whether the Indian law is sufficient to deal with the issues posed by the online vertical restraints.

[A] Law Relating to Vertical Restraints under Section 3(4) of the Indian Competition Act

Vertical Agreement/Restraint is covered mainly under section 3(4) in the form of anticompetitive agreements. The case of unilateral imposition of vertical restraints by an enterprise enjoying dominant position in the relevant market is covered under section 4 (discussed in Part B of the chapter):

(a) *Agreement* – While the provisions of section 3(4) require the presence of an agreement, it is not necessary that the party on whom vertical restraints have been imposed has agreed on the terms of the agreement wilfully, or has agreed at all. This is because the parties on whom the restraints are imposed would rarely agree to restraints being imposed on them. The Commission in deciding the cases before it has, time and again, clarified that agreement under section 2(b)[57] of the Act need not be in writing and includes any

55. Gunther (Dr.) et al., *Competition Law: European Community Practice and Procedures* (2008), Sweet and Maxwell.

56. *Coty Germany GmbH v. ParfümerieAkzente GmbH*, Case C-230/16.

57. Section 2(b) defines agreement as: 'agreement' includes any arrangement or understanding or action in concert – (i) whether or not, such arrangement, understanding or action is formal or in writing; or (ii) whether or not such arrangement, understanding or action is intended to be enforceable by legal proceedings; The Commission in *Director General (Supplies & Disposals), Directorate General of Supplies & Disposals, Department of Commerce, Ministry of Commerce & Industry*, observed that the definition of agreement under section 2(b) being inclusive and not

unwritten arrangement, understanding or action in concert. The same is in consonance with the view taken by more evolved jurisdictions. In *Automobiles Dealers Association* against *Global Automobiles Limited*,[58] the Commission accepted the Letter of Intent as an agreement between the Opposite Party[59] (OP) and its dealers. In *Honda Siel*,[60] while penalizing multiple automobile manufacturers for entering into anticompetitive agreements of a vertical nature with their authorised dealers, the Commission gave regard to the fact that several agreements were in the nature of an unwritten agreement between the dealers and the Original Equipment Manufacturers (OEM) which effectively resulted in dealers refusing to sell spare parts on the open market.

In *Fx Hyundai*,[61] it was argued by *Hyundai* that the case was merely that of consensual agreement and the dealers/distributors were not put under compulsion at any time. The Commission relied on circular dated 30 April 2010 issued by *Hyundai* to its dealers/distributors to come to the conclusion that Clause 5(iii) of the Dealership Agreement of Hyundai, does not result in imposition of de facto exclusivity. In refusing to construe Clause 5(iii) of the Dealership Agreement as a vertical restraint imposed, the Commission gave due regard to the fact that the circular did not instruct the OP's dealers/distributors to cease from taking up dealership of competing manufacturers *in toto*. Also in *Vishal Pande* against *Honda Motorcycle*,[62] the stand of the Commission taken in *Fx Hyundai*[63] was reiterated while noting that Clause 10.14 of the Dealership Agreement does not strictly set out an exclusivity clause creating an obligation on a dealer or preventing a dealer from dealing with competing dealerships or other businesses as dealer could do such activities with the prior written permission from the OP.

In *All India Chess Federation*[64] *(AICF)*, the Commission construed the undertaking prescribed by *AICF* regarding non-participation of its players in events not authorised by it as amounting to restraints in the nature of exclusive distribution and refusal to deal as defined in section 3(4)(c) and 3(4)(d) of the Act.

(b) *Appreciable Adverse Effects on Competition (AAEC)* – Section 3(4)[65] clearly states that a vertical arrangement shall attract the provisions of competition

exhaustive, is a wide one and that understanding may be tacit. The Commission went on to observing that the definition of agreement covers situations where the parties act on the basis of a nod or a wink.

58. Case No. 33 of 2011, Competition Commission of India.
59. Opposite Party in Competition Law in India is answering party against whom the information is filed under section 19(1) of the Competition Act, 2002.
60. Case No. 03 of 2011, Competition Commission of India.
61. Case Nos 36 & 82 of 2014, Competition Commission of India.
62. Case No. 17 of 2017, Competition Commission of India.
63. Case Nos 36 & 82 of 2014, Competition Commission of India.
64. Case No. 79 of 2011, Competition Commission of India.
65. Under section 3(4) any agreement among enterprises or persons at different stages or levels of the production chain in different markets, in respect of production, supply, distribution, storage, sale or price of, or trade in goods or provision of services, including (a) Tie in arrangement; (b)

law only if it causes or is likely to cause AAEC in India. Section 19(3)[66] acts as a guiding lamp in this regard. However, AAEC needs to be established on a case by case basis using the *rule of reason* approach.[67]

In the case of vertical agreements, the prospects of an agreement resulting in accrual of benefits to the consumers, bringing improvements in production, distribution of goods etc. or promoting technical, scientific and economic development weighs to tilt the scale in favour of the agreement being in compliance with law, indicating absence of AAEC. On the other hand, the likelihood that an agreement brings about negative effects on the market increases if the parties possess a degree of market power and the agreement in question contributed to the creating, maintenance or strengthening of market power or allows the parties to exploit such market power.[68]

The Commission, in a recent case, *Tata Power Delhi Distribution against National Thermal Power Corporation limited*[69] *(NTPC)*, dismissed the allegations of vertical restraints in relation to Power Purchase Agreements (PPA) entered between *NTPC*, an enterprise engaged in electricity generation, and *Tata Power Delhi Distribution*, an electricity distribution company. The Commission observed that significant investment made by the electricity generating companies required that the PPAs with distributors be for a longer

---

Exclusive supply agreement; (c) Exclusive distribution agreement; (d) Refusal to deal; (e) RPM; shall be an arrangement in contravening of sub-section (1) if such agreement causes or is likely to cause an AAEC in India.

66. Section 19 (Inquiry into certain agreements and dominant position of enterprise). Section 19(1) - The Commission may inquire into any alleged contravention of the provisions contained in subsection (1) of section 3 or sub-section (1) of section 4 either on its own motion or on - (a) receipt of any information, in such manner and accompanied by such fee as may be determined by regulations, from any person, consumer or their association or trade association; or (b) a reference made to it by the Central Government or a State Government or a statutory authority.

    Section 19 (2) - Without prejudice to the provisions contained in sub-section (1), the powers and functions of the Commission shall include the powers and functions specified in sub-sections (3)-(7). Section 19(3) The Commission shall, while determining whether an agreement has an appreciable adverse effect in sub-sections (3)-(7).

    Section 19(3) - The Commission shall, while determining whether an agreement has an AAEC under section 3, have due regard to all or any of the following factors, namely: - (a) creation of barriers to new entrants in the market; (b) driving existing competitors out of the market; (c) foreclosure of competition by hindering entry into the market; (d) accrual of benefits to consumers; (e) improvements in production or distribution of goods or provision of services; or (f) promotion of technical, scientific and economic development by means of production or distribution of goods or provision of services.

67. On the other hand, the presumption rule [as pertaining to horizontal agreements under section 3(3)] envisages that the competition authority would presume the conduct to be anticompetitive unless rebutted by the OP. While the simplest example of a presumptive approach (where the Commission presumes AAEC and it is for the OP to show that no AAEC flowed from its conduct) is that of a cartel where horizontal players collude and fix prices, territories etc., a case of a market player indulging into RPM, where the investigation has to show negative effects of RPM outweighing the procompetitive ones, depicts the rule of reason mode. Also *see* Mittal, D.P., *Anti-competitive Agreements* (2011), Taxmann Publication, 3rd edition.

68. Wijckmans, F., Tuytschaever, F. and Vanderelest, A., *Vertical Agreements in EC Competition Law* (2006), Oxford University Press, 3rd edition.

69. Case No. 20 of 2017, Competition Commission of India.

duration and that since the tariffs are independently determined by the electricity regulator, there was little possibility of harm to consumers.

In weighing the factors for arriving at anticompetitiveness (AAEC) in cases of restraints pertaining to vertically related parties, the Commission is also found to have considered factors such as limited duration of vertical restrictions.[70]

In *Ashish Ahuja* against *Snapdeal,*[71] the Commission gave importance of protection of brand image and goodwill to negate the likelihood of market foreclosure. The Commission observed that in a quality-driven market, brand image and goodwill are important concerns and it appears a prudent business policy that sale of products emanating from unknown/unverified/unauthorised sources are not encouraged/allowed.

(c) *Market Power – Presence* of significant (or not insignificant) market power by the player who imposes restraint vertically is important even to arrive at a prima facie view of anticompetitiveness. Market share provides the single most important proxy for market power, though other factors are also relevant. It is noteworthy that the Act does not expressly mandate the Commission to assess the market power of the supplier while assessing a case of vertical restraints. What assumes relevance as the deciding factor in cases of vertical restraints is that the enterprise enjoys sufficient market power to impose a restraint on a vertically related enterprise.

The Commission has shown a consistent approach of considering market power and position of the enterprise enforcing vertical restraints in deciding whether ultimately a case of market foreclosure is made out. Cases alleging foreclosure but not demonstrating ample extent of market power stand little chance of being penalised by the Commission. In *Ghanshyam Das Vij* against *Bajaj Corp,*[72] the Commission dismissed allegations of anticompetitive vertical restrictions imposed by a manufacturer of Fast Moving Consumer Goods products because the supplier enforcing the restrictions did not have sufficient market power.

The Commission has maintained the position that competition in the different levels of production-supply chain may possibly be adversely affected when both the entities to the agreement possess some market power in their respective spheres of market. In *Automobiles Dealers Association* against *Global Automobiles Limited,*[73] the Commission dismissed allegations of exclusive distributorship agreement because both the parties to the agreement had insignificant presence in the market in which they were operating and were fringe players, which diminished the likelihood of market foreclosure.

70. Himalya International against Himalya Simplot, Case No. 92 of 2013, Competition Commission of India.
71. Case No. 17 of 2014, Competition Commission of India.
72. Case No. 68 of 2013, Competition Commission of India.
73. Case No. 33 of 2011, Competition Commission of India.

(d) *Mere Contractual issues* – In *Akhil R Bhansali* against *Skoda Auto,*[74] the Commission held that while assessing whether a vertical restraint may cause an AAEC, the Commission is quite likely to examine the effect of the restraint on consumers interests as well. However, in practice, the Commission has been vigilant not to entertain consumer complaints disguised as vertical agreements posing competition issues.

In *Gateway Terminals India Private Limited,*[75] the Commission refused to investigate allegations of vertical tying of Container Freight Services (CFS) provided by the *AP Moller Maersk Group* along with container terminal services at *Jawaharlal Nehru Port.* The Commission, while refereeing to notification of the Customs Department stipulating that the usage of a particular CFS facility is the prerogative of a consignee, observed that the relationship between the consignees/shipping lines and CFSs is a purely commercial arrangement based on contractual understanding between the parties.

(e) *Tying in arrangements* – Section 3(4)(a) hits vertical restriction in the form of tying and bundling, provided the parameter of AAEC in India is met. In *Sonam Sharma* against *Apple Inc,*[76] although negating a case of sections 4 and 3(4), the Commission broadly laid down the conditions to be satisfied in the case of tying and bundling: (i) the presence of two separate products or services capable of being tied; (ii) the seller must have sufficient economic power with respect to the tying product to appreciably restrain free competition in the market for the tied product; and (iii) the tying arrangement must affect a not insubstantial amount of commerce.

(f) *Exclusive Distributor/Supply Agreement* – A particular mode of distribution, restricting the territory by means of an exclusive distributorship agreement, changes in existing practices of distribution or a selective distribution system restricting the supply of goods to enterprises other than those approved by the seller in the nature of exclusive supply or distribution agreements have been dealt with by the Commission under the *rule of reason* analysis under the Act and are hit by section 3(4), if it causes or is likely to cause, an AAEC in India. Recognising the likely benefits of an Exclusive Distributorship Agreement, the Commission, in *Ghanshyam Das Vij*[77] noted that such arrangement can be objectively justified on certain grounds such as protection from free riding, efficient management of sales of products, economic efficiency, etc. However, the Commission was mindful of the fact that such arrangements affect *inter* brand and *intra* brand competition. In *Honda Siel,*[78] the Commission comprehensively analysed anticompetitive conduct of the OEMs at the level of the

74. Case No. 44 of 2017, Competition Commission of India.
75. Case Nos 47 & 56 of 2016, Competition Commission of India.
76. Case No. 24 of 2011, Competition Commission of India.
77. Case No. 68 of 2013, Competition Commission of India.
78. Case No. 03 of 2011, Competition Commission of India.

macro automobile industry of India by assessing the composite effects of exclusive arrangements by all the OEMs, including warranty policies etc.

The Commission in *Keerthy Krishnan* against *Bharat Petroleum Corporation*[79] assessed a selective distribution system implemented by a state-owned oil and gas company, which prescribed certain eligibility criterion for parties to qualify for a tender to transport LPG cylinders. The Commission recognised that the OP had its own business liberty for any changes in the tender for its own interests and could procure services from the service providers other than the informant[80] and that such legitimate business decisions do not warrant any interference.

(g) *RPM* – While RPM is treated seriously in many jurisdictions, the Indian law envisages *rule of reason* analysis on a case by case basis. There are a large number of cases involving RPM that were looked at by the Commission during the last nearly ten years of its enforcement experience, the major ones being *ESYS Information Technologies against Intel,*[81] *Shubham Sanitary,*[82] *Fx – Hyundai,*[83] *Prime Magazine against Wiley*[84] and *Ghamshyam Das Vij against Bajaj Corporation.*[85] *Jasper Kaff*[86] is the most recent order of the Commission on online RPM (discussed later in the chapter).

Fx Enterprises against Hyundai,[87] marks the beginning of an era where the Commission directly ruled on RPM by holding that the restriction imposed by *Hyundai* on the maximum permissible discount that may be given by a dealer to the end-consumer, amounted to an act of RPM, which was in violation of the Act and slapped a fine of INR 870 million. The Commission found the restriction put in place by *Hyundai* to be stifling *intra*-brand competition, creating of barriers to the new entrants in the market and resulting in higher prices for the consumers and noted that the agreements/arrangements did not result into accrual of any consumer benefits; rather, the same resulted into denial of benefits to the consumers in the form of high prices. Further, the Commission was of the view that the agreements were not resulting into any improvements in production or distribution of goods or provision of services but were causing hindrance in the distribution of goods and provision of services in relation to new cars.

In deciding a case for RPM, the Commission's assessment is seen to focus on the freedom of the retailer to resell the product below the market

79. Case No. 08 of 2013, Competition Commission of India.
80. Informant under the Competition Act is the one who brings information under section 19(1)(a) of the Act to the Commission initiating the case before the Commission. The Commission can also take up a case *Suo moto* or on a reference from Central/State Government or Statutory Authority.
81. Case No. 48 of 2011, Competition Commission of India.
82. Case No. 09 of 2015, Competition Commission of India.
83. Case Nos 36 & 82 of 2014, Competition Commission of India.
84. Case No. 07 of 2016, Competition Commission of India.
85. Case No. 68 of 2013, Competition Commission of India.
86. Case No. 61 of 2014, Competition Commission of India.
87. Case Nos 36 & 08 of 2014, Competition Commission of India.

operating price (MOP).[88] If the retailer is able to sell the goods freely below the MOP, *intra* band competition would be vibrant. In *Shubham Sanitary Wares* against *Hindustan Sanitary ware*,[89] the Informant alleged that *Hindustan Sanitary ware* engaged into the vertical RPM by regulating the discount structure. However, the Commission observed that the practice of offering differential discounts to different categories of consumers i.e., less discount for retail buyers and a higher discount for bulk buyers (such as institutions, builders, colonisers and persons of importance) may not be construed as a violation of section 3(4) of the Act.

In *Vishal Pande against Honda Motorcycle*,[90] a case which is pending DG investigation, the Commission has been of the *prima-facie* view that RPM imposed by the OP, which includes monitoring of maximum permissible discount level through discount control mechanism and levy of penalty for non-compliance and appointment of mystery shoppers to collect data from dealers, amounts to contravention of section 3(4)(e) read with section 3(1) of the Act.

(h) *Exemption – Though* intellectual property rights (IPRs) constitute a conditional exemption from the ambit of the whole of section 3, the Commission has shown a somewhat conservative approach in extending the benefit of IPR to entities imposing vertical restraints. In *Honda Siel*[91] the OEMs relied upon the IPR exemptions stating that the restrictions on Original Equipment Supplier (OESs) for sales of the propriety parts to third parties without prior consent would fall within the ambit of reasonable condition to prevent infringements of IPRs. It was also contended that significant investments were made into research and development facilities by them based on which these products were manufactured. The Commission in interpreting 'reasonable' as mentioned under section 3(5) of the Act denied exemption under section 3(5)(i) due to being unconvinced regarding both the characterisation of IPRs claimed by the OEMs as well as insufficiency of evidence to establish claims over IPR. The Commission was watchful of the fact that even in cases where the OEMs had registered/applied for registration of certain designs, patents, the details of specific spare parts to which the IPRs corresponded, had not be furnished.

(i) *Remedy* – To remedy a restraint arising out of vertical relations of parties, the wide powers which range from power to impose fines on the violating enterprise to power to give direction to modify the agreement embodying the restraint under section 27 are available at the disposal of the Commission. In *Honda Siel*,[92] the Commission as a remedy directed the car manufacturer companies to allow the OESs to sell spare parts in the open market without any

88. Market Operating Price (MOP) is the actual price at which a product is made available to a retailer.
89. Case No. 09 of 2015, Competition Commission of India.
90. Case No. 17 of 2017, Competition Commission of India.
91. Case No. 03 of 2011, Competition Commission of India.
92. Case No. 03 of 2011, Competition Commission of India.

restriction, including on prices. The car manufacturing companies were also directed to develop and operate appropriate systems for training of independent repairer/garages, and also to facilitate easy availability of diagnostic tools.

[B] Law Relating to Vertical Restraints as a Unilateral Conduct under Section 4 of the Indian Competition Act

Besides section 3(4) of the Act, the Indian Competition law also envisages Vertical restraints to be read under section 4[93] as unilateral conduct when the enterprise enjoys a dominant position in the relevant market. Conspicuously, the use of the words AAEC are absent in section 4 implying that once dominance and abuse of the OP are proved, it is not open to the OP to argue that no anticompetitive effect flowed out of the unilateral act of the dominant enterprise to restrain the other party. However, what constitutes abuse under section 4(2)(a)(e) is open to detailed scrutiny so that the adverse effect on competition is duly, though indirectly, taken into account at this stage.

Vertical restraints under section 4 typically characterise cases where the OP, an enterprise dominant in the upstream market, imposes unfair or discriminatory conditions on the party in the downstream market, or denies market access, or imposes far from relevant obligations in the contracts on a firm in the same supply chain. Dominant position in the relevant market in this context is to be construed as signifying market power of a degree much more than that required for the purposes of section 3(4) and has to be proved having due regard to the factors contained under section 19(4) of the

93. Section 4 provides: (1) No enterprise or group shall abuse its dominant position:

(2) There shall be an abuse of dominant position 4 [under sub-section (1), if an enterprise or a group]–
  (a) directly or indirectly, imposes unfair or discriminatory–
    (i) condition in purchase or sale of goods or service; or
    (ii) price in purchase or sale (including predatory price) of goods or service.
  Explanation – For the purposes of this clause, the unfair or discriminatory condition in purchase or sale of goods or service referred to in sub-clause (i) and unfair or discriminatory price in purchase or sale of goods (including predatory price) or service referred to in sub-clause (ii) shall not include such discriminatory condition or price which may be adopted to meet the competition; or
  (b) limits or restricts–
    (i) production of goods or provision of services or market therefor; or
    (ii) technical or scientific development relating to goods or services to the prejudice of consumers; or
  (c) indulges in practice or practices resulting in denial of market access in any manner; or
  (d) makes conclusion of contracts subject to acceptance by other parties of supplementary obligations which, by their nature or according to commercial usage, have no connection with the subject of such contracts; or
  (e) uses its dominant position in one relevant market to enter into, or protect, other relevant market.

Act.[94] Market power here is such as to enable the enterprise to act independently of market forces, including consumers and competitors. The market power in the context of section 3(4) is more in terms of power over the existing consumers, by way of brand loyalty and other factors.

It is noteworthy that IPRs do not enjoy similar exemptions under section 4, as is the case with section 3. In *Honda Siel,* the Commission noted that unlike section 3(5) of the Act, there was no exception to section 4(2) of the Act in respect of IPRs.

In *Kansan* against *M/s Fast Way and Hathway*,[95] the Commission concluded that owing to its market power, the OP group denied the opportunity of transmission of the TV channel of the broadcaster by illegal termination of their contract. The Commission penalised the OP under section 27 and directed them to cease and desist from their conduct of denial market access to *Kansan*, a broadcaster of news and current affairs TV channel, in violation of section 4(2)(c) of the Act. The Competition Appellate Tribunal (COMPAT),[96] when vexed with an appeal filed by *Fastway and Ors*,[97] observed that the two services are separate services and are not in competition with each other and that by no stretch of imagination it could be established that by termination of a contract of interconnection of services between two service providers, there has been a denial of market access to the actual transmission of the channels to the viewers. Further, the COMPAT was of the view that there has been no denial of services to the viewers causing consumer harm.

The Hon'ble Supreme Court in case *Competition Commission of India v. M/s Fast Way Transmission Pvt. Ltd & others*[98] upheld the view of the Commission, and it overruled the COMPAT, holding that the words '*in any manner*' are of a wide import and should be given their natural meaning and that denial of market access vertically is covered under this provision. The Apex Court held that

> [O]nce a dominant position is made out on facts, whether a broadcaster is in competition with Multi System Operators is a factor that is irrelevant for the purpose of application of section 4(2)(c).

---

94. Section 19(4): The Commission shall, while inquiring whether an enterprise enjoys a dominant position or not under section 4, have due regard to all or any of the following factors, namely: - (a) market share of the enterprise; (b) size and resources of the enterprise; (c) size and importance of the competitors; (d) economic power of the enterprise including commercial advantages over competitors; (e) vertical integration of the enterprises or sale or service network of such enterprises; (f) dependence of consumers on the enterprise; (g) monopoly or dominant position whether acquired as a result of any statute or by virtue of being a government company or a public sector undertaking or otherwise; (h) entry barriers including barriers such as regulatory barriers, financial risk, high capital cost of entry, marketing entry barriers, technical entry barriers, economies of scale, high cost of substitutable goods or service for consumers; (i) countervailing buying power; (j) market structure and size of market; (k) social obligations and social costs; (l) relative advantage, by way of the contribution to the economic development, by the enterprise enjoying a dominant position having or likely to have an AAEC; (m) any other factor which the Commission may consider relevant for the inquiry.
95. Case No. 36 of 2011, Competition Commission of India.
96. Competition Appellate Tribunal is now National Company Law Appellate Tribunal (NCLAT).
97. Appeal No. 116 of 2012, Competition Appellate Tribunal, date of Judgment 02 May 2014.
98. Civil Appeal No. 7215/2014, Supreme Court of India, Order Dated 24 January 2018.

The Commission assessed a minimum guaranteed off-take requirement as imposing unfair and discriminatory conditions under the provisions dealing with abuse of dominance in *Re Faridabad Industries Association and Adani Gas Limited.*[99] While the Commission appreciated various business justifications associated with such contractual terms, it agreed with the DG that requiring the buyer to fulfil such minimum off-take obligations, even in the event of emergency shutdown, makes the terms 'unfair' and hence abusive. However, in *RICO Auto and Ors* against *GAIL,*[100] where the issue was whether the Long Term Re gasified Natural Gas (LTRNG) contracts entered into by GAIL are anticompetitive and forecloses competition, the Commission observed that considering the nature of the industry and the product involved as well as the fact that significant upfront capital investments for the exploration, design and construction of the facilities (which leads to hold up problem) making the buyer to take advantage of the investments made by the seller, it cannot be said that LTRNG entered into by the OP with its customers is inherently anticompetitive or entails foreclosure of competition. In arriving at a decision in the matter, the Commission recalled its own decision in *Tata Power* against *NTPC,*[101] wherein for the issue of Long Term PPA, the Commission held that there was a rational basis for binding the Informant and other procurers in long-term PPAs.[102]

It has also been found by the Commission in multiple cases that where the OP enjoys dominant position in the relevant upstream market, vertical restraints were imposed on the player in the downstream market, in the exercise of abuse of the dominant position by the OP. In *Three D* against *Verifone,*[103] the Commission was of the opinion that through the Software Development Kit agreement *Verifone* imposed unfair conditions on *Three D* which were in contravention of section 4(2)(a)(i) of the Act and restricted the provision of Value Added Software (VAS) services as well as limited/restricted the technical and scientific development of VAS services used in POS terminals in India in contravention of 4(2)(b)(i) and (ii) of the Act.[104]

99. Case No. 71 of 2012, Competition Commission of India.
100. Case Nos 16-20 of 2016, 45 of 2016, 02, 59, 62 and 63 of 2017, Competition Commission of India.
101. Case No. 20 of 2017, Competition Commission of India.
102. The Commission observed that: '...even if it is assumed that the OP was in a dominant position in the relevant market as identified by the Informant, a prima facie case of abuse of dominance in terms of the provisions of Section 4(2)(a)(i) of the Act is not made out in the instant matter because, firstly the Informant has entered into the PPAs with the OP being fully aware of the terms of the PPAs including the long term obligation stipulated thereunder, secondly there is a rational basis for binding the Informant and other procurers in the long term PPAs as the generating companies invest in establishing the generating stations based on allocation and the PPAs entered into with the parties (which are to be served through period agreed upon) and lastly, the Informant and other procurers have the option to approach the central government for reallocation of power allocated to them'.
103. Case No. 13 of 2013, Competition Commission of India.
104. The Commission, in this case, also observed that the purpose clause allowing licensee to develop the value added software only to be used on the licensor's products that the licensee had purchased was clearly restrictive and anticompetitive. Moreover, the Commission found the license restriction clause, *viz.* 'not use the licensed software to develop any payment software that directly or indirectly interacts with any acquiring bank' to be unfair and restrictive.

However in *Financial Software and Systems (FSS)* against *ACI Worldwide*,[105] the OP not being dominant in the relevant upstream market, the question of abuse was not gone into. The issue in the case pertained to the OP imposing unfair condition in the purchase or sale of goods or services through exclusive supply arrangements with ACI Banks and directing ACI Banks not to avail the integration services of *FSS*.

The Commission under section 4 uses its broad powers under section 27 to remedy a situation by passing order directing the OP to cease and desist from the conduct of denying market access to the competitors or consumers, or leveraging from upstream relevant market to the downstream relevant market, or imposing unfair terms and conditions, or imposing unrelated condition etc.

[C] Is the Indian Law Sufficient to Deal with Competition Law Challenges Posed by the Online World?

As the world witnesses the close of the second decade of the new millennium, terms such as *shopping cart, price on request, wishlist, payment options etc.* sound no longer new. With the world economy witnessing a tremendous upsurge, India, too, has seen new technological platforms which have revamped the traditional channels through which products or services were offered traditionally. E-commerce acts as a digital middlemen connecting millions of buyers and sellers where it is not convenient for them to meet. This technological era of e-commerce has ushered upon the Indian economy ravishing features such as online stores, online shopping, online booking services, e-books, comparison price sites, etc. In addition, e-commerce has flooded India with online portals which provide value added services,[106] e.g., logistics, warehousing, marketing and sales including provision of assistance to consumers in sorting and buying products, return/replacement services, tracking services for orders placed etc. Online shopping platforms facilitate connection of buyers through an online platform and deliver the products at customer doorstep.

On the lines of Competition authorities across jurisdictions, which are in constant pursuit to bring new challenges brought forth by e-commerce technology within their umbrella,[107] India, is also meticulously preparing itself to pin down foul online vertical restraints. However, being still in the first decade of competition law enforcement, jurisprudence is still evolving in this area. With the limited exposure the Indian Competition Authority has had with the online world, Indian law has given the clear signal that it is capable of dealing with assorted issues cropping up every now and then in the virtual arena. The legislature, while drafting of the Act, has been vigilant and watchful of the technological changes Indian economy was going through with the result that it provided adequate leverage in the provisions of the Act so as to

105. Case No. 52 of 2013, Competition Commission of India.
106. Jasper Kaff, Case No. 61 of 2014, Competition Commission of India.
107. Luis. O.G., and Fernández, M.M., *Most-Favoured Nation Clauses: A Business Need But Unresolved Topic in Mexico* (March 2016), CPI Antitrust Chronical, Volume 1, available at https://www.competitionpolicyinternational.com/wp-content/uploads/2016/03/Most-Favored-Nation-Clauses.pdf, accessed on 19 June 2018.

accommodate challenges thrown by the technological era. The net result is that the provisions of the Act seem clear and unambiguous in its application to the internet and online platforms.

The preamble to the Act specifies that the Act has been passed and the Commission has been established for the purposes of 'prevention of practices having an adverse effect on competition'. Further section 18 is couched in a manner so as to give the Commission the duty to not just prevent practices having AAEC on competition but also 'eliminate practices having adverse effect on competition.' The preamble read with section 18 bestows upon the Commission the broad mandate to bring to task various infringements of the Act to ensure that competition is well protected and sustained and markets function in a rather free but fair manner.

While the internet has transformed the relationship between the producer and the consumers to a large extent, it is not a myth to say that it also exerts a material influence on the distribution channels. While the bricks and mortar shop constitutes the offline channel of distribution, shopping websites and shopping apps constitute the online distribution channel. When it comes to anticompetitive agreements in the nature of vertical restraint, the Indian Act under section 3(4) uses the words '...enterprises or persons at different stages or levels of the production chain in different markets, in respect of production, supply, distribution, storage, sale....'

Responding to the technological era, the legislature has drafted section 3(4) in the most extensive and inclusive manner where terms such as production, supply, distribution, storage, sale etc. are all wide enough to extend their reach to the online platforms.

Use of the phrase 'provisions of services' following the term goods in section 3(4) brings under its domain 'online provisions of services'. Services in the nature of online accommodation booking, online ticket booking etc. come under the purview of provision of services. Apart from that, the term 'distribution' includes not only the offline modes of distribution but also the online means of distribution of goods bringing the shopping websites within the ambit of the Indian law. Not only is the definition wide enough to cover distribution channels involved in goods, but it is widely worded to subsume online platforms providing services.

While the online world fosters faster communication of orders, placing of orders and delivery thereof, it has also reduced the need for maintaining a minimum level of inventory with the distributors, thus having a bearing on inventory management/storage. In consonance with this, the Indian law, has used the word 'storage' under section 3(4), which seems wide enough to include an online maintenance/management of inventory or digital catalogue of products. While literal meaning of the word storage refers to the state of goods being stored physically, the Act possesses leverage to apply the same meaning to online maintenance of inventory. In the recent *Jasper Kaff*[108] case, the Commission gave regard to the fact that though the online platforms do not take possession of the goods in the literal sense of the word, it may not be appropriate to say that they do not form part of the value chain through

108. Case No. 61 of 2014, Competition Commission of India.

which ownership is transferred from the seller to the buyer. Moreover, the Commission in *Jasper Kaff* was mindful of the fact that owing to the nature of the high-tech digital markets, the principles of transit/movement of products in traditional market cannot be applied *strict senso* to digital markets.

The Act defines *agreements*[109] widely and can easily cover agreements on a virtual platform. In turn, the term agreement forms part of the definition of cartels under section 2(c) thereby suggesting that horizontal collusions which flow out of agreements are also covered. The definition of Service under section 2(u) is also kept inclusive by the framers of the legislation well accommodating online services.

Similarly, section 2(y) defines turnover as inclusive of value of goods and services which is broad enough to include revenue earned by the online platforms. In the online marketplace involving goods or products from multiple vendors where the vendors have to pay the fees to list their offering on the online market place, the revenue that can be extracted from the listing of products or services on the platform will fall under section 2(y) of the Act.

Section 19(3), which is the touchstone of measure of AAEC with respect to section 3 (anticompetitive agreements) in the Act, effortlessly accommodates online platforms while laying down the positives and negatives which constitutes the scales for balancing of adverse and beneficial effects to come to a conclusion regarding violation or otherwise of an alleged conduct. While stressing on positive factors, such as accrual of benefits to consumers, improvement in production or distribution of goods or provision of services, promotion of technical, scientific and economic development, to negate a case of anticompetitive agreements, the Act, naturally extends its reach to online cases. Section 19(3) in its application to online cases would take into consideration reduction/elimination of travel time and cost by overcoming geographical limitations and reduction of information asymmetry as visible benefits accruing to consumers. Besides, better technical support added with the features of better customisability would also add to benefits accruing to consumers. Similarly, decreasing cost of inventory management, lower advertising and marketing costs, and personnel cost is an improvement in production or distribution of goods or provision of services. Online facilities such as replacement/refund policies, parcel-tracking services etc. of shopping sites provide value added services which ultimately goes on to play a major role in further technical development. Moreover, foregoing the need of maintaining a physical store, insurance and infrastructure (as required under the analogue stores), plays its part to contribute towards scientific and technical development facilitating economic development while assessing factors under section 19(3).

Needless to say that the Commission is seen to be mindful of the fact that any analysis done in case of vertical restraints (online or offline) should concentrate on the impact on the market rather than the form in which the agreement has been couched. In fact, the crux of testing a conduct on the premise of *rule of reason* is to weigh the procompetitive and anticompetitive effects prior to labelling a conduct as anticompetitive. There may be cases where a combination of vertical restraints may lead to a

109. Agreements are defined under section 2(b) of the Competition Act, 2002.

favourable outcome rather than to increase the probability of anticompetitive outcome. In such cases, the Commission may not condemn the vertical restraint.

Market definition, as in every case of anticompetitive vertical agreement or abuse of dominance, assumes importance in cases of online vertical restraints too. Even though online markets are prone to competition issues similar to that of offline markets, the tools available to address many of the competition concerns need to be adjusted to account for the special characteristics of Internet markets such as their two/multi-sidedness. While two-sided markets are characterised by the presence of two groups of customers interacting with each other, multi-sided markets involve the presence of multiple groups. Since the general purpose of market definitions is to provide a context for examining the issues that arise in antitrust matters,[110] market definition should not be seen as an end in itself, but a first important step that helps assess competitive constraints, market power and the effects of the behaviour at stake.[111] Online markets throw up challenges which are more complicated than offline ones for two reasons. *First*, in many online markets consumers, not paying a positive price, at least not in monetary terms, pay an implicit price in the form of personal data and/or attention. In other words, platforms compete for consumer's attention and sell it to advertisers.[112] *Second*, to analyse market power in a two-sided market, examination of price cumulative to both the sides of the market should be necessarily above the marginal cost.

Market definition in the Indian antitrust cases is based on the broad contours of *price, intended use and physical characteristic*, which forms the very basis for its delineation. These broad parameters which assist the Commission to delineate the relevant market in offline cases are the ones which apply with equal vigour to cases concerning online challenges. Price,[113] which is one of the factors mentioned under section 2(t)[114] read with section 19(7)[115] of the Indian Act for delineating relevant market, assumes relevance when it comes to online cases as it seeks to account for the

110. Evans, D.S., *The Antitrust Economics of Two-Sided Markets*, available at SSRN: https://ssrn.com/abstract=332022, accessed on 04 July 2018.
111. Wismer, S. and Rasek, A., *Market Definition in Multi-Sided Markets* (June 2017), Directorate for Financial and Enterprise Affairs Competition Committee, DAF/COMP/WD (2017) 33, available at https://www.bundeskartellamt.de/SharedDocs/Publikation/EN/Diskussions_Hintergrundpapiere/OECD_2017_Competition_Committee_multi-sided%20markets.pdf?__blob=publicationFile&v=3, accessed on 04 August 2018.
112. Haucap, J., and Torben, S., *Competition and Antitrust in Internet Markets* (October 2015), Working Paper, Düsseldorf Institute for Competition Economics Discussion Paper, No. 199, available at https://www.econstor.eu/bitstream/10419/121420/1/837896487.pdf, accessed on 24 July 2018.
113. Price is defined under section 2(o) of the Competition Act, 2002 as 'price', in relation to the sale of any goods or to the performance of any services, includes every valuable consideration, whether direct or indirect, or deferred, and includes any consideration which in effect relates to the sale of any goods or to the performance of any services although ostensibly relating to any other matter or thing.
114. Section 2(t) provides: 'relevant product market' means a market comprising all those products or services which are regarded as interchangeable or substitutable by the consumer, by reason of characteristics of the products or services, their prices and intended use.
115. Section 19(7) provides: The Commission shall, while determining the 'relevant product market', have due regard to all or any of the following factors, namely: – (a) physical

implicit price paid by a consumer in the form of attention to a particular website even though the price paid in monetary terms may be zero. In *Google*,[116] it was argued that the consumers incur near zero search costs when surfing the web in order to gather information for making decisions on purchasing. The Commission, however, was of the view that the plea of *Google* that there is no sale or purchase of goods/services is not only flawed but altogether ignores the role of big data in the digital economy. The Commission noted:

> ... rise of new business models based on collection and processing of Big Data is currently shaping the world. With the development of data mining and machine learning, businesses are able to offer innovative, high-quality and customised products and services at low or even zero prices, with great gains for consumers. At the same time, it cannot be denied that the benefits of providing Big Data do not come without a cost. Consumers may be increasingly facing a loss of control over their data and are exposed to intrusive advertising and behavioural discrimination.

Thus, the Commission, negating the arguments of *Google*, observed that in markets that are characterised with more than one side, any market assessment that relies only on the side where the services offered are free to consumers distorts the true picture and leads to a biased assessment of the nature of competition in such markets. It was also observed that the revenue earned by search platforms through provisions of search based advertisers bears testimony not only to the potential of ad services offered by them but also negates the view that search services offered by such platforms are free.

Notably, the definition of price under the Act speaks of price to include consideration whether direct, indirect or deferred and includes *any consideration which in effect relates to sale of goods or performance of services although ostensibly relating to any other matter or thing*. Thus, the use of the phrase 'includes any consideration' and 'ostensibly relating to any other thing' in section 2(o) are seen to be sufficient to counter and reject the argument that consumer pays a zero cost when it comes to searching online as it constitutes neither purchase of goods nor provision of services under the Act. A careful reading of section 2(o) shows that time and attention paid by the end consumers to the online portal is enough to constitute 'any consideration' irrespective of the value.

When it comes to physical characteristics as a factor to be considered in determining the relevant market, the Commission in *Google* agreed with the DG that on account of vast differences in the characteristics of online and offline advertising, the two were not to be treated as substitutable and therefore not a part of the same relevant market. The Commission observed that online advertising is undertaken using internet as a medium which has a large coverage and is not substitutable for newspapers, radio or television for advertisers who seek to target areas or user groups with limited

characteristics or end-use of goods; (b) price of goods or service (c) consumer preferences; (d) exclusion of in-house production; (e) existence of specialised producers; (f) classification of industrial products.

116. Case Nos 07 & 30 of 2012, Competition Commission of India.

internet access. By maintaining a board distinction between online and offline advertising, the Act seems to include, under its ambit, advertising platforms in the nature of Facebook. Similarly, Facebook and Instagram, when integrated with enterprise's e-commerce site, to sell directly though enterprise's Facebook page will be amenable under the jurisdiction of the Act more so due to the coming up of Facebook's new feature of Facebook Marketplace which acts like a classified listings site with localised listings.

It was also observed as far as intended use as a factor in delineating relevant market is concerned, that price of search and non-search advertising are different from each other.

When it comes to the relevant geographic market, a conjoint reading of the definition of relevant geographic market and abuse of dominant position under section 4, makes it clear that the position of strength of the enterprise has to be in India. Although the internet knows no boundary and brings the world to a common platform, in dealing with online cases, the Commission has delineated the relevant geographic market in online cases within India.

Coming to the specific challenges posed by online vertical restraints, it is noticed that the Commission has practically not been vexed with any case pertaining to MFN, as on date. However, such an arrangement is likely to be assessed by the Commission under the '*rule of reason*' framework as and when it arises with the Commission balancing the pro-competitive and anticompetitive effects arising out of it and intervening if it finds the likelihood of AAEC in India. Similarly, IMAP, which has again never been encountered by the Commission, will face the same process as faced by MFN that of being tested on the touchstone of the *rule of reason* as embedded in section 19(3) of the Act.

The recent order of the Commission pertaining to *Jasper Kaff*[117] has pointed out to the fact the provisions of section 3(4) incorporating RPM as one of the vertical restraints, is fully geared up to deal with all substantial issues pertaining to online RPM. The DG, in the above said case, opined that since the Informant is only a market platform, it does not form part of the vertical chain and hence, cannot be subjected to a vertical restraint by the OP under section 3(4)(e) of the Act. In reaching the above said conclusion, the DG based himself on the following: *first,* the Informant/e-retailer/online portal did not perform any material function which could make it a part of vertical/supply chain; *second,* the Informant not being the buyer/purchaser of goods in the distribution chain, the basic ingredient for sustaining an allegation of RPM (i.e., presence of purchaser and seller) remained unfulfilled and, *third,* the Informant did not have any influence on price on its online platform. The Commission holding the observation of the DG inconsistent with the working of the technology-driven markets observed that considering the entry of digital markets and online platforms, the customary structure may not be present in every situation, especially in constantly evolving markets and that any entity/firm contributing value to product/service will be deemed to be a part of the value chain. In assessing AAEC for the above said case, the

117. Case No. 61 of 2014, Competition Commission of India.

Commission took into account the multiplied sales figures of chimneys and hobs of the OP as well as that of the other competing manufacturers on Informant's portal pointing at no deterrent effect of the notice in question. It was also held that the data on record did not show that the adverse effect of Caution Notice was sufficient enough to meet the criteria laid down under the Act i.e., AAEC.

As far as the issue of selective distribution channel is concerned, restricting the ability to sell *via* the online mode could be prohibited if the Commission finds such restrictions to cause, or be likely to cause, an AAEC in India. However in such cases, the Commission again would give due consideration to the sufficiency of market power of the OP in foreclosing the market or preventing entry of competitors. In *Mohit Manglani* against *Flipkart and Ors,*[118] the products were being sold exclusively through select internet platforms to the exclusion of offline channels and competing internet portals. It was alleged that e-commerce sites were having exclusive arrangements with sellers of goods/services. The Commission did not find any market foreclosure, because the products sold through these portals faced significant competitive constraints, and competition among e-portals was also thriving. In assessing the positives of section 19(3), the Commission gave due regard to the fact that the option of delivery right at the door steps of the consumers, convenience of the consumers and time saving in online distribution channel as compared with the bricks and mortar retail outlets, negate the case that exclusive arrangement between manufacturers and OPs lead to AAEC in the market.

In *Ashish Ahuja* against *SanDisk,*[119] the Commission assessed the allegations against *Snapdeal.com*, an e-commerce portal, and *SanDisk Corporation*, a manufacturer of electronic storage device. *SanDisk* insisted that only its authorised online channel partners shall sell its products through *Snapdeal*. Rejecting the allegations, the Commission noted that in a quality-driven market, the need to protect brand image justifies a business policy that discourages sale of products by unauthorised sellers.

Also in *Deepak Verma* against *Clues Network,*[120] the Commission while determining the dominance of an online retail portal, held that online and offline are not two different relevant markets, but are two different channels of distribution to the same relevant market. Similarly, in the case of *Confederation of Real Estate Brokers Association of India* against *Magicbricks.com,*[121] the Commission held that while determining the relevant market, the online and offline services of brokers cannot be distinguished, as both are alternative channels of delivering the same service.

As far as Indian law on restraints imposed as a result of an abuse meted out by the dominant OP is concerned, the cases of *Matrimony.com and CUTS* against *Google*[122] are clear examples that the law in its current form is capable of addressing the issue of double-sided markets and multi-sided markets. While dealing with cases of abuse of dominant position in the online platform in *Google,*[123] it was alleged that *Google* was

118. Case No. 80 of 2014, Competition Commission of India.
119. Case No. 17 of 2014, Competition Commission of India.
120. Case No. 34 of 2016, Competition Commission of India.
121. Case No. 23 of 2016, Competition Commission of India.
122. Case Nos 07 & 30 of 2012, Competition Commission of India.
123. Case Nos 07 & 30 of 2012, Competition Commission of India.

using its dominance in the market for general web search to impose restrictive conditions in online syndicate search agreements, in violation of section 4(2)(e) of the Act. The Commission observed that the exclusive agreement needs to be examined in light of the importance of scale and network effects in online search and online search advertising and *Google*'s substantial market shares in these markets. It was also observed that *Google* prevented partners with whom it entered into negotiated search agreements from implementing on their website any search services which are the same or substantially similar to *Google*'s search service. It was held that *Google* was using its dominance in the market for online general web search to impose restrictive conditions in online syndicate search agreement, in violation of section 4(2)(e) of the Act and that by restricting websites from entering into partnership with competing services, *Google* was denying its competitors access to the search business and further marginalising competitors and endangering their viability, while strengthening its own position.

§2.06 CONCLUSION

India has been a clear beneficiary of the advantages of e-commerce in almost all sectors of the economy. While e-commerce strengthens competition and reduces information asymmetries, it also throws up substantial challenges for the antitrust authorities to face. As a result, online vertical restraints are increasingly on the radar of competition agencies across the world owing, notably, to the emergence of online business transactions in larger and larger scales.

Such restraints when arising out of online transactions are much more difficult to assess, both in terms of violation and in terms of assessment of the extent of harm, given the characteristics of such transactions, their frequency, transparency and their tendency to transcend narrow geographical borders. Having regard to the fact that online vertical restraints are more subtle and nuanced, questions are, raised regarding the competence of domestic legislations which have been framed years, and in some cases decades, back to address the issue of such restraints effectively.

Vertical restraints under the Indian law are covered under two separate provisions: *first*, as part of section 3 related to anticompetitive agreements and *second*, as part of unilateral abusive conduct. Vertical restraints covered under section 3(4) are dealt with as per the provisions of section 19(3), which is the touchstone for AAEC. Here, the presence of significant market power has been identified as a condition precedent though not expressly mandated by the Act. While market power short of dominance makes a player capable of imposing vertical restraints, market power qualifying for dominance takes the case straight to the purview of section 4 making it a unilateral act of abuse of dominance. It is interesting to note that in India the issue of vertical restraints is structurally positioned under anticompetitive agreement provisions rather than the Abuse of Dominant position provisions. However, the Act possesses inherent ability to treat both the situations, first where as a result of the market power, the OP imposes restraints in the form of section 3(4) and second, where the OP being a dominant player in the upstream relevant market imposes unfair conditions on the downstream player, or denies market access to competitors/ consumers or imposes unrelated conditions on the other player.

Consistent with international best practice, the Indian law assesses vertical restraints falling under the purview of anticompetitive agreements (section 3(4)) using the lens of *rule of reason*, evaluating the net of adverse and beneficial effects of such restraints. While assessing online vertical restraints under section 3(4), the Commission has been looking at factors such as the existence of significant market power by the restraining enterprise and level of *inter* brand competition in the market.

As far as imposition of restraint as a result of unilateral abuse of dominant position is concerned, the same modality is used as is used in assessing other cases falling under Abuse of Dominant position. The stand of the Appellate Authority that vertical restraints are not covered under section 4 was overruled by the Supreme Court of India in *Competition Commission of India v. M/s Fast Way Transmission Pvt. Ltd & others.*[124]

Online vertical restraints can be assessed using the framework that applies to vertical restraints in offline markets, making the existing provisions of Competition Act sufficient and capable of tackling online vertical restraints. The Commission surely needs to adapt the established theoretical framework to the new e-commerce environment. However, when it comes to online markets, issues related to requirement of data and intensity of analysis are quite high. Thus, the rule of reason analysis in online cases would be much more involved than in the case of offline markets.

The issue of whether the Indian law is capable of addressing online vertical restraints has been answered in the positive in the Commission's decisions, especially in the cases of *Jasper Kaff* and *Google*. The argument of *Google* in *Matrimony.com and CUTS* against *Google*[125] that the Indian law in its current form is not capable of addressing the issue of double-sided markets and multi-sided was rejected by the Commission, and it was held that search services offered by *Google* are not free and thus constituted purchase or sale of goods or services. In the case of *Google*, the wide definition of 'agreements', factor based definition of relevant product market and dominant position, definition of price, all measure up to the task of addressing issues specific to online vertical restraints. Further, various definitions forming part of the Indian Law under section 2 are capable to cater to the requirements of the online world. Thus, price under section 2(o), storage, distribution etc. forming part of section 3(4) are seen to be adequately worded to cover cases of online world as and when they arise before the Commission.

The Commission in its more than nine years of journey of enforcement of the major provisions of sections 3 and 4 have dealt with cases of online RPM and exclusive distribution. However, no occasion has arisen for the Commission to pronounce a verdict on IMAP or on MFN.

There are no specific Safe Harbours for vertical restraints under the Indian law. Intellectual property defence provides exemption for section 3 as a whole when reasonable conditions are imposed for the legitimate enjoyment of the right by the right

124. Civil Appeal No. 7215/2014, Supreme Court of India, Order Dated 24 January 2018.
125. Case Nos 07 & 30 of 2012, Competition Commission of India.

holder. No market share threshold for market power has been provided by the Commission by way of guidance. Clearly such guidance in the form of Guidelines will have to wait as sufficient experience needs to be gained before venturing into it.

CHAPTER 3

E-commerce and Competition Law: Insights from the Mexican Experience

Carlos Mena Labarthe, Michel Narcia Martínez & Aleine Obregón Natera[*]

§3.01 INTRODUCTION

Nowadays, e-commerce has not only reshaped the way consumers shop at a global level, it has significantly improved competition levels and radically pushed forward innovation across all supply and distribution levels. In addition, the rise of e-commerce has changed our way of living in many aspects.

Paradoxically, recent technological developments in the e-commerce world have placed us closer to a scenario where it is no longer unthinkable to follow Orwell's advice: 'if you want to keep a secret you must also hide it from yourself'. Such advice could not be more applicable nowadays. We are living in a modern world, surrounded and supported by machines and algorithms that collect, learn, evolve and predict our thinking to suffice our needs (and those of others). We have built a technological world in which the new currency is based on data and is measured by those who are capable of exploiting such information.

Precisely, as explained in the following texts, this chapter aims to briefly analyse the symbiotic relationship between e-commerce and some of the most recent and advanced creations: big data and pricing algorithms. These technologies have the potential not only to reduce the levels of competition, but also to improve them and, in parallel, improve our way of living.

First, this chapter analyse the digital economy built as a result of the e-commerce, assessing the competition challenges surrounding these technologies. Second, we

* The views hereby expressed are exclusively of the authors and do not necessarily reflect those of the organisations involved.

focus on analysing the effect that the use of big data and pricing algorithms has to the competition that exists in the e-commerce world.

§3.02 COMPETITION AND DIGITAL ECONOMY

[A] Introduction to Digital Economy

In recent years, we are shifting into a digital world, where inevitably digital platforms have played a significant role in redefining the traditional economic criteria. Given the fast-growing nature of the digital sector, the traditional competition models have not been sufficient to meet the demands the digital markets need, therefore there is a challenge to adapt the regulation and strengthen the regulatory agencies, including the competition authorities, in order to balance privacy, equity and freedom of choice among market participants.

As Chakravorti[1] states, the transition into a global digital economy has passed three stages: (i) the denial phase, in the early 2000s where there was a strong scepticism to the internet´s use in business; (ii) global adoption after the economic crisis in the West mainly in 2007, when digital economy at a global level was emerging and rapidly evolving; and (iii) mobile connectivity from 2015 onwards, where billions are going online at a worldwide level and most of commerce is done through tablets or phones.

To get a full view of what constitutes the digital economy, many authors have focused on defining what such concept involves. Some consider it as 'the economic activity that results from the millions of online connections among people, businesses, devices and processes' or is seen as markets driven by digital technologies that enable consumers to trade goods and/or services through electronic commerce (known as e-commerce).[2] Besides enabling the trade of goods and services, the digital economy has effects on society and in the functioning of the markets that go beyond the development of digital technologies, which creates more difficulties to competition authorities when it comes to enforcement.

The main factor involved in digital economy is the use of digital technologies that facilitate the exchange of goods and services, considerably increasing the economy growth by eliminating geographical location barriers, a reduction of costs such as distribution due to the use of new technologies (i.e., e-books, music, television programmes, etc.), allowing the introduction of new economic agents that in normal based conditions would be considerably more difficult.

Notwithstanding the foregoing, competition in such sector has very specific characteristics such as the highly grown innovation, the importance of network effects, the tendencies toward 'winner takes all' competition for the market, the dynamism of

1. Chakravorti, Bhaskar *Where the Digital Economy is Moving Fastest* Harvard Business Review, 2016. http://www.digital-economy-lebanon.org/wp-content/uploads/2017/01/16259.pdf.
2. OECD Hearings, *The Digital Economy*, 2012, p. 5 http://www.oecd.org/daf/competition/The-Digital-Economy-2012.pdf [The OECD Hearings].

the market, the existence of multi-sided markets, platform-based models, among others.

[B] Types of Digital Platforms and Elements of the Digital Economy

Online businesses may operate in the form of marketplaces, which involves digital multiple-sided platforms where various retailers operate, generating a continuous contact between buyers and sellers through a well-known site. Similarly, advertising services may be offered, enhancing search rankings and facilitating the access to such platforms.

Marketplaces may operate as an intermediary or as a hybrid model. The former role is limited to offering hosting services for third-party sellers. Conversely, through the latter, the role is not limited to offering hosting services, but also to offering products and services.

In recent times, competition authorities' agenda around the world has been highly focused in the potential competition effects resulting from the collection of consumer data. The potential antitrust issues that could arise for this data collection have not been determined. Many commentators and even authorities have commented how they could function as a barrier to entry into the e-commerce sector or create other competition problems.

In addition, another important issue to analyse is the potential antitrust implications that advertising in digital economy could have. Advertising plays a very important role in digital economy and in e-commerce, and together with the data collection, it could allow targeting which advertising suits better with the preferences of each customer. Similarly, minimum advertising price polices that could be imposed by the supplier may function to negate the price transparency that makes e-commerce competitive.[3]

Lastly, advertising provides a key link between e-commerce and other central component of the digital economy which are less lucrative, also called the key monetised element of digital economy, such as online searches. This element is presented to the user without a cost, but generally is financed by online advertisers.[4]

[C] Competition Challenges

Historically, competition in digital markets has been cyclical, which means that digital platforms can acquire at some point significant market power. Nonetheless, based on this cyclical nature, such dominance can be vulnerable and defeated by the next cycle of innovation, development or any disruption. In this regard, neither the optimal market structure of digital economies (which seeks to incentive investments and innovation), nor the impact of digital economies to other areas of the economy have

3. OECD Dictatorate for Financial and Enterprise Affairs Competition Committee, *Implications of E-Commerce for Competition Policy-Background Note*, 2018, pp. 11–12 http://www.oecd.org/daf/competition/The-Digital-Economy-2012.pdf [The OECD Implications of E-commerce].
4. *Ibid.*

been defined for purposes of determining at which point an enterprise with market power is damaging the market. The foregoing has increased the importance and study of the competition issues that digital economies could arise.[5]

The main task for competition authorities is to make sure that the exchange of goods and services is efficient, regardless of the environment where it occurs. This means that the aim of authorities should be that the digital economy benefits both the economic agents and the consumers, preventing and sanctioning any conduct that affect the e-commerce markets from horizontal collusions to any vertical restraints. For instance, the Mexican Federal Commission for Economic Competition (COFECE) started an investigation regarding potential problems to competition, stating that in Mexico more than 3% of the total retail sales are made online but the market is growing. Without differentiating expressly the e-commerce from the brick and mortar markets, implicitly the COFECE and other authorities are already differentiating between environments and segmenting the markets which may be inaccurate.

Although competition authorities are working to ensure competition in digital markets, based on the technical knowledge required and the constant evolution of the digital economy, it is difficult to apply the traditional competition laws and economic concepts in this sector. In this regard, although competition authorities have to improve their technical knowledge in digital economy, this represents a continuous challenge because they will not only face technical difficulties, but also geographical problems due to the global scope of digital economies which requires cross-border cooperation between national competition authorities.

As previously mentioned, the nature of the digital economy requires constant investments and innovation for the continuous development of digital markets. In this regard, one of the main issues when it comes to enforcement of competition law in digital markets is when is the appropriate moment to consider a firm is dominant or holds a monopoly position and therefore when the antitrust authorities should intervene.[6]

Moreover, although many of the important players in the digital markets are large and profitable firms, there is a vigorous competition among the companies and together with the cyclical nature of the markets, it is very rare that a company can sustain a dominant position which makes more difficult to be able to determine when is the correct time to presume that there is a market leader and for competition authorities to intervene.[7]

The continuous evolution of digital economy brings two main challenges to competition authorities when it comes to enforcement of competition law in this market: The first challenge is to be able to conduct the analysis in a dynamic environment where the current situation could be rapidly modified with the competitive pressures from other participants in the market. The second challenge is to be able

5. OECD Hearings, *supra*, pp. 5-6.
6. *Ibid.*, p. 7.
7. *Ibid.*

to determine when the dynamics of the digital economy become a competition problem and in which situations the enforcement of competition law is (more) effective.[8]

Based on the above, when it comes to the application of competition law in digital economy, there are many elements that must be analysed to determine if all of the concepts currently used in competition law reflects the reality of digital markets or how the traditional concepts need to be adjusted.

As previously mentioned, one of the characteristics of digital markets that represents a challenge for the enforcement of competition is the dynamic nature of digital economy. Given its intrinsic characteristics, competition law interventions may not ensure competition for future markets and an ex-ante intervention, which could restrain innovation, could create more harm than efficiency in digital markets.[9]

One difficulty for competition authorities is the expertise they need to acquire to apply the law effectively and if such expertise will help in the near future due to the fast-moving nature of the digital economy. Another difficulty is the jurisdictional problems that could arise to identify which authority should have jurisdiction over the case. Moreover, when it comes to the application of the established concepts of competition law in the digital area, it could be a challenge to identify the relevant market.[10]

As previously mentioned, in digital economy there is not only a change in the interaction between economic agents and customers, but also a change in the interaction between platform owners and/or entrepreneurs that could become potential rivals. The designers of platforms can facilitate the development and innovation of follow-on technology if they open their platforms to enable third-party innovation but can also raise competition concerns if the owner of the platforms seek to exclude third-party applications to protect its vertical integrated applications or, if the owner of the platform first seeks not only to capture investment of third-party developers but only to try to copy their applications.[11]

A balance between innovation and competition regulation needs to be found to be able to keep innovation and investment, but at the same time protect any potential harm to the markets. Therefore, the role of competition authorities in the following years will be to adapt the traditional concepts of competition to the specific characteristics of the digital economy and to keep updating them at the same speed of the changes in technology and in the digital world.

8. Ezrachi, Ariel, *EU Competition Law Goals and the Digital Economy*, University of Oxford, 2018, p. 1.
9. *Ibid.*
10. OECD Hearings, *supra*, pp. 7–8.
11. *Ibid.*, p. 10.

§3.03 E-COMMERCE AND COMPETITION

[A] Definition of E-commerce

E-commerce in general terms refers to the activity of buying and selling products online.[12] In broader terms, e-commerce includes all business activities happening in electronic networks, including the purchase and sale of products, services, transfer of funds, online marketing activities and the collection and processing of data.[13]

E-commerce has become an important and popular retail channel for the purchase of goods and services and therefore, operators of online platforms receiving such purchaser orders have become extremely relevant in the increase of competition in retail markets, but also it has become relevant for competition authorities to ensure that these operators respect competition law.

E-commerce has not only revolutionised the way in which consumers purchase products, but also modified and increased the variety of providers from which the consumers can acquire the goods or services and the logistics of commerce in general.

According to the OECD, online selling goods can be classified into three broad categories.[14] First, tangible consumer goods, such as books, clothing, furniture, among others. In this sector, there is a need to have a physical delivery of such items, through any type of delivery system that could be directly from the same platform (such as Amazon) or through third parties that provide such service. In this sense, some people are reluctant in the use of this kinds of platforms (mainly when it involves a cross-border purchase) since in many cases, even though there is not a clear geographical limitation, some products are available only in certain regions.[15] Second, services for offline consumption, that includes those services that are sold online, such as transportation, events and accommodation. These types of services normally do not need any physical delivery of a proof purchase (*e-tickets are normally enough*), and the main characteristic is that said services are rendered offline. Third, digital content services, which are both sold and rendered online. In digital content services, in many cases there are geographical limitations, such as different pricing and different content services, but such are mainly due to local regulations or intellectual property rights (a clear example is *Netflix* that offers different content and similarly the pricing changes in different jurisdictions).[16]

12. OECD Implications of E-commerce, *supra*, p. 1.
13. *Ibid.*, p.6.
14. *Implications of E-commerce for competition Policy* Organization for Economic Co-operation and Development Directorate for Financial and Enterprise Affairs Competition Committee, 4 May 2018, p. 7.
15. This characteristic known as geo-blocking prevents online cross-border shoppers to purchase goods or access digital content services. In the European Union, some of these practices may be considered as vertical restraints, therefore many elements such as market power and non-compete clauses shall be evaluated. EUROPEAN Parliament, *The Geo-Blocking Proposal: Internal Market, Competition Law and Regulatory Aspects*, January 2017, p. 14 http://www.europarl.europa.eu/RegData/etudes/STUD/2017/595362/IPOL_STU(2017)595362_EN.pdf
16. Comisión Federal de Competencia Económica (COFECE), *Rethinking Competition in the Digital Economy*, February 2018, p. 16 https://www.cofece.mx/wp-content/uploads/2018/03/EC-EconomiaDigital_web_ENG_letter.pdf#pdf

E-commerce activities are developed through different channels and business models. Many manufacturers of goods or service providers decide to vertical integrate, operating their own goods or services directly to the customer, which provide them control over the sales and prices of their products. Although the vertical integration of manufacturers or service providers could be cost efficient, the online sales come with additional responsibilities and activities that must be developed mainly for the marketing and delivery of the product to the consumer.[17]

[B] Multisided Platforms

One of the challenges for the competition analysis of e-commerce is the recognition of retail multi-sided platforms. First, it is important to understand what and how a multi-sided platform works. Evans[18] provides an analogy of the multi-sided platforms with a matchmaking club. A matchmaking club offers a platform where men and women can meet and potentially match. In order for it to work, it needs to be an equivalent number of men and women, since too many men would not attract women and vice versa. In addition, the club needs to determine how much to charge for each group, for it to be profitable, but at the same time to maintain the balance among men and women, and in case they are short in supply, a club may offer discounts in drinks or other benefits to men or women.

On e-commerce, marketplaces are an example of multi-sided platforms, since they unite retailers that seek to sell their products and/or services, customers who are willing to buy, and advertisings seeking to draw attention to the said groups (in the same way a matchmaking club connects and coordinates the possible couples). The variation in retail multi-sided platforms online is the interaction of different groups of customers, each one with specific demand, but interlinked, since the conduct of one group may alter the conditions of the other groups. Multi-sided platforms normally involve different pricing among them since the platform may make charges to one group, and another may have significantly lower charges and even none. Frequently, platforms charge the advertisers, while users are not charged at all.

In a competition law perspective, in order to determine the market power for any of these economic agents may be complicated, or at least the conventional monopolistic test would be less effective than in other markets. This, since a platform may have free services for customers because the price is covered by the advertisers, which means that there are unequal payment structures in the online platforms which makes the different users interdependent.[19]

As previously mentioned, in multi-sided platforms there are different issues to assess if any firm has market power. The first problem is that the different groups of

17. OECD Implications of E-commerce, *supra*, p. 9.
18. Evans, David S. (2003) "The Antitrust Economics of Multi-Sided Platform Markets," Yale Journal on Regulation: Vol. 20: Iss. 2, Article 4. Available at: http://digitalcommons.law.yale.edu/yjreg/vol20/iss2/4. Evans, David S. and Schmalensee, Richard (2007) "The Industrial Organization of Markets with Two-Sided Platforms" Competition Policy International (print ISSN 1554-0189, online ISSN 1554-6853): Spring, Vol. 3, No. 1.
19. OECD Implications of E-commerce, *supra*, p. 14.

customers with their individual demands exist and interact through the platform. Nonetheless, their demands are interdependent because the price increase or the quality decrease in one group has effects on the others, reducing the general demand on the platform.[20]

The second problem is cross-subsidies between participants in the platform, where some groups can access the platform without a cost, while some other groups are charged for using the platform. A common example is online retail platforms, where third-party retailers are charged for selling their products through the platform and customers are not charged additionally for using the platform and purchasing the products. As previously mentioned, this unequal payment structures make the Small but Significant Non-Transitory Increase in Price (SSNIP) test or hypothetical monopolistic test less effective.

The third issue refers to innovation; multi-sided platforms are continuously subject to incremental innovation, seeking to improve their offer or services to attract more users to all different channels of the platform, or to disruptive innovation where leading platforms are displaced by alternative business models. Although dynamic competition is less important in e-commerce (compared with other areas such as social media), the interconnectedness of the digital ecosystem means that dynamic considerations which drives innovations are also present in e-commerce and therefore need to be considered.[21]

[C] Vertical Restraints

With the continuous growth of e-commerce markets, the competition concerns of vertical restraints is one of the most important concerns in competition law in many jurisdictions and has put into perspective the approach to vertical restraints in e-commerce markets. The competition concerns that are usually associated with vertical restraints are the risk of facilitating collusion and the risk of softening competition, concerns which also apply for e-commerce.[22]

For the vertical integrated manufacturers that chose to operate their own online sites to have more control over distribution, usually the application of competition law is not required. Nonetheless, in those cases where the manufacturer is not vertical integrated and tries to limit or control the online resale of its products or impose contractual limitations such as exclusivities or requirements to offer the lowest prices through the platform could be considered anticompetitive.

There are two important distribution models used by manufacturers for online sales, which need to be analysed case by case to determine if they have significant anticompetitive affects to consider them illegal. The first is the exclusive distribution model which refers to vertical arrangements by which a supplier contracts to sell its

20. *Ibid.*
21. *Ibid.*
22. OECD Dictatorate for Financial and Enterprise Affairs Competition Committee, *Vertical Restraints for On-line Sales*, 2013, p. 6 http://www.oecd.org/competition/VerticalRestraintsForOnlineSales2013.pdf [The OECD Vertical Restraints].

products to one single distributor in one specific territory; which limits competition between different manufacturers by limiting the online retailer to sell only one specific brand.[23] The second is the selective distribution model which refers to vertical arrangements by which a supplier establishes minimum standards for admitting the manufacturer in its distribution network. One of the practices that have been implemented in e-commerce is the inclusion of so-called internet addendums which includes more restrictions for online sales.[24]

[D] Antitrust Implications of Data Collection

As previously mentioned, collection of consumer data is a key element in e-commerce because it allows to learn consumer preferences, among many other features. In this regard, the most current and popular questions among competition authorities, scholars and practitioners are whether data constitutes an essential facility and whether a policy for limiting its collection is necessary. An important factor to keep in mind is that the simple collection of data is not by itself harmful to competition, as it can result in innovation of products and services.

Having said that, considering that data collection can constitute a very strong tool for the use of competition mechanisms which could facilitate collusion or unilateral conducts by operators of digital platforms, it has become relevant for competition authorities to analyse at what point the use of data collection becomes an illegal practice and how competition law could address some of the risks that could be caused by data collection.

For instance, advertising is a key feature and plays an important role in e-commerce and in general in digital economy. It has become an essential component of e-commerce and currently is highly integrated in almost all digital companies involved in the e-commerce sector or in other digital platforms such as social networks. Together with data collection, advertising becomes 'tailored-made' for each customer. Data collection is used by retailers to attract consumers based on their preferences obtained from their recent searches. Therefore, it allows specific targeting and personalisation of advertising efforts.[25]

Another crucial component of digital economy and e-commerce are search engines. In particular, this search tools may represent a competition problem in the event that a platform provider benefit from its own customers or users by giving an advantage to a specific retailer or firm. Precisely this situation was analysed and fined by the European Union, by imposing Google a fine of EUR 2.42 billion for abusing its dominant position as search engine. In its decision, the European Commission

23. OECD Implications of E-commerce, *supra*, p. 16.
24. *Ibid.*, p.17.
25. *Ibid.*, *supra*, p. 11.

concluded that Google provided an illegal advantage to the products of its own corporate group over the products of its competitors.[26]

Furthermore, due to the amount of information available in online platforms, there is a high degree of price transparency among different retailers. Due to this particular condition, price transparency may make easier for companies to monitor prices quoted by competitors and even their own retailers. For instance, in a recent competition sector inquiry launched by the European Commission, it was identified that nearly two-fifths of retailers in Europe received recommended prices by its manufacturers.[27] However, some of those retailers confirmed that in those cases that they decided to sell lower than the recommended prices, they would immediately receive an e-mail from the manufacturer threatening their business relationship if they did not set the prices back up again.[28] Such price transparency, together with the use of price-tracking software and price-setting algorithms makes the analysis of these practices even more challenging for competition authorities.

§3.04 THE ROLE OF BIG DATA AND PRICING ALGORITHMS IN THE AGE OF E-COMMERCE

We are leaving a new stage of economic evolution. The new currency of the e-commerce world is based on data and is measured by those who are capable of exploiting it. Nowadays, the new economy's driver of growth and change is no longer a battle on who the owner of more oil is, but who owns and benefits from data.[29] For these reasons, data has become the 'oil of the digital era'.[30] Nonetheless, similar to oil, data is almost useless in its rawest form.[31] It is when data is 'refined' – once extracted, processed and combined – when it can be much more valuable.[32] Under such particular conditions, we are referring to the so-called big data.

Based on the above, companies nowadays understand that gathering, tracking and analysing big volumes of information about the products and services they offer (typically collected by data companies such as Nielsen, Google, Facebook, etc.) can allow them to provide a more valuable and targeted experience to their customers, thus increasing its presence in the e-commerce market.

26. European Commission, *Antitrust: Commission Fines Google €2.42 Billion for Abusing Dominance as Search Engine by Giving Illegal Advantage to Own Comparison Shopping Service*, June 2017, http://europa.eu/rapid/press-release_IP-17-1784_en.htm.
27. Vestager, Margrethe, Speech: *Getting the Best Out of Technology*, CEPS Corporate Breakfast, Brussels, September 2018, https://ec.europa.eu/commission/commissioners/2014-2019/vestager/announcements/getting-best-out-technology_en.
28. *Ibid.*
29. The Economist, *Fuel of the Future: Data Is Giving Rise to A New Economy*' (Economist.com, 2017) https://www.economist.com/news/briefing/21721634-how-it-shaping-up-data-giving-rise-new-economy.
30. The Economist, *Regulating the Internet Giants: The World's Most Valuable Resource Is No Longer Oil, But Data* (Economist.com, 2017) https://www.economist.com/news/leaders/21721656-data-economy-demands-new-approach-antitrust-rules-worlds-most-valuable-resource > .
31. Chandrasekaran, Natarajan, *Is Data the New Currency?*, World Economic Forum, 2015, https://www.weforum.org/agenda/2015/08/is-data-the-new-currency/.
32. *Ibid.*

Companies are adopting data-driven models to obtain a more competitive advantage over their competitors. Such competition is based on the customer's data that they hold in comparison to the one held by their competitors, which ultimately has the purpose of materialising into more efficient business policies and provide better products and services to their customers, while maximise companies' profits.

All the above situations are of utmost relevance to competition law and, until very recently, competition watchdogs, lawyers and scholars have started to assess and understand that big data, as well as other related tools (such as pricing algorithms) have impact into competition, especially in the e-commerce market.

[A] Understanding Big Data in a Nutshell

The use and exploitation of data by companies and business people is not a new situation as it has taken place since many years ago, even before the rise of big data or Internet. However, the current ways on how data is collected in the e-commerce world can result in the creation of new entry barriers.[33] For instance, new relatively-small players in a market not being able to collect data or have access to the type of information that is used by bigger and more consolidated players are placed under a less-favourable position and will find it difficult to compete against the latter.

Many decades have passed since companies realised that the use of data is essential to efficiently run their businesses, to improve the quality of their products and services, as well as to properly address advertisements to their target customers.[34] Nevertheless, the most recent developments in the technological sector, particularly those involving the use of data through the big data capabilities, were considered science fiction less than twenty years ago. Nowadays, we can safely say that we are living a very early stage of a (technological) revolution.[35]

Defining and understanding the concept of big data is a complex task and goes beyond the scope of this work; however, it is not possible to discuss the implications of big data in the e-commerce world without having a general understanding of such concept. There are more than twelve different definitions of big data.[36] In a nutshell, big data is generally associated with large volumes of data, obtained from a wide array of sources at different speeds and that require powerful processors and algorithms to be handled.[37]

In a report published by McKinsey in 2011, big data was defined as 'data-sets whose size is beyond the ability of typical database software tools to capture, store,

33. *Ibid.*
34. Autorité de la Concurrence, Bundeskartellant, *Competition Law and Data*, 2016, pp. 8-9 http://www.autoritedelaconcurrence.fr/doc/reportcompetitionlawanddatafinal.pdf, [The EU Report].
35. Forbes, *Big Data: 20 Mind-Boggling Facts Everyone Must Read* (Forbes.com, 2015) https://www.forbes.com/sites/bernardmarr/2015/09/30/big-data-20-mind-boggling-facts-everyone-must-read/#2c39bdc017b1.
36. Forbes, *12 Big Data Definitions: What's Yours?*, Forbes.com, 2014 https://www.forbes.com/sites/gilpress/2014/09/03/12-big-data-definitions-whats-yours/#3d0aee4913ae.
37. EU Report, *supra*.

manage, and analyse'.[38,39] Microsoft defines big data as 'the term increasingly used to describe the process of applying serious computing power – the latest in machine learning and artificial intelligence – to seriously massive and often highly complex sets of information'.[40] In addition, Gartner defines big data as 'high-volume, high-velocity and high-variety information assets that demand cost-effective, innovative forms of information processing for enhanced insight and decision making.'[41]

The use of big data can result in improvements of products and services.[42] In particular, this can be achieved by learning effects, similarly to what happens with search engines: based on the number of searches made by a user, together with the collection of data of which specific results were chosen, a search engine is capable of adjusting, refining and predicting future searches by such particular user; this ultimately results in a higher quality on the search engine's results, and ultimately, more consumers feeling attracted to keep using such platform.[43] On the other hand, data can also be used to learn about user's usage of certain products and services (e.g., web browsers, websites and operating systems constantly assess their users' activity to identify and minimise technical problems).[44]

Nowadays companies are able to adopt business models that rely completely on information obtained from their customer's personal data.[45] This situation regularly takes place between multi-sided platforms[46] (e.g., Uber, Airbnb, eBay etc.). Under such models, companies offer certain products or services to their customers by obtaining, in parallel, personal data that is further provided to advertisers with the aim of building more individualised advertisements, products and services.[47]

It is based on this new business model that big data reveals patterns of information that are learned by companies in order to understand their customers' behaviour and preferences, thus giving them the ability to improve and target their products and services accordingly. For this particular reason, the availability of big data to all players in the market has become so relevant, as big data is now providing a competitive advantage to all types of companies.[48]

38. Mckinsey Global Institute, *Big Data: The Next Frontier for Innovation, Competition, And Productivity*, McKinsey Global Institute, 2011, p. 1 http://www.mckinsey.com/business-functions/digital-mckinsey/our-insights/big-data-the-next-frontier-for-innovation, [The McKinsey Report].
39. It is relevant to mention that in defining such concept the McKinsey Report recognised that such definition was built over a subjective basis thus allowing the definition to evolve through time-based on how big a data-set needs to be in order to be considered big data.
40. Arxiv, *The Big Data Conundrum: How to Define It?*, MIT Technology Review, 2017, https://www.technologyreview.com/s/519851/the-big-data-conundrum-how-to-define-it/.
41. Gartner, '*Big Data*' definition Gartner IT Glossary https://research.gartner.com/definition-whatis-big-data?resId=3002918&srcId=1-8163325102.
42. EU Report, *supra*, pp. 8-9.
43. *Ibid.*, p. 9.
44. *Ibid.*
45. Ezrachi, Ariel and Stucke, Maurice, *Virtual Competition: The Promise and Perils of the Algorithm-Driven Economy*, 1st edn, Harvard University Press, 2017, p. 20.
46. *Ibid.*
47. EU Report, *supra*, p. 10.
48. Ocello, Eleonora, Sjödin, Cristina and Subočs, Anatoly, *What's Up with Merger Control in The Digital Sector? Lessons from The Facebook/WhatsApp EU Merger Case*, 2015, http://ec.europa.eu/competition/publications/cmb/2015/cmb2015_001_en.pdf, p. 6.

The use of big data by companies has resulted not only in better quality of products and services, but also in measurable financial and operational benefits. According to a study by the Massachusetts Institute of Technology (MIT), companies that have adopted a more data-driven approach in conducting their businesses have outperformed their financial and operational results: 'companies in the top third of their industry in the use of data-driven decision making were, on average, 5% more productive and 6% more profitable than their competitors.'[49]

Hence, the acquisition and exploitation of big data already has a tremendous (positive and potentially negative) effect on competition on a global basis throughout all types of sectors and markets, and some measures need to be adopted to assure a fair playing field for all competitors.

[B] Big Data and Its Effects over the Competition Process

The use of data and big data has clearly affected the traditional concept of competition - 'the invisible hand that distributes the necessities of life'[50] - has been replaced by the so-called digital hand.[51] This new force is not a typical market force; it is based and determined by algorithms designed by men or women and, consequently, can result in anticompetitive behaviours that require evolved tools to be used by competition authorities.[52] It is undisputed that the acquisition, use and exploitation of data and big data are not only an essential basis of competition for already existing companies, but it is also a key basis for the creation of new and strong competitors.[53] In the following years, any competitor that is not able to adapt to the big data world will not be able to compete.[54]

However, in the e-commerce world not all 'refined' data is as valuable as money. Particularly, data such as customers' information and purchasing behaviour actually is the crown jewel in the big data world.[55] For instance, nowadays consumers are offered opportunities to obtain cash rewards or discounts in exchange for providing valuable information about their personal interests, Internet and web-surfing habits, preferences between brands, as well as recent and future purchases.[56] Further, such information is sold to advertisers in order to create more efficient and targeted

49. Mcafee, Andrew and Brynjolfsson, Erik, *Big Data: The Management Revolution*, Harvard Business Review, 2012, https://hbr.org/2012/10/big-data-the-management-revolution.
50. Ezrachi, Ariel and Stucke, Maurice, *supra*, p. viii.
51. *Ibid.*
52. *Ibid.*
53. McKinsey Report, *supra*, p. 13.
54. *Ibid.*, p. 6.
55. Harris, Derrick, *Data Isn't Just the New Oil, It's The New Money: Ask Zoë Keating*, Gigaom.com, 2012, https://gigaom.com/2012/11/20/data-isnt-just-the-new-oil-its-the-new-money-ask-zoe-keating/.
56. *Ibid.*

behavioural advertising.[57] All of these exchanges of data have resulted in the creation of a new type of e-commerce.

There is another good example involving the bank industry's scheme: retail companies provide banks with information regarding the specific types of customers they would like to target. Further banks, using their own data base - which includes their customers' personal data such as their shopping habits - profile those most suitable customers and send them the retailers' offers and discounts; if such customers 'catch' the deal, then banks get a commission.[58] This, in particular, is highly relevant considering that just in 2015 - in accordance with a report published by Aite Group - such commission scheme generated USD 1.7 billion dollars in revenues to banks.[59]

At its initial stage, competition concerns over the use of big data in the e-commerce were primarily focused over the five tech giants: Alphabet (Google's parent company), Amazon, Apple, Facebook and Microsoft. However, recent cases evidence that competition authorities are starting to look to other key players. In particular, there is a growing claim among both public and private sectors for such tech giants to be broken up, similarly to the measures adopted in the old ages of Standard Oil.[60] Specifically, there is an increasing concern that these companies, while seeking to acquire or preserve their competitive advantage, will be highly interested in limiting their rivals' access to that useful data, design mechanisms to prevent data-sharing and will attempt to block data-portability to other competitors.[61]

A good example is the acquisition of WhatsApp by Facebook - which was valued in approximately USD 19 billion - that was successfully closed in October 2014. The transaction in itself was very relevant in the competition community due to its potential effects on competition and privacy.[62] It is particularly relevant to note that, on May 2017, in a recent EUR 110 million fine imposed to Facebook by the European Commission,[63] the latter identified that Facebook provided incorrect or misleading information about the acquisition of WhatsApp. Essentially, in its pre-merger filing Facebook informed that it would not be able to match WhatsApp users' accounts with their Facebook's accounts,[64] however, that information was not accurate. In fact, on August 2016, WhatsApp informed about certain amendments to its privacy policy, as well as its future plans for using and transferring WhatsApp's users' phone information with Facebook, in order to be linked to Facebook's profiles, thus to enable the ability of showing better and more attractive advertisements to Facebook's users. Such ability

---

57. Harris, Derrick *Will Consumers Trade the Keys to The Data Castle for A $5 Gift Card?*, Gigaom.com, 2012, https://gigaom.com/2012/11/07/will-consumers-trade-the-keys-to-the-data-castle-for-a-5-gift-card/.
58. Ellis, Blake, *The Banks' Billion-Dollar Idea*, CNNMoney, 2011, http://money.cnn.com/2011/07/06/pf/banks_sell_shopping_data/index.htm.
59. *Ibid.*
60. The Economist, *The Fuel of the Future, supra.*
61. Ezrachi, Ariel and Stucke, Maurice, *supra*, p. 40.
62. Stucke, Maurice E. and Grunes, Allen P., *Big Data and Competition Policy*, 1st edn, Oxford University Press, 2016, p. 75.
63. Vestager, Margrethe, Speech: *Commission Fines Facebook €110 Million for Providing Misleading Information About WhatsApp Takeover*, European Commission, 18 May 2017, http://europa.eu/rapid/press-release_IP-17-1369_en.htm.
64. Stucke, Maurice E. and Grunes, Allen P., *supra*.

existed since 2014 and Facebook's staff was aware of that information and even acknowledge the infringement of the merger procedural rules.[65] However, considering both the fact that there are other alternative suppliers which also offer targeted advertising (e.g., Google, Adobe, Microsoft, Yahoo, Apple, Amazon, eBay, Twitter, etc.[66]), and that a large amount of information is not controlled by Facebook, the European Commission held the clearance of the transaction.[67]

It is also argued that breaking up tech giants will not stop the unique characteristics of data and the networks effects arising thereto: ultimately, as The Economist considers, a broken tech giant will become a new tech giant again.[68] It is for these reasons that more evolved approaches could be useful: on one hand when assessing the effects of a transaction, competition regulators could move from the traditional approach of assessing the parties' size and market power to now consider the data assets owned by the relevant companies.[69] On the other hand, it is also argued that stricter policies need to be implemented over the data that is used by online service providers (e.g., forcing such companies to disclose to consumers the data they hold and the revenues they obtain from such information).[70]

It is based on the above that companies are highly incentivised to obtain and strengthen the competitive position they have obtained in the e-commerce markets through the assessment and application of big data results.[71] For these purposes, companies are encouraged to prevent its competitors from accessing to the data-sets they use as well as to engage in speed battles for being the first in obtaining valuable information.[72]

Although the use and collection of data can both enhance consumers' and companies' experience, in some cases it may be used solely for the purpose of benefitting companies[73] (e.g., through certain targeted price discrimination practices by using pricing algorithms, as discussed below). Under increasingly growing speeds, data is becoming a relevant asset and the effects of competition of using and exploiting data are turning highly relevant.[74]

Nonetheless, the aforementioned should not be misinterpreted: companies should be able to have access to a large and variable amount of information to be able to compete and offer better products and services. The use of data by companies has taken place since many years ago, even before the rise of big data or Internet. However,

65. *Ibid.*
66. Facebook/WhatsApp Decision C (2014) 7239 final, 3 October 2014, paragraph 34.
67. Vestager, Margrethe, Facebook's fine, *supra*.
68. The Economist, *The Fuel of the Future, supra*.
69. *Ibid.*
70. *Ibid.*
71. OECD, *Data-Driven Innovation for Growth and Well-Being: Interim Synthesis Report*, 2014, http://www.oecd.org./sti/inno/data-driven-innovation-interim-synthesis.pdf, p. 6 and 42.
72. Schep, Nils-Peter and Wambach, Achim, *On Big Data and Its Relevance for Market Power Assessment*, Journal of European Competition Law & Practice 2016, https://academic.oup.com/jeclap/article/7/2/120/2357794/On-Big-Data-and-Its-Relevance-for-Market-Power?searchresult=1.
73. Schepp, Nils-Peter and Wambach, Achim, *supra*, p. 122.
74. EU Report, *supra*, p. 11.

such collection of data can amount to entry barriers.[75] For instance, new relatively-small players in a market not being able to collect data or have access to the type of information that is used by bigger and more consolidated players.

[C] Pricing Algorithms and E-commerce

We are living in the blooming of the e-commerce era and market players are fully aware about its tremendous economic potential. Just based on the latest estimates published by the European Commission, the e-commerce market in Europe is already worth more than EUR 500 billion.[76] In this particular era, the rise of technological events and personalised services has led us to become open books, almost accessible to anyone, about our lives, preferences and purchasing habits.

For instance, online advertisements addressed to children differ from those addressed to parents, teenagers, among others, to the point that is not possible to identify if current advertisements reflect Internet enquiries, previous purchases or information disclosed through instant messaging services (e.g., WhatsApp) or even text messages.[77] Similarly, pricing algorithms allow companies to automatically extract the value of the data obtained from their customers to improve their pricing policies, customise their services and predict competitors' movements,[78] thus potentially resulting in market efficiencies, innovation and fostering competition.[79]

However, pricing algorithms are the current concern of several competition authorities due to their potential to allow competing companies to reach pricing collusion without even the need of reaching an agreement.[80] In particular, pricing algorithms are automatically capable to assess complex data (including prices offered by competitors) and determine in real time prices at speed and sophistication levels that are above human capabilities.[81]

The above situation has misled companies to assume that their price-setting policies are automatically machine-driven. However, it is nowadays clear that the human element of pricing algorithms – the one that designs the computer code ruling the algorithm – is the one that generally leads to an anticompetitive practice.[82] Such misconception has already been identified by competition authorities. For instance, the

75. *Ibid.*
76. Vestager, Margrethe, Speech: *Commission Fines Four Consumer Electronics Manufacturers for Fixing Online Resale Prices*, European Commission, 24 July 2018, http://europa.eu/rapid/press-release_IP-18-4601_en.htm
77. *Ibid.*
78. Capobianco, Antonio and Gonzaga, Pedro, *Algorithms and Competition: Friends or Foes?*, Competition Policy International, 14 August 2017, https://www.competitionpolicyinternational.com/algorithms-and-competition-friends-or-foes/.
79. OECD, *Algorithms and Collusion, Competition Policy in the Digital Age*, June 2017, p. 34, http://www.oecd.org/daf/competition/Algorithms-and-colllusion-competition-policy-in-the-digital-age.pdf.
80. *Ibid.*
81. Baer, Billy, Kuester P., Sonia and Musick Vesselina H., *Pricing Algorithms: The Antitrust Implications*, Arnold & Porter, 17 April 2018, https://www.arnoldporter.com/en/perspectives/publications/2018/04/pricing-algorithms-the-antitrust-implications.
82. *Ibid.*

European Commission has already encouraged companies 'to ensure antitrust compliance by design' and warned that arguments aiming to blame algorithms or employees' limited computer skills will not be valid excuses if the use pricing algorithms led to an anticompetitive behaviour.[83]

Precisely, in a recent case involving the sale of cinema posters sold through Amazon's online marketplace, David Topkins and other competitors were prosecuted and fined by the US Department of Justice as a result of using an enhanced-algorithm software that allowed them to fix prices of their posters.[84] In particular, Mr Topkins and his co-conspirators designed a pricing algorithm that was capable of collecting prices offered by other competitors in order to coordinate any modifications to their pricing strategies regarding the sale of their posters through Amazon.[85] This case represents the first criminal antitrust prosecution of its kind.[86]

Furthermore, the new digital world we are living is characterised for being personalised and tailor-made to our personal needs.[87] Nowadays, websites analyse users' patterns and behaviours and show different versions of their web to the different users they access their platform.[88] For instance, price discrimination may potentially assist companies to supply products or services to final consumers and, in parallel, result in exclusionary effects on a particular market.[89]

Accordingly, price discrimination can take different forms. For instance, a firm is capable to charge different customers with different prices depending on their ability and willingness to pay. In addition, companies are able to assess customers' purchasing habits, sort them in different groups and further offer them a specific array of products and services.[90] Under the latter scenario, companies are able to sort products and services that are rather similar, but including brands that are more heavily marketed.[91]

The use of data-based price discrimination is not a hypothetical situation. In fact, as previously mentioned, as part of the on-going trend among competition authorities, on 1 February 2018, COFECE initiated an *ex-officio* investigation for potential abusive

83. Snoep, Martijn, et al., *Know Your Algorithms – or Pay the Price*, Mondaq, 20 April 2017, http://www.mondaq.com/x/587304/Antitrust+Competition/Know+your+algorithms+or+pay+the+price.
84. *United States v. Topkins*, No. CR 15-00201 (N.D. Cal. 2015). Also known as the 'Poster Cartel'.
85. *Ibid.*
86. Lynch, David J., *Policing the Digital Cartels*, The Financial Times, 8 January 2017, https://www.ft.com/content/9de9fb80-cd23-11e6-864f-20dcb35cede2.
87. Valentino-Devries, Jennifer, Singer, Jeremy and Soltani, Ashkan, *Websites Vary Prices, Deals Based On Users' Information*, Wall Street Journal, 2012 https://www.wsj.com/articles/SB10001424127887323777204578189391813881534.
88. *Ibid.*
89. Armstrong, Mark, *Price Discrimination*, University College London Department of Economics 2006, p. 2, http://else.econ.ucl.ac.uk/papers/uploaded/222.pdf.
90. Hovenkamp, Herbert et al., *IP and Antitrust: An Analysis of Antitrust Principles Applied to Intellectual Property Law*, 2nd edn, Aspen Publishers, 2010, Appendix F.
91. Desai, Deven R, Lianos, Ioannis and Weber, Spencer, *Brands, Competition Law and IP*, Cambridge University Press, 2015.

practices in the market for e-commerce platform services in Mexico.[92] Accordingly, COFECE informed that this was the first time an investigation on digital markets was opened.[93]

Different effects can stem out from this type of (digital) price discrimination. On one side of the ledger, using big data to price discriminate can result in a breach of consumer equality.[94] The above is typically contested by arguing that consumers are fully able to switch to other suppliers in order to combat unfair price discrimination practices, however, this can trigger a parallel effect by increasing the costs of searching different alternatives that ultimately reduce the possibility of choosing other substitutes.[95] On the other side, price discrimination can also redistribute income form the poorer to the richer,[96] resulting in a scenario where some customers will pay higher prices, but some others will receive better prices in comparison to scenarios where price discrimination is absent.[97] Among the latter scenario, it could be possible to identify customers not able to afford certain products or services if only a single-identical price was allowed.[98]

Furthermore, pricing algorithms fed on big data input can both enhance and reduce competition.[99] For instance, aware of the competitive levels in a particular market and through the use of big data, a firm is able to establish lower prices to customers that have strong preferences for certain competitive products or services, thus resulting in an increase of price competition.[100] This is the case of the latest EUR 100 million fine imposed by the European Commission to four consumer electronics manufacturers: Asus, Denon & Marantz, Philips and Pioneer.[101]

Nonetheless, it important to clarify that the likelihood of reaching a 'perfect' stage of price discrimination is unlikely.[102] This argument relies on two actual facts. First, companies' lack of sufficient data to be able to identify each customers' reservation price, which is constantly fluctuating.[103] Second, even considering the latter impediment, there are several factors affecting customers' purchasing decisions and in many

92. Comisión Federal de Competencia Económica, *COFECE Probes the Market of E-commerce Platform Services in Mexico*, file number IO-002-2017, 1 February 2018, https://www.cofece.mx/wp-content/uploads/2018/02/COFECE-06-2018-COFECE.pdf.
93. *Ibid.*
94. EU Report, *supra*, p. 21.
95. *Ibid.*
96. Whish, Richard and Bailey, David, *Competition Law*, 8th edn, Oxford University Press, 2015, p. 803.
97. EU Report, *supra*, p. 21.
98. *Ibid.*
99. *Ibid.*
100. Armstrong, Mark, *supra*.
101. Vestager, Margrethe, *supra*, press release regarding fine to four consumer electronics manufacturers, *supra*.
102. This scenario means that companies are able to implement price discrimination policies that are able to charge customers with the maximum price they are willing to pay; thus those companies are able to capture all consumer' surplus. *See also* Ezrachi, Ariel and Stucke, Maurice, *supra*, p. 86.
103. *Ibid.*

cases consumers do not even know their own reservation price, making almost impossible to predict their purchasing behaviour.[104]

§3.05 CONCLUSIONS

This chapter touches on the various issues that can arise in a completely new world with completely new challenges deriving from technological changes and evolution of the markets into a digital economy. E-commerce is not in itself a different market but poses challenges for traditional and new means of commerce.

The different channels and alternatives to sell products and services, together with the challenges to privacy and the accumulation of data are immense. We consider and agree with many commentators in that data is the new currency and it is becoming the foundation of the digital economy. For this reason, it is necessary to understand that its relevance is not only a competition concern, but also an issue affecting all aspects of our life and needs to be addressed by different types of regulation depending on the market failure or social concern being considered.

Furthermore, it is essential to understand that data is the new driver over which companies are nowadays incentivised to compete and strengthen their market position. If the use of customers' data is not properly regulated, including the use of tools such as big data and pricing algorithms, companies may be able to implement abusive practices, such as price and behavioural discrimination, which ultimately distort market conditions and amount to consumer harm.

We consider current competition rules around the world should be reassessed by legislators considering these changes and consider if changes are necessary. Modernising our criteria and educating competition authorities, practitioners and scholars regarding the importance of healthy competition in the e-commerce, as well as regarding an adequate use of big data and pricing algorithms should become a top priority for all countries and international organisations.

104. *Ibid.*, p. 97.

CHAPTER 4

Digital Swords Versus Digital Shields in Cartel Enforcement: Insights from Russian Experience in Electronic Procurements*

Alexey Ivanov & Ekaterina Semenova

§4.01 INTRODUCTION

Competition law has been changed by digital innovations as almost any other part of economic life has. In his well-known painting "The Bosses of the Senate," Joseph Keppler has subtly defined the main challenges for the competition policy in the industrial age—corporate trusts in steel, oil, sugar, coal and other tangible goods. Digitalization creates new challenges for competition policy as special algorithms are used more and more frequently in electronic procurement and for trading on digital marketplaces. "Digital invisible hand"[1] becomes omnipresent in the modern economic life. Market participants take advantage of new technologies to collude on business-to-government platforms while governments capitalize on opportunities brought by the software for cartel detection. Moreover, companies exploit pricing algorithms in order to engage in anticompetitive behavior such as resale price maintenance in cases where it would have been impossible in the past.

Competition authorities around the world are trying to adjust antitrust enforcement to the new reality. Digitalization is of great interest to the Federal Antimonopoly

* The authors are grateful to Dr. Mikhail Erofeev (Lomonosov Moscow State University, Ph.D. in Computer Science) for providing thorough advice and expert opinion on this chapter.

1. This term was dropped by Ariel Ezrachi and Maurice E. Stucke in their book "Virtual Competition: The Promise and Perils of the Algorithm-Driven Economy" (Harvard University Press, 2016).

Service of the Russian Federation (FAS Russia) and drives its practice and potential legislative initiatives.[2]

In this chapter, we analyze the enforcement practice with regards to one of the hot topics in the competition law and policy domain—the unsettled relations between algorithms and collusive market behavior. We try to look at this topic from both competition authorities and companies' perspectives. While self-learning digital cartels are still a matter for the future, we focus on the current state of digital technologies' application in facilitating bid-rigging and other forms of collusion.

In §4.02 of the chapter we discuss new software tools for cartel detection used by the competition authorities around the world. These software applications attract the attention of competition enforcers as they provide novel opportunities to automatically find signs of cartels while processing myriads of bids in electronic procurement. In its recent workshop, the Organisation for Economic Co-operation and Development (OECD) has highlighted the increasing role of software tools for cartel detection in the digital age.[3] After detailed analysis of Russian, Korean, Brazilian and UK approaches to software screening tools application, we show possible ways for these software tools' advancement based on big training data sets gained through competition authorities' cooperation.

Section §4.03 of the chapter is devoted to the analysis of recent cases illustrating how companies use digital technologies to get anticompetitive advantage in procurement. We analyze FAS Russia pioneering cases on "auction robots," or bots, signifying the evolution of bid rigging in the digital age. Auction bots are a piece of software automating the routine process of bid submission. This software is typically built in the e-procurement platforms and is not *per se* illegal. However, FAS Russia cases revealed that some companies used auction bots to automate collusive practices at auctions. The review of these cases showed that classic overt collusion might be facilitated by auction bots. Nevertheless, we conclude that auction bots which companies might use for collusion ironically also help competition enforcers since this software creates additional evidence of collusive intent and behavior.

§4.02 SCREENING SOFTWARE TOOLS: INNOVATION IN CARTEL DETECTION

Digital technologies are a double-edged sword, as they affect both market competitors and competition enforcers. While companies use algorithms either to foster competition, e.g., by service customization, best market prediction and other advancements, or to harm competition by cartelization via digital tools, competition authorities might enjoy benefits by using algorithms for cartel detection.

2. *See* Press Release, Federal Antimonopoly Service of the Russian Federation, Andrey Tsyganov: suppressing digital forms of violations is a new challenge in antimonopoly regulation (September 14, 2018), http://en.fas.gov.ru/press-center/news/detail.html?id=53358.
3. OECD. Workshop on Cartel Screening in the Digital Era. January 30, 2018. http://www.oecd.org/competition/workshop-on-cartel-screening-in-the-digital-era.htm.

To date, the most prominent examples of digital technologies in the service of competition enforcement are anonymous software tools for detecting cartels, and online whistleblowers and leniency tools for submitting online applications.[4]

Whistleblowers tools are online web applications that inform authorities about competition law violations. Although the idea seems simple, only several competition authorities have implemented the anonymous tool for whistleblowers[5]. For example, the EU Commission introduced this tool only in 2017, noting that: "Inside knowledge can be a powerful tool to help the Commission uncover cartels and other anti-competitive practices. With our new tool it is possible to provide information, while maintaining anonymity."[6]

Another example of a modern tool for competition enforcement in the digital age is software to detect cartels. This tool is more advanced than tools for whistleblowers and leniency applications.

To detect cartels, competition authorities use retroactive methods, such as signals from whistleblowers, leniency programs, as well as proactive methods like screenings, industry monitoring, or a combination of both methods.[7]

Screenings are empirical methods which economists apply to input data to decide whether it has patterns of collusive behavior.[8] Thus, typical screening relies on an econometric analysis of data: economists provide routine analysis of cartel signs.

However, 'by-hand' econometric analysis has limitations, as it solely depends on human resources. As the Korean Fair Trade Commission (hereinafter KFTC) explains, investigation of possible collusive bidding solely by humans is difficult, as the information "was usually sent in written form which made it physically impossible for the KFTC to thoroughly review and analyze it."[9] The spread of electronic bidding systems together with digital technology development in general shifts the manual analysis of data to automatic cartel detection.

According to Commissioner Terrell McSweeny and her attorney advisor Brian O'Dely at the US Federal Trade Commission, "Competition enforcers must recognize the possibility that algorithms might facilitate cartel formation and maintenance.

4. European Commission. Press release. March 2019. https://europa.eu/rapid/press-release_IP-19-1594_en.htm.
5. In 2012 Bundeskartellamt implemented anonymous online whistleblower tool in Germany. See https://www.bundeskartellamt.de/EN/Banoncartels/Whistle-blower/whistle-blower_node.html.
6. European Commission. Press release. March 2017. http://europa.eu/rapid/press-release_IP-17-591_en.htm.
7. *See* OECD. Roundtable on Ex Officio Cartel Investigations and the Use of Screens to Detect Cartels, p. 7, https://one.oecd.org/document/DAF/COMP(2013)14/en/pdf. For example, FAS Russia and the Brazil Administrative Council for Economic Defense use both retroactive and proactive methods for cartel detection.
8. *See*, for example, Rosa Abrantes-Metz, and Patrick Bajari. "Screen for Conspiracies and Their Multiple Applications." Antitrust 24 (2009): 66.
9. https://one.oecd.org/document/DAF/COMP(2013)14/en/pdf, p. 61.

Detection of such arrangements may require novel investigative approaches or additional resources.[10] Screening software tools has become this novel approach in cartel detection.

Screening software tools providing the possibility for automatic data analysis signify a revolution in cartel detection, as they use data automatically collected from bidding institutions and rely on machine learning methods to predict the likelihood of collusion. As Rosa Abrantes-Metz puts it: "Doctors regularly screen their patients for diseases even though their methods exhibit both false positives and negatives. Even so, they screen patients because the expense of testing all patients for a rare disease is prohibitive. The process of screening identifies a subset of patients that are at a higher risk than others, which then allows the doctor to engage in more extensive testing for a select few. Analogously, a good antitrust screen will narrow the set of possible conspiracies to a manageable few that merit further review."[11]

Such screens help competition authorities to identify suspicious behavior in myriads of bids from government e-procurement platforms. Notably, manual analysis of such amounts of data is infeasible and can be done only with help of automation tools.

Canadian Senior Deputy Commissioner of Competition Matthew Boswell at the Forum on innovation in public procurement in November 2017 highlighted that *innovation* in cartel detection starts in the development of screening software tools:

"The Bureau uses a wide range of tools and approaches to fight cartels, and that includes working to leverage new technology. For detecting bid-rigging, that means the development of bid-screening algorithms—algorithms that are able to sift through electronic bidding data for possible signs of collusion."[12]

Matthew Boswell stated that the Canadian competition bureau is currently developing its own screening software and emphasized that the Bureau is "looking for opportunities to collaborate with other domestic and international partners in this area."

To our mind, collaboration between competition authorities is the next step required to build a big-data-intensive screening software tool of a new generation. In subsection B of Section 1, we discuss this issue in more detail.

[A] Screening Software Designs: National Approaches

Software screening tools for cartel detection are applied by competition authorities in Russia, Korea, Brazil and the UK. Software screening tools are currently under

10. https://www.ftc.gov/system/files/documents/public_statements/1286183/mcsweeny_and_odea_-_implications_of_algorithmic_pricing_antitrust_fall_2017_0.pdf, p. 76.
11. Rosa Abrantes-Metz and Patrick Bajari. *supra*, p. 66.
12. https://www.canada.ca/en/competition-bureau/news/2017/11/bid-rigging_detectionandpreventionensuringacompetitiveandinnovat.html.

development in Spain[13] and Canada[14]. Non-software screenings are also applied in Italy,[15] Sweden[16], Switzerland[17], Mexico[18], India[19] and other countries.

One of the first software screening tools was implemented in Korea in 2006. This software called Bid Rigging Indicator Analysis System (BRIAS) automatically analyzes bid information obtained from 332 Korean public procurement agencies.[20] Amongst the successful BRIAS cases has been the detection of collusion in Seoul Subway Line 7 construction worth $5 billion.[21]

In 2017, two more software tools for cartel screening were introduced: FAS Russia announced the successful implementation of such software in mid-2017, and the UK Competition and Markets Authority (CMA) shared their open Screening for Cartels tool at the end of 2017. [22]

To date, the FAS Russia tool detected eighty cartels in e-procurement, including the most serious bid rigging in construction and medical supply e-procurements, which amounted to 197 billion rubles (circa $2 billion).[23] The success of the FAS Russia screening resulted in institutional changes: a new department working solely with the software screening tool is created in FAS Russia.[24] This software tool also was dubbed with a new title—"Big Digital Cat," as it detects that "mouse," that is cartels, in the digital age.

13. In May 2018 Spain National Authority for Markets and Competition (CNMC) officially reported the development of screening software in collaboration with professionals in statistics, computer and data science, https://www.cnmc.es/node/368434.
14. Matthew Boswell. Bid-Rigging Detection and Prevention: Ensuring a Competitive and Innovative Procurement Process. Speech at Canadian Public Procurement Council Forum 2017: Innovation in Public Procurement. November 2017. Matthew Boswell in his November 2017 speech at Canadian Public Procurement Council Forum on innovation announced the development of software screening tool URL: https://www.canada.ca/en/competition-bureau/news/2017/11/bid-rigging_detectionandpreventionensuringacompetitiveandinnovat.html.
15. http://ec.europa.eu/competition/ecn/brief/05_2013/bidrig_it.pdf.
16. Josef Ålander. Swedish Competition Authority. Screening for Cartels in Procurement Procedures—Lessons Learned. https://www.competitionpolicyinternational.com/assets/Uploads/EUSept14-2.pdf, Mihály Fazekas and Bence Tóth. Assessing the Potential for Detecting Collusion in Swedish Public Procurement. Swedish Competition Authority Commissioned Research Reports 2016:3, October 2016, http://www.govtransparency.eu/index.php/2017/08/08/assessing-the-potential-for-detecting-collusion-in-swedish-public-procurement/.
17. D. Imhof Y. Karagök and S. Rutz. Screening for Bid Rigging—Does It Work?. Journal of Competition Law & Economics, 14(2) (2018), 235-261.
18. https://www.competitionpolicyinternational.com/assets/Cartel-Column-June-New-Format-Full.pdf.
19. Competition Commission of India. Towards Competitive Tenders. Diagnostic Tool for Procurement Officers. https://www.cci.gov.in/sites/default/files/whats_newdocument/Final%20Diagnostic%20Tool%2019032018-1.pdf.
20. Korea Fair Trade Commission, Current Status of Operation of Bid Rigging Indicator Analysis System, http://www.ftc.go.kr/www/cmm/fms/FileDown.do?atchFileId=FILE_000000000079626&fileSn=0, Roundtable on Ex Officio Cartel Investigations and the Use of Screens to Detect Cartels, OECD, https://one.oecd.org/document/DAF/COMP(2013)14/en/pdf, P. 62.
21. Korea Fair Trade Commission, Current Status of Operation Bid Rigging Indicator Analysis System, p. 6.
22. https://www.gov.uk/government/news/cma-launches-digital-tool-to-fight-bid-rigging.
23. https://fas.gov.ru/news/1690/export_to_file.pdf (in Russian).
24. https://fas.gov.ru/news/26154 (in Russian).

The Brazil Administrative Council for Economic Defense (CADE) developed the screening tool Projeto Cérebro, integrated into the federal electronic procurement system Comprasnet in 2018.[25] Projeto Cérebro helped CADE to effectively detect bid rigging in the supply of implantable cardiac pacemakers.[26]

The above-mentioned countries demonstrate different approaches in software screening tools. First, screening tools address different stakeholders: CMA developed screening tool not for CMA itself, but for public and private procurers.[27] This tool should help procurers to flag suspicious procurement exercises in their tenders and notify CMA for further investigation. However, both the decisions to use this tool and CMA notification are at the discretion of procurers.

On contrast, in Korea, Russia and Brazil, software tools for cartel detection aim at competition authorities. Only competition authorities have direct access to the software tools implemented into electronic public bidding systems. These software tools automatically transfer bidding information to the competition authorities. Procurers do not have access to the software screening tools.

Second, most competition authorities keep their screening tools private and share neither its source code nor binary executable. Unlike most other countries, the UK screening software is open-source software available for download by interested persons upon request. The black-box approach chosen by most competition authorities is beneficial in the sense of non-disclosure of implementation details to colluders. The presence of mysterious digital software able to detect collusion in some unknown way works as the sword of Damocles, making colluders surrender voluntarily. As Korea FTC reports, during the period of BRIAS operation, "voluntary reporting by cartel participants has increased significantly, and some of this increase is attributed to the raised awareness and fear of being caught, generated by the implementation of the BRIAS system." [28]

Third, software tools developed by competition authorities have different designs, as they differ in both the set of collected bidding information and the indicators they analyze.

Strong and weak points of the above-mentioned software screening tools do noticeably variate. Our analysis of these tools[29] shows that criteria analyzed by screening tools might be grouped into four major categories:

---

25. Cartel screening in the digital era—CADE Brazil—January 2018 OECD Workshop. https://www.slideshare.net/OECD-DAF/cartel-screening-in-the-digital-era-cade-brazil-january-2018-oecd-workshop See also http://www.lickslegal.com/clientalert/Newsletter_Antitrust_January2018.pdf P. 5; http://www.oecd.org/officialdocuments/publicdisplaydocumentpdf/?cote=DAF/COMP/LACF(2016)19&docLanguage=En p.3.
26. http://www.cade.gov.br/noticias/superintendencia-instaura-processos-para-apurar-cartel-no-mercado-de-orteses-proteses-e-materiais-medicos-especiais.
27. CMA launches digital tool to fight bid-rigging. Press release. https://www.gov.uk/government/news/cma-launches-digital-tool-to-fight-bid-rigging.
28. Country case: Korea's Bid Rigging Indicator Analysis System (BRIAS). https://www.oecd.org/governance/procurement/toolbox/search/korea-bid-rigging-indicator-analysis-system-brias.pdf.
29. CMA provided access to the software screening tool source code for the authors of this paper, as the CMA screening tool is open software available for download upon request. Thus, we analyzed the CMA screening tool source code in details. Other software screening tools are not

(1) number and pattern of bidders;
(2) suspicious pricing patterns;
(3) low endeavor and similar submissions; and
(4) tenders' history data.

Let's start with CMA screening tool analysis. To find suspicious tenders, CMA screening tool analyses eight criteria and four combination tests. The category *Number and pattern of bidders* carries out the following tests: low number of bidders, which is triggered when the number of bidders is less than three; and a single bid test.

The category *Suspicious pricing patterns* includes: 1. "winning price is outlier" test, which is triggered when the winning price is more than one standard deviation away from mean price of all bids; 2. "similar pricing across bids" test is triggered when the ratio of prices mean to standard deviation is less than fifteen; 3. the last criterion analyzed in this category is made-up costs. This test verifies that all prices in the bid conform to Benford's law. This criterion is unique across software tools developed by other countries. By analyzing the frequency of the first digit, it allows to find out that distribution of costs listed in the bid consists of made-up numbers rather than real prices.

The next category analyzed by CMA software tool is *Low endeavor and similar submissions*. This category has the following tests: 1. same authors in more than one bid, which analyses author name according to metadata of files submitted by bidders. 2. "Low endeavor losing bids" test evaluates ratio of submitted documents revision count to time spent editing the document. Both values are extracted from submitted documents' metadata. 3. "Similar text in losing bids" test compares word frequency of two losing bids weighted by the inverse of overall word frequency in all bids.

Since the CMA tool analyses data of a single tender only, it does not carry out any tests from *Tenders' history data* category.

Each criterion is associated with its weight, which is added to the tender's "suspicion score." Due to limitations of such a simple linear score computation model, tool developers enriched the list of criteria by four combination tests. Each combination test relies on two basic tests and is triggered when both basic tests are triggered.

CMA combination tests are the following: similar text and word count in losing bids; low number of bidders and made-up prices; winning price is outlier and made-up prices; made-up prices and low effort.

While the linear "suspicion score" model appears to be used in all screening tools under review, only CMA tool employs combination tests to overcome the limitations of the linear model, thus making CMA tool more flexible.

Now let's proceed to the FAS Russia screening tool analysis. The FAS Russia tool developers declare that it relies on analysis of fifty criteria.[30] Unfortunately, only few

---

publicly available, and we revised them based on the information publicly disclosed by FAS Russia, KFTC and CADE in the conferences' proceedings and other publications.

30. Andrey Tsarikovskii, Alexey Ivanov, Elena Voinikanis, Ekaterina Semenova, Andrey Tenishev and Mukhammed Khamukov. "Antitrust Regulation in the Digital Age. Competition Enforcement in the Context of Globalization and the Fourth Industrial Revolution" p. 153. doi: 10.17323/978-5-7598-1750-5 (in Russian).

criteria are disclosed. Unlike the CMA tool, FAS software analyses tenders' history data besides data of current tender. This feature enables FAS Russia to detect bid rigging techniques that cannot be discovered by analysis of single tender, for example, bid rotation and bid suppression.

In *Number and pattern of bidders* category, the FAS tool executes only a "low number of bidders" test. In "Suspicious pricing patterns" category, FAS tool analyzes difference between winning bid price and market price.

The FAS tool compares bidders' IP addresses, sets of fonts used in submission, number of characters in submitted documents, and performs rich analysis of metadata (compares authors name, time of creation and software version).

We believe that the FAS Russia software tool performs the most thorough analysis of bids' metadata.

There is no evidence that the FAS Russia tool analysis text similarities (unlike the CMA tool), it appears to perform the deepest analysis of implicit similarities (e.g., IP address, fonts, metadata). This approach turns out to be fruitful, as it helped to detect dangerous collusion in the supply of medical expendables' procurement, which amounted to 197 billion rubles (circa $2 billion).[31]

Thanks to analysis of historical data, the FAS tool can perform tests from the *Tenders history data* category and detect bid rotation and companies which often win tenders.

Korean BRIAS is a non-public software tool used internally by Korean FTC. The tool automatically collects information from the Korean e-procurement system KONEPS, used by multiple Korean procurers. To detect suspicious behavior, BRIAS checks low number of bidders' criteria, and winning price is outlier criteria. More specifically, the winning price is outlier criteria computes the gap between the winning price and the prices of the second and the third bidders.

In the *Suspicious pricing patterns* category, it also analyses the number of bids above the market price, similarly to the FAS tool. The tool also carries out the test from the tender's history data category and detects companies with a high winning rate.

A strong point of BRIAS is the integration with the national e-procurement system, enabling a completely automated screening pipeline.

Projecto Cerebro developed by CADE Brazil collects data for analysis from 40 databases including prices and public procurement databases.[32] The collected data is used to perform tests from the suspicious pricing patterns category, such as cover bidding and superfluous losing bidders. It also detects low endeavor and similar submissions by searching for text and metadata (author, IP address) similarities (*see* Table 4.1). The tool is also advertised to analyze historical data and detect bid rotation, bid suppression and stable market share.[33]

31. FAS Russia Deputy Head Andrey Tsarikovskii emphasized the role of FAS Russia software screening in the detection of collusion behavior in the "VALERIA" and "Egmed" bid rigging case.
32. Latin American and Caribbean Competition Forum, Session III: Promoting effective competition in public procurement—Contribution from Brazil—12-13 April 2016. P.4. http://www.oecd.org/officialdocuments/publicdisplaydocumentpdf/?cote=DAF/COMP/LACF(2016)19&docLanguage=En.
33. Slides Cartel screening in the digital era—CADE Brazil—January 2018 OECD Workshop.

Table 4.1 Summarizes the Main Features of the Discussed Software Screenings

Analyzed Criteria\Screening Tool	*UK CMA*	*Russia FAS*	*Korea BRIAS*	*Brazil CADE Projecto Cerebro*
Number and pattern of bidders	+	+	+	
Low number of bidders	+	+	+	
Single bid	+			
Suspicious pricing patterns	+	+	+	+
Winning price is outlier	+		+	
Non-market bids		+	+	+
Winning price is close to start price		+		
Similar pricing across bids	+			+
Made up costs	+			
Low endeavor and similar submissions	+	+		+
Text similarities	+			+
Similar word count	+	+		
Low endeavor losing bids	+			
Metadata similarities	+	+		+
Same fonts		+		
History of participation		+	+	+
Bid rotation		+		+
Bid suppression				+
Stable market share and/or constant winner		+	+	+
Combination tests	+			

As our analysis shows, no screening tool outperforms others, since each tool has its strong and weak points. For example, the FAS Russia's main advantage is deep metadata analysis (e.g., fonts analysis). The Korean BRIAS tool's strong point is seamless integration with the e-procurement system, uniting administrative agencies, local governments and government companies.[34] The CMA tool uses combination tests, allowing overcoming the limitations of a linear model.

This observation highlights the need for collaboration between competition authorities to develop new generation software screening tools. Moreover, all the tools rely on a large amount of rather simple tests that can be simply fooled by aware

34. P. 62. OECD 2013.

colluders. For example, metadata can be simply forged by bidders, thus rendering metadata-based tests useless. Colluders can also fool the made-up prices test by generating fake costs according to Benford's law.

The wider use of screening tools inevitably leads to growth of colluders' awareness and the number of attempts to fool these tools. This once again emphasizes the importance of competition authorities' collaborative development of new tools based on smarter tools.

The next section discusses possible avenues for collaborative improvement of screening tools.

[B] Avenues for Further Screening Software Tools Development

Existing software screenings rely on a linear model and use simple tests mostly easy to deceive by aware colluders. Big data and advanced machine learning techniques might be a possible solution to this issue, as they provide the possibility to find nontrivial collusive patterns that econometrics could not foresee and build nontrivial tests on these patterns. As we mentioned above, the main advantage given to competition authorities by current screening tools is the analysis of large amounts of procurement data, which are impractical for analysis by human. Moreover, advanced machine learning techniques should give such tools one more strong point: employment of effective cartel detection criteria which are unknown to econometrics.

However, transition from a linear model with hand-crafted weights to advanced machine learning techniques (such as neural networks or random forests) requires big training data sets containing the examples of collusive and competitive behavior.

Creation of such data sets demands a huge number of man-hours to analyze procurement data and annotate whether it is competitive or not, and thus collaboration between competition authorities is desirable. Rosa Abrantes-Metz analyses possibilities of machine learning aiding in cartel detection and asks whether "such a data set exist today—with a sufficient number of cases of both collusion and not-collusion, with the necessary data on price, cost, and drivers of supply and demand—or will we have to wait for it?"[35]

To our mind, to create a training data set containing collusive examples for neural networks and other machine learning methods, competition authorities should share data on cartels gained by operation of current software screenings, such as Korea BRIAS, Brazil Projecto Cérebro and FAS Russia software screening tools. Moreover, new suspicious behavior criteria found during analysis of such a data set should also be shared across borders to improve screening tools of all countries. Thus, the artificial intelligence age requires a deepening of competition authorities' collaboration in the digital sphere.

Notably, improvement and wider usage of the software screening tools will make colluders refine bid-rigging techniques to make them invisible to these tools. In its turn,

35. Rosa M. Abrantes-Metz & Albert D. Metz. Can Machine Learning Aid in Cartel detection? CPI Antitrust Chronicle July 2018. P. 3, https://www.competitionpolicyinternational.com/wp-content/uploads/2018/07/CPI-A-M-Metz.pdf.

the improvement of bid-rigging methods will require the development of better screening tools. Therefore, we are at the beginning of yet another sword and shield competition.

Finally, to discourage over-optimistic expectations from screening tools, we want to emphasize that disregarding any progress made in their improvement, screening tools enable to find only *suspicious* behavior. The final decision whether this is *collusive* behavior should remain the call of the competition authority.[36]

§4.03 RISE OF AUCTION ROBOTS IN ELECTRONIC PROCUREMENT

Electronic procurement is a step toward pro-competitive public procurement aiming at enhancing and innovating public auctions by the means of digital technologies.[37] Furthermore, electronic procurement platforms are catalyst for the development of cartel detection software screening tools, since these platforms accumulate historical bidding data in a machine-readable format.

Russia launched its electronic procurement system in 2012. Nowadays 9 trillion rubles (circa USD 133 billion) volumes *electronic* public procurement, while the annual public procurement volume is 25 trillion rubles (circa USD 369 billion, 30% Russian GDP).[38] Thus, e-procurement volume is up to 10% of Russian GDP.

Electronic procurement systems improve bidding transparency and availability of information for competitors. As the World Bank explains, "Automation of the procurement transactions reduces human error, enhances the integrity of the data, brings in transparency to the Government procurements and facilitates standardization of processes."[39] E-procurement systems mostly coped with the task.

Nevertheless, e-procurement systems failed to completely eliminate bid rigging from the procurement process. In Russia, bid rigging is still up to 85% of cartel offenses.[40] According to FAS Russia, cartel damages amounted to 1.5%–2% of Russian GDP in 2017. Thus, bid-rigging damages constituted 1.3%–1.7 % of Russian GDP.

Recently FAS Russia uncovered some atypical cases on bid rigging in e-procurement, in which colluders relied on auction robots.

Auction robot (auction dynamic pricing agent or dynamic bidding software) is a piece of software typically built in the procurement system that auction participants

36. See about this, for instance: Lianos, Ioannis and Genakos, Christos, Econometric Evidence in EU Competition Law: An Empirical and Theoretical Analysis (October 1, 2012). CLES Research Paper series 06/12. Available at SSRN: https://ssrn.com/abstract=2184563 or http://dx.doi.org/10.2139/ssrn.2184563.
37. See OECD (2017), Public Procurement for Innovation: Good Practices and Strategies, OECD Public Governance Reviews, OECD Publishing, Paris, https://doi.org/10.1787/9789264265820-en.
38. Head of FAS Russia Cartel Office Andrei Tenishev Shared an Experience on Fighting Digital Cartels, https://fas.gov.ru/news/24373 (in Russian).
39. World Bank Group. Case Study on eProcurement in GoAP, http://siteresources.worldbank.org/INTEGOVERNMENT/Resources/APeProcurement.doc.
40. Federal Antimonopoly Service of Russia. Twelfth Annual Report on Competition In Russian Federation. August 2018, http:/d-russia.ru/wp-content/uploads/2018/09/12_Doklad_o_razvitii_konkurentcii_FAS.pdf (In Russian).

can program for minimum price and reduction step. The pre-configured auction 'bot' automatically submits bids on behalf of the participant, eliminating the need to watch price during the whole auction process and submit bids manually. Thus, it saves a lot of manpower for companies that participate at multiple auctions at once.

Auction robots might be either built-in software (like auction robots built in Russian e-procurement systems Sberbank-AST and RTS-Tender, which automate bid submission), or standalone third-party software agents, which run on user's premises and automate bid submission by communicating with procurement platform. Such standalone agents were described in US patent[41] and are also widely used as eBay auction snipers (e.g., Auction Auto Bidder).[42]

The use of auction robots is not illegal. However, auction robots appear to be not only a tool to automate competitive behavior but a tool to automate collusive behavior as well. FAS Russia and its regional branches had to deal recently with four relevant cases in this area. Further we review these cases in more details and then discuss prospective developments of e-procurement tools and their influence on competition law evolution.

[A] Cases on Bid-Rigging with Auction Robots at Reverse Auctions

Pioneer cases on bid rigging automation via auction robots handled by FAS Russia are cases at "reverse auctions" [43] that are auctions in which suppliers compete for the buyer and decrease price.

First case on collusion facilitated by the use of auction robots was decided by the Murmansk regional office of FAS Russia (hereinafter Murmansk OFAS Russia) in May 2016.[44] In this case, two bidders ("ORKO-Invest" LLC and "TSOO" LLC) colluded at 25 e-procurement auctions on solid domestic and medical waste removal. At these auctions, "ORKO-Invest" and "TSOO" agreed to maintain high uncompetitive price by implementing bid rotation—classic bid-rigging technique. This classic bid-rigging scenario might be performed without any specific software tools.

What makes this case special is the auction robots that the companies used to facilitate bid rigging. "ORKO-Invest" and "TSOO" used auction robots built in the

41. See patent US7461024B2 "Bidder-side auction dynamic pricing agent, system, method and computer program product," https://patents.google.com/patent/US7461024B2/en, and patent application US20130211946A1 "Bidder automation of multiple bid groups or cascades for auction dynamic pricing markets system, method and computer program product".
42. Auction Auto Bidder, http://auctionautobidder.com/.
43. Ray Hackney, Steve Jones & Andrea Lösch (2007). Towards an e-Government efficiency agenda: the impact of information and communication behavior on e-Reverse auctions in public sector procurement, European Journal of Information Systems, 16:2, 178-191, DOI: 10.1057/palgrave.ejis.3000677.
44. Decision of Murmansk OFAS on "ORKO-Invest" LLC and "TSOO" LLC bid rigging. Case No. 05-03-16/6, http://solutions.fas.gov.ru/to/murmanskoe-ufas-rossii/05-03-16-6-ebc701b6-df71-4ef4-bb18-4bb972d58ae9 (in Russian). See also Murmansk OFAS decision as of 19 April 2017, https://solutions.fas.gov.ru/to/murmanskoe-ufas-rossii/05-04-17-5-0e9cea0e-e192-42fd-863a-1eeb6f4a98a7 (in Russian).

electronic procurement system Sberbank-AST.[45] This procurement system provides an opportunity for all bidders either to submit bids manually or to use auction robots to automate bids submission. In the case at hand, colluders preferred to use auction robots in 22 of 25 auctions.

Under the Rules of the Sberbank-AST e-procurement system, any auction participant may use auction robots.[46] Intent to use such a robot and be bound by the bids submitted by this robot is demonstrated by the electronic signature of the participant. To activate a robot, the participant should set the price decrement step and the minimum price. During the auction, the robot submits bids once every two minutes. If more than one participant uses robots, these robots submit bids sequentially (i.e. one after another) in the order these robots were created. However, at any time during the auction the participant may switch from automatic to manual bid submission.

In 22 auctions "ORKO-Invest" and "TSOO" created auction robots right after they submitted an application to participate in the auctions. Once the auction robots are set, colluders are able to sit back and relax. No further work needs to be done. Hence, auction robots help colluders to automate bid submission and make the process of bid rigging much easier.

Thus, auction robots helped colluders to submit bids saving time and effort. However, "ORKO-Invest" and "TSOO" ignored the flip side of the bid rigging via auction robots, as these robots provide additional evidence of collusive behavior for competition authorities.

In particular, Murmansk OFAS Russia concluded that these colluders used a bid rotation technique: in some auctions "ORKO-Invest" was the winner, as it programed the robot for a 1% decrease from the start price, while "TSOO" programed its robot for only 0.5% decrease, and vice versa. In each of 22 auctions, these companies used the same collusive technique preselecting the winner and contract price at the moment of application creation. Murmansk OFAS Russia also found that the robots' configurations and bids for both companies were submitted from the same static IP address.

Furthermore, Murmansk OFAS Russia found suspicious behavior patterns of the companies: these companies used the bid rotation scenario via auction robots only when no other companies participated at the auction. However, if other independent bidders took part in the auction, "ORKO-Invest" and "TSOO" actively competed in manual mode decreasing the starting price more than twice.

Thus, Murmansk OFAS Russia concluded that these evidences together with other evidence (e.g., auction documents submitted by colluders had text similarities, a head of "TSOO" is a deputy director of "ORKO-Invest") show that the companies entered into collusive agreement on price maintenance.

Another case on auction robots automating bid rigging provides further details on the evolution of both companies' collusive behavior and competition authorities' approaches to prove bid rigging in the digital age.

45. Sberbank-AST is an automated trading system integrated with the official unified information system on procurement zakupki.gov.ru, http://utp.sberbank-ast.ru/ (In Russian).
46. Sberbank-AST Regulations on Electronic Auctions, https://www.sberbank-ast.ru/Docs/Reglament44FZ_2018.pdf (In Russian).

In the case decided by FAS Russia in April 2018[47] two companies ("VALERIA" LLC and "Egmed" LLC) colluded at 14 auctions for the supply of medical expendables for the operations of stenting of coronary, carotid arteries and other operations in 2016.[48] These companies were awarded contracts for 197 billion rubles.

In this case, "VALERIA" and "Egmed" preferred to facilitate bid rigging via auction robots in 12 of 14 auctions. As in the previous case, colluders used built-in auction robots of the electronic procurement platform Sberbank-AST. However, in the case at hand colluders exposed various tactics in different auctions switching between manual bidding or automatic bidding and implementing either bid rotation or bid suppression techniques.

Thus, "VALERIA" and "Egmed"'s collusive tactics were the following: firstly, in five auctions both companies set their robots for a 0.5% decrease in the start price. According to the rules of the Sberbank-AST procurement platform, in case the bids are equal, the winning bid is the bid that is submitted earlier. The rules clarify that auction robots submit bids sequentially depending on the robot's ID assigned at the moment of the robot's creation. In these 5 auctions "VALERIA" was awarded the contracts, as its robots were created earlier than "Egmed" robots, and "VALERIA" robots considered to submit bids earlier than "Egmed" robots according to Sberbank-AST rules.

Secondly, in four other auctions "VALERIA" and "Egmed" used the *bid rotation* technique by setting their robots either to a 0.5% decrease for "VALERIA" and a 1% decrease for "Egmed" or a 1% decrease for "VALERIA" and a 0.5% decrease for "Egmed," Thirdly, in yet another auction "VALERIA" and "Egmed" used the *bid suppression* technique, since "Egmed" set robot at a 1% decrease whilst "VALERIA" abstained from submitting any bids. Fourthly, in the other auction "Egmed" set the robot for a 0.5% decrease of the start price, and "VALERIA" set the price at a 1% decrease, *manually*.

Moreover, in one more auction, "VALERIA" set a 0.5% price decrease and "Egmed"—a 1% price decrease. However, independent parties which took part in this auction continued to compete and decrease the price. This made "Egmed" manually set the price decrease at 11%.

Hence, in contrast to the previous case decided by Murmansk OFAS in 2016, when colluders used auction robots to automate only the bid rotation technique, in the case at hand "VALERIA" and "Egmed" used algorithms for more complicated tactics, including bid suppression automation.

Similar to the previous case decided by Murmansk OFAS in 2016, in the case at hand FAS Russia found that "VALERIA" and "Egmed" robots submitted bids from the same IP address, and both companies used this IP address to sign awarded contracts. Furthermore, companies' auction applications had text similarities (e.g., in most

---

47. FAS Russia Case No. 1-11-166/00-22-17, https://solutions.fas.gov.ru/ca/upravlenie-po-borbe-s-kartelyami/ats-30960-18 (in Russian). *See also*: The Russian Competition Authority Opens a Proceeding Against a Cartel That Used Auction Robots (EGMED), https://www.concurrences.com/en/bulletin/news-issues/november-2017/the-russian-competition-authority-opens-a-proceeding-against-a-cartel-that-used.
48. Case against a cartel that used auction robots, https://en.fas.gov.ru/press-center/news/detail.html?id=52369.

auctions both companies use the same account—Tanya—to create or modify applications). FAS Russia also proved that the Head of "Egmed" was the cofounder of "VALERIA."

Significantly, this case provides further details on auction robots' contribution to prove collusive intent of companies by competition authorities: in the case at hand both companies set auction robots, however they preferred to disable robots and switch to manual mode to actively compete and decrease price when independent participants took part in the auction. The question is whether such a suspicious behavior is intentional or might be justified by market reasons: for example, for all intents and purposes companies could not decrease the price in some auctions more than 1% due to costs and other expenses while in other auctions (which were auctions with independent participants only by random coincidence) companies could significantly decrease the price, as contract costs were not very high for them.

Disabling of robots and switching to manual mode by colluders provided further evidence for FAS Russia, as a robot's pre-programmed settings demonstrated colluders' initial intent to fix the price at certain level (at a 1% decrease to the start price). Having robots pre-programmed, colluders could not justify their suspicious behavior (such as only 1% price decrease of the start price in absence of other participants, and significant price decrease when independent companies participated in the auctions) referring to market reasons, since robots settings programed before the beginning of the auction showed that companies intended to fix the price as they used to do in previous auctions, and only independent participants which continued to compete made colluding companies to further decrease price.

Notably, this case is one of the cases detected by the FAS Russia software screening tool.

In 2018, the regional offices of FAS Russia dealt with two more cases on auction robots automating bid rigging. Perm OFAS identified suspicious pricing patterns in 10 auctions on the supply of materials for medical laboratories: two companies set auction robots identically at a 0.5% decrease to the starting price.[49] As bids were similar, the winner was a company which created an auction robot earlier, because this robot submitted a bid first according to the rules of the procurement system. In the case at hand, both colluders cooperated with Perm OFAS and made full confessions.

One more case on auction robots is at the time of writing under consideration by Yaroslavl OFAS. In April 2018 Yaroslavl OFAS opened a proceeding against a cartel: as reported by Yaroslavl OFAS, two companies colluded at 49 auctions on the supply of reagents and diagnostic preparations.[50] These companies implemented a bid rotation technique facilitated via auction robots set at a 0.5% and 1% decrease to starting price. Notably, in this case companies colluded at two electronic procurement platforms (Sberbank-AST and RTS-Tender) using auction robots built into these platforms.

49. Auction robots helped Perm OFAS Russia Identify Bid Rigging at Auctions, http://perm.fas.gov.ru/news/15409 (in Russian).
50. Yaroslavl OFAS Order on Cartel Proceedings Initiation as of 29 March 2018, http://solutions.fas.gov.ru/to/yaroslavskoe-ufas-rossii/b-n-63c28800-094e-40f7-bc18-5424a43acaf1 (in Russian).

[B] Discussion and Further Work

The review of these four cases shows the evolution of bid rigging in the digital age. It demonstrates that collusion in e-procurement might be facilitated by auction robots. In all four cases, the collusion was classic "Smoke-Filled Room" bid rigging (overt collusion),[51] as colluders entered into cartel agreement beforehand. Despite the classic nature of the collusion, colluders used new tools—auction robots—to implement bid rigging.

However, the review shows that built-in auction robots also facilitate competition authority work, since to use an auction robot the company must submit its settings to the e-procurement platform before the auction begins, and thus create extra evidence, which might help authority to prove intent to collude. Notably, the use of third-party standalone auction robots (in contrast to built-in robots) does not create such evidence since the robot runs on the colluders' premises and its settings can be erased by the colluder once the auction is finished.

Russia is not the only country where auction robots are used. 18F (the office of United States General Services Administration tasked to build digital services for US Federal agencies) has experimented with enabling micro-purchase auction participants to bid via API (i.e., allowing bidders to use standalone auction robots).[52] 18F noted that bidding activity in the very first auction opened to robots was much higher than in previous auctions (7 unique participants submitted 70 bids versus 5-7 bids submitted by 3-4 participants in previous auctions). However, the final price was higher than the price of previous auctions. In 18F's opinion, the high final price might be explained by the change of auction type due to robot's presence. Since most of the bids were submitted by robots (including the winning bid which was submitted just ~ one second before the auction end), the final price was effectively determined by the robots' minimum prices which were set by the participants before auction started, thus the open reverse auction collapsed to a sealed bid auction. Nevertheless, 18F does not give up and wants to use learnings from this auction to make electronic bidding platforms convenient for both manual and automatic bidding. In particular, 18F in its future experiments wants to push forward the auction deadline if the last second's bid is submitted thus giving human-participants time to react to the new bid.

While auction robots at the Russian e-procurement systems Sberbank-AST and RTS-Tender implement the simplest autonomous bidding strategy known as proxy bidding,[53] there is a place for a number of more advanced autonomous bidding strategies that might be employed by the companies in the future. For example, scholars have shown that machine learning methods can be employed to predict bids

51. See, for example, Ariel Ezrachi and Maurice Stucke. From Smoke-Filled Rooms to Computer Algorithms — The Evolution of Collusion, http://clsbluesky.law.columbia.edu/2015/05/14/from-smoke-filled-rooms-to-computer-algorithms-the-evolution-of-collusion/.
52. Michael Torres and Alan de Levie. The Role of Bot-Bidding in Micro-Purchase Auctions. 2016, https://18f.gsa.gov/2016/08/09/the-role-of-bot-bidding-in-micro-purchase-auctions/.
53. Roth, Alvin E., and Axel Ockenfels. "Last-Minute Bidding and the Rules for Ending Second-Price Auctions: Evidence from eBay and Amazon Auctions on the Internet." American economic review 92.4 (2002): 1093-1103.

at government procurement auctions.[54] Such predictions can be used by companies to asses multiple auctions and take part only in the most profitable ones, thus effectively allocating business capacity. Nevertheless, the impact of such advanced techniques on competition conditions is yet to be researched.

§4.04 CONCLUSION

It is evident that the automation of the tasks which previously belonged to the domain of human labor brings to competition authorities and market participants new opportunities and challenges alike. Auction robots can facilitate bid rigging in electronic procurement. This is all clear now. The cases of FAS Russia covered in this chapter demonstrate how robots are used for bid rotation and suppression.

Screening software already allows competition authorities in Russia, Korea, Brazil, and UK to detect cartels by analyzing vast amounts of data. Authorities in these countries use different approaches by either using software themselves or, as in the case with UK, encouraging public and private procurers to use these instruments as well. Moreover, the UK software is open-source and is available for download upon request. However, it is difficult to rank these digital enforcement tools by effectiveness as FAS Russia employs deep metadata analysis while the Korean BRIAS is tightly integrated into e-procurement systems and the UK's CMA capitalizes on combination tests. Needless to say, market participants will continue to collude and such technologies as machine learning advances are set to level the playing field in this digital race between the competition authorities and cartel builders. It is probably a time to watch closely how this arm race going to advance.

54. J.-M. Kim and H. Jung (2018), "Predicting Bid Prices by Using Machine Learning," Applied Economics, http://facultypages.morris.umn.edu/~jongmink/research/AE_bidding_2018.pdf.

Part II Challenges in Traditional Economy

CHAPTER 5

Cracking 102 RPM Cases in a Single Programme: A Success Story in Mauritius

Deshmuk Kowlessur

§5.01 INTRODUCTION

What does a Competition Authority do when it is faced with the prospect of having to investigate a whole economy where Resale Price Maintenance (RPM) is rife and common practice among market players? This is the question the Competition Commission of Mauritius (CCM) had to ask itself after it had conducted an investigation on one enterprise for RPM practices with its resellers in the chicken industry. The Commission imposed fines of nearly USD 1 million on the enterprise in year 2017. Although the case is now on appeal in front of the Supreme Court of Mauritius, one fact was clearly established by the investigation that the practice of RPM is widespread in Mauritius among enterprises, ranging from Fast Moving Consumer Goods (FMCG) to electronics and construction goods. Worse still, the CCM gathered that a majority of enterprises practiced RPM as a long established and 'accepted' conduct and they were not even aware that RPM is a per se prohibited conduct under the Mauritian Competition Act.

The CCM has been in existence since year 2009 and in nearly 10 years of existence, it has conducted more than 45 investigations and more than 300 enquiries. The CCM has completed around 7 cartel investigations and the Commission has imposed financial penalties in 2 cases, namely, in a case concerning market sharing between 2 breweries where penalties of approximately USD 1 million was imposed and the other one, as mentioned earlier an RPM case, in the chicken industry, where the fines were slightly lower than USD 1 million (case currently under appeal in the Supreme Court of Mauritius). In another case concerning agro-chemicals, the Executive Director of the Competition Commission has recommended fines of approximately

USD 2 million to be imposed on the two offending enterprises in that case. The commissioners are yet to give their decision on this matter.

Although the CCM has a respectable track record when it comes to anti-cartel enforcement, it nevertheless has limited resources, and with those limited resources in mind, the CCM had to decide how to eradicate the problem of RPM on the market which was inevitably harming consumers. Was full-fledged investigations and imposition of fines the best solution? Would the CCM be able to cope with the number of investigations it had open? Finally the CCM thought that the best way to eradicate RPM conduct in Mauritius was through advocating and educating enterprises about the ill effects of RPM conduct and in so doing, encourage them to change their conduct to be compliant with the Competition Act, and it did so by harnessing its enforcement endeavours in the investigation on RPM in the chicken industry to advocate about RPM through an uniquely tailored amnesty programme whereby enterprises which committed to change their RPM conduct would get immunity from financial penalties. The programme which was moulded on the CCM's leniency and immunity programme was named RPM Amnesty Programme, yielded results which were both surprising and unexpected to the CCM. On preliminary estimates, the CCM was at most expecting approximately 20 applications to come through. However, through a well-planned and all-encompassing, advocacy around the programme, enterprises embraced the RPM Amnesty Programme and, in the end, the CCM received more than 100 applications. In this chapter, we endeavour to explain how the CCM achieved such a feat and how we combined effective enforcement together with advocacy to make it happen.

§5.02 THE ENFORCEMENT AND ADVOCACY ENDEAVOURS OF THE CCM

As stated earlier, the CCM has been fairly active regarding anti-cartel enforcement. Apart from South Africa, Mauritius is the only other African country which has had relative success regarding leniency applications in cartel cases. The Breweries cartel case was completed in about 3 months thanks to a leniency application from one of the parties, which assisted the CCM in conducting its assessment. The leniency in that case was the first obtained by the CCM back in 2013. Since then, we have received around 5 more leniency applications. The cartel case in agro-chemicals was also completed on the basis of leniency application by one of the parties. The CCM is currently investigating 5 other cartel cases where leniency applications have been received.

This relative success in leniency applications is the fruit of a multi-pronged approach combining effective enforcement of the provisions of the Competition Act and advocacy with different stakeholders. The CCM has over the years built a respectable enforcement history, and enterprises are aware that the institution is on the lookout for anticompetitive behaviour by enterprises. On the other hand, the CCM has also had a steady advocacy programme, building healthy cooperation with the press, trade associations, public authorities and other important stakeholders such as lawyers and the Chamber of Commerce.

Lawyers have been a strong link in our leniency programme. The CCM recognises that enterprises will not willingly come for leniency unless they have assessed the likelihood of their conduct being discovered by the authority and after they have been advised of their likelihood of success in the event of an investigation. The CCM has engaged thoroughly with lawyers to explain to them the leniency programme and the benefits to their clients. It would be safe to say that almost all leniency applications we received were by enterprises whose lawyers understood the leniency programme and advised them to take advantage of the programme.

§5.03 THE LAW CONCERNING RPM IN MAURITIUS

The Mauritian Competition Act has a specific provision on RPM. Section 43 of the Act deals with vertical agreements involving RPM and makes RPM a per se prohibition and one where fines of up to 10% of annual turnover of an enterprise can be imposed on the enterprise. The Act however allows a supplier or producer to recommend a minimum resale price to a reseller of goods or services provided that the recommendation is not binding. However, section 43(3) of the Act stipulates that where a supplier or producer has recommended a minimum resale price to a reseller of goods and the resale price appears on the goods, the words 'recommended price' shall appear next to the resale price.

By the wordings of the Act regarding RPM, we can deduce that the legislators intended RPM to be a per se prohibition as opposed to a conduct that is assessed under the rule of reason.

It has been observed that RPM concerns in Mauritius can be categorised in three broad categories:

(1) First, where there are agreements or clauses in contracts between a dealer and a reseller about the price to be practiced on the market.
(2) Second, where suppliers issue pricelists to resellers stipulating the resale price to the dealer.
(3) Third, where suppliers affix prices as determined by the supplier itself directly on the products without any mention of 'recommended price' as stipulated in the Act.

Very often, dealers simply acquiesce to the prices as are stipulated in the price lists provided by suppliers. This, among others, was one of the concerns in the chicken RPM case. While conducting interviews during the investigation it came to our knowledge that many suppliers were practicing RPM, and these were accepted by retailers. We were also made aware that these practices were very commonly practiced since long. In fact, before year 2009, when the Competition Act came into force in Mauritius, there was no law which prevented RPM in Mauritius. Suppliers were free to practice it and over the years it became a way of doing business in Mauritius. Even after the coming into force of the Competition Act 2007, enterprises continued with the practice. The CCM further gathered that the provisions of RPM in the Competition Act were largely unknown to enterprises. We will not venture here as to why those provisions were unknown to enterprises, but suffice to say that the Executive Director of the CCM, in the Chicken RPM case, took this into account in setting the fines. The Executive Director was of the view that it would be unfair to penalise one enterprise for such practice when other enterprises were still practicing them on the market. The question which arose then was how the CCM was to tackle the other hundreds of RPM conducts still happening on the market since consumers were invariably being harmed by such practice as RPM usually has the effect of chilling competition on the market.

Surely, it would have been practicably impossible for an institution of the size of the CCM to commence investigations on all those practices, even though they were to our knowledge. Also, the CCM wanted to expeditiously curb such practices and effectively restore competition dynamics in various markets for the betterment of consumers; hence, the idea of the RPM Amnesty Programme (the RPM Amnesty).

§5.04 THE RPM AMNESTY

Effective as from 5 June 2017 and valid up to 20 October 2017, the RPM Amnesty was a unique window of opportunity being provided to any enterprise involved in RPM to come forward during the limited amnesty period and disclose its participation in any RPM conduct in exchange for complete immunity from financial penalties.

The programme also concerned RPM agreements which pre-dated the coming into force of the Act, but which nevertheless continued to exist (whether by object or by effect) after the Act came into force as they would still amount to a breach. The RPM Amnesty was therefore a one-off opportunity for any enterprise involved in RPM, irrespective of the nature or form of the RPM conduct, to come forward and provide evidence of such conduct in order to assist the CCM in detecting and enforcing the Act against RPM conducts, and benefit from immunity from fine.

Any enterprise involved in a RPM conduct, be it the supplier or the dealer (reseller), were able to benefit from immunity from financial penalties, on the condition that they applied for the CCM RPM Amnesty Programme and complied with all the following conditions:

(a) they admit participation in, and inform the CCM about the RPM;
(b) they provide the CCM with all the information, documents and evidence available to them regarding the RPM, as required by the CCM;
(c) they maintain continuous and complete cooperation until the conclusion of any action by the CCM in relation to the matter; and
(d) they provide the CCM with undertakings ('commitments') that satisfactorily address all the concerns that the CCM had regarding the adverse harm to competition.

An enterprise which wished to take advantage of the CCM RPM Amnesty offer had to contact the CCM and make an application through various channels:

(i) directly, in which case any person representing the enterprise must have had the authority to represent the enterprise;

(ii) through a legal adviser; or
(iii) through the assistance of the Mauritius Chamber of Commerce and Industry (MCCI).

§5.05 ADVOCACY AROUND THE PROGRAMME

Although the launch of the programme was disseminated through various means, namely, mass mailing to enterprises in Mauritius, through the press via media releases and communiques, one-on-one contact with selected enterprises, one-on-one contact with lawyers active in the field of competition law among others, it is apposite to note the collaboration of the MCCI in making the RPM Amnesty programme a success.

The MCCI partnered with the CCM to act as a bridge between the business community and the CCM. The CCM was alive of the fact that enterprises might be reluctant to approach the authority and divulge their RPM activities outright. Thus, the CCM had various working sessions with the MCCI to explain to them the RPM amnesty programme and how it would work. Once the MCCI was comforted about the programme, they became a strong advocate of the programme vis-à-vis the business community. The MCCI even set up an RPM cell within the organisation so that they could respond expediently to the queries of enterprises regarding the amnesty programme. Nearly half of the RPM amnesty applications received by the CCM were as a result of the involvement of the MCCI.

The CCM also approached lawyers who practice in the field of competition law. One-on-one meetings were organised with at least 10 major law firms in Mauritius to explain the programme to them. Some law firms even advertised the programme on their online newsletters. Lawyers also became a strong advocate of the programme in giving reassurance to their clients about the well-foundedness of the programme.

A thorough and detailed guidance document was prepared by the CCM to explain how the programme worked, the conditions to be met, the law on RPM and what types of conducts could be caught by the law as RPM conduct. The guidance document also contained template application forms and sample undertakings which enterprises could tailor to their needs to fit their business conducts. All these, of course, were available to the public via the CCM's website.

Whereas the CCM-MCCI collaboration aimed to render the CCM RPM Amnesty programme more widely accessible to enterprises and facilitate their application process, this in no way impinged on the discretion of enterprises to contact the CCM directly.Various enterprises and associations, mostly in the retail trade, contacted the CCM and requested for one-on-one meetings to understand better the programme and to explain to them how to apply for the amnesty. The CCM prepared bespoke advocacy sessions with associations such as the Association of Mauritian Manufacturers. Furthermore, the CCM worked in close collaboration with various enterprises in reviewing their applications before they were finalised.

By the end of 4 months, during which the programme ran, the CCM had received around 75 applications for amnesty. However, the CCM was requested by the MCCI and various other stakeholders to extend the validity of the programme because there were many other enterprises which wanted to apply for the amnesty but needed more time to complete their applications. The CCM therefore extended the programme by another 2 weeks. In the end, the CCM received 102 applications in total.

§5.06 THE RPM AMNESTY APPLICATION ASSESSMENT PROCESS

All 102 applications have been scrutinised by the Executive Director in batches. The assessment comprised of an enquiry to determine whether there are reasonable grounds to determine whether the reported conduct may amount to RPM as defined under the Act, and where reasonable grounds were found, an investigation was launched into the application to assess whether the application fulfils the conditions for the grant of RPM Amnesty. The Executive Director submitted a preliminary report of his findings to the applicant concerned and invited its views on same. Once the views were received, the report was finalised and submitted to the Commission for determination.

The RPM Amnesty Programme was launched by the CCM in an endeavour to curtail such restrictive business practices within various sectors of the Mauritian economy which might have been existing since long. RPM conducts are sanctioned by financial penalties under the Competition Act. The Programme therefore proved to be an effective way to address such restrictive business practices whereby the enterprises themselves admitted their participation to a conduct which may amount to RPM and voluntarily proposed measures which would cease such conducts.

§5.07 RESULT OF THE RPM AMNESTY PROGRAMME

The RPM Amnesty programme was highly successful and impactful, more so for a relatively small economy like that of Mauritius. Mauritius is a small Island of 2040 km^2 with a gross domestic product of MUR 485 billion (USD 14 billion) and with a population size of 1.3 million. It generated 102 applications for RPM Amnesty in form of leniency applications, and additionally acted as an effective advocacy of competition law through interaction with several hundreds of enterprises, leaving a robust footprint of the Competition Commission in the business community.

The 102 applications for RPM Amnesty received by the Competition Commission emanated from enterprises of varying sizes and operating in various sectors including FMCG, construction, manufacturing, electronic goods, information technology products, books, pharmaceutical and cosmetic products.

By its very definition RPM involves both suppliers and resellers. 52% of applications received were from suppliers and 48% emanated from resellers. The suppliers include mainly large distributors, wholesalers, importers and manufacturers. The resellers who applied for the RPM Amnesty are mainly hypermarkets and supermarkets.

Out of the applicants, 36 are from top 100 companies or are part of Groups which forms part of the top 100 companies in Mauritius in terms of turnover. That is, they are part of the largest enterprises in Mauritius. The turnover of 43% of applicants exceeds

MUR 1 billion (approximately USD 30 million) per year. This clearly shows that the applications are from important enterprises in the Mauritian economy. Thus, the impact of the programme is significant for an economy like Mauritius.

Most of the RPM conducts for which applications for Amnesty have been made are in the form of contractual agreements between suppliers and resellers containing clauses which restrict the ability of the reseller to reduce price lower than thresholds agreed between the supplier and the reseller. Several of such clauses pertain to agreements on the minimum price to be practiced by the reseller. Another common clause is an agreement between the supplier and reseller for the reseller not to sell at a price which is lower than the 'recommended price' of the supplier.

Several applications related to the practice for the suppliers to affix on the products a resale price as determined by the suppliers themselves. Such prices become the resale price of the product practiced by resellers. This practice eliminates competition among resellers as a single resale price has already been determined by the supplier.

The nature of RPM for which Amnesty has been sought can be classified as shown in Table 5.1.

Table 5.1 Reported Conducts

Nature of RPM	*% of Applications*
RPM in price list which was mostly spread across Retail segment, FMCGs and Pharmaceutical sectors	31%
RPM via written contracts, of which 70% occurred in the Retail supply sector	28%
RPM through price labeling in the Retail and Pharmaceutical sectors	24%
RPM through e-mail communications mostly in the FMCGs sector	4%
Other forms of RPM	13%

The Competition Commission has also received application for more complex practices which not only involved RPM but also intertwined with potential collusive horizontal agreements. These conducts are also being assessed.

Most of the applicants applied for more than one RPM conduct and for different periods.

§5.08 THE EXPECTED IMPACT

As a condition to benefit from the RPM Amnesty, applicants have to ensure that they cease to be party to such practices and offer undertakings to the CCM in which they commit on actions they will take to ensure they cease such practices. The elimination of the RPMs for which Amnesty have been requested is expected to boost the level of competition in the retail sector to the benefit of consumers, new entrants and the economy at large.

The applications concern several thousands of products with turnover of several billions of rupees. Most of the RPM practices for which Amnesty have been claimed are practices whereby the reseller was not allowed to lower prices. This practice was such common in relation to certain products that several resellers considered it a normal practice for the supplier to decide on the resale price for the product and as such nearly all resellers were practicing the price as determined by the supplier instead of competing on the price of such products. Agreements on minimum prices were also very common, hindering the ability of the reseller to reduce prices.

It is expected that the elimination of such RPMs will boost competition and result in lower prices. The cumulated price effect over several thousands of products is likely to be important for consumers and the economy at large. Even a minor effect on the price of each product will be significant overall given the number of products involved.

More importantly the programme will trigger a new level of competition among resellers by removing the price latency established by previous practices. As resellers would compete more fiercely for their resale prices, the dynamic of competition will be boosted for the whole sector.

Curtailing of RPM in Mauritius will also facilitate entry. One particular case which was pretty interesting was from a reseller. The reseller complained that he wanted to enter a market in which there existed several well-established competitors. So, he chose as entry strategy to offer products in that market at a lower price which argued that there would be no reason for a customer to purchase the product from it rather from a long-established supplier unless it is able to sell at a lower price. Eventually the reseller entered the market and started to offer the product at a lower price. However, after few days the supplier asked the reseller to increase its price to the recommended price otherwise it would cease supply. Upon query the reseller gathered that one of the largest players on the market asked the supplier to ensure that the new entrant does not undercut price else it would cease buying from the supplier. Elimination of such RPM will clearly facilitate entry into markets. On a side note, the typical RPM defence did not apply in this case.

It is usually said that enforcement is the best advocacy. Through this programme, the Competition Commission has reached several hundreds of enterprises in Mauritius and not only the 102 applicants. Their involvement has been more than merely attending a workshop or going through an advocacy programme. They have given serious consideration on whether their business practice may fall foul of the RPM provision of the Competition Act and conducted compliance programmes. The RPM Amnesty programme has thus been an effective advocacy campaign for the Competition Commission, building upon its repute and establishing a new level of awareness of competition law among the business community.

The RPM Amnesty programme has and is continuing to generate further leniency applications and investigations into non-RPM conducts. As such the 'spillover' effects will add to the success of the programme, further increasing the effect of competition enforcement to the benefit of the economy and consumers.

Although the CCM has not made a quantitative estimation of the benefits of the result of the RPM Amnesty programme on consumers and the economy at large, such benefit is expected to be significant. More so given that nearly all the applications, if not all, are in relation to RPMs which are likely to be harmful to consumer without having the beneficial side of certain RPM.

§5.09 CONCLUSION

Cracking 102 RPM cases in a period of 2 years is a spectacular result in itself, which would have not been achievable without the RPM Amnesty programme and the accompanying advocacy. The Executive Director of the CCM has completed his review on all applications and the Commissioners have issued their decision with respect to most of the applications. Absent such a programme it would have not only been time consuming to detect and investigate these RPMs, while consumers continue to be harmed, but it would have been a challenge to detect all those RPMs and to be able to gather the required evidence. The benefits brought through the Amnesty programme are likely to outweigh the potential fines, and this, without frustrating the efficacy of the leniency programme of the CCM. The RPM Amnesty programme was a one-off offer, and this was made clear to the business community.

The RPM Amnesty programme has demonstrated that enforcement can also be done in an innovative and collaborative way, without impeding on other enforcement tools. On the contrary, the RPM Amnesty programme is expected to increase on the efficacy of other enforcement tools driven by increased awareness of the law and augmented trust in the Competition Commission and its enforcement work.

The RPM Amnesty programme has marked an important milestone in the history of the Competition Commission in its way to consolidate its presence and repute in Mauritius and in the region as a robust enforcer of competition law.

CHAPTER 6

Exclusion and Margin Squeeze: The Nippon Telegraph and Telephone East Corporation Case (2010)

Yosuke Okada & Junko Shibata

§6.01 INTRODUCTION

In August 2001, the Nippon Telegraph and Telephone East Corporation (hereafter NTT East) started an optical fibre telecommunication service to residential buildings, *fibre-to-the-home* (FTTH) service, in eastern Japan. In this chapter, we explore a ruling of the Supreme Court of Japan on exclusionary conducts of NTT East with respect to the FTTH service.[1] The Japanese Antimonopoly Act (hereafter AMA) Article 3 regulates exclusionary practices through the prohibition of *private monopolisation*, and AMA defines *exclusionary private monopolisation* in Article 2(5).[2] The Supreme Court passed a ruling for this case in December 2010 based on the tribunal decision taken by the Japan Fair Trade Commission (JFTC) in March 2007 and the appeal court decision by the Tokyo High Court in September 2009.[3] This was an important case that constituted the first ruling of the Supreme Court regarding whether a refusal to deal with a competitor can result in private monopolisation.

In section 2, we provide an overview of the NTT East case. In section 3, we discuss the Supreme Court ruling and its relevance of the exclusionary private

1. Supreme Court, 17 December 2010, 57-II, *Shinketsu-shu*, 215 (*NTT East*).
2. Article 2(5) defines the private monopolisation as follows: 'Such business activities, by which any enterprise, individually or by combination or conspiracy with other enterprises, or by any other manner, excludes or controls the business activities of other enterprises, thereby causing, contrary to the public interest, a substantial restraint of competition in any particular field of trade.' For a concise explanation of the Japanese Antimonopoly Law, *see* Masako Wakui (2018), *Antimonopoly Law: Competition Law and Policy in Japan* (2nd ed.), Design Egg Co., pp. 61–74.
3. Tokyo High Court, 17 December 2012, *Minshu* 64, 2067.

monopolisation. Section 4 compares the ruling with similar ones in Europe and the United States. Section 5 applies an economic analysis to this case. Section 6 concludes the chapter.

§6.02 NTT EAST CASE

[A] Background

The first provider of FTTH service in eastern Japan is the USEN Broad Networks (hereinafter USEN Broad) which started its service from May 2001, though its FTTH service was concentrated in a fairly small number of districts in Tokyo and Yokohama. Shortly after the entry of USEN Broad, NTT East made a full-scale entry to the FTTH market in eastern Japan from August 2001. In the following months, Tokyo Electric Power Company Holdings, Incorporated (hereinafter TEPCO) expressed the intent to start providing FTTH services in March 2002, using their own optical fibre infrastructure which had been used for its electricity business. Furthermore, USEN Broad planned to enlarge its service area to include prefectural capitals in eastern Japan from March 2002. This resulted in mainly a three-way battle among USEN Broad, NTT East and TEPCO to attract more subscribers of FTTH services.

Figure 6.1 Market Structure of the FTTH Service: The NTT East Case

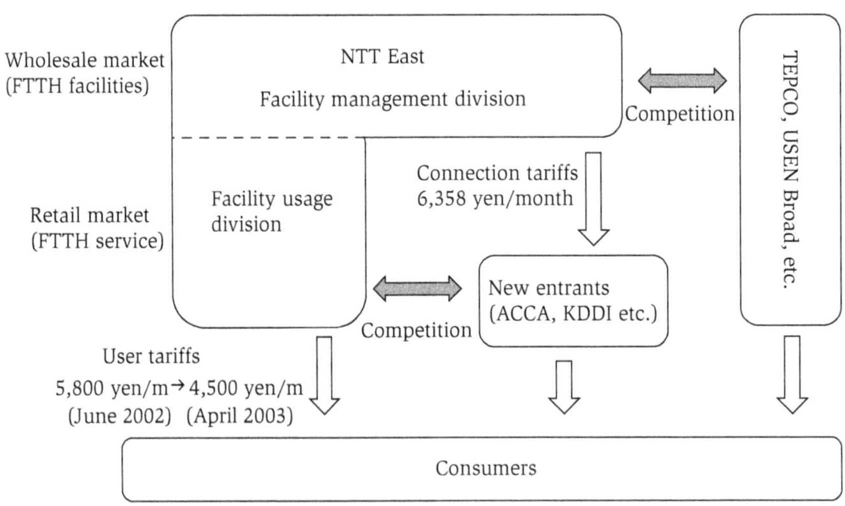

Note: The connection and user tariffs in Figure 6.1 are based on a core direct connection system (*see* the main text).

Figure 6.1 depicts the vertical relation between the wholesale and retail markets for FTTH services. Wholesale and retail divisions of TEPCO and USEN Broad were vertically integrated. On the other hand, though NTT East is also a vertically integrated operator, it has been granted a business license as a 'Type 1 Telecommunications

Carrier', indicating that NTT East is obliged to provide connection services of upstream optical fibre networks to downstream retailers (Article 38, Telecommunications Business Act).[4] Therefore, operators who provide FTTH services in competition with NTT East are classified to belong to either of the following two types: those with vertically integrated services using their own FTTH facilities (TEPCO, USEN etc.) and those with retail service borrowing optical fibre from NTT East (ACCA, KDDI etc.).

Although the Telecommunications Business Act had stipulated no detailed regulations concerning the relation between the connection tariffs and user tariffs, the governing agency of the Act, the Ministry of Internal Affairs and Communication (hereafter MIAC), released a review of connection rules at the Telecommunications Council in December 2000, which stated that 'regarding the relation between the connection tariffs and user tariffs, when considering that connection tariffs are wholesale prices and user tariffs are retail prices, the connection charges going below that of user tariffs is not generally considered appropriate in terms of fair competition'. Based on the report, the MIAC provided administrative guidance, necessitating that the user tariffs of Type 1 Telecommunications Carriers, such as NTT East, should not become lower than the connection tariffs. This administrative guidance is referred to as an *imputation rule*.

[B] Overview of the NTT East Case

In August 2001, when NTT East started an FTTH service in eastern Japan region, it provided this service in which a single-core optical fibre was dedicated to each user (*core direct connection system*) for a monthly tariff of JPY 9,000. In addition, in March 2002, TEPCO started to provide the same kind of communication system for a monthly tariff of JPY 9,900. In the very same year, in June 2002, NTT East unveiled a new service, 'New Family Type', based on a *branching system* in which a maximum of thirty-two users shares one core optical fibre. In this branching system, because the communication speed would be lower than that of the core direct connection system, the connection tariffs were set to decrease as the number of sharing users increased, thereby enabling NTT East to offer a cheaper user tariff. Assuming that the usage rate of New Family Type service would be 60% which amounts to sharing a single-core optical fibre by ninenteen users, NTT East set the monthly user tariff to JPY 5,800 in June 2002.[5]

4. Article 38 of the Telecommunications Business Act stipulates that businesses that possess 'Type 1 Telecommunications carriers' licenses, upon receiving the petition of other carriers, should connect their telecommunications equipment. Type 1 Telecommunications Carriers who instal 'Category 1 designated telecommunications equipment' shall determine the interconnection tariffs with respect to the connection tariff and conditions and shall receive approval from the Minister of Internal Affairs and Communication.
5. In addition to the service tariffs, users of NTT East's network must pay the Internet Service Provider (ISP) tariffs for using the internet services, because NTT East is not allowed to offer ISP service bundled with its network service by the NTT Act (which was enacted when NTT was privatised in 1985).

In January 2003, after TEPCO reduced its user tariff to JPY 7,800, NTT East reduced the monthly tariff for its New Family Type to JPY 4,500. By the time this new service started, the number of users who were requesting access to the FTTH service had not completely expanded; thus, a branching system was required only in rare cases.[6] Accordingly, NTT East did not instal the equipment required to change the core direct connection system to the branching system even though the service was sold to New Family Type users.

The core direct connection system and the branching system are compared in Table 6.1. The method that is used to calculate the connection tariffs in the branching system is rather complicated. For example, if the connection tariff for the branching system in which a maximum of thirty-two users can use one core is provided to only one user using one of the thirty-two branched lines, this would result in a cost of JPY 17,145; however, if twenty of the thirty-two branched lines are used, the connection tariff per user becomes JPY 2,335. The user tariff of JPY 5,800 for the New Family Type service, which was notified by NTT East to the MIAC, was calculated based on ninenteen users per core, with sales costs being added to the connection tariff per user (approximately JPY 4,906).

Table 6.1 Comparison of the Core Direct Connection System (Basic Type) and Branching System (New Family Type)

	Core Direct Connection System (Basic Type)	*Branching System (New Family Type)*
No. of users per core	*1 user*	*1 + (up to 32 users)*
Monthly connection tariff (per user)	JPY 6,328 or more (fluctuates depending on the number of users who are sharing facilities other than the core)	Initial JPY 20,130–JPY 2,326/From March 2003, JPY 17,145–JPY 1,746 (the tariffs decrease as the number of users increases)
Monthly user tariff	JPY 9,000	Initial JPY 5,800/ From April 2003, JPY 4,500
Communication speed	100 mbps	Maximum 100 mbps (may decrease in case of multiple simultaneous users)

Note: Commentary on Supreme Court Ruling (p. 805).

The entrants in the retail market who intended to sell the FTTH service using the optical fibre of NTT East were selling services based on the core direct connection system instead of the branching system. At that time, the retail telecommunication carriers who were using the optical fibre of NTT East paid a total connection tariff of

6. For example, the Supreme Court ruling confirmed the facts determined in the original decisions that the appellant NTT East 'as of the end of March 2003 ... owned approximately 3.8 million optical fibre cores, of which the appellant is using approximately 840 thousand cores for its own FTTH service, with approximately 20 thousand cores connected to other telecommunications carriers, and the other 2.85 million cores (75% of the total) currently being unused (*dark fibre*)'.

JPY 6,328. Because NTT East had set the monthly user tariffs of the New Family Type (though provided as directly connected core lines) to JPY 5,800 in June 2002 and then JPY 4,500 from April 2003, it was difficult for other retail telecommunication carriers to meet competition with NTT East. This situation continued until the end of March 2004.

In November 2003, the MIAC provided administrative guidance to NTT East, requesting an investigation and reporting accommodative connection charges for new entrants. Consequently, from April 2004, NTT East stopped providing FTTH service under the core direct connection system to New Family Type users, and articulated the plan to move the current New Family Type users under the core direct connection system to the branching system.

[C] Rulings by the JFTC and Tokyo High Court

The JFTC ruled that NTT East, while setting the connection and user tariffs for the New Family Type based on a branching system that was not actually being used, sold the New Family Type via the core direct connection system, thereby excluding FTTH service providers of the retail market by setting a user tariff lower than the connection tariff. JFTC ruled this conduct as *substantial restraint of competition* in the relevant market, as is specified in Article 2(5) of the AMA, thereby resulting in exclusionary private monopolisation.[7] In the appeal trial, the Tokyo High Court acknowledged the fact that new entrants were subjected to a negative margin between the connection charge and the user tariff and that they were forced to incur a significant loss; that NTT East effectively deterred the new entrants to provide FTTH services, therefore confirmed the violation of the AMA.

§6.03 RULING OF THE SUPREME COURT

[A] Applicability of the Exclusionary Conducts

An important point of contention in the lower court rulings is the applicability of the exclusionary private monopolisation which involves substantial restriction of competition. According to the mainstream legal theory in Japan, substantially restricted competition would result in the establishment, maintenance and consolidation of market dominance.[8]

Exclusionary private monopolisation is applicable to an extensive range of conducts which set off the substantial restriction of competition. However, while determining the illegality of such activities, it is not always easy to distinguish between the normal conducts of competition and exclusionary behaviours which may constitute private monopolisation. Needless to say, exclusion as a result of free and fair competition does not fall the scope of private monopolisation. According to the Supreme Court ruling and some lower court precedents in Japan, conducts that would

7. Tribunal Decision of JFTC, 26 March 2007.
8. Wakui, *supra*, Section 1.3.3.

fall into exclusion are equal to the anticompetitive conducts by the *means to be condemned*, or evoked by the *artificial method in the sense that such method is beyond the normal method of competition.*[9] However, there are no certain common criteria regarding what these words exactly mean.

It is worth noting that exclusionary conducts can fall into a category of *unfair trade practices* (prohibited under Article 19 and defined in Article 2 section 9) as well as private monopolisation.[10] If an exclusionary conduct that is capable of restricting competition fall the category of unfair trade practices, it could be found to be an anticompetitive conduct and may also be certified as an exclusionary conduct in terms of private monopolisation. In such a case, the conduct in question is not regarded as normal competition. Meanwhile, although it is generally acknowledged that some exclusionary conduct not being categorised as unfair trade practices may constitute private monopolisation, it would be difficult to set a clear judgmental standard for illegality in such cases. Current (rather narrow) common understanding about the judgmental criterion would be that efficiency-enhancing practices in terms of price or quality of products or services are not considered exclusionary private monopolisation due to artificial method beyond the normal method of competition.

The Supreme Court ruled that the NTT East's conduct was exclusionary private monopolisation 'despite receiving approval (from the MIAC) for connection tariffs and also notifying the MIAC the user tariffs on the assumption of using the branching system, when providing New Family Type services, the core direct connection method was actually implemented and user tariffs were set lower than the connection tariffs based on the core direct connection method'. In this respect, the court said, a different connection format from the one for which approval was granted under the Telecommunication Business Act was evidently implemented, resulting in deviating from the Act; despite implementing the core direct connection system, NTT East did not indicate this fact and advertised its communication service as the branching system which was an inferior communication system to the core direct connection system.[11] Consequently, the user tariffs were lower than the actual connection tariffs, and if new entrants who were competitors of NTT East in the retail market had to set tariffs to compete with this company, it would not be possible for their business to be profitable, regardless of the efficiency with which they conduct their business. Based on these facts, the ruling confirmed that other potential operators in the FTTH retail market were effectively excluded.

9. Relevant cases are as follows: Conducts that interfere with the business activities of other operators (*Japan Medical Foods Association* case, Tribunal Decision of JFTC, 8 May 1996, *Shinketsu-shu* 43, 209); Deceptive activities related to the exercise of authority by public institutions (*Paramount Bed* case, Tribunal Decision of JFTC of 31 May 1998, *Shinketsu-shu* 44, 362); Exclusionary private monopolisation by bundling numerous music copyright licenses (*Japanese Society for Rights of Authors, Composers and Publishers [JASRAC]* case, Supreme Court, 28 April 2015, 69-III, *Minshu* 518).
10. The AMA provides for two concepts in regulating dominant firms: private monopolisation and unfair trade practices. Article 2(9) specifies five categories of practice as unfair trade practices, including concerted refusal to deal and resale price maintenance, and Article 2(9)(vi) authorises the JFTC to designate additional prohibited practices.
11. *Commentary on Supreme Court Ruling*, p. 842.

According to the Supreme Court ruling, to determine whether the conducts are regarded as exclusion in terms of private monopolisation, 'it is necessary to find whether independent and unilateral refusal to deal and price cutting, from the perspective of establishing, maintaining, and consolidating their market dominance, constitute artificial method in the sense that such method deviates from the scope of normal means of competition, and whether it is likely to make it significantly difficult for competing companies to enter the FTTH service market'. Thus, the Supreme Court determined that NTT East used their position as the sole supplier in the subscriber optical fibre equipment market to impose economically unreasonable connection conditions on retail competitors and thereby deterring new entries; that the conducts of NTT East were deemed to be an exclusion deviating from the scope of normal methods of competition.

Moreover, the Supreme Court ruling suggests that the conducts of NTT East constitute both unilateral refusal to deal and predatory price cutting. However, the court did not clearly state which of these be designated as a form of illegal conducts. According to the commentary on the ruling (written by a Supreme Court legal officer), NTT East's conducts were supposed to be investigated within the framework of unreasonable refusal to deal.[12] However, the ruling implemented no concrete assessment as to the relevance of refusal to deal, and just concisely described the exclusionary behaviour as an 'artificial method which is beyond the normal method of competition.' The ruling appears to define the anticompetitiveness of the negative spread between the connection and user tariffs as the *combination* of unilateral refusal to deal and predatory price cutting.

In response to this reasoning, NTT East claimed that, based on the branching system calculation, they entered the market on the assumption that they would incur a deficit for the time being, whereas other retail competitors would be able to, despite their high retail prices, appeal to the potential customers using the superior quality of the core direct connection system, thereby ensuring that the competitive conditions were equal and it was not deviating from the 'normal methods of competition'. However, the Supreme Court stated that, during the period in which the demand for FTTH was very low, it was almost impossible that NTT East would provide FTTH services using the branching system; practically only using the core direct connection method was viable at that time. Therefore, the ruling negated the claim of NTT East.

[B] Characterisation of the Illegal Conducts

The nature of the exclusionary conducts in this case can be understood as one pertaining to *margin squeeze*. The Supreme Court ruling describes the conducts of NTT East as 'independent and unilateral refusal to deal and price cutting,' and Commentary on Supreme Court Ruling (pp. 816–817) states that the question of whether to call this a 'price squeeze' is 'simply a terminology issue'. However, the NTT East case caused

12. *Ibid.* p. 818.

much discussion as to whether the conduct pertain to an existing type of illegal conducts or it can be understood as an original type of illegal conduct.[13]

In the *Guidelines for Exclusionary Private Monopolization under the Antimonopoly Act*,[14] JFTC refers to margin squeeze as follows: 'when operators in upstream markets providing necessary products to enable business activities in downstream markets conduct business activities in their own downstream markets', and the 'price of products in the upstream market provided to supplied operators is set to a higher level than the product prices in their own downstream markets or a price such that the supplied operators cannot compete with reasonably economical business activities', this pertains to exclusionary private monopolisation under Article 2 paragraph 5 of the AMA. This can also be judged as relating to exclusion from the same perspective as 'refusal to supply and discriminatory dealing'.

As previously mentioned, the Supreme Court ruling did not discuss this point in detail even though the ruling referred to margin squeeze as a hybrid of refusal to deal and price cutting. In addition, in terms of the standard for illegality, the detailed judgment criterion was not clarified in the ruling, even though the focus remained on the negative spread of upstream and downstream prices. In the next section, we review several cases pertaining to margin squeeze in Europe and the United States from a comparative law perspective.

§6.04 DISCUSSIONS FROM COMPARATIVE LAW PERSPECTIVES

[A] Cases in Europe: Margin Squeeze as Independent Abuse

A typical case of margin squeeze in Europe is one that involved *Deutsche Telekom* (DT).[15] This company set a higher tariff for the connection for subscriber lines in the wholesale markets than the tariff in the retail markets. The focus was on whether the relevant margin (difference between the wholesale price to competitors and their own retail price) was insufficient to cover the relevant costs for the existing operator (DT). The wholesale price set by DT received an ex ante approval from the regulatory authority. However, because DT could apply a price to avoid margin squeeze (higher retail price), competition law was deemed to be applied to this case. The European Court of Justice ruled that margin squeeze is an independent abuse and there is no need to prove that wholesale or retail prices are in themselves abusive. In addition, in this case, the long-run average incremental cost (LRAIC) of the downstream sector of the

13. *See* Noboru Kawahama (2011) "Exclusive Private Monopolisation through Price Squeeze," *Jurist*, no.1419, p. 106 (in Japanese). Kawahama argued that for the purpose of Article 2(5) of the AMA, exclusion cannot be clarified just on the basis of merits or efficiency criterion. He elaborated that exclusion is typically found where an enterprise employs tactics that raise rivals' costs without efficiency-based justification (such as exclusive dealing) or that would not make sense if rivals are not excluded (such as predatory pricing).
14. JFTC released the guidelines in October 2009 in response to the amendment of AMA to introduce administrative fine against private monopolisation in June 2009.
15. *Deutsche Telekom*, European Court C-280/08, Case collection I-9555.

vertically integrated operator (DT) is considered to be the relevant benchmark cost to judge the viability of the retail competitors.

Another salient example of margin squeeze in Europe is the case of *TeliaSonera*.[16] TeliaSonera had a monopoly position in fixed-line local telephone networks in Sweden. The European Court ruled that margin squeeze is in itself capable of constituting an abuse. That is, margin squeeze occurred in Asymmetric Digital Subscriber Line (ADSL) connection service[17] if 'the spread between the wholesale prices for ADSL input services and the retail prices... were either negative or insufficient to cover the specific costs of the ADSL input services which TeliaSonera has to incur in order to supply its own retail services to end users, so that the spread does not allow a competitor which is as efficient as that undertaking to compete for the supply of those services to end users.'

Note that, in the TeliaSonera case, there were no ex ante price regulations at either the wholesale or retail market. In addition, there were no conditions under which a duty was imposed based on the business law to provide connection services at the wholesale stage; further, no consideration was made that the upstream connection services at the wholesale stage were *essential* for the retail service.

Based on the European cases, margin squeeze is defined as an independent, stand-alone abuse setting for both upstream and downstream tariffs by a vertically integrated operator; even though predatory pricing and refusal to deal are recognised to be similar in terms of their effect to margin squeeze,[18] they are strictly separated in terms of their forms of conduct.[19]

[B] Cases in the United States: Priority Application of Business Laws

In the United States, margin squeeze itself is not considered to violate Article 2 of the Sherman Act; this will be examined in terms of either the refusal to deal at the wholesale stage or predatory pricing at the retail stage. In *linkLine* case,[20] Pacific Bell owned a monopoly status over the subscriber line network which was to be used by a DSL service in the retail market. Pacific Bell set a high wholesale price for the subscriber line network to a competing internet DSL service provider, while they simultaneously set a low retail price for their own DSL service to downstream customers.

16. *TeliaSonera Sverige AB*, European Court C-52/09, EuZW, 2011, 339.
17. ADSL is a form of digital subscriber line, which enables faster data transmission over copper telephone lines but much slower than FTTH.
18. The guidance published by the European Commission (Guidance on the Commission's enforcement priorities in applying Article 82 of the EC Treaty to abusive exclusionary conduct by dominant undertakings Report 2009 C45, p. 2) states that margin squeeze can be used in place of refusal to deal, and that it explains the same area as refusal to deal.
19. Refer to Walter Frenz, *Die Kosten-Preis-Schere im Licht aktueller Entwicklungen*, NZKart, 2013, from p. 60. With respect to the standards under which the margin squeeze is regulated based on the EU guidance, the setting of prices in the upstream market that makes it impossible to engage in profitable business activities, even by equally efficient competitors, in the downstream market is considered to be a problem.
20. *Pacific Bell Telephone Co. v. linkLine Communications Inc.*,129 S.Ct.1109 (2009).

The Supreme Court denied *monopolization* that resulted in an infringement of Article 2 of the Sherman Act. Because Pacific Bell did not have a duty to deal with the competitors in the upstream market and because their conducts were not recognised as predatory pricing in the downstream market, the operator did not have a duty to consider margin with their competitors. That is, margin squeeze would not be interpreted as an independent act of infringement under the antitrust law; if a specific business law is preferentially applied to a certain market, it is deemed to be no complementary scope of antitrust liability for business conduct in the market.

The ruling of the Supreme Court in the linkLine case is fundamentally different to that in Europe. The stance of the US Supreme Court is that upstream and downstream markets should be separately considered, and they are not particularly considered to be the conducts of a vertically integrated operator. In the United States, refusal to deal upstream could be illegal only when a duty to trade is apparently stipulated. Further a duty to deal under a sector specific business law is not necessarily a priori taken into account in judging whether refusal to deal is against the US antitrust law. Therefore, wholesale price regulations under a sector specific law would negate a complementary application of the Sherman Act. This view is based on the understanding that, under a sector specific business law, margin squeeze is not likely to be caused by a vertically integrated operator but be triggered by a regulatory authority.[21]

[C] Relation Between the Business Law and the Antimonopoly Law

Margin squeeze is typically caused by the pricing of a vertically integrated operator at both the wholesale and retail stages, and, in many cases, wholesale prices for the services provided by the operator are regulated under the business law. How the regulation of the business law affects the judgment of the antitrust law is related to a wide range of issues where the two types of laws intersect.[22]

In the NTT East case, the Supreme Court found that the MIAC provided administrative guidance on the facility configuration and connection tariffs of the New Family Type; that the MIAC did not favour the connection tariff by NTT East which caused negative spread between wholesale and retail tariffs; and that NTT East had actually maneuvered the imputation rule imposed by the MIAC by the offering of the branching system in appearance but actually the core direct connection system. The Supreme Court clarified that the fact that MIAC had not issued an instruction for the change of facility configuration or the rate revision order for connection tariffs according to the Telecommunications Business Act did not demonstrate that Minister for the MIAC regarded the conducts to be legal under the Antimonopoly Act. The

21. Niamh Dunne, *Margin Squeeze: Theory, Practice, Policy – Part II*, ECLR(2012), p. 66.
22. In Japan, the relationship between the business law and the AMA has been a controversial issue. In the *Osaka Bus Association* case (Tribunal Decision of JFTC, 10 July 1995), for example, JFTC determined that, exempting exceptional circumstances in which the regulations of the business law are hamstrung for some reason, price agreements within the range of illegal fares prohibited under the business law shall, in principle, is contravention of the AMA.

Supreme Court confirmed that the liability of the AMA does not depend on the regulatory judgment under the Telecommunications Business Act.

The ruling suggests that if appropriate regulatory measures under the business law are not undertaken, the regulated firms should not be exempt from the antimonopoly law. In the present case, if the administrative orders and/or guidance of the MIAC worked properly, the negative or insufficient spread between retail price and wholesale price could not happen in the first place; under the ineffective regulatory measures, NTT East had some room for changing tariffs at their own discretion, which can be regarded as the grounds for applying the AMA. In this light, the application of the AMA to this case does not contradict the regulatory obligations taken by NTT East under the Telecommunications Business Act. NTT East is able to apply for the revision of connection tariffs to be permitted by the MIAC and is also allowed to notify the MIAC the rate revision of user tariffs on its own will.

The way of understanding the relation between business law and antimonopoly law in the NTT East case is different from the cases in Europe and the United States. In the United States, competition-related problems which can be resolved by taking measures based on the business law are not within the remit of antitrust law. For example, in *Trinko* case,[23] the US Supreme Court found that Verizon failed to meet its duty to share its network with AT&T customers under the Telecommunication Act. However, the court held that the alleged breach of Verizon's duties by the Telecommunication Act did not state a claim under the Sherman Act. In fact, the conducts of Verizon were examined and resolved through regulatory measures based on the Telecommunication Act. The court reasoned that 'the existence of a regulatory structure designed to deter and remedy anticompetitive harm' is of particular importance to judge the remit of antitrust, even if the regulatory regime becomes a mere façade; the US Supreme Court ruled that the remedial antitrust measures 'beyond the practical ability of a judicial tribunal to control' should be executed primarily by a regulatory agency.

In Europe, even though the objective of both the competition law and the regulatory law is common in terms of promoting competition, each law is subject to an independent legal enforcement mechanism. In addition, the broadly established principle in Europe is that the dominant operators have a *special responsibility*; they have already distorted competition due to their very existence, thereby having a responsibility not to further distort the competition. In DT case, the ruling suggests that the dominant operator bears the responsibility for not causing a margin squeeze when it was possible to adjust at least one side of vertical tariffs, either directly or indirectly through regulatory authorities. That is, the wholesale tariff was already set by the regulatory authorities indicating that it was not freely set by the dominant operator; on the other hand, the price-cap for the retail tariffs continued to decrease over the period

23. *Verizon Communications Inc. v. Law Offices of Curtis V. Trinko*, LLP, 540 U.S. 398 (2004). For existing telecommunications operators, the duty to connect to regional networks for other operators is applied based on Federal Communications Commission's (FCC) regulations; however, in this case, it was judged that refusal of the request from their competitors (AT&T, among others) was not in contravention of Article 2 of the Sherman Act. There is no duty for Verizon to release their infrastructure which is not owned or used by other competitors.

in question; and DT could change the retail price on its own decision with the approval of the regulator but did not do so. The court weighed this fact more heavily as a violation of the competition law than the conformity with the regulatory enforcement.

In the United States, the margin squeeze under regulations of the sector specific regulations shall be primarily subject to the business law; the vertical price structure will not be deemed illegal unless the conducts are predatory or in violation of the duty to deal under the antitrust law. On the other hand, in European Union and Japan, even though their respective rationales are slightly different, many cases are assessed under both the business law and the antimonopoly law in a mutually complementary manner. In other words, even if competitive situation is basically formed by the business law (exempting the cases where all the possible strategic behaviours are dictated by the government or the business law), as long as there is a room for some competition, the competition law could be applied. In the NTT East case, Commentary on Supreme Court Ruling (p. 832) said that the conducts which conform to the Telecommunication Act are not necessarily abide by the AMA, which is consistent to this view. Assuming that they are mutually complementary, it is necessary to contemplate the application of the antimonopoly law from its own perspective which might be different from that of the business law.

§6.05 ECONOMIC ANALYSIS OF THE NTT EAST CASE

[A] Exclusion and Exploitation Through Margin Squeeze

As is shown in the NTT East case, margin squeeze is referred to an action by a dominant upstream provider which is vertically integrated in retail markets. It is a form of predation or vertical foreclosure by setting the combination of high upstream and/or low downstream prices that obstructs downstream competition. Key question here is whether this type of conducts gives rise to a certain anticompetitive effect from the viewpoint of economic theories.

The restraint of competition under the vertical market structure in the NTT East case can fall under either *exclusion* of downstream competitors or *exploitation* where market dominance can be exercised using their upstream monopoly position. As for exclusion, there is a well-known Chicago critique indicating that exclusion of efficient downstream retailers is improbable because a monopolistic upstream operator is able to appropriate downstream profits using wholesale prices; hence it is not a reasonable conduct for the upstream monopolist to exclude efficient downstream operators. However, many economists have clarified the possibility of exclusion as a reasonable conduct of vertically integrated operators (*market foreclosure*).[24] Under a vertical market structure, exclusion can occur in the following cases: (i) exclusion from horizontal markets (*tie-ins/bundling*); (ii) exclusion from vertical markets (*input*

24. *See* Patrick Rey and Thibaud Vergé (2008) "Economics of Vertical Restraints," in Paolo Buccirossi ed., *Handbook of Antitrust Economics*, MIT Press, 353–390 for more comprehensive discussions on vertical restraints.

foreclosure); and (iii) exclusion from adjacent markets.[25] The conducts of the NTT East can be considered as the second case (input foreclosure).

As for exploitative monopolisation (specified as *private monopolisation by control* in Article 3 of the AMA),[26] margin squeeze may provoke substantial restraint of competition through exploitation which means that the vertically integrated companies with upstream bottlenecks exercise their market power to increase the wholesale price, thereby increasing monopoly rent. In the exploitative monopolisation case, efficient downstream competitors are not necessarily excluded; exploitation could be regarded as a typical case of monopoly pricing.[27]

[B] Margin Squeeze and Equally Efficient Competitors Test

As stated in section 4, the EU Guidance tests the anticompetitive effects owing to margin squeeze based on the concept of *equally efficient competitors*; margin squeeze occurs when vertically integrated companies with significant market power provide upstream services to equally efficient downstream competitors but the downstream retailers cannot compete with the integrated service provider. This can be explained using Figure 6.2 showing a typical market structure in which margin squeeze is likely to occur.

Figure 6.2 Exclusion Through Margin Squeeze

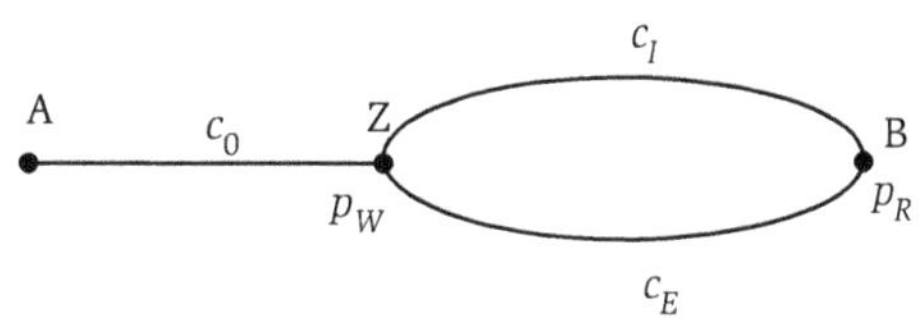

A vertically integrated company (I) provides a communication service from point A to point B. Here, a downstream company (E) aims to enter the market to provide service from relay point Z to B. The downstream company E also aims to provide an end-to-end service from A to B; however, company E need to purchase or borrow a communication line service ranging from A to Z from company I. Assume that the marginal cost of company I from A to Z is c_0 and that from Z to B is c_I and the marginal cost of company E from Z to B is c_E. The wholesale price when company E purchases an upstream service (A to Z) from company I is p_W. Finally, the retail tariff for the retail

25. *See* Bruno Jullien, Patrick Rey, and Claudia Saavedra (2014) "The Economics of Margin Squeeze", *IDEI Report*, Institut D'Economie Industrielle. *Guidelines Concerning Distribution Systems and Business Practices under the Monopoly Act* as of 16 June 2017 by JFTC represent various types of conducts of exclusion, refusal to deal and exploitation as margin squeeze.
26. This concept comes from the Sherman Act and is different from the concept of 'abuse of dominant position'.
27. However, it is not clear from a theoretical point of view the impact that prohibiting margin squeeze has on economic welfare. For example, the restrictions may weaken competition at the retail stage. For details, *see* Jullien et al. *supra*.

customers is p_R. Note that the imputation rule is applied to the upstream company I (like Type 1 Telecommunications Carriers such as NTT East). If the connection tariff is p_W and the user tariff is p_R, the imputation rule is satisfied by $p_R > p_W$. Margin squeeze cannot occur for as long as this condition is satisfied; the positive margin ($p_R - p_W$) is guaranteed to company E.

Broadly adopted benchmark by which to judge rivals' efficiency is of the dominant firm in the downstream market. This is broadly referred to as *equally efficient competitors* test. This criterion reflects the fact that the wholesale price p_W should be lower than the sum of marginal cost c_0 plus the *opportunity cost* for the incumbent firms to offer a connection service to a new entrant. That is, according to the equally efficient competitor test, the connection tariff should be set to satisfy the following condition:

$$p_W < c_0 + (\text{opportunity cost}) = c_0 + (p_R\text{-}c_0\text{-}c_I) = p_R - c_I.$$

The opportunity cost (per unit service) for the existing company I is equivalent to the lost profit (p_R-c_0-c_I).[28] If $c_I > c_E$, company I would set the wholesale price p_W to p_R - c_E rather than p_R - c_I. In this case, the incumbent firm I has no incentive to exclude the efficient downstream competitor E.

In the equally efficient competitors test, the incumbent's downstream marginal cost c_I is referred to *average avoidable cost* of the vertically integrated operator.[29] If this test is passed, margin squeeze will not occur; however, it is hard to verify whether the unit cost c_I of the existing company is efficient without further information. Furthermore, even if the equally efficient competitors test is cleared, it is still possible that the retail price p_R amounts to be exploitative. Thus, the efficiency of retail price (p_R) and the long-run incremental cost (p_R-c_I) should be separately tested according to the vertical market conditions.[30]

To summarise, we should investigate whether the vertical tariff structures facilitate market foreclosure in a situation where there are no regulations on connection tariffs. On the other hand, when there are connection tariff regulations, it is appropriate to use the equally efficient competitors test to evaluate anticompetitive effect. If this test fails to identify the anticompetitive effect of margin squeeze, we should concurrently examine whether the tariff structure is exploitative.

On the connection tariff regulation in the Japanese telecommunication market, the MIAC has adopted the *total element long-run incremental cost rule* instead of the abovementioned criteria of average avoidable cost. This rule is defined as 'a method for calculating costs based on the lowest price and most efficient facilities and technologies

---

28. The rationale behind this EU guidance is essentially the same as the Efficient Component Pricing Rule (ECPR). *See* William Baumol, Janusz Ordover, Frederick Warren-Boulton and Robert Willig (2003), Brief of amici curiae economics professors to U.S. Supreme Court in *Verizon v. Trinko*.
29. Average avoidable cost corresponds to the cost that would not have to be borne if an operator decides to stop providing product or service. Normally, this is equivalent to average variable cost. However, in the long run, in which all inputs can be regarded as variable, the average avoidable costs are equivalent to average total costs. The average avoidable cost in the EU Guidance can be interpreted as based on the idea that sunk costs are not included as part of fixed costs.
30. With this in mind, ECPR only provides a *partial* rule. Baumol et al. *supra*.

that can be used at the current time that is being newly constructed, rather than the actual costs occurring in the network'.[31] If the connection tariffs set by NTT East are based on the cost of 'lowest price and most efficient' technologies, margin squeeze should be possible for as long as a considerably low retail price is set by NTT East (i.e., predatory pricing).

In reality, under the market conditions in which the FTTH service was introduced in eastern Japan, it can be inferred that NTT East really wanted to set low monthly user tariffs to attract customers. That is, there are two main incentives for margin squeeze in this case: (i) 'hunting' for new users via a low user tariff (penetration pricing) and (ii) the exclusion of competitors by setting low prices (predatory pricing). If these circumstances have been sufficiently understood and shared between NTT East and the MIAC, there may have been a larger effort to introduce fine-tuned regulation on connection tariffs, given the penetration of the branching system at that time when an insufficient number of people were available to share a core optic fibre.

[C] Market Definition of Broadband Access Market

Another point of contention in the court and tribunal decisions was whether FTTH service market for residential homes could be regarded as a *particular field of trade* (i.e., the relevant market).[32] For example, the initial JFTC's tribunal decision stated that regarding three types of internet connection services over FTTH, ADSL and cable television (hereinafter 'CATV'), 'it was recognised that the users have common objectives to transmit large volumes of data, each user selects the service among them based on the facilities, services and prices, and it is recognised that each aforementioned service responds in different ways to the individual demands of users'. The tribunal court recognised the FTTH service for residential homes as the relevant market. The Supreme Court confirmed this decision.

However, the substitutability between these services (FTTH, ADSL and CATV) is an empirical issue. Several empirical studies estimating broadband access demand in Japan suggest that it may be difficult to define the FTTH service as an independent market.[33] In Japanese court and tribunal decisions, sufficient attention has not been devoted to the demand structure in terms of defining the relevant markets.

The initial tribunal court decision by the JFTC emphasised the supply side substitutability and stated that 'for the FTTH service, which needs to lay new optical fibre facilities, a gap exists in terms of the time and cost required to start provision of

---

31. The Ministry of Posts and Telecoms (current MIAC), *Report on Total Element Long-run Incremental Cost Model*, 20 September 1999.
32. Defining a *particular field of trade* is a statutory requirement in Article 2(5) of the AMA.
33. *See* Takanori Ida and Toshifumi Kuroda (2006) "Discrete Choice Analysis of Demand for Broadband in Japan," *Journal of Regulatory Economics* 29, 5–22, Mitsuru Sunada, Masato Noguchi, Hiroshi Ohashi, and Yosuke Okada (2011) "Coverage Area Expansion, Customer Switching, and Household Profiles in the Japanese Broadband Access Market," *Information Economics and Policy* 23, 12-23. These studies suggest that the various broadband services of FTTH, ADSL and CATV are regarded as substitutes, and strongly so between FTTH for residential areas and high-speed ADSL.

a service, compared to ADSL and CATV internet access using existing telephone lines (metal lines) and TV networks'. Therefore the court ruled that the substitutability on the supply side is low. However, it is worth noting that the supply side issues relate to investment incentives, thus we need to explore a dynamic *facility based* competition between NTT East, TEPCO and USEN Broad, as is mentioned in section 2. There are various factors that affect the investment incentives, not least regulatory rules of connection charges having a major effect on future investment decisions. In the NTT East case, we should evaluate the exclusionary effect from the viewpoint of not only competition through resale/mixed-bundling but also facility-based competition.

§6.06 CONCLUSION

The NTT East case is the first ruling by the Supreme Court on whether refusal to deal with competitors constitutes exclusionary private monopolisation. In the ruling, there was no explicit examination about the statutory requirements of refusal to deal; instead, the focus was on the existence of anticompetitive conducts evoked by 'artificial method beyond the normal method of competition'. It is rather difficult to state at this moment that clear legal standards have been presented by this ruling; the Supreme Court ruling stated that the conducts constituting margin squeeze are considered as a hybrid of refusal to deal and predation. Note that the regulation of connection tariffs strongly defined the characteristics of the NTT East's conduct in this case. Furthermore, we should also note that the equally efficient competitors test does not, in itself, clarify the extent of exploitation of the vertical tariff structure.

CHAPTER 7

The 'Car Wash Operation' in Brazil: Challenges and Perspectives in the Fight Against Bid Rigging

Paulo Burnier da Silveira & Victor Oliveira Fernandes[*]

§7.01 INTRODUCTION

In the last decade, the fight against bid rigging has become a priority under the Brazilian competition enforcement.[1] The new Competition Law (Law no. 12,529/11) has clarified that companies involved in public procurement crimes would be eligible for Leniency Programmes, which has enhanced the incentives of violators to admit participation in bid rigging schemes.[2] The Brazilian competition authority (Portuguese acronym 'CADE') has also created a special unity for bid rigging investigations and a

* The views expressed in this chapter are personal and do not reflect those of the organizations involved.

1. This was recently recognized in the OECD's 2019 Peer Reviews of Competition Law and Policy: '*the prosecution of bid rigging in public procurement has long been a priority for Brazil's competition authorities*'. Organisation for Economic Co-operation and Development, OECD PEER REVIEWS OF COMPETITION LAW AND POLICY: BRAZIL 184 10 (2019), available at: www.oecd.org/daf/competition/oecd-peer-reviews-of-competition-law-and- policy-brazil-2019.htm.
2. This change in the legal framework was intentionally designed to address an uncertainty about the scope of competition law leniency programs in Brazil. As explained by Paulo L. Casagrande: '*there was a significant doubt about whether the leniency applicant could obtain immunity related to the crime of 'fraud to competition in public procurement proceeding' – provided for in art. 90 of the Public Procurement Law. This is because such crime was not mentioned in the leniency rules of the previous antitrust statute*'. Paulo L Casagrande, *Brazilian Antitrust Policy Towards Bid Rigging: History and Perspectives*, COMPET. POLICY INT., 4 (2018). The 2015 CADE's Antitrust Leniency Program Guidelines expressly provide that Leniency Agreements apply to antitrust conspiracies aimed to affect '*prices, conditions, advantages, or refraining from participating in a public bidding*'. Administrative Council for Economic Defense, CADE GUIDELINES ANTITRUST LENIENCY PROGRAM 1–60 10 (2015).

screening laboratory (so-called CADE's *Cerebro Project*) to detect cartels through data-mining of public procurement databases.[3]

Bid rigging prosecution address the widely known negative effects of these practices, such as the enormous wastes of public funds and the diminishing of public confidence in the competitive process and in the government. Those effects are even more harmful in developing economies such as Brazil, where the strict control of public expenditure still remains a key factor for sustaining the domestic economy.

Despite all the accomplishments in bid rigging fighting, there is an undisputed understanding that conventional antitrust are constantly being challenged by increasingly complex schemes worldwide. As recently pointed out by Anderson, Jones and Kovacic, while competition law enforcement remains critical in this field, there is an inevitable trade-off between refining corrective measures needed to deter corruption or implementing tools to avoid supplier collusions.[4] The risks of over-reliance on leniency regimes and sub-optimal cartel detection must also be taken into account by competition agencies. Moreover, cooperations with other national agencies with jurisdiction over corruption in public procurement remains a paramount for antitrust enforcers.

The challenges faced by CADE in the fight against bid rigging have become exponential in the context of the world-famous 'Car Wash' investigation, the largest corruption scheme uncovered in Latin America. This chapter addresses the key competition aspects of this investigation. First, the chapter describes the inception of the investigations with preliminary investigations into a minor money laundering suspicion in 2013. The chapter then analyses two major challenges to competition policy emerging from car wash investigations: (i) the need to align the incentives of multiple leniency systems and (ii) the importance of better defining the benefits resulting from the adoption of compliance programmes antitrust. Finally, the chapter sets out the likely future implications of these investigations, in particular in relation to public government procurement in Brazil and certain positive externalities to other Latin American economies.

§7.02 INCEPTION

The 'Car Wash' (or '*Lava-Jato*' in Portuguese) operation consists in a set of ongoing investigations in Brazil, covering a wide range of topics that include corruption, money laundering and competition issues. It started in 2013 with a preliminary investigation into a minor money laundering suspicion. The name 'Car Wash' was given because the investigation began focusing at a small office of foreign currency exchange and money

3. For a description of how CADE has been using screens for public procurement data analysis, *see* Lucas F. Roquete & Felipe L. V. Silva, *The use of screens to prevent and detect bid rigging in public procurement – Contribution from Brazil*, PROMOT. EFF. COMPET. PUBLIC PROCUREMENT. LAT. AM. CARIBB. COMPET. FORUM. 4 (2016).
4. Robert D. Anderson, Alison Jones & William E. Kovacic, *Preventing Corruption, Supplier Collusion and the Corrosion of Civic Trust: A Procompetitive Program to Improve the Effectiveness and Legitimacy of Public Procurement*, KING'S COLL. LONDON LAW SCH. RES. PAP. NO. 19-14 (2019). The paper discusses ways in which the effectiveness of the conventional tools used in bid rigging enforcement can be strengthened.

transfer services located at a gas station in Brasilia, which also provided car wash services for its customers. The initial phase of the investigation aimed to uncover illicit payments and foreign transfers operated by this office in Brasilia.

In March 2014, through lawful telephone and e-mail interceptions, a first corruption flag was identified when it was uncovered that one of the main persons under investigation for money laundering had apparently given an expensive, imported automobile to a senior director of Petrobras, the Brazilian state-owned company. This development, later confirmed through criminal plea bargain agreements in 2014, marked the first shift from a small financial investigation to a wider money laundering and possible corruption scheme investigation. The possible corruption scheme included politicians appointing key persons to senior positions at Petrobras, and those persons, in turn, supposedly serving as intermediaries in bribe negotiations. The bribes consisted of a certain 'commission' in government contracts that would later serve to finance certain political parties, including for campaigning purposes. In addition, the investigation uncovered signs that certain construction companies were colluding during public tenders to divide the market and raise both their profits and the corresponding bribes to politicians.

In total, the investigations targeted four groups that could have been involved in these schemes: financial operators, managers at Petrobras, politicians and businessmen mainly from the construction industry.

§7.03 COMPETITION SCOPE

As mentioned earlier, although the 'Car Wash' operation was not originally related to competition issues, the investigations suggested that construction companies were colluding to divide markets and fix prices in several government procurements. This explains the involvement of the Brazilian Competition Authority (CADE) in the investigations carried out by different government bodies, including the Public Prosecutor's Office, the Comptroller General's Office and CADE itself.

In 2016, the CADE announced that it was investigating more than thirty alleged cartels arising from the 'Car Wash' investigations. At a first stage of investigations, constructions companies were accused of bid rigging in oil and gas related markets, such as the construction of power plants. Petrobras argued that it was a victim of cartels among constructions companies as they had divided markets and fixed prices. At a second moment, the investigations lead to other construction projects. Notable examples concern the construction of football stadiums and railroads – all of them with significant public investments and wide public interest, relating to both the planning of the 2014 Fédération Internationale de Football Association (FIFA) World Cup in Brazil and the 2016 Olympic Games in Rio de Janeiro.

[A] Increase of National Leniency Applications

The 'Car Wash' operation is responsible for the significant increase in CADE's numbers of leniency applications in the past years in Brazil. More than forty-two leniency agreements were signed in 2015–2017, which corresponds to approximately half of the total number of the leniency agreements ever signed by CADE since the first one in 2003 (Figure 7.1).

Figure 7.1 Leniency Agreements in Brazil

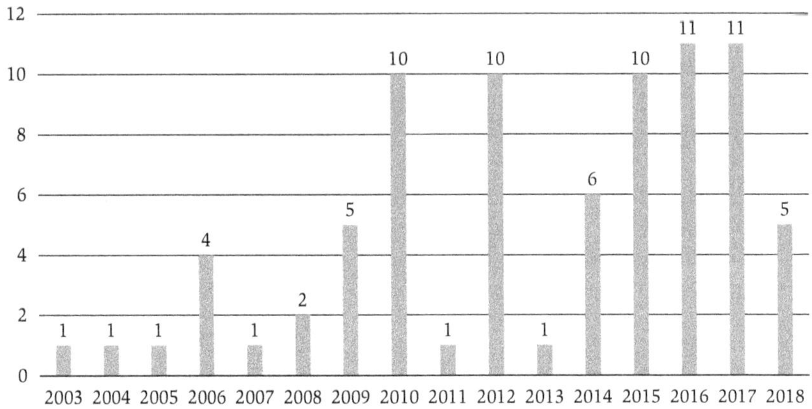

Source: CADE.

CADE has reached the mark of eighty leniency agreements in its sixteen years history of the leniency programme for cartel enforcement. More than half of these leniency agreements were signed in the past five years largely due to 'Car Wash' investigations. The numbers above include only the first-in applicants, as subsequent applicants may apply for settlements, but not for leniency in Brazil. The leniency programme may grant full immunity in both administrative and criminal matters, whereas the settlements programme only allows for a fine reduction. The numbers include neither leniency plus agreements nor additions to the main leniency agreements. This has strongly changed the trend of leniency policy in Brazil, which was much related to international cartels in its first years. Nowadays, national cartels represent approximately 2/3 of CADE's marker requests.[5]

Consequently, requests for settlements have also reached record levels in Brazil. In November 2018, the first set of settlements were concluded with CADE and led to a pecuniary contribution of approximately EUR 200 million, which will be paid by four construction companies. The companies have admitted participation in cartels for public construction, including contracts to build railways, a major nuclear power plant and soccer stadiums used for the 2014 FIFA World Cup. In addition, companies are also committed to collaborate during the investigations with evidences, further clarification or other means necessary to the understanding of the illegal scheme.

5. Amanda Athayde & Marcela Fernandes. 'A glimpse into Brazil's experience in international cartel investigations: Legal framework, investigatory powers and recent developments in leniency and settlements policy'. *Revue Concurrences*. Paris, 2016.

[B] Cooperation Between Investigation Bodies

The Car Wash Operation reinforces the notion that cooperation between national enforcement agencies with jurisdiction over collusion and corruption in public procurement is a paramount to provide an efficient enforcement.[6] In the years following the beginning of the investigation, some reforms in the anti-corruption and criminal legal framework have imposed an indispensable dialogue between these policy fields.[7]

In August 2013, right after Car Wash scandal was disclosure, a new Brazilian Anticorruption-law (Law no. 12,846 of 2013) was adopted. This legislation provided a legal regime for administrative and civil responsibility of private entities for anti-competitive acts of bribery.[8] In what concerns to public bids and contracts, the new legislation considered illegal[9]:

(i) to frustrate or defraud, by means of collusion or any other expedient, the competitive nature of a public bid;
(ii) to prevent, hinder or defraud the performance of any act within the scope of a public bid;
(iii) to remove or seek the removal of a bidder, by means of a fraud or by offering advantage of any kind; and
(iv) to defraud a public bid or the contract resulting thereof.

The Anti-Corruption Law was vividly inspired in the Competition Law, in at least two aspects. First, the new legislation has granted to a centralized agency, the Brazilian Comptroller General (*Controladoria Geral da União* - CGU), the power to initiate administrative proceedings against private entities when the acts are possibly carried out against a Federal public body. Second, the new legislation has allowed public bodies to engage in Leniency Agreements with private entities responsible for anti-corruption acts - the so-called Anti-*Corruption Leniency Agreements*. As pointed out by N. Monebhurrun, the leniency programmes as a legal tool originally pertaining to the competition law sphere 'has thus been used as a model and its logic and spirit have been efficiently transposed to the anti-corruption field'.[10]

6. The need to endorse formal cooperating between these agencies through formal mechanisms of evidence-sharing was long recognized. OECD, POLICY ROUNDTABLES: COLLUSION AND CORRUPTION IN PUBLIC PROCUREMENT 509 11 (2010).
7. Douglas Costa Ribeiro, Néfi Cordeiro & Denis Alves Guimarães, *Interface between the Brazilian Antitrust, Anti-corruption, and Criminal Organization Laws: The Leniency Agreements*, 22 LAW BUS. REV. AM. 195–244, 103 (2016). (arguing that '*the emergence of Operation Car Wash (operação lava jato) as one of the biggest corruption scandals of all time has called attention to the interface between the antitrust and anti-corruption leniency regimes*').
8. For a comprehensive analysis of these provisions, see Ribeiro, Cordeiro, and Guimarães, *supra* note 7.
9. Law no. 12,846/2013, Article 5.
10. Nitish Monebhurrun, *Fighting Corruption and Promoting Competition in Brazil, in* INTERNATIONAL COOPERATION AND COMPETITION ENFORCEMENT: BRAZILIAN AND EUROPEAN EXPERIENCES FROM THE ENFORCERS' PERSPECTIVE. CARVALHO, V. M. (EDITORS) RAGAZZO, C. E. J. E SILVEIRA, P. B., 84 (2014).

The anti-corruption leniency agreement can grant firms up to 2/3 reduction in the applicable pecuniary penalty,[11] which can range from 0.1% to 20% of the gross revenues earned in the financial year preceding the financial year in which the administrative proceeding was commenced, excluding taxes, which penalty fine shall never be less than the advantage obtained, whenever such advantage may be estimated.[12] The agreement can also immunize alternative non-pecuniary penalties, such as the prohibition of receiving incentives, subsidies, grants, donations or loans from public agencies or entities and public financial institutions or from financial institutions controlled by the government, for a minimum period of one and a maximum period of five years.[13]

Besides the new Brazilian Anticorruption-law (Law no. 12,846 of 13), also in August 2013 it adopted a new Organized Crime Law (Law no. 12,850 of 2013). This legislation provided a third leniency regime – the so-called *Criminal Leniency.*[14] There is no consensus among the commentators on whether criminal leniency could cover crimes unrelated to the formation of criminal organizations. The Public Prosecution Office is using this tool to address several crimes possibly related to bid rigging violations, such as the crimes described in the Public Procurement Law (Law no. 8,666 of 1993) and in the Economic Crimes Law (Law no. 8,137 of 1990), including cartel crimes.

During the five years of Car Wash operation, the Federal Public Prosecution Office has already executed 183 criminal leniency agreements.[15] Most of them are related to infringements which are also investigated by antitrust and anti-corruption agencies. It is clear that the Public Prosecution Office and the Police Chief Investigators have the power to execute leniency agreements in a much broader range of activities than CADE and CGU.[16]

The coexistence of antitrust, anti-corruption and criminal law regimes improves bid rigging enforcement, as it significantly increases the chances of detection and punishment of such practices.

There are, however, relevant at least two institutional challenges emerging from the coexistence of these three regimes. This multiple punishment system inevitably requires (i) an alignment of the incentives of the leniency regimes and (ii) an improvement of cooperation between the enforcers agencies.

Regarding the incentives of leniency regimes, one should bear in mind that decisions of economic agents to disclose and collaborate with investigations are determined by the legal incentives derived from the multiple available regimes considered together and not in isolation. The absence of coordinated forms of leniency

11. Law no. 12,846/2013, Article 16.
12. Law no. 12,846/2013, Article 6, I.
13. Law no. 12,846/2013, Article 19, V.
14. In fact, several previous Brazilian criminal laws already regulated the use of leniency agreements. However, Law no. 12,850 in 2013 has brought significant advances in the use of leniency in combating economic crime.
15. These data are available at: https://exame.abril.com.br/brasil/cinco-anos-da-lava-jato-os-resultados-e-desafios-da-operacao/.
16. Ribeiro, Cordeiro, and Guimarães, *supra* note 7 at 144.

can lessen the incentives to collaborate with the authorities. As Luz and Spagnolo point out: 'the involvement of multiple authorities in leniency cases makes it difficult to limit disclosures and to preserve privileges, thus reducing the effectiveness of existing leniency provisions in inducing whistleblowing'.[17]

The main weakness of the multiple leniency system in Brazil seems to derive from the fact that lenient applicants in competition law and anti-corruption spheres can remain exposed to criminal sanctions even if they engage in full collaboration with CGU or CADE. The Anti-corruption leniency agreements are applicable only to firms and not to individuals. It also does not grant any criminal immunity. This shifts the incentives of the firms to negotiate leniency agreements with CGU, as the evidence brought by the applicant firm in an anti-corruption leniency may expose the involved individuals to criminal sanctions. As the new anti-corruption law did not provide for penalties applicable to individuals, it was presumed that individuals could not benefit from the leniency agreements entered into with the CGU. However, as Ribeiro, Cordeiro and Guimarães explain 'there is no doubt that when a company negotiates a leniency agreement, it is providing authorities evidence of corrupt acts performed by individuals'.[18] This lack of criminal immunization, therefore, can undermine the effect of the Brazilian Anti-corruption Law on wrongdoers' incentives to blow the whistle.[19]

Contrary to the Anti-Corruption Law, the Antitrust Leniency clearly grants criminal immunization, but the extension of this immunization is puzzling. The Antitrust Law provides that leniency grant criminal immunity for Crimes Against the Economic Order (defined by the Law no. 8,137 of 1990), and for other crimes 'directly related to cartel practice', such as the ones defined by the Public Procurement Law (Law no. 8,666 of 1993) and the Criminal Code (Decreto-Lei no. 2,848 of 1940).[20]

Nevertheless, there is no strong consensus as to what the term 'related crimes' actually means. Martinez and Tavares explain that, although the law does not appear to be exhaustive in defining the crimes that may be immunized by the agreement, 'some prosecutors have already stated that a leniency letter signed with CADE may only protect leniency recipients from criminal conviction regarding the offenses explicitly mentioned by the law'.[21] Others commentators such as Athayde and De Granis argue that the antitrust leniency agreement covers all criminal offenses 'that represent a normal prior or necessary to the formation of the cartel'.[22]

In order to ensure greater legal certainty, the antitrust leniency agreements signed with CADE in the car wash operation started to provide for a specific clause that establishes the scope of criminal immunity. Clause 7.9 makes it clear that the benefits of the agreement do not apply 'to crimes not directly related to cartel practice, such as

17. Reinaldo Diogo Luz & Giancarlo Spagnolo, Leniency, collusion, corruption, and whistleblowing Journal of Competition Law and Economics (2017).
18. Ribeiro, Cordeiro, and Guimarães, *supra* note 7 at 171.
19. Luz and Spagnolo, *supra* note 17 at 746.
20. Law no. 12,846/2013, Article 87.
21. Mariana Tavares de Martinez & Ana Paula Araújo, *Anti-cartel Enforcement in Brazil: Status Quo & Trends*, *in* Overview of Competition Law in Brazil 257–274, 12 (2015).
22. Amanda Athayde & Rodrigo De Grandis, *Programa de Leniência Antitruste e Repercussões Criminais: Desafios e Oportunidades Recentes*, *in* A Lei 12.529/2011 e a Nova Política de Defesa da Concorrência 287–304, 293 (2015).

the crimes of corruption and money laundering, although related to the cartel offenses covered by the agreement'.[23]

The provision of this clause in leniency agreements helps to undo misunderstandings in the interpretation of legislation. However, balancing the incentive structure of multiple leniency systems remains a clear challenge to antitrust policy.

[C] Proliferation of Compliance Programmes

Another great effect of the Car Wash operation in Brazil and likely in Latin American countries is a revolution on compliance corporate programmes. Companies have realized that prevention is the best medication. This has increased the demand for compliance assistance services as well as discussions on if and how should compliance programmes be taken into consideration by competition authorities. As professor Vicente Bagnoli has explored, Car Wash investigation has become a 'true turning point of corporate culture in Brazil'.[24]

Even though in the past some initiatives aimed at encouraging the adoption of competition law compliance programmes have taken place,[25] it was only after the Anti-Corruption Law was edited that the incentives of adopting compliance programmes both for antitrust and anticorruption proposes became evident.[26] Although the Brazilian Competition Law does not contain specific provisions on compliance programmes, CADE published in 2016 the 'Guidelines on the structuring and benefits of adopting competition compliance programs'.[27] These Guidelines have established non-binding instructions for these programmes and have clarified the advantages of implementing them.

As it occurs in other jurisdictions, under Brazilian Competition Law there is still much controversy about whether companies which have adopted a compliance programme should be granted antitrust immunity or a reduction in the fine for antitrust infringements. As S. Frubing and K. Huschlrath point out that 'it becomes apparent that competition authorities have different opinions (or possibilities set by law, respectively) on whether to allow fine reductions for the (ex-ante and ex-post)

23. This scope of this clause is discussed at Eduardo Frade, Diogo Thomson & Amanda Athayde Martins Linhares, *A Operação Lava Jato e a Investigação de Cartéis no Brasil: Evolução ou Revolução?*, *in* A REVOLUÇÃO DO ANTITRUSTE NO BRASIL. CESAR MATTOS (ORG.) 223-254 (2018).
24. Vicente Bagnoli, *Business strategies to improve antitrust compliance in Brazil and the approach of CADE to advocacy: the Car Wash Investigation*, 33-34 REV. CONCORRÊNCIA E REGULAÇÃO 299-304, 299 (2018).
25. The aim of improving the enforcement of competition law thought encouraging the adoption of compliance programs was first addressed in Brazilian Competition Law in 2004, when the former Secretariat of Economic Law (SDE) of the Ministry of Justice issued the Resolution 14/2004.
26. Paulo Burnier da Silveira & Victor Oliveira Fernandes, *Compliance Concorrencial*, *in* MANUAL DE COMPLIANCE 463-476, 465 (2018).
27. Brazil, GUIDELINES COMPETITION COMPLIANCE PROGRAMS 42 (2016).

implementation of a CLCP or not'.[28] The so-called 'main jurisdictions' seems to be still reluctant in rewarding compliance programmes with fine reductions.[29]

In Brazil, this controversy has been addressed, at least in part, in the context of Car Wash investigations. Under the Brazilian competition law, the question of whether the antitrust watchdog is authorized to grant fines reductions is puzzling. The 2016 CADE's Compliance Guidelines points out that 'the mere existence of compliance programs is not sufficient to hinder the application of administrative fines'. It states notwithstanding that CADE's Tribunal might take compliance programmes as a signal of companies' good faith under the criteria provided for in Article 45 of the Law no. 12,529/11, which can lead to lower antitrust fines.[30] In the same vein, the Guidelines for Cease and Desist Agreement for Cartel Cases assess compliance programmes as a mitigating circumstance in the calculation of the pecuniary contribution.[31]

It is not clear, however, whether the CADE's Guidelines allows fines reductions for the simple commitment of the firms to adopt *ex-post* compliance programmes in the future. Under the 2016 CADE's Compliance Guidelines, to be eligible for such benefit, companies must prove that its compliance programme meets all the requirements listed in section 3.2 of the Guideline. It means that the compliance programmes should involve a genuine commitment of the governing bodies with the programme, and it should have the appropriate resources and independence; it should be preceded and followed by risk analysis, it should be well monitored and documented and it should be continuously reviewed. The simple task of checking these high-standard requirements however might be unsuited with the mere commitment of the firms to adopt a compliance programme in the future.

In settlement agreements policy, the Guidelines for Cease and Desist Agreement for Cartel Cases explains that eligible compliance programme should be before the infringement and that it should be directly related to the decision to propose a settlement or to the cooperation within the scope of the agreement.[32] This last provision opens the possibility of grating benefits due to the further implementation of compliance programmes. Nevertheless, this option seems to remain limited to cartel investigations in which the parties agree to collaborate with the ongoing investigation. It means that fines reductions for future adoption of compliance programmes may not

28. Stefan Frübing & Kai Hüschelrath, *Competition Law Compliance Programmes: A Law and Economics Perspective, in* PAHA, JOHANNES. COMPETITION LAW COMPLIANCE PROGRAMMES: AN INTERDISCIPLINARY APPROACH., 26 (2016).
29. In the United States, the Department of Justice (DoJ) has been very restrictive in giving fine reductions for the implementation of competition law compliance programs, even though the US Sentencing Guidelines expressly authorizes this fine reduction. In Europe, even though the European Commission has granted those benefits in remote cases, since 2001, the authority has been standing that strong compliance programs should be seen as part of regular order and no reward should be granted to companies for the simple fact of having these measures in place. For an compressive analysis, see Nathalie Jalabert-doury et al., *Enforcers 'Consideration of Compliance Programs in Europe: A Long and Winding – but Increasingly Interesting – Road'*, 2015 (2015).
30. Brazil, *supra* note 27 at 41.
31. Brazil, GUIDELINES CEASE AND DESIST AGREEMENT FOR CARTEL CASES 53 30 (2016).
32. *Id.* at 30.

be guaranteed in monopolization practices investigations or in 'pay-to-go' settlement agreements.

Despite the lack of clarity in the CADE's procedures and Guidelines, since the release of 2016 Compliance Guideline, the authority has signed up to twenty-three Cease and Desists Agreements in which companies have agreed to implement *ex-post* Compliance Programmes. These cases are summarized in the Table 7.1. In most of them, CADE has not disclosed to which extend the commitment of adopting compliance programmes has reduced the pecuniary contributions.

Table 7.1 Cease and Desist Agreements with the Commitment to Adopt Compliance Programmes in CADE's Case Law from January 2016 to January 2019

	Requirement	*Firms*	*Antitrust Investigation*	*Settlement Date*
1	Requirements nos. 08700.001200/2016-70, 08700.007539/2016-80, 08700.007859/2016-30, 08700.007862/2016-53, 08700.007863/2016-06, 08700.007864/2016-42, 08700.007865/2016-97, 08700.007866/2016-31, 08700.007868/2016-21, and 08700.007869/2016-75	Sindicato dos Estabelecimentos de Serviços de Saúde do Estado do Espírito Santo (SINDHES) and others	Collective negotiation of prices and contractual conditions practiced by SINDHES and hospitals in the face of operators of health plans in the state of Espírito Santo.	06/07/2017
2	Requirement no. 08700.004602/2016-26 (0318671)	Elson Cascão, Luis Imbriosi Filho, Antônio José Matias De Souza, Laudenor De Souza Limeira, Cascol Combustíveis Para Veículos Ltda.	Cartel in the markets of distribution and resale of liquid fuels of the Federal District.	04/05/2017
3	Requirement de TCC no. 08700.003071/201735 (0380739)	Sindicato do Comércio Varejista de Derivados de Petróleo do Estado de Minas Gerais – Minaspetro	Cartel in the market of resale of liquid fuels in Minas Gerais.	09/06/2017
4	Requirement de TCC no. 08700.005133/2017-43	Requerentes: Conselho Federal de Corretores de Imóveis (Cofeci) and others	Influence of uniform commercial conduct on the real estate brokerage services market in Brazil.	03/14/2018

	Requirement	*Firms*	*Antitrust Investigation*	*Settlement Date*
5	Requirement no. 08700.005312/2017-81	Sofape Fabricantes de Filtros Ltda. ('Sofape')	Cartel in the national market of automotive aftermarket filter ('aftermarket' or 'IAM').	08/08/2018
6	Requirement no. 08700.005349/2017-17	Jorge Zandoná, Elias Antônio Piva, AM Combustíveis Ltda., Posto JA Ltda., Posto LC Ltda. Posto Zandoná Ltda., Posto Z10 Ltda.	Cartel in the market of resale of liquid fuels in Joinville-SC.	04/25/2018
7	Requirement no. 08700.003794/2018-15	Sindicato das Empresas de Compra, Venda, Locação e Administração de Imóveis e dos Condomínios Horizontais, Verticais e de Edifícios Residenciais e Comerciais no Estado de Goiás - Secovi-Go	Influence of uniform commercial conduct on the real estate brokerage services market in Brazil.	09/19/2018
8	Requirement no. 08700.004337/2016-86	Construtora Norberto Odebrecht S.A., João Antônio and others	Cartel in the market of services of engineering, construction and industrial assembly 'onshore', in Brazil, in invitations to bid realized by Petrobras.	11/21/2018
9	Requirement no. 08700.004341/2016-44	Construtora Norberto Odebrecht S.A., Adolfo de Aguiar Braid, Fábio Andreani Gandolfo e Henrique Pessoa Mendes Neto	Cartel in the market of works of assembly electronuclear of the Angra 3 Plant in bid of Eletrobrás Termonuclear S.A. - Eletronuclear.	11/21/2018

	Requirement	*Firms*	*Antitrust Investigation*	*Settlement Date*
10	Requirement no. 08700.005078/2016-19	Construtora Norberto Odebrecht S.A., João Antônio Pacífico Ferreira, Pedro Augusto Carneiro Leão Neto e Ricardo Roth Ferraz de Oliveira	Cartel in the market for civil works of infrastructure and railway superstructure, special works of art and engineering services for the implementation of Railways tendered by Valec - Engenharia, Construções e Ferrovias S.A. ('Valec').	11/21/2018
11	Requirement no. 08700.007077/2016-09	Construtora Norberto Odebrecht S.A., Odebrecht Engenharia e Construção Internacional S.A. e Odebrecht Participações e Investimentos S.A.	Cartel in the national market for construction works, modernization and/or renovation of sports facilities ('football stadiums') for the 2014 World Cup in Brazil ('World Cup').	11/21/2018
12	Requirement no. 08700.008158/2016-18	Construtora Norberto Odebrecht S.A e Carlos José Vieira Machado da Cunha	Cartel in a bidding process for the company Petróleo Brasileiro S.A. - Petrobras for the contracting of engineering and civil construction services of 'Large Porte Buildings with Special Characteristics'.	11/21/2018
13	Requirement no. 08700.008159/2016-62	Construtora Norberto Odebrecht S.A.	Cartel in public bids for engineering and construction services for the Complexo do Alemão, Manguinhos Complex and Rocinha Community in Rio de Janeiro/RJ ('PAC - Favelas').	11/21/2018

	Requirement	*Firms*	*Antitrust Investigation*	*Settlement Date*
14	Requirement no. 08700.003188/2018-08	Sindicato das Empresas de Transportes de Carga de São Paulo (SETCESP)	Sham litigation and price discrimination in the national markets for receipt, transport and delivery of correspondences and express orders.	01/30/2019

Source: Prepared by the authors.

It was only in six agreements, all of those related to the so-called 'Car Wash Investigation,' that CADE has explicitly granted from 2% to 4% of the reduction in the pecuniary contributions that the companies were obligated to pay. The authority has acknowledged that the reductions for the adoption of compliance programmes shall not be higher than those conceded due to the provision of documents that prove violations. Also, CADE's decisions have considered that this maximum percentage was in line with the discounts applied by the Federal Comptroller General's Office in the execution of Leniency Agreements disciplined by Law no. 12,846/2013, regulated by Decree no. 8,420/2015.[33]

Even though it is undisputed the relevance of compliance programmes to enhance competition law enforcement, there is still much controversy about whether companies which have adopted a compliance programme should be granted antitrust immunity or a reduction in the fine for antitrust infringements.[34] In that sense, it is not clear if the discounts granted to the firms investigated in the Car Wash operation represent an exception or a new paradigm in CADE's compliance programmes policy. This discussion shows up a real policy trade-off between, on the one hand, a strict liability regime that fails to reward the existence of effective programmes and, on the other hand, an absolute negligence regime that may end up underestimating the risks of palliative compliance programmes.[35]

33. For all, see Requeriment n° 08700.008159/2016-62.
34. In recent years, conflicting proposals raised in the literature. The most important arguments that support each one of these policies regimes are acknowledged by the distinguishing scholars Wouter P.J. Wils and Damien Geradin. Wouter Wils argues that compliance programs should not be considered as a mitigating factor for reducing the amount of antitrust fines because it would raise the companies' incentives to set out those programs with the sole proposal of receiving lower penalties. Wouter P.J. Wils, *Antitrust Compliance Programmes & Optimal Antitrust Enforcement*, 1 J. ANTITRUST ENFORC. (2013). On the other hand, Damien Geradin that competition authorities are able to evaluate compliance programs in an objective way and without incurring excessive costs, as these authorities typically collect a large amount of market information, including information on the culture and values of companies and on the circumstances leading to antitrust infringements. Damien Geradin, *Antitrust compliance programmes and optimal antitrust enforcement: A reply to Wouter Wils*, 1 J. ANTITRUST ENFORC. 325–346 (2013).
35. Anne Riley & Daniel D. Sokol, *Rethinking compliance*, 3 J. ANTITRUST ENFORC. 31–57, 39 (2015).

§7.04 FINAL REMARKS

The 'Car Wash' investigations have caused a significant effect in cartel enforcement in Brazil. The investigations have highlighted the importance of leniency programmes to detect cartels. They have also captivated the attention of a greater audience, including the business community, political stakeholders and consumers, as high-profile cases were reported by both specialized and general press. In addition, the 'Car Wash' operation has had a regional effect on neighbouring countries. Some of these countries have already initiated related investigations based on facts and allegations that surfaced during the 'Car Wash' investigations, including bid rigging and corruption allegations.

Another effect of 'Car Wash' cases is the investment on compliance programmes. Companies are now more aware that prevention is better than cure, as cartel sanctions often include hefty fines. In Brazil, CADE has attempted to encourage and support the compliance efforts by the private sector. CADE considers that a neutral and comprehensive competitive environment is the utmost goal of competition authorities. One concrete example of this effort is the Guidelines on Compliance Programmes published in 2016 by CADE in both Portuguese and English.

The success of leniency programmes powered by the 'Car Wash' cases has also led to new challenges. The main point of concern is the need for internal cooperation with other investigative bodies, including the Public Prosecutor's Office, the Comptroller General's Office and the Court of Accounts. These are the institutions with jurisdiction to investigate certain aspects of the illegal practices at issue, such as fraud on tender proceedings and corruption allegations. Recently, leniency instruments have been introduced in these institutions to serve as additional enforcement tools. This creates the possibility of having multiple leniency applications among different investigative bodies, which highlights the need for cooperation between CADE and these institutions.

In conclusion, the 'Car Wash' investigations have transformed the way leniency agreements are perceived in Brazil. The investigations have also fostered significant support for the fight against cartels, in particular bid rigging. Follow-up damages claims will also increase, which will require careful legal treatment of documents in order to preserve the proper incentives for future leniency applications. The full effect of these investigations is yet to be determined but certain benefits are already widely observed.

CHAPTER 8

Anti-competitive Practices in the Context of Public Tenders: Recent Peruvian Experiences

Elizabeth Servan & Andrés Valdivia[*]

§8.01 INTRODUCTION

During the last few years, the number of cases related to anticompetitive conducts sanctioned by INDECOPI,[1] the Peruvian Competition Authority, has risen, in particular regarding horizontal collusion practices.[2] It is important to mention that many of these anticompetitive conducts have taken place in the context of the Peruvian State's public procurement activities.

This chapter summarizes three of the most recent cases regarding these markets and highlights its most relevant aspects:

(i) medicinal oxygen (2013);
(ii) Peruvian Engineers Professional Body (PEPB) and Peruvian Consultancy Association (PCA) (2017); and
(iii) hemodialysis clinics (2018).

Finally, the main lessons learnt from these cases in order to persecute and sanction future anticompetitive practices in the context of public procurement activities are summarized in this chapter.

* The views hereby expressed are exclusively of the authors and do not necessarily reflect those of the organizations involved.

1. The National Institute for the Defense of Free Competition and the Protection of Intellectual Property (INDECOPI, in its Spanish Acronym).
2. An increase of approximately 150% in accumulative terms from 2010 to 2017 of concluded cases that lead to the imposition of sanctions.

§8.02 MEDICINAL OXYGEN

Case summary

In 2013, INDECOPI's Tribunal[3] for the Defense of Competition (hereon, the Tribunal) upheld the Competition Commission's decision[4] to sanction three companies—*"Praxair Perú S.R.L."*, *"Aga S.A."* and *"Messer Gases del Perú S.A."* (hereon, Praxair, Aga and Messer)—for infringing Article 6 of Legislative Decree 701,[5] the former Peruvian Competition Law.[6] According to the Tribunal's decision,[7] these suppliers engaged in bid rigging practices from January 1999 to June 2004, in order to split and share the market in the public bids called by the Peruvian government entity in charge of social security (hereon, EsSalud) for the acquisition of medicinal oxygen to be used in health centers nationwide.

Due to the scope and duration of the anticompetitive practice, as well as the fact that the involved product is relevant for the life and health of social security affiliates, the Tribunal also upheld the Commission's decision to classify this infringement as "very severe" and to sanction the defendants with fines equivalent to USD 4,368,277 (Praxair), USD 1,466,498 (Aga) and USD 562,217 (Messer).[8]

Regarding the execution of the anticompetitive practice, it is important to notice that the Competition Authority identified two different periods during which it took place:

(i) One first period that went from 1999 to 2002 and in which EsSalud's bids presented the following characteristics: (a) the country was divided into four different geographic areas for the provision of medicinal oxygen (north, center, south and Lima[9]); (b) liquid and gaseous oxygen were demanded jointly; and (c) the bidders experience was valued taking into account income values that were not associated to the value of the required item.

(ii) A second period that went from 2003 to 2004 and in which a series of changes were introduced by EsSalud to the public bids' rules: (a) the medicinal oxygen provision geographic areas were increased to twenty-four regions;[10] (b) liquid and gaseous oxygen were demanded independently; and (c) the bidders experience was valued taking into account income values that were associated to the value of the required item.

3. Decision No. 1167-2013/SDC-INDECOPI.
4. Decision No. 051-2010/CLC-INDECOPI.
5. This article prohibited bid rigging practices.
6. In 2008, Legislative Decree 701 was repealed and replaced by Legislative Decree 1034. However, in this case the anticompetitive practices took place from 1999 to 2014, before the enactment of Legislative Decree and while Legislative Decree 701 was still in force.
7. Decision No. 1167-2013/SDC-INDECOPI.
8. Taking into account the Peruvian Soles (S/) to US Dollars (US$) average exchange rate for the year 2018.
9. The Peruvian political capital and largest city.
10. The Peruvian territory is divided in twenty-four different political regions.

The Competition Authority concluded that throughout the first and the second period the three companies agreed to share the medicinal oxygen market, so that each one of them supplied a different geographic area. This way, Aga supplied the northern part of the country, Messer supplied the center and Praxair supplied both Lima and the south. In order to execute this market division agreement, the two companies that were not intended to attend EsSalud's demand in a certain geographic area presented economic bids that were over the maximum level accepted by the public auction's rules during the "first period", with the objective of being disqualified.

Even though, as it has been pointed out, in the "second period" (2003–2004) EsSalud modified the rules of the mentioned auctions so as to increase the level of competition among bidders, the three companies continued to be selected in the regions corresponding to the same geographic areas as during the "first period". However, instead of self-disqualifying in the auctions that corresponded to the regions that formed part of the geographic areas allocated to their competitors through the market sharing agreement, they abstained from participating in these tenders.

It is relevant to highlight that, in this case, the Competition Authority did not find any direct evidence on the existence of the bid rigging agreement, but based its decision on the joint analysis of a series of circumstantial pieces of evidence, which were valued in the context of a market that presented a series of characteristics that facilitated the adoption of this type of agreements, summed up to the analysis and dismissal of the alternative explanations that were offered by the defendants to question the existence of the anticompetitive practice, as explained in the following texts.

Market structure

As it has been previously pointed out, the market structure in this case allowed the adoption and implementation of the agreement:

- Entry barriers
  The Authority found high entry barriers that prevented the entry of new competitors into the market, these barriers were related to: (i) high plant installation costs (approximately USD 20 million), (ii) the existence of industry specific assets (valves, vaporizers, etc.) and (iii) high fixed costs, such as electricity and equipment depreciation.
- Concentration
  In addition, the market presented high levels of concentration during the investigation period (1999–2006). Each year the Herfindahl-Hirschman Index (HHI) was located over 2,500, reaching its highest point (7,490.07) on the year 2000, as it is shown in Table 8.1. These high levels of concentration prevented new firms from entering the market.

Table 8.1 Market Share and Concentration According to Oxygen Volumes Purchased by EsSalud, 1999–2006

Year	*Aga (%)*	*Messer (%)*	*Praxair (%)*	*Others (%)*	*HHI*
1999	10.35	4.20	75.45	0.00	7,426.74
2000	10.98	3.23	85.78	0.00	7,490.07
2001	12.10	2.73	83.86	0.31	7,139.79
2002	20.13	5.55	70.57	3.75	5,430.40
2003	23.12	2.59	66.80	7.48	5,060.12
2004	29.45	1.17	65.06	4.32	5,120.33
2005	38.86	2.49	49.86	8.79	4,079.73
2006	15.89	1.92	66.28	15.92	4,901.83

Source: Decision No. 1167-2013/SDC-INDECOPI.

- Other market conditions

  Since all of the processes organized by EsSalud were public, there were almost no costs involved in the supervision of eventual collusive agreements. In the case of tenders, the companies were able to verify if others followed the agreement without incurring in supervision costs.

  Moreover, considering the defendants knew that EsSalud organized processes to purchase medicinal oxygen within a year gap and that these processes were repeated over time, due to the importance of the involved services for its patients' health.
- Supply features

  In terms of supply, the homogeneity of the product required by EsSalud allowed the agreement to be a simple one and therefore to reduce transaction costs between firms. At the same time, the market presented symmetry among firms, since all three firms used the same technology and faced the same costs to attend EsSalud's demand. The authority concluded that all of these characteristics reduced the possibility of deviation from a collusive agreement and, consequently, facilitated collusion.
- Demand features

  The Authority found low product substitutability and an increasing demand during the analyzed period (1996–2004). In addition, the pressure that the implicated firms performed over EsSalud eased the adoption of a collusive agreement. As it is shown in Figure 8.1, EsSalud was the biggest buyer of medicinal oxygen in Perú. Even though EsSalud had purchasing power over this product, in the short term the Social Security needed to be permanently supplied with medicinal oxygen, because the life and health of patients depended on it. On that note, EsSalud only used its purchasing power from 2003 to 2004, when some changes were introduced into its contracts and auction rules, situation that favored the entry of new firms into this market.

Figure 8.1 Medicinal Oxygen Demand Nationwide—2002

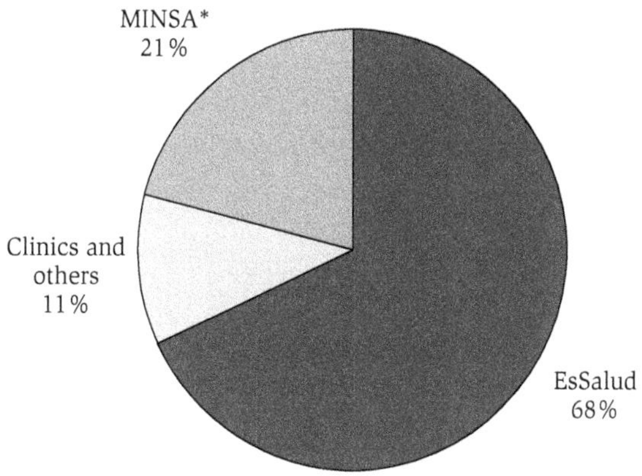

Source: Decision No. 1167-2013/SDC-INDECOPI.

* Peruvian Ministry of Health (MINSA, in its Spanish Acronym).

The employment of circumstantial evidence

Throughout the procedure, the Competition Authority gathered evidence of, among others, the following facts:

(i) From 1999 to 2004, the defendants won EsSalud's auctions for the acquisition of medicinal oxygen in the same geographic area: Aga in the north, Messer in the center and Praxair in both Lima and the south.
(ii) During the "first period", the defendants obtained prices that equaled or were close to 110% of the public bid's referential value in their corresponding geographic areas, that is, the maximum possible contract value according to Law.[11]
(iii) The defendants presented bids that were more than the maximum legal value for those areas that they did not supply, which lead to their automatic disqualification.
(iv) The defendants did not supply medicinal oxygen in their influence areas, that is, those areas where they already had installed their infrastructure (oxygen production and filling plants) and, therefore, should have been more convenient to attend.
(v) Since September 2002, after EsSalud adjusted the auctions' rules, encouraging the entrance of new competitors, the defendants modified their behavior. They kept supplying the same geographic areas, but in most cases their

11. According to the Peruvian public procurement legal framework, the referential value represents the contract price and economic bids cannot surpass 110% of this value.

economic bids were far lower than the maximum possible legal value and, in some cases, they even equaled the minimum possible legal value (which was 70% of the reference value), while they abstained from participating in the auctions that corresponded to the other two companies' geographic areas.

In addition, the Competition Authority dismissed the alternative explanations offered by the defendants to justify the above-mentioned facts which, among others, consisted of the following:

(i) The defendants argued that they did not have the financial and productive capacity to profitably supply the other geographic areas. However, not only did they not present evidence in order to support this argument, but the authority also verified that during the investigated period they had available oxygen production and supply capacity that would have enabled them to attend additional geographic areas.

In addition, the authority verified that the defendants abstained from supplying medicinal oxygen in their influence areas, that is, those areas where they had already installed their infrastructure.

(ii) The defendants sustained that the auctions' rules contained a series of entry barriers—such as the requirement to jointly supply liquid and gaseous oxygen, as well as the obligation to supply very large areas of territory—that limited their participation in the different geographic areas. Despite this, the authority verified that during the investigated period the three companies did comply with all of these rules, which therefore only represented entry barriers for new economic agents who were less capitalized and, unlike the defendants, did not own oxygen production and filling plants in different locations throughout the country.

Furthermore, even though during the "second period" the auctions' rules imposed higher entry costs, the defendants were willing to supply medicinal oxygen to EsSalud for prices that were considerably lower than the ones obtained during the "first period".

(iii) The defendants stated that, during the "first period", they presented economic bids that were more than the maximum level accepted by the public auction's rules as a "signaling" strategy in order to encourage EsSalud to increase the reference values. However, even though EsSalud increased the reference values up to a level that was even above the one required by the companies, they kept self-disqualifying in those bids that corresponded to the geographic areas they did not supply.

Moreover, this alleged "signaling" strategy did not take place during the "second period" in which the referred values were significantly reduced.

Consequently, the Competition Authority concluded that the only possible explanation for the defendants' conduct was the existence of an anticompetitive agreement to split and share the market in the public bids called by EsSalud for the acquisition of medicinal oxygen.

§8.03 PEPB AND PCA

Case Summary

In 2017, INDECOPI's Tribunal[12] upheld the Competition Commission's decision[13] to sanction the PEPB and the PCA—for infringing Article 11.1.a of Legislative Decree 1034,[14] the Peruvian Competition Law.

According to the Tribunal's decision,[15] the PEPB, in coordination with the PCA, carried out horizontal collusive practices aimed at increasing the referential values that corresponded to the staff fees and overhead costs that were established in the public bids called by the Special National Transport Infrastructure Project (hereon, "*Provías Nacional*"[16]) for the hiring of engineering consultancy services.[17]

It is important to notice that the Peruvian legal framework establishes that engineers must be associated to the PEPB in order to exercise their profession and are obliged to comply with its rulings when practicing their profession, otherwise they can be suspended or even expelled from it.

In addition, according to its Bylaws, the PEPB had the power to regulate the fees charged by its members for engineering services, and, according to Article 54.f of its Code of Conduct, associates who fixed or influenced on the fixing of professional fees for engineering services that were inadequate considering their importance and degree of responsibility could be suspended for up to six months from this association which meant they would not be allowed to practice their profession during that period.[18]

In this case, the Competition Authority verified that the PEPB and the PCA adopted a joint decision on which they considered should be the level of the mentioned staff fees and overhead costs and spread it through a series of documents and printed communications among their associates, including engineers and consulting firms who participated in the auctions called by *Provías Nacional*, plus engineers who worked as civil servants in *Provías Nacional* and were in charge of establishing the referential values in the public bids called by this entity.

In these documents and communications, the PEPB and the PCA not only established what they considered should be the level of these values, but also pointed out that they were compulsory for all engineers and included a reference to Article 54.f of the PEPB's Code of Conduct.

12. Decision No. 508-2017/SDC-INDECOPI.
13. Decision No. 040-2014/CLC-INDECOPI.
14. This article prohibits any agreement, decision, recommendation or concerted practice among competitors aimed at directly or indirectly fixing prices.
15. Decision No. 508-2017/SDC-INDECOPI.
16. The Peruvian Government entity in charge of the construction and maintenance of the national road network.
17. Specifically, these consultancy services consisted on the elaboration of definite engineering studies and on the supervision of construction works.
18. It is important to notice that both the PEPB's Bylaws and Code of Conduct constitute its internal regulations and, therefore, cannot contravene or enable this association to act against Peruvian laws, such as Legislative Decree 1034, the Peruvian Competition Law.

The Competition Authority sanctioned each of the PEPB and the PCA with a fine equivalent to USD 1,246,154.[19] Plus, it ordered a series of remedies, including the following:

(i) the PEPB and the PCA should stop spreading any document or communication containing their decision on the level of the staff fees and overhead costs;
(ii) the PEPB should repeal those articles of its Code of Conduct which established that associates who fixed or influenced on the fixing of professional fees for engineering services that were inadequate considering their importance and degree of responsibility could be suspended for up to six months from this association;
(iii) the PEPB should also eliminate Article 2.09.p which established that this association had the power to regulate the fees charged by its members for engineering services from its Bylaws; and
(iv) both associations should elaborate a comprehensive explanatory memorandum on anticompetitive conducts, approved by the Competition Commission's Technical Secretariat and disseminate it among their associates.

As it can be noticed, the existence of professional associations and the legal obligation for all engineers to form part of the PEPB in order to practice their profession played a key role in the above-mentioned infringement. Further details on this matter are provided below.

According to Article 11 of Legislative Decree 1034, the Peruvian Competition Law, collusive practices can be materialized not only through direct agreements, but also through other mechanisms such as recommendations, decisions or collusive practices.

Regarding decisions and recommendations, they usually take place in the context of associations, unions, syndicates, professional bodies or any organization in which independent economic agents participate and consist on statements or indications aimed at standardizing the behavior of its members, restricting competition between them or against third parties, with negative effects as a result of this behavior.

As indicated by the OECD, any associations must include diverse forms of cooperation and interaction between individuals and companies, for the purposes of competition rules, any association must have the following elements:

(a) A structural/organizational element: the presence of a corporate structure is relevant and allows: (i) distinguishing between associations and their members; and, (ii) distinguishing the association's activities from those performed by its members in the market.
(b) A functional element: an association must have the capacity to influence on the development of an economic activity, even though it is not necessary for it to have an active participation in the market. However, its activities must, in any form, have an effect over competition.

19. Taking into account the Peruvian Soles (S/) to US Dollars (US$) average exchange rate for the year 2018.

Therefore, within many types of associations with any relevance in the application of the rules of free competition, we can find: associations, professional bodies and other self-regulated associations.

Business associations represent an industry and their members are companies that compete among them. Typically, they make public relationships for their industry, representing their member's opinions before the government and pressing for policy changes; establishing ethic codes; making standards and certifications for their products and services, conducting educational programs (workshops and certifications), gathering and spreading industry information, organizing fairs, conventions and reunions, among others.

On the other hand, *professional bodies* provide an official certification so that professionals can legally exercise their professions. For certification, associations establish standards (typically education requirements and other trainings), take entrance exams, and, establish and enforce conduct rules. These associations usually intervene in the establishment and implementation of rules that affect professional practice, as well as in the elaboration of new regulations for the approval of involved public authorities.

In that context, professional associations and business associations can be employed as a vehicle for information exchange. In consequence, according to specialized literature, given their cooperative forms and the interaction between their members, professional bodies and associations can adopt practices that may increase the probability of collusion. Due to the potential effect of those practices, which may promote coordinated behavior among competitors through information exchange and/or other incentives,[20] they are denominated enabling practices.

Similarly, when a membership is required, whether legally or *de facto*, rules to remain as a member, conduct codes or ethic codes, certifications and quality standards can be used to implement and enforce collusive agreements. In those cases, the expulsion from the association in case the collusion agreement is broken by one of its members is quite effective, because it might put him or her out of professional practice or business.[21]

Therefore, regarding cases involving professional bodies, INDECOPI's Tribunal indicated: "Professional bodies, such as groups of professionals, are important in the field of competition law not only for the business activity developed by themselves, but mainly because associations have an organizational structure, that supported on conventions or laws, constitutes the means for decision making which might determine or influence its members' behavior".[22]

20. Church, J. and Ware, R. Industrial Organization: A Strategic Approach. McGraw-Hill, 2000 pp. 348–349.
21. Church, J. and Ware, R., 2000 *supra*, pp.349.
22. Decision No. 229-97/TDC, November 12, 1997, p.5.

The discussion around the *Noerr-Pennington* doctrine

Throughout the procedure, both the PEPB and the PCA argued that in its past decisions INDECOPI's Tribunal had established that, according to the *Noerr-Pennington* doctrine,[23] the attempts of a private entity to influence administrative or legislative authorities' decisions, even when these attempts had anticompetitive goals, were not punishable under competition legislation, since they were part of its constitutional right of petition.

Moreover, the defendants alleged that, since the documents and communications that were sent to the engineers who worked as civil servants in *Provías Nacional*—and were in charge of establishing the referential values in the public bids called by this entity—represented a simple requirement in order for this entity to adjust these values, its conduct constituted a manifestation of their right of petition, protected by the *Noerr-Pennington* doctrine and, therefore, was not punishable under the Peruvian Competition Law.

Regarding these arguments, the Tribunal specified that the conduct that was being questioned and sanctioned was not the delivery of the mentioned documents and communications, but the decision that was adopted jointly by the PEPB and the PCA to establish the level of the staff fees and overhead costs that should be considered in the public bids called by "*Provías Nacional*" for the hiring of engineering consultancy services. In that sense, the documents and communications only constituted a means to spread and enforce their decision.

In addition, the Tribunal pointed out that, the fact that the referred communications were not only directed to PEPB's engineer associates who worked as civil servants in *Provías Nacional* and were in charge of establishing the referential values in the public bids called by this entity, but also included a reference to Article 54.f of the PEPB's Code of Conduct, that, as has already been mentioned, established that PEPB associates who fixed or influenced on the fixing of professional fees for engineering services that were inadequate considering their importance and degree of responsibility could be suspended for up to six months from this association.

In this regard, the communications in question were not simple petitions directed to the above-mentioned engineers, but a coercion mechanism to guarantee the enforcement of PEPB and PCA's joint decision to rise the indicated values.

For these reasons, the Tribunal concluded that the defendants' conduct did not represent the exercise of their constitutional right of petition and was therefore not protected by the *Noerr-Pennington* doctrine.

23. This doctrine was established by the Supreme Court of the United States of America in *Eastern Railroad Presidents Conference v. Noerr Motor Freight, Inc.*, 365 U.S. 127, 135 (1961) and was further developed in *United Mine Workers v. Pennington*, 381 U.S. 657, 670 (1965), It is based in the First Amendment of the US Constitution (protection of political speech) and, according to it, private entities are immune from liability under the antitrust legislation for attempts to influence the approval of laws, even if these laws could reduce competition in the market.

§8.04 HEMODIALYSIS CLINICS

Case Summary

In March 2018, INDECOPI's Tribunal[24] upheld the Competition Commission's decision[25] to sanction thirty-one hemodialysis clinics for infringing Article 11.1.a of Legislative Decree 1034,[26] the Peruvian Competition Law, as well as one of their representatives for infringing Article 2.1 of this Law.[27]

According to the Tribunal's decision,[28] these hemodialysis centers engaged in a horizontal collusive practice in order to increase the referential values—this value represents the contract price and, according to the Peruvian public procurement legal framework, the contracting entity must gather market data in order to establish it[29]—in the public bids called by EsSalud (the Peruvian government entity in charge of social security) for the hiring of hemodialysis services for its affiliates in the cities of Lima and Callao, during the years 2010–2012.

The Competition Authority based its decision on the joint analysis of a series of pieces of evidence—among others, interviews to the centers' representatives, e-mails, the defendants' claims and numerous quotations for the provision of hemodialysis services. This joint analysis demonstrated that the hemodialysis clinics held diverse meetings and coordinations, aimed at agreeing on the price of the quotations that they presented to EsSalud, in response to the requirements made by this entity for the calculation and determination of the referential values that were applied in the public bids called by it for the hiring of hemodialysis services.

Moreover, these pieces of evidence demonstrated that, since EsSalud did not consider the values contained in their agreed upon quotations, the hemodialysis clinics agreed to jointly abstain from participating in the mentioned auctions, with the objective of convincing this entity that they would not take part in them unless it adjusted the referential values in accordance with their quotations, thus reinforcing the effectiveness of their anticompetitive agreement.

This forced EsSalud to declare these auctions void and to make successive calls for them during a period of more than two years. Nevertheless, with the objective of avoiding a shortage of the hemodialysis service for its affiliates during this period (2010–2012), EsSalud had to hire this service through direct contracts with private clinics and, in some cases, called for last minute emergency minor auctions in which, unlike what happened in the regular auctions, these clinics did participate.

---

24. Decision No. 068-2018/SDC-INDECOPI.
25. Decision No. 019-2016/CLC-INDECOPI.
26. This article prohibits any agreement, decision, recommendation or concerted practice among competitors aimed at directly or indirectly fixing prices.
27. This article establishes that the Competition Law is also applicable to the infringer's managers and representatives.
28. Decision No. 068-2018/SDC-INDECOPI.
29. Among other possibilities, the entity can require the presentation of quotations from potential bidders.

The Competition Authority sanctioned the thirty-one hemodialysis clinics with a global fine equivalent to USD 1,888,309 and their representative with a fine equivalent to USD 55,237,[30] due to his role in the planning and execution of the price fixing agreement.

Description of the service and demand

The hemodialysis process is made through a dialyzer and a hemodialysis machine that simulates the kidney of a patient with End Stage Renal Disease (ESRD). People treated for this condition must receive at least three to four hours of hemodialysis sessions three times per week in order to survive.

Even though EsSalud has some public installations to serve its patients, due to an increase in the number of patients with ESRD, it was necessary to cover this unsatisfied demand with the services provided by private hemodialysis clinics.

In 2012, the coverage of this service in Lima was distributed among fifty-four hemodialysis clinics that supplied 59.9% of EsSalud's patients, the remaining 40.1% was provided by this entity's public healthcare network. It is also important to notice that thirty-four out of these fifty-four private clinics were involved in this investigation (*see* Figure 8.2).

Figure 8.2 Participation in the Provision of the Hemodialysis Service During 2012 (% of EsSalud Patients)

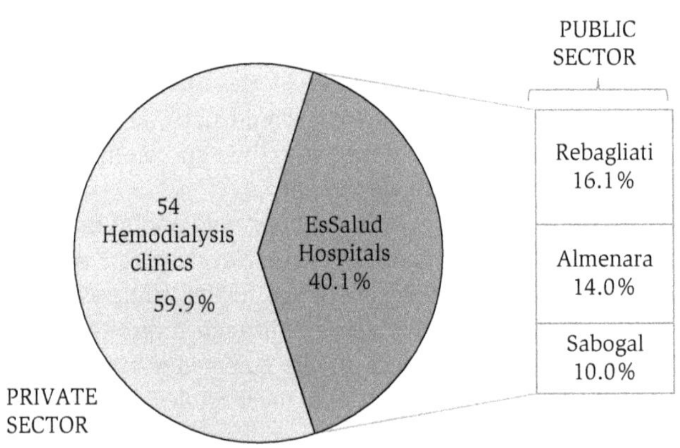

Source: Decision No. 068-2018/SDC-INDECOPI.

In this context, it should be noted that demand for the referred hemodialysis service, being of high complexity and considering that the life and health of patients depends on its due provision, is inelastic regarding its price. Hence, if there was an increase in the price offered by private hemodialysis clinics, either justified or based on their unilateral decisions, their demand would not be affected.

30. Taking into account the Peruvian Soles (S/) to US Dollars (US$) average exchange rate for the year 2018.

Price fixing agreements in the context of public bids

Throughout the procedure, the defendants argued that it was not possible to fix prices in the context of a public auction for the following reasons:

(i) it is the entity and not the bidders who finally establishes the referential value, since EsSalud was not legally obliged to employ the prices contained in the quotations presented by potential bidders; and
(ii) the referential value is not the equivalent of a price.

Because of this, they alleged that the charges against them—the violation of Article 11.1.a of Legislative Decree 1034, the Peruvian Competition Law, that prohibits price fixing agreements among competitors—were not valid.

Regarding these argument, the Tribunal indicated that Article 11.1.a prohibited both direct and indirect price fixing agreements. This meant that those agreements among competitors aimed at coordinately establishing any aspect that influenced or was a part of the price formation process—for example, profit margins or discount policies—constituted an infringement to the Peruvian Competition Law.

The Tribunal also specified that, according to the Peruvian public procurement legal framework, the referential value represented the maximum price that the public entity was willing to pay for a given goods or service, which meant that this value determined the price that the State would finally pay for it.

Therefore, an agreement aimed at influencing on the establishment of the referential value in the context of a public bid did constitute a punishable price fixing practice, since it qualified as an indirect mechanism to clout on this determination.

With regard to these ideas, the Tribunal indicated that, according to the above-mentioned Peruvian public procurement legal framework, in order to establish the referential value to be applied in a public bid, the entity must gather market data and, among other possibilities, can require the presentation of quotations from potential bidders.

Consequently, in this case, by agreeing on the price of the quotations that they presented to EsSalud, the defendants distorted the market information that this entity would employ to establish the applicable referential value, which, as has been noticed, would finally determine the price that this entity would pay for the hemodialysis service to be provided to its affiliates.

§8.05 CONCLUSIONS

These proceedings enable us to arrive to some general conclusions regarding the investigation and sanctioning of anticompetitive practices in the context of the Peruvian State's public procurement activities:

(i) Authorities must pay attention to all the stages involved in public tenders, including their design, calling and execution. Particular emphasis must be put on the process for the establishment of the referential value, since potential bidders might agree to distort market information gathered by the contracting entity during this process or might engage in strategic collusive behavior aimed at manipulating its fixation in accordance to their private interests.

(ii) Associations, unions, syndicates, professional bodies or any organization in which independent economic agents—who might be linked to the State's public procurement activities— participate have not necessarily developed a "free market economy and competition" culture. Therefore, it is important for authorities to pay attention to their behavior regarding public tenders and to perform activities aimed at developing the mentioned culture.

(iii) The Competition Authority should generate and disseminate among public entities involved in the State's public procurement activities accessible documents and instructions, directed to illustrate them on the different patterns of conduct that might constitute evidence of potential anticompetitive practices throughout the different stages involved in public tenders.

In line with these appreciations, INDECOPI's Competition Commission has recently published its project of "Guidelines for the promotion of competition in public tenders" in order to receive comments from any interested party. These guidelines have been designed as a tool to aid public servants who participate in public procurement related activities to achieve two objectives: (i) scheming efficient and competitive public tenders; and (ii) identifying potential anticompetitive practices throughout the different stages involved in public procurement.

CHAPTER 9

Supranational Leniency Programs: The Latin American Experience with the Tissue Paper Cartel Case

Jorge Enrique Sánchez Medina

§9.01 INTRODUCTION

In May 2018, the General Secretary of the Andean Community (SGCA)—an international integration organization whose members are Bolivia, Colombia, Ecuador and Peru—exercised its power for the first time regarding antitrust topics by sanctioning competition restrictive practices by two companies with operations in the subregion.

The fact that a sub-regional body joined the efforts that several Latin American countries have been making on their own during the last years to enforce the laws that protect free competition would have been great news for those of us who promote this protection in the region.

However, the SGCA's sanction, as well as the resolution that initiated the investigation that preceded it, produced great concern in the legal, academic and institutional competition regional community.

The general confusion arose from the fact that SGCA's sanction involved companies that had already been investigated by the national competition authorities of the member countries, within the framework of their respective leniency programs.

Moreover, the SGCA's sanction was based on the facts that these companies revealed and on the evidence they provided during such leniency programs' process.

With good reason, this circumstance has raised many doubts and concerns regarding the regional leniency programs advances and strengths, which find its foundation on strict confidentiality and trust principles, and has put at risk the Andean Community member countries competition protection policies.

The SGCA's sanction supposed a disincentive for the leniency programs within the Andean Community member countries, specifically, regarding companies with operations in several of these nations. The situation has been considered with a great deal of seriousness, some have even seen this decision as a "deadly blow" to this type of programs in countries that until now, are starting the path for its implementation.[1]

It is therefore relevant to raise a question regarding the truthful effect of the SGCA's intervention on the leniency programs. This, to determine if their competence in terms of competition protection should end, as some people promote it, or on the other hand, there might be ways to prevent that from happening and to the contrary, strengthen a supranational tool that can be fundamental for the future protection of markets.

The following supposes a more or less detailed view on the specific case, its effect on the national leniency programs and how it can be compatible with competition protection supranational tools.

§9.02 SGCA'S RESOLUTION NO. 2006 OF 2018 AND ITS IMPACT ON LENIENCY PROGRAMS

[A] SGCA's Resolution No. 2006 of 2018

In application of the Andean Community Decision No. 608 of 2005,[2] by Resolution No. 1883 of November 11, 2016,[3] the SGCA decided to initiate an investigation regarding anti-competitive conducts committed by four companies with operations in Colombia and Ecuador: Kimberly's and Familia's respective branches in those countries, manufacturers, among others, of soft paper/tissue products.

The Decision No. 608 of 2005 represents a binding rule for the Andean Community Member States, whose Article 5 allows the SGCA to investigate and sanction anti-competitive behaviors that take place in a member country territory and whose real effects are produced in another member country territory. This means SGCA's

1. The decision of the SGCA was massively rejected by the academic and legal community, not only in Colombia, but also in Latin America. For example, on the subject, the Colombian Association of Competition Law, an association of private lawyers and public scholars of the subject, held a round table to discuss whether a competition regime in the Andean region was justified. (Available at: https://www.youtube.com/watch?v=igmSmdRFWTc&disable_polymer=true). On the other hand, academics and former officials of the region provoked the debate through publications in different specialized publications such as Global Competition Review or Competition International Policy.

   The issue has even received attention from the Organization for Economic Cooperation and Development (OECD) Competition Committee and the International Chamber of Commerce Competition Committee.
2. *See* Andean Community. Decision No. 608 of 2005. Official Gazette of the Cartagena Agreement. Year XXII-Number 1180. Lima, April 4, 2005, pp. 1–9. Available at: http://intranet.comunidadandina.org/Documentos/Gacetas/Gace1180.pdf.
3. *See* Andean Community. SGCA Resolution No. 1883 of 2016. Official Gazette of the Cartagena Agreement. Year XXXIII-Number 2871. Lima, November 14, 2016, pp. 1–19. Available at: http://intranet.comunidadandina.org/Documentos/Gacetas/GACE2871.pdf.

jurisdiction excludes behaviors with origins and effects in the same Andean Community member country.[4]

The SGCA's investigation began with a hypothesis: that the companies had come to an agreement in Colombia for price fixing and market distribution, with real effects in both Colombia and Ecuador.

The SGCA's procedure started with a complaint made on October 20, 2016 by the Ecuadorian competition authority, the Superintendency of Market Power Control (SCPM).

The SCPM's complaint was based on confidential documents that were on their possession and had been declassified to be sent to the SGCA. These documents had been obtained during the leniency's process before the Ecuadorian authority to which Kimberly had agreed.

In addition, SCPM's complaint connected these documents with some facts discovered in the investigation carried out by the Colombian competition authority against the Colombian branches, and that, at that time, were of public knowledge during the imposition of several sanctions on these companies in May 2016 by the Colombian authority.

In this regard, it is important to note that in both Colombia and Ecuador, as well as other countries of the region (such as Peru), Kimberly and Familia were already involved and assured their participation in the leniency programs of each jurisdiction, in order to disclose their involvement in anti-competitive conducts in each of those markets. This was also to obtain the benefits established in each legislation.

In fact, Kimberly was the first company to have access to a total exemption of fines imposed by the Colombian[5] and Peruvian[6] competition regimes. That is to say, in both cases, the sanctions took origin on their participation in the respective leniency programs.

---

4. Andean Community Decision No. 608 of 2005:

> Article 5.—The purpose of this Decision is those conducts practiced in:
>
> a) The territory of one or more Member Countries and whose actual effects occur in one or more Member Countries, except when the origin and effect occur in a single country; Y,
> b) The territory of a country that is not a member of the Andean Community and whose actual effects occur in two or more Member Countries. The national laws of the respective Member Countries shall govern other situations not provided in this article.

5. *See* Superintendence of Industry and Commerce. Resolution SIC 31739 of May 26, 2016. Available at: http://www.sic.gov.co/sites/default/files/estados/022018/RES_31739_DE_2016.pdf Confirmed by Resolution SIC 69906 of October 19, 2016. Available at: http://www.sic.gov.co/sites/default/files/estados/022018/RES_69906_DE_2016_RECURSO_RES_31739_DE_2016.pdf.
   In this regard, you can also consult the Motivated Report of the investigation submitted by the Deputy Superintendent for Competition Protection in the file SIC 14-151027.
6. *See* National Institute for the Defense of Competition and the Protection of Intellectual Property. Resolution INDECOPI 010/2017 / CLC-INDECOPI. *See*: https://www.indecopi.gob.pe/inicio/-/asset_publisher/ZxXrtRdgbv1r/content/el-indecopi-desarticulo-y-sanciono-en-primera-instancia-al-cartel-de-papel-higienico-conformed-by-companies-kimberly-clark-peru-y-protisa? inheritRedirect = false.

In Ecuador's case, once Kimberly began its national leniency program application, the SCPM informed the company that it was also eligible for its own program. However, after eighteen months of investigation, the SCPM ruled out the investigation and closed the case, then reopened and closed it again, just before referring the case to the SGCA, based on documents and evidence that the SCPM had obtained during the leniency application process.

After the investigation had started, the SGCA developed a brief procedure in which the defendants presented their arguments. During that time, the SGCA practiced some tests through the competition authorities of the member countries, based on documents and evidence that the SCPM had obtained during the leniency program.

Decision No. 605 of 2005s procedure, in addition, foresees the preparation of a SGCA's investigation technical report, with the purpose that the Defense Competition Andean Committee, composed by Member States of the Andean Community competition authorities, pronounces itself and presents recommendations, before a potential sanction imposition.

According to Decision No. 605 of 2005, the SGCA must address the Committee members' opinions in the final decision and explain the reasons for which it departs from them.

In the specific case, the competition authorities of Colombia, the SIC, and Peru, the National Institute for the Defense of Competition and the Protection of Intellectual Property (INDECOPI), presented their opinions against the technical report and requested the SGCA not to sanction the investigated.

Despite this, on May 28, 2018, that is, just eighteen months after the investigation began, the SGCA, through Resolution No. 2006 of 2018, resolved to sanction the companies investigated with penalties of close to 18 million dollars each.[7]

It is worth to point out that, in the final decision, the SGCA did not address the SIC's and INDECOPI's opinions against the sanction imposition.[8]

Andean Community's rules that regulate the procedure before the SGCA[9] include the possibility that those interested in an administrative procedure result can request a reconsideration of it.

---

7. SGCA's Resolution No. 2006 of 2018 states:

> Article 6.—Sanction for the commission of the conduct typified in letter a) of Article 7 of Decision No. 608 to companies:
>
> - Colombian Kimberly Colpapel S.A. and Kimberly Clark of Ecuador S.A., with the sum of $ 18,344,916 (eighteen million three hundred and forty-four thousand nine hundred and sixteen dollars of the United States of America) to be paid in a joint and several manner.
> - Productos Familia S.A. and Products Familia Sancela of Ecuador S.A. with the sum of $ 16,857,278 (sixteen million eight hundred and fifty-seven thousand two hundred and seventy-eight dollars of the United States of America) to be paid in solidarity.

8. Andean Community Resolution 2018 of the SGCA. Paragraphs 558 and 559.
9. Andean Community Decision 425 of 1997. Official Gazette of the Cartagena Agreement. Year XVI. Number 314. Lima, December 18, 1997. pp. 12–23. Available at: http://intranet.comunidadandina.org/Documentos/Gacetas/gace314.pdf.

Thus, both sanctioned companies, as well as the SIC and INDECOPI (through the Ministry of Foreign Trade and Tourism of Ecuador) submitted reconsideration appeals, in which they reiterated the opinions expressed during the entire process and requested the revocation of the initial decision.

The companies investigated and INDECOPI as well, requested the Resolution No. 2006 of 2018s effects suspension, while the appeals were resolved.

SIC's opinions are summarized in the following texts, most of which can be identified with those expressed by INDECOPI and those sanctioned by the SGCA.[10] They show the SGCA's failures during the process, which are not exclusively related with national leniency programs' impact.

Based on the Andean rules and the community court jurisprudence, the SIC noted that the SGCA's Resolution No. 2006 of 2018 is affected by nullity regarding: (i) justification defect, (ii) a non-entitled involvement defect and (iii) formal defects, in addition to having serious effects on the Andean Community Member States' national competition protection policies:

(i) First, after analyzing the evidence in the file, the SIC concluded that the evidence did not support the conclusions from which the SGCA imposed the sanction.

The SIC affirmed that although the evidence did account for an autonomous price fixing cartel existence in the Colombian soft paper market -tissue- (sanctioned by the SIC) and, possibly, the existence of similar cartel in the Ecuadorian market (the one that the SPCM decided to not address), in no way demonstrated the hypothesis of the investigation, that is, the existence of an agreement that occurred in Colombia with real effects in Ecuador.

Thus, the SIC highlighted the differences between the markets of each country; the fact that the evidence showed that pricing was established in each market and in relation to different marketing lines (in Colombia, in the consumer and institutional lines, and in Ecuador, only in the latter); and the lapses of the illegal agreement in both countries (in Colombia, until 2013, in Ecuador, according to the evidence, until 2011).

In this regard, the SIC noted, "the soft paper market of both countries is so different that it would even seem irrational that the agreement made in Colombia would even seek to affect the Ecuadorian market."[11]

In addition, the SIC pointed out that all the testimonies, including those that the Ecuadorian authority sent with the complaint to the SGCA, pointed out that the agreements in each country only had a national scope. In fact, it warns of the seriousness that some of the testimonies collected by the SGCA were not fully addressed in the resolution that imposed the sanction, but only in the favorable parts to the verification of the investigation hypothesis.

10. The SIC's Reconsideration Appeal is part of the File of the SGCA filed with No. 002 / LC / SG / 2016.
11. *See*. SGCA file filed with No. 002 / LC / SG / 2016. SIC Reconsideration Resource. P. 4.

In any case, as it had been done before, during the investigation and sanction in its charge, the SIC emphatically affirmed that none of the evidence made public with which companies were punished, also used by the SGCA, served to demonstrate that the price agreement sanctioned in Colombia had real effects in Ecuador.

On the other hand, the SIC also criticized the economic exercises on which the SGCA based their rationing to conclude that the Colombian market price agreement had effects on the Ecuadorian market. On the subject, the SIC pointed out that there was not robust economic evidence or analysis in the file to verify this relationship.

Regarding the Resolution No. 2006 of 2018s economic analysis, it is important to highlight that, based on it, the SGCA concluded that a price parallelism between the companies investigated in the Ecuadorian market between 2011 and 2016 existed. From that parallelism derived, without any other analysis or evidence, the existence of an agreement between the companies investigated during that period.

The SIC forcefully pointed that such price parallelism's studies suffered from significant methodological flaws and the conclusion the SGCA presented based on those (i.e., the existence of the agreement), without any other type of evidence to indicate its effective occurrence, was completely foreign to the international doctrine on the subject and the one used by the SIC.

(ii) Second, the SIC affirmed that Resolution No. 2006 of 2018 had a non-entitled involvement defect, since the SGCA lacked competence to impose a sanction in the case.

In accordance with the analysis of the already mentioned evidence, the SIC points out that the SGCA's research hypothesis was not corroborated, so the price agreement between the investigated companies that initiated in Colombia, did not have real effects in Ecuador, a requirement demanded by Article 5 of 608 Decision of 2005, which grants the competence to the SGCA.

As an additional argument, the SIC notes that, in this case, the SGCA's sanctioning capacity had prescribed, in accordance with Article 43 of 608 Decision of 2005, which provides a term of three years.[12]

For this purpose, the SIC stated that the record proved that the agreement between the companies in the Ecuadorian market only lasted until 2011 and not 2016 as the SGCA intended to demonstrate based on poor economic studies and without taking into any account international standards.

(iii) Finally, the SIC warned about the formal defects of Resolution No. 2006 of 2018, which translates into different irregularities and due process breaches,

12. Andean Community Decision No. 608 of 2005:

> Article 43.—Free competition infringement provided for in this Decision shall be time-barred within three (3) years after the conduct was carried out. In the case of continued behavior, the three years mentioned above, will begin to count from the day after the one in which the behavior ceased.

in the recollection and practice of evidence, as well as in the violation of the investigated defense, contradiction and self-incrimination rights.

The SIC warned that the evidence transferred to the SGCA by the SCPM, collected during the leniency program's process of that country, in which one of the investigated parties participated, is invalid and illegal.

Indeed, due to the special circumstances in which they were presented to the SPCM, it is clear that such evidence was completely confidential and its use by the Ecuadorian authority, or by any other authority such as the SGCA, for any purpose other than the one of the nature of the leniency program in which it was obtained, implies a serious self-incrimination right breach for the company that presented it.

For the same reasons, the SIC also considered SCPM's behavior, in which it "declassified" the documents provided by the company during the process of the complaint, with the sole purpose of transferring them to the SGCA, is illegal.

The SIC criticized the fact that the SGCA failed to analyzed the origin of the evidence sent to the SPCM. If it had done so, it would have realized that this delivery was illegal and implied a serious violation of the companies' rights.

In this regard, the SIC noted with surprise, that the SGCA, in Resolution No. 2006 of 2018, had indicated that, in any case, the companies could not allege the breach of any human right, because in their opinion, companies cannot be holders of these. The foregoing, even against Article 3 of 608 Decision of 2005, which establishes that due process should be a guarantee to all people.[13]

On the other hand, the SIC clarified that some of the evidence used by the SGCA to draw its conclusions and support the sanction was not contradicted by the companies investigated, which violated their right to a defense.

Thus, the SIC warns that the SGCA carried out depositions without the presence of the companies and did not grant any access to the information that served as the foundation for the Ecuadorian market prices parallelism existence thesis. A matter that allowed maintaining the SGCA's sanction capacity, otherwise, it would have prescribed.

Regarding these irregularities, the SIC even stated that "the SGCA's performance was so nontransparent that it is not even possible to be certain of how much of the evidence was carried out without the presence of the companies investigated, since it is even indicated that during the investigation, the SIC carried depositions (...) that didn't even happened."[14]

Finally, in the appeal, the SIC warned about the serious effects of the decision regarding the leniency programs implemented by the Member States and, in general, its

13. Andean Community Decision No. 608 of 2005:

> Article 3. Due process, in the sense of assuring all natural or legal persons a fair process that allows them to fully exercise their right of defense, respecting the rights of the parties to present arguments and evidence before the agencies, administrative entities or competent courts, within the provisions of this Decision's framework, as well as a duly motivated statement.

14. *See* SGCA file filed with No. 002 / LC / SG / 2016. SIC´s Reconsideration Resource. P. 35.

effects on competition protection public policies, issues that are addressed later on this chapter.

It remains to point out that the companies' and the Peruvian and Colombian authorities' appeals have not yet been resolved.

However, it is noted that the SGCA (through Resolution No. 2017 dated August 6, 2018) decided to suspend the Resolution No. 2006 of 2018s effects, since it considered that allowing its execution, that is, allowing the companies' fine payment, without resolving the reconsideration remedies first, would mean a serious economic damage against them.

In addition, in the same resolution, and at the request of Kimberly on its reconsideration appeal, the SGCA decided to suspend the entire process before the Andean Community, until all the legal actions initiated by the company before the Ecuadorian judicial authorities were resolved.

The company's request had to do with the demands presented before the Ecuadorian judicial authorities in order to declare the illegality of both the "declassification" of the documents provided during the Ecuadorian leniency program's process, as of its delivery to the SGCA.

In this regard, it has been recent news that the Second District Court of Administrative Contentious matters with headquarters in Guayaquil, Ecuador, declared on a first instance decision that the SPCM's decision to send information offered by Kimberly in the Ecuadorian leniency program's framework was illegal, since it was not communicated to the company in a timely manner and represented a serious defense right violation.[15]

The reasons why the SGCA's sanction seriously affected not only the Member States leniency programs but also their competition protection public policies (reasons shared by the SIC and other national competition authorities as well as the rest of the legal community) are indicated in the following texts.

[B] Leniency Programs' Difficulties Posed by the SGCA's Resolution No. 2006 of 2018

SGCA's investigation and sanction circumstances call into question the recent Latin American leniency programs' reliability.

Indeed, as is well known, leniency programs are the most effective tool on the fight against cartels. These programs' success relies on the trust and transparency principles in which they operate. In such a way, that any flaw that affects companies' will to enter some of these programs, not only affected its functioning, but also the policies on the matter' success.

In addition to the irregularities stated in the previous section, at least two procedure's facts and specifically the SGCA's sanction affected the national member countries leniency programs' credibility:

15. In this regard, among others, you can see the news that appeared on the website of the Ecuadorian law firm Pérez, Bustamante and Ponce, available at: http://www.pbplaw.com/es/#.

First, in order to sanction companies, the SGCA used the information revealed by Kimberly to the SCPM during the Ecuadorian leniency program's application, as well as the evidence that it provided for this purpose during the entire process.

This situation may be the most concerning to leniency programs, since the facts revealed and the evidence offered in a legitimate trust context that originated in a negotiation between the administrated and the authorities, under the promise of a potential benefit, were later used against them, in a strictly sanctioning context procedure without its consent, and before a completely different authority from which they had made an agreement with in the first place.

This situation calls into question the seriousness of the SCPM's leniency program implementation. It also eliminates the trust and confidentiality conditions that are required for these programs in order to work.

Second, the SGCA' sanction supposes that the national leniency programs' benefits be annulled and left them with no effect.

Thus, Kimberly, for example, who thanks to its involvement in the Colombian and Peruvian leniency programs benefited from the total exoneration of the millionaire fine imposed in each country, now is obligated to pay the economic sanction, which it had avoided in the first place, due to the SGCA's decision.

This situation constitutes a serious disincentive for companies with operations in Andean Community countries when taking part in regional leniency programs, and it also causes an effect on the companies' legal certainty that already participated in these programs and had previously obtained the corresponding benefits.

No offender will be persuaded in obtaining benefits in exchange of disclosing their involvement in a restrictive practice and collaborating with its dismantling within a leniency program's framework, if they know that due to their engagement, a supranational authority such as the SGCA can impose millionaire sanctions. Much less when it comes to an authority such as the SGCA, which in addition to a precarious research capacity does not have its own leniency program.

On the other hand, the SGCA's investigation and sanction circumstances weaken the Andean Community national public policies for competition protection. This is because such circumstances have eroded their leniency programs, which are the most effective tool for cartel's detection and dismantling, as the international community has said.

Some go even further and state that this case also affected Andean community non-member countries' leniency programs.[16] They argue that SGCA's specific behavior

16. *See* Mena-Labarthe, Carlos; Barahona, Jaime; Marques de Carvalho, Vinicius; and Frade Eduardo. (2018). The end of leniency programs in the Andean Region? Competition Policy International. April 18. Available in: https://www.competitionpolicyinternational.com/the-end-of-leniency-programs-in-the-andean-region/.

In the same sense, *see* Mena-Labarthe, Carlos; Barahona, Jaime; Marques de Carvalho, Vinicius; and Frade Eduardo. (2018). Call to Arms in Defense of the Leniency Programs in Latin America. Competition Policy International. Julio, 23. Available in: https://www.

discourages not only companies with operations in Andean Community countries on taking part in the member countries' leniency programs, but also for those who can access Mexico's, Argentina's or Brazil's leniency programs and have businesses in the Andean countries.

In this way, they also point out that SGCA's decision not only affected countries with younger national leniency programs, but also affected those with more or less consolidated leniency programs.[17]

§9.03 SGCA'S OPERATION AND ITS COORDINATION WITH NATIONAL LENIENCY PROGRAMS

As noted, the SGCA's investigation and sanction imposed on two companies in the Resolution No. 2006 of 2018 produced confusion and concern among the members of the legal, institutional and academic regional community.

Moreover, this concern was extended to other scenarios such as the OECD's Competition Committee[18] round table, as well as in the International Chamber of Commerce Competition Committee, which addressed the topic at their meetings.[19]

Those who have expressed their concern, wonder for example, about SGCA's powers limitation when it comes to scenarios where companies have already benefited from a national leniency program.[20]

Others even ask about the real justification of having an Andean system of competition protection and suggest its total suppression, since, in their opinion, the Andean Community's economic integration purpose has not been fulfilled after almost fifty years and each day, that purpose seems even more unattainable.[21]

Other people warn that a sanction, such as the one imposed by the SGCA in Resolution No. 2006 of 2018, goes against one of the integration purposes that inspired

competitionpolicyinternational.com/called-a-las-armas-en-defensa-de-los-programas-de-clemencia-en-america-latina/.

17. *Ídem.*
18. The negative impact of the performance of the SGCA was put forward by Colombia and Peru in the round table held in June 2018 within the OECD Competition Committee, called "Roundtable on challenges and co-ordination of leniency programs." The Colombian contribution can be seen in: https://one.oecd.org/document/DAF/COMP/WP3/WD(2018)14/en/pdf The Colombian contribution can be seen in: https://one.oecd.org/document/DAF/COMP/WP3/WD(2018)18/en/pdf.
19. Ver Mena-Labarthe, Carlos; Barahona, Jaime; Marques de Carvalho, Vinicius; and Frade Eduardo. (2018). Llamado a las Armas en Defensa de los Programas de Clemencia en América Latina. Competition Policy International. Julio, 23. Available at: https://www.competitionpolicyinternational.com/llamado-a-las-armas-en-defensa-de-los-programas-de-clemencia-en-america-latina/.
20. *See* Competition Law Colombian Association Roundtable Decision No. 608: Is a community competition regime justified? Attorney Alfonso Miranda Londoño intervention. Available at: https://www.youtube.com/watch?v=igmSmdRFWTc&disable_polymer=true.
21. *See* Colombian Association of Competition Law. Roundtable Decision No. 608: Is a community competition regime justified? Intervention lawyer Gabriel Ibarra Pardo. Available at: https://www.youtube.com/watch?v=igmSmdRFWTc&disable_polymer=true.

the Andean Community creation: the member countries national laws harmonization.[22]

However, there are also those who warn about the convenience and necessity of having a competition protection supranational authority, but at the same time, they request that these efforts respect the national policies that include tools such as leniency programs.[23]

We share this last perspective, which is why the reasons for a competition protection supranational authority's existence is convenient and necessary are exposed in the following section. In addition, some considerations regarding the conditions under which an authority of that competence can coordinately work with consolidated national competition authorities or in the process of consolidation are also presented next.

[A] Supranational Authorities' Convenience and Need

Those of us who are enthusiastic about competition protection should welcome any national or supranational effort to establish tools against competition restrictive practices that may affect markets' efficiency and consumers' welfare. In the Latin American case, the Andean Community established a supranational regime in Decision No. 608 of 2005.

Despite some apocalyptic visions, understandable due to the SGCA's Resolution No. 2006 of 2018s repercussions, there is consensus among the Andean Community countries on the need to maintain the essence of this effort with some necessary reforms in order to avoid some failures that surfaced during the first investigation and punishment's case.

The fact that the economic integration proposed in the 1969s Cartagena Agreement has not been achieved just yet does not mean that we should desist from the idea of it or the Andean Community's existence importance for Andean markets' regulation.

Furthermore, it is wrong to interpret the Andean Community as an international organization with purely economic purposes; since its creation was inspired by principles similar to those that were the basis of the European integration process, according to which, behind economic integration would come a political coexistence among the states.

In this sense, the Andean Community stands out from other international organizations that promote integration since its Member States established the possibility of their bodies to issue direct and prevailing supranational norms application regarding national regulations.

---

22. McConnell, Charles (2018). Peru joins Colombia in Andean leniency fight. Global Competition Review. May, 23 Available in: https://globalcompetitionreview.com/article/1169896/peru-joins-colombia-in-andean-leniency-fight.
23. *See*, for example, McConnell, Charles (2018). Leniency fight divides Colombia from regional body. May 10. Available in: https://globalcompetitionreview.com/article/1169321/leniency-fight-divides-colombia-from-regional-body.

It is true that, unlike what happened in the Andean Community, where economic integration has suffered several setbacks, in the European case this seems to occur naturally. The above perhaps since the geographical relationship between the different European markets has deep historical roots and due to the communications' development. In this matter, the possibility of having direct and preferential common legal regimes over national legal regimes application was particularly important, in order to facilitate the integration's objective.

Therefore, the importance of a supranational authority's existence that investigates and sanctions behaviors that, for territorial jurisdiction's reason, are beyond the reach of national competition authorities is undeniable. Even more now, regarding the Latin American's growing economies' internationalization.

Consider, for example, how beneficial it would have been for Latin American countries to have a supranational tool in order to address the serious corruption problem at the behest of Brazilian company Odebrecht, and in this order, articulate the negotiation mechanisms for the dismantling of these corrupt practices.

From this point of view, it is necessary to assure that the problems that have arisen due to the Andean Community's competition authority powers, such as those proposed in Resolution No. 2006 of 2018, cannot be resolved with the suppression of such powers. This would have serious repercussions, not only regarding a backward path in the integration process, but also on a lower institutional capacity to discipline markets in cases in which businessmen's illegal behaviors go beyond state borders.

This has been noted not only by the State of Colombia, but also by the SIC, its national competition authority, which, in recent years, at the same time that supranational mechanisms such as Decision No. 608 of 2005s existence was extolled, proactively participated in the Andean competition system reforms proposal, in order to strengthen the fight against anti-competitive practices at a sub-regional level.[24]

---

24. The Colombian State has thus referred to Decision No. 608 of 2005:

> "The Republic of Colombia, through a communication sent by its Ministry of Commerce, Industry and Tourism, presented as its considerations those issued by the Delegate Superintendent for the Promotion of Free Competition of the Superintendence of Industry and Commerce. In particular, he highlighted that within the objectives of integration and economic cooperation among the Andean Community member countries, they include facilitating the member countries participation in the regional integration process, with a Latin American common market view gradual formation", in addition to "tending to reduce external vulnerability and improve member countries position in the international economic context," as the Cartagena Agreement in its Article 1 indicates.

Likewise, the Republic of Colombia affirmed that, as special mechanisms for the implementation and execution of such objectives, it was stipulated that "the gradual harmonization of economic and social policies and the approximation of national legislations in the pertinent matters", as it refers expressly the Cartagena Agreement in its Article 3.

Under these considerations, the Republic of Colombia affirmed that, to these objectives and mechanisms, there are underlying concerns expressed in the Cartagena Agreement which states as distortions of competition in the subregion to: "undue manipulation of prices, maneuvers intended to disturb the normal supply of raw materials and others of equivalent effect", as indicated in Article 93.

Below are a few proposals on the conditions in which an authority can coordinately work with consolidated national competition authorities, specifically, regarding the need to maintain the leniency programs trust.

[B] Towards a Transnational Leniency System in the Andean Community (Proposals)

So far, the importance of a supranational anti-competitive conducts investigation and punishment tools, which suppose the inability of the national authorities to discipline markets that go beyond their state borders, has been addressed.

In addition, the need for such tools to not affect other national authorities' tools, such as leniency programs.

It is now necessary to consider the scenarios in which it seems feasible to achieve the necessary coordination between the SGCA and the Andean community member countries' competition authorities, especially regarding the leniency programs' effectiveness.

These scenarios, which can be complementary, are limited to the SGCA's exercise of powers reform and to a supranational leniency programs' establishment.

[1] SGCA's Exercise Power Regulation in Competition Matters Regarding Companies That Have Benefited from National Leniency Programs

In 2016, the Competition Defense Andean Committee discussed some regime reforms established in the Decision No. 608 of 2005, under some Andean Community member's conviction regarding the supranational tool utility for competition protection in the region.

In this scenario, the SIC made some proposals in order to strengthen the supranational authority functioning. The proposal came with a warning: the reform's purpose cannot be established to replace the prerogatives of the national competition authorities, but to facilitate SGCA's action regarding cases that have a serious subregional interference and are in line with Article 5 of the Decision.

As principles reforms guidance, the SIC proposed the following: (i) the need to homogenize the Andean Community member countries competition regimes, in compliance with the international organization's objectives; (ii) permanent coordination and cooperation mechanisms between national competition authorities; and (iii) sufficient national authorities participation in a supranational authority power exercise.

In this regard, the SIC proposed the extension of the SGCA's investigative faculty and the clear definition of the moment in which this prescription is interrupted; the evidentiary term suppression established in Decision No. 608 of 2005, in order to strengthen the SGCA's investigative capacity; the SGCA's extension term to prepare the

---

See Opinion No. 03-2009 of the General Secretariat of the Andean Community. Official Gazette of the Cartagena Agreement. Year XXVI. Number 1723. Lima, June 10, 2009.

investigations results report presented to the Competition Defense Andean Committee; and the need to include a preliminary investigation process, in which the national authorities play a preponderant role by conducting surprise inspection visits (dawn raids).

However, as demonstrated by what happened with SGCA's Resolution No. 2006 of 2018, in order to avoid the loss of the Andean competition regime legitimacy, regulation of these situations is urgent, in which the national competition authorities' decisions are based regarding the information generated in their leniency programs' framework.

It is urgent to adopt reforms that categorically prohibit the SGCA's faculty to initiate investigations based on facts revealed by an informer in a national leniency program's framework or supported in the depositions that itself contributed during the process.

Furthermore, and in order to strengthen the national leniency programs, it is convenient to establish that anti-competitive conducts investigations and sanctions committed by those who have been recognized as informers and benefit creditors in the national leniency programs are completely excluded from SGCA's knowledge.

It is also important that the SGCA cannot initiate any type of investigation in these cases, without the national competition authority's opinion and approval that grants the respective benefits, since evidently in this case national competition protection policies are involved.

[2] A SGCA's Supranational Leniency Program

In addition to the foregoing, in order to strengthen competition in the region, it is convenient to create a leniency program for conducts that fit into Article 5 of Decision No. 608 of 2005, which defines SGCA's strict powers.

As it has been said, leniency programs represent an effective tool in the fight against cartels, so they should be included in an Andean competition protection regime.

The introduction of an Andean leniency program was proposed in the Defense Competition Andean Committee, during the discussion of Decision's No. 608 of 2005 reform.

During this discussion, the SIC drew attention to the need to establish precise rules to avoid SGCA's and national authorities' power duplication in the respective leniency programs.

In addition, it is necessary to coordinate the benefits offered by each authority, so that incentives are not set to promote or avoid the use of any of the supranational or national leniency programs.

§9.04 CONCLUSIONS

The study of what happened with Resolution No. 2006 of 2018, its effect on the member countries of the Andean Community leniency programs and the proposals for the coexistence of these with a supranational competence authority lead us to the following conclusion.

The Decision No. 608 of 2005 regime's reform set to regulate national leniency's subjects, as well as the introduction of an Andean leniency program and, in general, the SGCA's investigative and sanction powers, require the establishment of cooperation, coordination and information permanent tools exchange between the national authorities and between these and the SGCA.

In fact, what happened with the Resolution No. 2006 of 2018 shows that, at present, the SGCA lacks the regulatory and technical tools, as well as the institutional capacity to develop an investigation within the powers attributed by Andean Community. In addition, the SGCA discarded without any explanation the observations made regarding the effects of its behavior, opinions made by the Colombian and Peruvian competition authorities.

For this reason, the national competition authorities' participation is urgent; especially those with more experience who have consolidated tools and policies set to fight anti-competitive practices.

The Andean Community has to forge its own path in the search for competition community tools. The integration process advances in the European Union's case may be a good example to watch and study.[25]

Unlike what happens in Europe, where the community leniency program gave rise to the more or less standardized national leniency programs, in Latin America the SGCA's tools must look after the national competition's policies advances and

25. EU law aims to ensure a consistent application of competition rules in the Member States through a mechanism of cooperation between the Commission and national competition authorities. This mechanism is called "the European Competition Network" (REC). In 2006, the REC adopted, at European level, a model leniency program. In subsequent years, several national authorities' members of the REC and the Commission adopted similar programs of denunciation within their corporations.

Regarding competition, these respective of benefits' programs for collaboration of the Union of the Member States coexist in an autonomous manner, with the Commission being competent to know behaviors with effects in several of the member territories of the Union, and the national authorities on derivative effects of conducts carried out in their corresponding territories.

As above mentioned, the leniency programs application of both the commission and the European national authorities are completely independent and autonomous from each other.

In this regard, the European Court of Justice' ruling can be seen in the litigation between DHL Express, DHL Global, Agility Logistics and Shenker for allegedly having consolidated a cartel in the national and international merchandise transport market, in which ruled that the information and requests submitted to both the Commission and the European national authorities enjoy absolute independence. Incidentally, the Court finally ruled that (i) there is no legal link between the application for the leniency program admission filed with the Commission and the application filed with the corresponding national authority, (ii) the national authority is not obliged to review the applications they receive in light of the one presented to the Commission, as the two are totally independent, (iii) the authority does not have to contact the Commission to obtain information corresponding to the object and development of the investigations, (iv) a high request before a national authority can be accepted even if it has not been submitted to the Commission and, furthermore, (v) a company could benefit from the reduction of a sanction imposed by the national authority and at the same time, can be exonerated from the total fine imposed by the Commission if it is the first applicant for admission to the leniency program.

strengths, since, in some cases, such as the Colombian and Peruvian authorities, the competition protection regimes have taken decades to develop.

Thus, while these community tools are consolidated, the current Andean Community competition integration's struggle involves the construction of a genuine cooperation network among national competition authorities and the establishment of assistance channels. These mechanisms are designed for the SGCA, as a supranational authority, to execute its functions in the best possible way, which is, in true benefit of the regional competition protection.

However, it is also fundamental, and so is required by the legal, institutional and academic community, that the SGCA clearly recognizes the progress, policies and efforts that national authorities in a national level have carried through. Efforts such as the national leniency programs that Resolution No. 2006 of 2018 put in risk without any justification and in detriment of the regional competition protection policies.

Part III Challenges with Competitive Neutrality and Public Interest

CHAPTER 10

Competitive Neutrality and the Role of Competition Authorities: A Glance at Experiences in Europe and Asia-Pacific

Deborah Healey

Competition law traditionally focused on the conduct of business enterprises which had an anticompetitive effect on market competition. It is clear, however, that the effect of government actions on competition in markets is likely to be significant and lasting:

> ... for harms to competition, the State is the biggest culprit because it can erect impenetrable barriers and privilege itself, its businesses and its friend as no private actor can do without the help of the State. But, of course, the State is also a guardian of the public good.[1]

It is only relatively recently that the anticompetitive effect of government in the market has been fully recognised and law and policy steps taken to address the issue. While some jurisdictions such as the European Union (EU) and Australia have had formal structures in place for some time to address competitive neutrality issues, the pace of acceptance has been slower in others, particularly in developing jurisdictions. At the time of a research project led by the author with results published in 2014, for example, of seven countries involved in the research (China, India, Malaysia, Pakistan, Russia, Switzerland and Vietnam), only India showed any real appetite for competitive neutrality policy reform.[2]

1. Eleanor M. Fox and Damien Gerard, EU Competition Law: Cases, Texts and Context (2017) Edward Elgar Cheltenham UK, 333.
2. *See* Deborah Healey (ed.) Competitive Neutrality and its Application in Selected Developing Countries (2014) United Nations Conference on Trade and Development, available at https://unctad.org/en/Pages/DITC/CompetitionLaw/ResearchPartnership/Competitive-Neutrality.

This chapter briefly examines competitive neutrality policy frameworks in several developed and developing jurisdictions to show the diversity of approaches currently being delivered.[3]

§10.01 INTRODUCTION: THE ROLE OF GOVERNMENT IN THE MARKET

Competition law and policy assume that a level playing field will deliver the most efficient competitors who will provide goods and services at the lowest prices, stimulating innovation, to the benefit of the economy generally and to consumers.[4]

Governments affect markets by the laws and regulations which they make, and by their policy decisions and other market interventions. Governments also conduct business in the market by way of their state-owned enterprises (SOEs) and other bodies which they own, control or influence. SOEs and other bodies affect markets when they are engaged in business in competition with private businesses or are engaged in business which might otherwise attract private players to the market. Government influence in markets may be inadvertent or by design and may include market impact by way of the implementation of industrial policy.

A number of meanings are attributed to 'competitive neutrality'. The Organisation for Economic Co-operation and Development (OECD) has addressed the issue by stating that '...the legal and regulatory framework for state-owned enterprises should ensure a level playing field in markets where state-owned enterprises and private sector companies compete in order to avoid market distortions.'[5]

The OECD approach focuses on the application of the same legal and regulatory frameworks to SOEs and private market participants and the application of the competition law of the jurisdiction to SOEs where they are engaged in business. The Australian approach assumes that competition law applies to government business activity and focuses on the idea that '...government business activities that are in competition with the private sector should not have a competitive advantage merely by virtue of government ownership and control.'[6]

---

aspx. China did have its administrative monopoly provisions but has since embarked on a much broader policy to deal with the issue – *see* later.

3. It takes an expansive view of the problem in examining the issue and includes some reference to policies and laws dealing with anticompetitive regulation and policy making.
4. Different jurisdictions take an individual approach to the goals of competition law and there is current debate on the appropriateness of some goals, such as privacy. However, this chapter takes a fairly traditional simple economic approach as the backdrop to the discussion. See, for example, the views expressed in Frederick Hilmer and Independent Commission of Inquiry into Competition Policy in Australia, National Competition Policy Review (1993) (Hilmer Review, 2-4.
5. OECD, OECD Guidelines on Corporate Governance of State-Owned Enterprises, (2005), 18, noted in Thomas K. Cheng, Competitive Neutrality from an Asian Perspective, OECD, DAF/COMP/WD (2015)49, 2. For the updated 2015 Guidelines see https://www.oecd.org/corporate/guidelines-corporate-governance-soes.htm
6. Deborah Healey, Competitive Neutrality: the Concept, in UNCTAD Research Partnership Platform: Competitive Neutrality and Its Application in Selected Developing Countries (2014), 12. Other authors have suggested that competitive neutrality also applies to the behaviour of regulators in the selection and enforcement of competition law provisions. This chapter assumes that this will be the case. *See* Nicolas Petit, Implications of Competitive Neutrality for Competition

Several approaches to implementing competitive neutrality are explored in this chapter. The structural models can be placed along a continuum from the most comprehensive to the most light-handed, the models discussed here being: a specific competitive neutrality policy, either alone or as part of a comprehensive competition policy; a specific law, regulation or agreement (enforceable or not); and addressing the problem by advocacy, with or without a legislative mandate for the regulator, and with or without accountability of government.

§10.02 HOW BIG A PROBLEM IS THIS?

Historical, cultural, political and economic factors will dictate the nature of government involvement in markets. Given the number of jurisdictions which have now adopted initiatives around competitive neutrality, it is clear that the competition issues involving government and competitive neutrality are well recognised. Notably in the Russian Federation, for example, it is acknowledged that more than 50% of antitrust complaints considered by the Federal Antimonopoly Service (FAS) annually relate to government agencies and SOEs.[7] It is likely that competitive neutrality issues will be prominent in jurisdictions which have a large number of SOEs, but the nature of other government market interventions will also be important in determining the significance of competitive neutrality issues in a jurisdiction. In China, for example, a country with a very large number of SOEs at all levels of government, and with a history of laws and regulations protecting government and SOEs, particularly at a provincial level, powerful initiatives in law and policy are now being implemented to address government market interventions.[8] Both developed and developing countries now recognise competitive neutrality as an important competition law and policy issue.

§10.03 WHAT IS COMPETITIVE NEUTRALITY?

The most basic step in levelling the playing field for competition between government bodies and private companies is the application of the competition law to government businesses. Most jurisdictions apply competition law to SOEs where they are engaged in trade or carrying on business.[9] Second, laws, regulations and policies should not advantage SOEs or other government bodies. As noted earlier, competitive neutrality policy in some jurisdictions also recognises the advantage which government

---

Agencies: A Process Perspective, OECD RoundTable on Competition Neutrality, (2015) DAF/COMP/WD(2015) 50, 2. The chapter does not address ideas relating to competitive neutrality involving issues of privatisation or where government is not involved. *See* Cheng, n. 5, 3.

7. Response to research questionnaire by Federal Antimonopoly Service of the Russian Federation, Eleanor Fox and Deborah Healey, Competition Law and the State Part II, on-going project, UNCTAD Research Partnership Platform.
8. *See* below.
9. Eleanor Fox and Deborah Healey, When the State Harms Competition: The Role for Competition Law 79 Antitrust Law Journal 769 (2014). *See also* International Competition Network, Annual Conference, Special Project of Moroccan Conseil de la Concurrence, State-Owned Enterprises and Competition, Marrakesh 23–25 April 2014, 14.

businesses often have when competing in markets. It recognises that significant government businesses in competition with the private sector should not have a competitive advantage merely because they are owned and controlled by government. Competitive neutrality policy in this context is thus the steps or mechanisms put in place to ensure that the market is 'neutral' in respect of SOEs.

Many examples of these competitive advantages exist. SOEs may have advantages linked to immunity from taxes, charges and regulatory requirements; explicit or implicit government guarantee of debt; concessional interest rates on loans; no accounting for depreciation expenses; no expectation of achieving a commercial rate of return; effective immunity from bankruptcy; and pricing policies which do not fully account for production costs. In some countries, SOEs find it much easier than other companies to get bank finance. Of course, and depending upon the circumstances, there are also potential disadvantages of being a government business: greater accountability; community service obligations; reduced managerial autonomy; compliance with other government policies. These also need to be factored into any assessment of competitive neutrality.

Finally, competitive neutrality has both national and international implications. Within a jurisdiction where SOEs are advantaged, more efficient private competitors may be driven out of the market because of the advantages of their SOE competitor. Internationally, SOEs supported by their government may enter foreign jurisdictions and disadvantage or drive out more efficient local competitors. Competitive neutrality has an interesting relationship with industrial policy and the whole idea of 'state capitalism'.

The next section discusses current approaches to the issue of competitive neutrality with specific case studies from representative jurisdictions.

§10.04 COMPETITIVE NEUTRALITY: ADOPTION OF A POLICY

A competitive neutrality policy can be implemented either alone or as part of a more comprehensive competition policy.[10] A competition policy may be binding on participants if it forms part of an agreement between them. The outcomes which can be achieved will depend upon the extent to which the policy is enforceable.

Australia

Australia, which has been described as having the 'most comprehensive competition policy' worldwide by the OECD,[11] has had a working competition law for more than forty years. It is important to note, however, that competitive neutrality in Australia is contained in a competition *policy,* and that the competition regulator, the Australian

10. 'Competition Policy refers to government policy to preserve or promote competition among market players and to promote other government policies and processes that enable a competitive environment to develop. UNCTAD, the relationship between competition and industrial policies in promoting economic development', TD/B/C. I/CLP/3, 27 April 2009.
11. OECD, Competitive Neutrality: Maintaining a Level Playing Field between Public and Private Business: Report on OECD and National Best Practices in Competitive Neutrality (2012), 64.

Competition and Consumer Commission, does not enforce it. Australia undertook a comprehensive and influential review of competition law and policy in 1992.[12] The Hilmer Review, as it became known after the leader of the review group, recommended reform to the competition law (then known as the Trade Practices Act) to ensure that all market participants, including most government bodies engaged in business at Commonwealth, State, Territory and local government levels, were subject to its provisions. The review also made many recommendations about competition policy, many based on the idea of creation of true national market, including competitive neutrality. It recommended both retrospective and on-going prospective review of the anticompetitive effect of laws at both national and state level, and made recommendations on the reform, and restructure and privatisation of SOEs and other government bodies. It recommended the implementation of competitive neutrality policy for government bodies at state and national levels.[13] Competitive neutrality was to be applied to significant business activities charging for goods and services, with an actual or potential competitor, when its application would result in a net benefit to society. For many years financial rewards based on estimated efficiency gains of policy implementation were given by the Commonwealth government to state and territory governments as incentives for implementation of these and other national competition policy (NCP) reforms, although this has now ceased.

Most Hilmer recommendations were accepted and implemented by governments. The nature of Australia as a federal system of government with states and territories raised constitutional issues about how a national competition policy including competitive neutrality might be implemented. Ultimately, the national competition policy as a whole, including competitive neutrality and regulatory review (NCP), was implemented under an agreement between the Commonwealth, the states and territories. Each of these parties was free to implement the competitive neutrality policy under its own agenda, subject to their agreement to specified basic elements.[14]

Competitive neutrality in this context is achieved by the initiatives addressing the advantages of SOEs, such as by the payment of taxes or tax equivalents by significant government bodies engaged in significant business activities. SOEs should achieve a commercial rate of return on assets, should pay commercial interest rates or debt neutrality charges, and comply with regulations which apply to private sector competitors. Pricing should account for all costs.

However, competitive neutrality policy does not prevent government from pursuing other legitimate policy objectives.

12. See fn 5. A full discussion of the Australian position, including history and current issues can be found in Deborah Healey and Rhonda Smith, Competitive Neutrality in Australia: Opportunity for Policy Development 25 Competition and Consumer Law Journal 223–248 (2018).
13. *See* generally Deborah Healey, Competitive Neutrality: Addressing Government Advantage in Australian Markets in Josef Drexl and Vicente Bagnoli, State Initiated restraints of Competition Edward Elgar (2015) 3–39.
14. *See* Council of Australian Governments, Competition Principles Agreement (11 April 1995) as amended (13 April 2007).

In practical terms, the implementation of competitive neutrality policy in Australia is undertaken in the following way: competitive neutrality complaints at Commonwealth, state and territory level are dealt with by independent units, by existing regulators or government departments. It should be remembered that under the Competition Principles Agreement [15] each jurisdiction was free to approaches the implementation of competitive neutrality policy in its own way subject to some conditions. The remainder of this part focuses on competitive neutrality at Commonwealth level.

At Commonwealth level, competitive neutrality complaints are dealt with by the Australian Government Competitive Neutrality Complaints Office (AGCNCO), which is an autonomous unit within the Australian Productivity Commission. AGCNCO accepts complaints, assesses them and provides advice to the parties including the government body involved. If a suitable resolution of the complaint cannot be achieved, AGCNCO may inform the Treasurer of its conclusions, but the government is not obliged to comply with the AGCNCO advice. AGCNCO may recommend a public inquiry. There are no penalties for non-compliance with competitive neutrality policy, but transparent examination of conduct and publication of outcomes increases the accountability of government businesses and portfolio ministers.[16]

Various complaints about competitive neutrality have been considered by the Commonwealth, the states and territories. Complaints surrounding the implementation of the National Broadband Network (NBN), for example, led to a detailed review by AGCNCO, [17] and it found that NBN Co had breached competitive neutrality policy in a number of respects. AGCNCO also found that there were a number of issues of policy uncertainty arising from the NBN Co circumstances. Issues arising related to policy for pricing of infrastructure in greenfields developments and appropriate rate of return on government assets. Other issues which have arisen in relation to competitive neutrality policy, and which are currently under review by the on-going Treasury inquiry, include review of the definition of 'significant business activity'; the nature of the 'public interest test'; lack of certainty that non-compliance will be addressed; lack of compensation for private sector firms injured by the conduct; and relatively high cost in dollars and time for businesses which pursue complaints.[18]

Competitive neutrality is generally regarded in Australia as a very positive initiative.[19] The Treasury Review outcome is awaited with interest.

---

15. Above n.14.
16. The process has been reviewed several times: Productivity Commission Review of National Competition Policy Arrangements, 21 June 2004; Competition and Infrastructure Reform Agreement (CIRA)1.4,6.1 in 2006 enhanced and clarified obligations of State, Territories and Commonwealth; Competition Policy Review 2015 (Harper Review). Arising out of the Harper Review recommendations Treasury commenced a Review of Commonwealth Government's Competitive Neutrality Policy in March 2017 (Treasury Review), which is on-going. Treasury proposes to release a revised competitive neutrality policy and supporting statement that reflects submissions from stakeholders and the Secretariat's report following completion of the review.
17. AGCNCO, NBN Co, Investigation NO 14, 2011, https://www.pc.gov.au/inquiries/completed/nbnco/report14-nbnco.pdf.
18. *See* Healey and Smith, above n. 14 for further discussion of these issues.
19. *See* reviews mentioned at n. 16.

[A] Philippines

The Philippine Competition Act was implemented in 2015 and its competition regulator is the Philippines Competition Commission. Its objectives include to:[20]

> ... enhance economic efficiency and promote free and fair competition in trade, industry and all commercial economic activities, as well as establish a National Competition Policy to be implemented by the Government of the Republic of the Philippines and all of its political agencies as a whole.

In short, the Act is aimed at steering regulations and administrative procedures of government agencies toward promotion of competition, as well as strengthening the enforcement of antitrust laws and ensuring competitive neutrality.[21]

The Philippine Development Plan ('Development Plan') (PDP) 2017–2022 is a broad and impressive economic initiative which among other things foreshadows the NCP.[22] The Development Plan expressly 'seeks to enhance market competition by fostering an environment that penalizes anti-competitive practices, facilitates entry of players and supports regulatory reforms to stimulate investments and innovation.'[23] The Development Plan aims to level the playing field for competition and in this context refers to review of laws and regulations, enforcement and competitive neutrality. The Development Plan states:

'Competition law and the corresponding mechanism to enforce it is an essential component of a national competition policy. In formulating the NCP, the other equally essential components, such as policies relating to competitive neutrality, consumer protection, government regulations that do not impede competition, and removal of structural barriers are established, and that an effective institutional mechanism to coordinate and oversee the implementation of these inter-related components is put in place.'[24]

In the context of government in the market, the Philippine Development Plan refers to specific existing areas of preferential treatment enjoyed by government-owned and controlled corporations (known as GOCCs in the Philippines) and notes that they currently also enjoy tax exemptions and other incentives. In the circumstances, the Plan concludes that

> ... measures must be made to ensure that they are not given undue advantage when they directly or indirectly compete with firms in the provision of goods and services.[25]

The Plan also refers to State-enabled policies and barriers which have created distortions in the market such as by government monopolies, government authorised

20. Philippine Competition Act, section 2(a).
21. Philippine Development Plan 2017–2022 (Philippine Development Plan), 246. available at http://extwprlegs1.fao.org/docs/pdf/phi169293.pdf.
22. Philippine Development Plan.
23. *See* Philippine Development Plan, 245.
24. Philippine Development Plan, 246.
25. Philippine Development Plan, 247.

private monopolies, government control of entry and expansion of market players, and government provision of goods and services in competition with private participants. Reference is made to government actions which not only address important social objectives but also create market distortions by limiting the entry and expansion of current players and protecting vested interests; other government-authorised monopolies; controlled pricing of some essential foods; and discriminatory laws and regulations.

The Philippines is targeting a move to the top 25% of all economies for market efficiency and consumer welfare by the end of the Plan following the implementation of the NCP.[26] To ensure that these results will be achieved the Philippine Competition Commission (PCC) will undertake the following activities:

- review legislation and policies that may substantially prevent, restrict or lessen competition;
- analyse competition issues in priority sectors;
- investigate conduct and agreements that may substantially prevent restrict or lessen competition;
- promote competition-related policies and best practices;
- conduct capacity building activities;
- institutionalise a mechanism for the implementation of NCP.

Competitive neutrality is a pillar of NCP, and there is commitment to holding SOEs to the same standards as private sector businesses and not allowing them to enjoy any competitive advantages over private sector businesses simply by virtue of public sector ownership, unless it can be clearly demonstrated that the greater public interest will be served and there is a lack of commercial viability.[27]

The NCP is still under development and it is expected that it will be adopted by Executive Order in early 2019. There is significant commitment to the implementation of NCP within the jurisdiction.

In addition to the NCP, the Philippines envisages a significant role for regulator advocacy. The PCC has specific advocacy roles under the Competition Act in relation to competition issues generally, and in relation to competitive neutrality. In addition to enforcement and other roles, the PCC is charged with reviewing economic and administrative regulations and advising government on competitive implications of its policies and programmes (Philippines Competition Act, section 12(r)). It is also required to assist the National Economic and Development Authority in the formulation of the NCPs and programmes (Philippines Competition Act, section 12(o)).

Thus, in the Philippines the PCC has legislative roles in relation to NCP (including competitive neutrality) and in relation to advocacy in areas which include competitive neutrality. The Philippines thus takes a broad approach to competition law and policy and has taken huge steps towards the creation of a level playing field for competition in a short period.

26. Philippine Development Plan, 249.
27. Philippine Competition Plan, 251.

Both Australia and the Philippines have taken a comprehensive approach to competition law and policy and to addressing government involvement in markets. They both apply competition laws to SOEs and other government businesses. They have NCP initiatives addressing anticompetitive laws, regulation and policies favouring government. NCPs also address competitive neutrality in the context of the advantages maintained merely because a body is owned or controlled by government.

§10.05 TREATMENT UNDER A SPECIFIC LAW

The second category of approach is to address competition concerns by way of statute.

[A] European Union

The EU is a good example of a jurisdiction with specific legal provisions covering competitive neutrality, which it does in the context of its laws on state aids and also under various internal trade provisions of the Treaty on the Functioning of the European Union (TFEU).[28] In the case of the EU, the policy really has its basis in the need to maintain a level playing field not only in the context of both public and private competitors but also in the context of the goal of a single market. The TFEU prohibits the grant of state aids which have the capacity to distort competition in the internal market (Articles 107–109).[29] Basically, any aid granted by a Member State or through state resources which distorts or threatens to distort competition by favouring certain undertakings or the production of certain goods is incompatible with the internal market if it affects trade between Member States. It is important to note that these provisions apply to state aids provided to both government and private bodies. Certain specific exemptions are listed for aids which are declared to be compatible with the internal market, such as aids of a social character granted to individual consumers or aids to make good damage caused by national disasters or exceptions occurrences (Article 107(2)). Other aids may be permitted such as those to remedy a serious disturbance in the economy of a Member State, which was invoked in relation to financial institutions following the Global Financial Crisis of 2008 '...so that Member States could adopt measures to safeguard the stability of their financial systems without unduly distorting competition.'[30] Article 107(3) provides for the balancing of benefits from addressing a market failure or other objective in the common interest against the distortionary effect of the conduct, with the Article only being contravened

28. *See* Article 107–109 TFEU on state aids.
29. SOEs and government bodies are caught by the TFEU if they are classified as 'undertakings'. Article 106 prohibits Member States from adopting, with regard to public undertakings and undertakings which have been given exclusive or special rights any measure which would lead to infringement of provisions including Articles 101, 102 or the free movement provisions. However, Article 106(2) provides that Services of General Economic Interest (SGEI) are excepted to the extent that the conduct is necessary to achieve the purposes entrusted to them.
30. *See* Richard Whish and David Bailey, Competition Law, 7th Edition (2012) Oxford University Press, 246-247.

if the balance is negative.[31] Block exemptions have been enacted to permit conduct which falls within particular listed categories and which allows the Commission to concentrate on cases which are more important.[32]

State aids may be approved prior to implementation for reasons listed in Article 107(2) and 107(3). If permission is not granted or permission is not sought, the Commission must direct the State to abolish or alter the conduct and to recover aid granted. If the state fails to comply, the Commission or an interested Member State may refer the matter to the Court of Justice.[33]

The Treaty importantly institutes a system '...ensuring that competition in the internal market is not distorted.'[34] Member States are obliged to conduct their economic policy in accordance with the principles of an 'open market economy with free competition'.[35] Member States must take all appropriate measures to fulfil Treaty obligations[36] and abstain from all measures that would jeopardise Treaty obligations. The TFEU also guarantees four freedoms. These are the free movement of goods[37] and persons;[38] the freedom of establishment to provide services;[39] and the free movement of capital.[40]

State aids account for half of the enforcement activity of the Directorate-General for Competition in the EU.[41] One important example where state aids were found not to be involved was the Altmark case.[42] It involved provision of services to the state by a private business, in the form of a privatised transport service, where the state continued to cover the costs of public service operations. The state thus required the business to supply services not otherwise provided by the market to meet social policy objectives. The European Court of Justice found that compensation for public services in that context does not constitute state aid where:

- the universal or public service obligation is clearly defined;
- the parameters for compensation are objective, transparent and established in advance;

31. *See* OECD, Roundtable on Competitive Neutrality in Competition Enforcement: Note by European Union (16–18 June 2015) 9–13, referred to in Healey and Smith, above n, where specific examples of state aids are noted.
32. *See* General Block Exemption Regulation 651/2014, which includes aid for environmental protection, risk capital, research and development and innovation, newly created small enterprises and broadband rollout.
33. Eleanor M. Fox and Damien Gerard, EU Competition Law: Cases, Texts and Context (2017) Edward Elgar Cheltenham UK, 313.
34. Protocol on the internal market and competition (Protocol to the Lisbon Treaty).
35. Article 119(1) TFEU.
36. Article 4(3)(2) TEU (Treaty on European Union).
37. Articles 28–37 TFEU.
38. Articles 45–55 TFEU.
39. Articles 56–62 TFEU.
40. Articles 63–66 TFEU.
41. Eleanor M. Fox and Damien Gerard, EU Competition Law: Cases, Texts and Context (2017) Edward Elgar Cheltenham UK, 311.
42. *Altmark Trans GmbH and Regierungsprasidium Magdeburg v. Nahverkehrsgesellschaft Altmark GmbH* (C-280/00) [2003] ECR I-7747.

- compensation does not exceed the costs, including reasonable profit; and compensation is determined either through public procurement or on the basis of the typical costs of a well-run company.

While a full consideration of these EU provisions is beyond the scope of this chapter, and they have been thoroughly considered in a number of well-known publications, it is important to understand that various issues relating to competitive neutrality are thoroughly addressed under EU law.

[B] China: Law and Policy

This material has emphasised that the nature of the political economy of a jurisdiction will dictate vastly different approaches to issues of competitive neutrality.

The Constitution of China designates SOEs as a leading force of the national economy. China has adopted a hybrid system for dealing with the issue of competitive neutrality, having specific provisions in its competition law and implementing a sweeping policy of regulatory review. The latter is important because very many of the beneficiaries of anti-competitive laws, regulations, rules and policies are SOEs or other government bodies. Given the very large number of SOEs in the country and the existing issues surrounding the level playing field, the two-pronged structure of ex ante and ex post regulation is well-justified.

Crucially for this chapter, it has recently been reported that:

> The seemingly unfamiliar expression 'competitive neutrality' has entered public discourse in China. On 14 October [2018] Yi Gang, the governor of the People's Bank of China, told a G-30 meeting that China would accelerate domestic reform and opening-up to the rest of the world, strengthen protection of intellectual property, and consider treating state-owned enterprises (SOEs) with the principle of 'competitive neutrality' in order to solve the structural problem of the Chinese economy.[43]

The use of the words 'competitive neutrality' in the context of economic reform is particularly important as it foreshadows a significant change of approach to the role of SOEs in the marketplace in China.

China implemented its Anti-Monopoly Law (AML) in 2007 and it became operative in 2008. It is a competition law for a socialist market economy, with broad and somewhat unusual objectives, and provisions which in some parts reflect its political economy.

The AML applies to SOEs, but a number of provisions give great discretion to regulators and courts, particularly in circumstances involving industries which are seen to be important to the economy. Using merger analysis as an example, a number of the merger factors do not focus on competitive effect and consider issues such as the effect of the merger on the national economy. The merger process is not always

43. http://www.xinhuanet.com/money/2018-10/15/c_129971267.htm.

transparent; under the AML, the regulator only needs to produce a written determination if the merger is rejected or approved subject to conditions. Most mergers are allowed, so there are relatively few written determinations to assess. Many of these involve SOE mergers.

On the other hand, the AML contains very unusual and detailed provisions on 'administrative monopoly' which attack laws and regulations at provincial and local level which erect barriers, favour locals and establish exclusive contracts and arrangements in an anti-competitive way. Many beneficiaries of this local protectionism are SOEs. These administrative monopoly provisions are regularly enforced. However, under the AML there are no penalties for those breaching the provisions. The process is administrative: recommendations are made to the authorities which oversee the dealings of the authorities or SOEs which breach the administrative monopoly provisions. The latter may be instructed to rectify their behaviour. There is no formal oversight of whether this type of anti-competitive conduct is actually rectified or amended, and no compulsion on administrative superiors to act on the recommendations of the enforcer. Administrative monopoly behaviours are also so pervasive and wide-spread that it is difficult to know the true effect of administrative monopoly provisions in the context of the economy as a whole, despite apparent active attempts to enforce it.

In addition to the administrative monopoly provisions, however, an ex ante Fair Competition Review SystemFCRS was implemented in 2016 by Opinion.[44] The FCRS addresses restrictions on competition by laws, regulations and directives and to that extent it 'pre-empts' the administrative monopoly provisions. The FCRS addresses both existing and new regulation. It requires a review of all new laws, policies, regulations and rules to ensure that they have no anticompetitive effect prior to implementation, in the interests of supporting a national market. Drafts of laws and regulations cannot be submitted to the State Council for implementation without such a review. The FCRS applies to all levels of government, and very significant progress has been made in implementing the programme since its inception.[45]

The Opinion which sets out the processes for the FCRS requires the review issuesareas such as market entry, industrial development, attraction of foreign investment, tendering and bidding, and government procurement in the context of standards on market entry and exit; standards on the free movement of goods and production factors; standards that affect production and operating costs; and standards that affect

44. Opinion on Establishing a Fair Competition Review System during the Development of Market -Orientated Systems, State Council, 1 June 2016. *See* Xiaoye Wang, Promoting the Fair Competition Assessment to Restrain Administrative Monopoly, 1 Competition Law and Policy Review 3 (2016).
45. At the end of 2018, all departments in the State Council and provincial governments, 98% of municipal governments, and 85% of county governments had adopted the system. Seventeen provinces (including the municipality and prefecture) including Beijing, Tianjin and Hebei had reached province-municipality-county three-level implementation of the system. *See* China's State Administration for Market Regulation discloses implementation of FCRS System in 2018, (in Chinese) available at http://www.gov.cn/xinwen/2019-01/27/content_5361519.htm. (SAMR Report).

production and business operations. Exceptions are allowed in areas such as safeguarding national security, national defence construction, poverty alleviation, national development, and energy and resource conservation. Public interest is relevant, and a very broad view of public interest is taken.

Adjustments have been made to the implementing organisation, the system and rules. A SAMR Report in late 2018 [46] indicates that a guide for implementing third party assessment of the FCRS will be released and random audits of departments and provinces are proposed to check on progress. SAMR also proposes to strengthen supervision of processes. While it is difficult to assess the overall effect of the FCRS, it is clear that a huge effort is being made to implement it. It is an enormous task given the number of laws, regulations, rules and policies, and the size and power of the bureaucracy in China.

Thus, the EU approaches competitive neutrality issues by various provisions of the TFEU, and the TEU and the provisions are actively enforced. China has adopted both legislative and policy approaches to these issues and appears to proactively enforce the law and impose the FCRS.

§10.06 ADVOCACY

The final method of dealing with issues of competitive neutrality is advocacy. Advocacy is a key activity of competition regulators, and the activities of governments, including their business operations via SOEs and other entities, is generally an important part of competition law and policy advocacy. Various international bodies see a very broad role for competition advocacy by competition regulators.[47]

Much has been written about the importance of advocacy and its political challenges. The independence of the regulator is generally an important factor in successful advocacy. Several templates for advocacy exist in competition laws. Competition regulators may have a specific mandate in the legislation establishing them to assist governments with drafting laws, regulations and policies. Regulators may have a general mandate to advocate for competition and that role would include advocacy in relation to government and its activities. Finally, even without a specific advocacy role mandated in legislation, many regulators advocate for competition generally. The political challenges of advocacy are acute where commentary on government and its activities is involved, particularly where the regulator makes findings which are critical of government. The independence of the regulator is particularly important in this context, and it is difficult for those regulators which are set up as part of government departments to fulfil this advocacy role effectively, although it is possible to do so.

46. *See* SAMR Report above.
47. *See* World Bank and OECD, A Framework for Design and Implementation of Competition Law and Policy (1998), 93; International Competition Network, Advocacy and Competition Policy, Report prepared by the Advocacy working Group (ICN Conference, Naples, Italy, 2002, i. Both reports are referred to in Hon Mr Robert French AC, former Chief Justice of Australia, Regulatory Advocacy, in Pamela Hanrahan and Ashley Black (eds) Contemporary Issues in Corporate and Competition Law (2018)LexisNexis, 75 at 80.

However, even where regulators are independent there is a basic conflict between the right of the government as elected representative of the citizens of a country to implement laws and policies in what it considers to be the best interests of citizens, and goals such as the impact of government conduct on competition. The role of government requires balancing multiple policy goals, of which competition policy is just one. This feature sometimes leads to a clash of objectives. The subsequent material gives examples of the advocacy roles of some competition regulators.

Specific competition law provisions on advocacy vary greatly between jurisdictions. Jurisdictions with a formal advocacy role include the following:

- In the Czech Republic, the regulator can impose fines on public authorities for distortion of competition and the law includes a list of practices of government which cannot be undertaken without legitimate reasons.
- In French Polynesia, the regulator may advocate where the government asks for comment or on its own initiative. The regulator may give its opinion on any matter related to competition.
- In Indonesia the regulator, the KPPU, may advocate on very many specified initiatives, and it appears that the government is increasingly adopting the KPPU views on issues raised.
- In Mexico, the regulator can give its views to government, but they are not necessarily adopted.
- In New Caledonia, the regulator consults on draft legal texts and any other matter in relation to competition. The regulator may be asked for its views on competition issues or may offer them of its own initiative. The government has an obligation to consult the regulator on issues such as price regulation and price setting.
- In Serbia the regulator is able to give opinions, but they have no binding effect.

Many other regulators take on advocacy where the laws establishing them do not specifically give them an advocacy role at all, or only give them a specific but limited role.[48] Thus, advocacy is a tool which may be used by all regulators and its effect will depend upon a number of factors, which may not include the logic of the proposal or the damage occasioned by the conduct under consideration.

§10.07 POLICY AND ADVOCACY: ENSURING OUTCOMES

This chapter has explored approaches to competitive neutrality ranging from competition policy to specific legislative provisions to advocacy. Each has its shortcomings.

Laws are enforceable but there must be sufficient enforcement actions by the regulator to act as a deterrent to governments and SOEs in relation to their anticompetitive conduct. Even where these provisions exist, it may also be politically difficult

48. As to the limits of regulatory advocacy in this context *see* Hon Mr Robert French AC, former Chief Justice of Australia, Regulatory Advocacy, in Pamela Hanrahan and Ashley Black (eds) Contemporary Issues in Corporate and Competition Law (2018) LexisNexis, 75, where the author examines the advocacy role of the Australian Competition and Consumer Commission.

for regulators to enforce laws against governments and their SOEs, which may, for example, be very powerful or contribute substantially to government funds, thus making government reluctant to support the competition regulator.

Policy and advocacy alone do not generate enforceable outcomes. Often change following advocacy is left to the goodwill of governments, which may or may not feel inclined to adopt recommendations or change their behaviour.

But should government have an obligation to rectify conduct or take other action?

This chapter accepts that government does not have an obligation to adopt all recommendations of regulators but argues that where competition policy mandates investigation of a competition issues such as those involving competitive neutrality, or where regulators are obliged under laws to advocate on specific issues, government should provide a response to the regulator in a particular case in the interests of transparency.

[A] Australia

As noted earlier, Australia's NCP, which is implemented by agreement between the Commonwealth, the states and territories, contains competitive neutrality obligations. The numbers of complaints about competitive neutrality at all levels in Australia are relatively small. Some of the problems in relation to competitive neutrality policy were highlighted in the earlier section. There is no obligation for the relevant government body or SOE to do anything if a negative finding is made about its conduct following the investigation of a competitive neutrality complaint. Given that a system of complaints and formal investigation is set out in the Competition Principles Agreement,[49] it would seem reasonable that should a breach of the policy be found, the owner or controller of the SOE or other government body should accept the determination, consider it and then act to address or to justify its conduct. However, there is generally no obligation to do so. In this context it should be remembered that competitive neutrality is a policy and not a law in Australia. One must accept that the government has policy imperatives other than competitive markets and that it has been elected to prioritise its activities for the benefit of citizens. Ultimately it is answerable to citizens at the ballot box. But where does this leave the complainant whose complaint has been verified?

Two possibilities might address this situation. The first would be for government to take a matter of competitive neutrality to the Australian Competition Tribunal (in relation to Commonwealth complaints) where it disagrees with the finding of an investigation for review (or to other state or territory tribunals in respect of findings in their jurisdictions). However, this would be a quasi-judicial reconsideration of the implementation of government policy, which would be highly unusual.

Alternatively, an obligation might be imposed on the government body and its minister to formally notify the investigating agency and the complainant of the reasons for its inaction following the successful complaint. The minister might be obliged to lay

49. *See* n. 15.

the notification and reasons for inaction before parliament, and also to include them in the annual report of the organisation.

Such obligations imposing transparency might have the effect of changing behaviour in circumstances where the government involved was under an obligation to apply competitive neutrality policy under the Competition Principles Agreement.[50] Of course, these obligations would need to be the subject of amendment between the parties to the Competition Principles Agreement.[51]

The lack of obligation on governments to act on regulator advocacy is also a frustration in the context of the issues discussed in this chapter, particularly in circumstances where regulators have a legislative obligation to contribute to legislative development or have a general obligation to advocate more generally on competition issues, including competitive neutrality. As is recognised earlier, it is not argued here that governments should necessarily adopt the views of regulators advocating for competition. But it is suggested that transparency of decision making in this area is important given the potential effect of government in the market.

In both examples noted earlier, this chapter argues that adding transparency would significantly improve the current models for competition policy and for mandated advocacy.

§10.08 CONCLUSION

This chapter has provided a detailed examination of mechanisms employed under three structural models in various jurisdictions to deal with issues of competitive neutrality under its broad and narrow constructions.

Of course, none of this works where concerted industrial policy is implemented in a jurisdiction, where governments choose to encourage and promote a specific industry or sector with an array of policy tools. Traditionally, the absence of competitive neutrality policies for government and its SOEs and other bodies meant that the benefits of effective competition would be decreased within that jurisdiction. Given globalisation, however, the impact on competition of this failure is now greater where competitive neutrality does not exist in the jurisdiction of the foreign competitor. The impact has gone from inside the jurisdiction to another jurisdiction.

Ultimately addressing competitive neutrality is an important feature of competition law and policy which must be addressed to level the playing field for competition.

50. *See* n. 14.
51. It appears that such a commitment has been given by the Government of Ireland in relation to recommendations of the Competition Commission arising from market studies. The Government has stated that it will act on recommendations contained in reports of the Competition Authority within nine months of their publication. *See* Program for Government, 10 October 2009. However, it is unclear whether this commitment involves transparent consideration or is limited to intra governmental consideration.

CHAPTER 11

Public Interest, Industrial Policy and Competition Law Remedies: The South African Experience

Dennis M. Davis

Through the long period of the dominance of Chicago economics, the prevailing view was that competition lawyers had reached a consensus that, if appropriately implemented, competition law would maximise consumer welfare, enhance economic growth and assist those who were among the lower income groups in society. On this basis, it was suggested that it made little difference whether one was dealing with an advanced or developing country; similar rules would yield similar results. Extend competition law beyond these confines, and whether by way of false positions or false negatives, consumer welfare would be jeopardised.

When the South African Act[1] was introduced in 1998, it went against this grain by including as part of its purpose, the promotion of employment, the advancement of the social and economic welfare of South Africans, the promotion of a greater share of ownership and, in particular, the imperative to increase the ownership stakes of historically disadvantaged persons.

Contrary to Robert Bork who wrote in the Antitrust Paradox[2] about a revolution in antitrust law that transformed it from social policy to legal rules, the South African drafters saw a need to introduce an element of social and industrial policy into competition law.

Initially the nod towards both industrial and social policy concerns within the South African Act was relatively modest and, generally, took place within the context of mergers. In other words, the standard test as to whether a merger will substantially prevent or lessen competition was supplemented by a series of public interest factors

1. The Competition Act 89 of 1998.
2. Robert Bork *The Antitrust Paradox: A Theory at War with Itself* (1983).

of which courts were required to take into account in assessing whether to permit or refuse a merger; hence industrial policy was confined in the main to this limited area.

The introduction of these public interest provisions followed a report in 1997 by the Department of Trade and Industry (DTI) entitled Proposed Guideline for Competition Policy. In this document, DTI argued that a coherent competition policy would lead to more competitive and efficient economic outcomes, including lower costs along the value chain, enhancement of the attractiveness of South Africa to foreign investors, it would allow for a more balanced regional economy, the stimulation of entrepreneurial activity, the promotion of international competitiveness in South African firms, and through its influence on production processes, the assistance in the furtherance of government's overall socio-economic policy.

§11.01 THE ACT AND PUBLIC INTEREST

Three particular sets of legislative provisions relate to public interest. The preamble of the Act canvasses the context and purposes for enacting this legislation. Public interest is directly referred to therein, particularly in the provision that 'the economy must be open to a greater spread of ownership, in particular to historically disadvantaged persons of South African's'. The Act seeks to promote an efficient, competitive environment, balancing the interest of workers, owners and consumers and focussing on development which will benefit all South Africans.

Section 2 of the Act, the purpose section, sets out a range of objectives, several of which are directly related to public interest concerns. These include the promotion of employment, the advancement of the 'social and economic welfare of South Africans', the expansion of opportunity for South African companies in world markets, the provision of equitable opportunities for small and medium sized enterprises (SMEs), the promotion of a greater spread of ownership, particularly with respect to the historically disadvantaged individuals.

But, as indicated in the introduction, it is the concept of public interest with regard to mergers that has proved to be critical to the development of South African competition jurisprudence. These provisions are directly relevant to a consideration of whether a merger should be approved. Section 12 A provides that, in addition to competition and efficiency considerations traditionally considered by competition authorities, it is necessary to assess that a merger can or cannot be justified on substantial public interest grounds by assessing a range of factors, set out in section 12 A (3) which provides thus:

> When determining whether a merger can or cannot be justified on public interest grounds, the Competition Commission or the Competition Tribunal must consider the effect that the merger will have on –
>
> a) a particular industrial sector or region
> b) employment
> c) the ability of small businesses or firms controlled or owned by historically disadvantaged persons to become competitive
> d) the ability of national industries to compete in international markets.

§11.02 THE INITIAL REACTION

David Lewis, in his extremely thoughtful book on the history and early development of competition jurisprudence in South Africa, writes that the inclusion of interest grounds in merger review, in particular, elicited huge controversy[3]. He notes further 'that no matter how controversial and no matter how much business community in particular would have preferred the omission, everyone involved in the negotiating process recognised that no major piece of socio-economic legislation would have passed muster without incorporating job creation and BEE (black economic empowerment) into the overall objectives of the policy and statute.'[4]

In reflecting on the first decade of the Competition Act, and the jurisprudence that was developed by the authorities, Lewis contends that text book orthodoxy notwithstanding, public interest issues can be incorporated credibly into a core competition evaluation, without doing violence to the principle objectives of a competition agency, namely the promotion of competition. He argued that this has been done principally in two ways; the Competition Tribunal[5] resisted extravagant expansions of the ambit of public interest and that because the public interest criteria had been incorporated into the Act, it was possible for the competition authorities to achieve a balance between traditional cognisable competition considerations and public interest criteria.

A decade into the operation of the Act, James Hodge et al.[6] contended that public interest is primarily served by competition itself and direct consideration in merger proceedings is secondary. They suggest that one of the original motivations for a completion law in South Africa was the recognition that competition enforcement would in and of itself be in the public interest simply by reducing prices to the poor and entry barriers to economic participation by SMEs and historically disadvantaged persons. This benefit is generated with every robust competitive assessment, but is even more visible following the Competition Commission's decision deliberately to focus their efforts in sectors of economy that have more direct relevance to the poorer members of society. The broad political and social support enjoyed by the competition authorities reflects that they are serving the public interest well in their actions. This assessment must be read within the context of the key cases in this area, whether delivered by the Competition Tribunal or the Competition Appeal Court.

§11.03 THE KEY PUBLIC INTEREST MERGER CASES

In *Metropolitan Holdings Limited/Momentum Group Limited*[7] the Competition Tribunal gave considerable attention to the scheme of section 12 A. The Tribunal held that

3. *Thieves at the Dinner Table* (2012).
4. At 118.
5. Lewis was the first chair of the Competition Tribunal, the adjudicator of first instance from where there is a right of appeal to the Competition Appeal Court.
6. James Hodge, Sha'ista Goga and Tshepiso Moahloli *Public Interest Provision in the South African Competition Act: A Critical Review*. In K Moodaliyar and S Roberts (eds) *The Development of Competition Economics in South Africa* (2012).
7. [2010] 2 CCLR 337 (CC).

initially it was required to determine the competition effects of a merger. If a merger was not likely to substantially prevent or lessen competition, it was still required to consider its effect on the public interest.

The Tribunal was required to decide the question of what was to occur once a substantial public interest ground had been raised and, accordingly, whether the merging parties faced an evidential burden of justification. It held 'once a prima facie ground has been alleged that a merger may not be justifiable on substantial public interest grounds, the evidential burden will shift to the merging parties to rebut it.' In the filing of the relevant documents in the *Metropolitan* case, the merging parties indicated that 'as a worst case scenario', the merger could lead to a net amount of 1,000 retrenchments.

This was the backdrop to a Tribunal's consideration of public interest questions in this case; in particular employment. Employment losses were of a considerable magnitude and the short-term prospect of re-employment for a substantial section of this effected class was extremely limited. It was fair to presume that the merger would have a potentially substantially adverse effect in respect of the public interest provision of protecting employment.

An evidential burden lay upon the merging parties, which according to the Tribunal, were required to satisfy two criteria:

(1) a rational process has been followed to arrive at the determination of the number of jobs to be lost, ie that the reason for the job reduction and the number of jobs proposed to be shed are rationally connected; and
(2) the public interest in preventing employment loss is balanced by an equally weighty, but countervailing public interest, justifying the job loss and which is cognisable under the Act.[8]

The Tribunal held that, even if the merging parties made good on efficiency arguments in respect of job losses, the efficiency argument in a case, where the job losses were as substantial as in this case, had to be justified on a ground that was public in nature in order to gainsay the public interest in preserving jobs.[9] As an example of a justification that the Tribunal was not prepared to accept, it cited an employment loss caused by cost saving, justified solely by ensuing benefits to the shareholders. Hence, it took the view that purely private efficiency gains could not be taken into account as countervailing factors to a lessening of a competition.

Significantly, the Tribunal acknowledged that what was required in terms of the section was a balancing exercise; in this case between the private interests of shareholders and what was referred to as 'the weightier public interest' in preventing employment loss as a result of the merger. In this balancing exercise, other aspects of public interest would have to be taken into account. For example, if it was found that the merger had an adverse effect on employment, in circumstances where the maintenance of a factory in a region, which suffered from considerable unemployment,

8. At paragraph 70.
9. *See* paragraphs 68–71 of the judgment.

this would be a countervailing factor which could trump an argument raised on public interest considerations to refuse the merger or to impose particular conditions.

In this case, the Tribunal found that there were no countervailing public interest considerations which would represent an obstacle to the imposition of conditions. For this reason the Tribunal approved the merger, subject to a moratorium on all merger-related retrenchments for a period of two years, excluding senior employees as defined in the order.

In *Minister of Economic Development and others v. Wal-Mart Stores Inc. and others*[10] both the Competition Tribunal and, on appeal, the Competition Appeal Court held that the merger of Wal-Mart and Massmart Holdings Ltd, a company which had an African footprint on a vastly smaller scale but similar to Wal-Mart, raised no adverse competition issues. It prompted certain public interest concerns which the parties urged the Court to deal with by way of the imposition of conditions. The Tribunal and the Court were in agreement that Wal-Mart raised no cognisable competition considerations. It had not competed in South Africa prior to the merger and its only presence in the country was a procurement arm which did no more than purchase South African produce for an export market.

Two sets of public interest considerations were triggered by this transaction. In the first place, the relevant trade union contended that 574 of its workers, who had been dismissed prior to the merger, had lost their jobs in anticipation of a merger and, accordingly, reinstatement was justified in terms of section 12 A (3). Further, in regard to labour matters, the question arose as to the future of the rights of the relevant unions in terms of agreements which had been entered into with Massmart prior to the merger.

These labour issues were dealt with by way of a range of concessions that were made by the merging parties. The second public interest consideration raised a far more difficult question namely, the argument that, as a result of the merger, it was contended that there would be a significant shift in purchasing away from South African manufacturers towards foreign low cost Asian producers which, in turn, would have a significant effect upon small- and medium-sized businesses in South Africa and a consequent loss of jobs.

The Tribunal concluded, notwithstanding a clear concern regarding the effect of the merger upon local producers and jobs, that the possible losses which flowed therefrom had to be weighed against the consumer interest in lower prices and job creation at Massmart. As consumers would benefit from the lower prices associated with the merger and these were low-income consumers or consumers without any means of support of their own, being the poorest of the poor in South Africa, it followed that a public interest in lower prices was compelling.

Both before the Tribunal and the Court, the argument was raised about the introduction of certain procurement conditions. These were rejected. In order to impose procurement conditions, there would have to be a determination of the local procurement levels of Massmart premerger, followed by a requirement to hold Massmart to these levels for some period in the future. This would clearly be very

10. [2012] ZACAC 6 (9 October 2012).

difficult to implement and, in addition would be a discriminatory practice, unless similar procurement conditions were imposed upon Massmart's competitors, in particular, large supermarket chains that operate in South African and beyond its borders.

One of the great challenges facing the Competition Appeal Court was that the cost advantages that Wal-Mart were able to secure depended, to a large degree, on the way it had managed its own value chain globally. Wal-Mart's 'coordinating' global purchasing operations and superior infrastructure for exploiting global value chains would result in an inevitable importation of goods which could offer considerable benefits by way of cheaper products for local consumers as well as greater choice. In short, the national competition authority was faced with a significant public interest problem of a clear threat to local manufacturing caused by the broader consequences of globalisation and the rapid expansion of global value chains. Within this context, the Court required further evidence to find some meaningful set of conditions, having decided, as had the Tribunal, that it could not disallow the merger on traditional increased cost or reduced output grounds.

In its initial finding, the Court ordered the reinstatement of the 503 workers who had been retrenched in 2009 and 2010 and further ordered the merged entity to honour existing labour agreements, including the recognition of the existing trade union and its right to represent the bargaining units for at least three years from the date of the transaction.

It then ordered the merging parties to commission a study to determine the most appropriate means, together with a mechanism by which local South African supplies could be empowered to respond to the challenges posed by the merger and hence participate in the benefits thereof. The study was to be conducted by three experts, one to be appointed by the union, another by the merging parties and the third by the three government ministers who had opposed the merger.

The experts prepared two reports, which were not unanimous. Having considered these reports, the court decided to create a fund in the amount of ZAR 250 million which was designed to ensure the integration of small- and medium-sized South African businesses from historically disadvantaged communities into Wal-Mart's global value chain, a task which would be done by way of technical assistance by Wal-Mart, using its expertise and the necessary funds.

Within the first year of the funds' inception, 164 small-scale South African farmers had been successfully lined to Massmart's fresh supply chain and 337 farmers were trained to link into the supply chain. Approximately 514 tons of goods were supplied to Massmart by small-scale farmers.[11] The Commission's analysis of the effect of the Walmart merger was:

> Based on the observations above, we find that (Walmart Fund) has addressed both competition and industrial policy concerns; specifically, attention to vulnerable sectors, encouraging entry and expansion of SMMEs into the Massmart's supply chain, as well as adhering to local procurement commitments. From the analysis of its performance, it appears that the fund has addressed the merger-specific

11. Thulani Mandirza, Thembalethu Sithebe and Michelle Viljoen *An Ex-post Facto Review of the Walmart: Massmart merger* Competition Commission working paper CC 2016/03.

> concerns raised. The fund has contributed to the achievement of industrial policy objectives, each of these which are contained in the public interest provisions of the Competition Act.[12]

The Walmart decision proved to provide a framework for further merger control, of major acquisitions that followed shortly thereafter.

The Coca-Cola Company sought to merge with Independent Bottlers of Coca-Cola production. This merger was approved subject to various conditions which were proposed to address certain public interest concerns. The conditions imposed were binding commitments to open company-sponsored display unit spaces in small spaza shops to competitors, and extensive employment, localisation and small business development conditions, which included the attainment of a 30% BEE ownership target in the South African operations within a specified period. There was also a commitment to a ZAR 800 million development fund as well as the retention of the Appletiser operations in South Africa.[13]

AB InBev's acquisition of SABMiller was approved by the Competition Tribunal subject to extensive public interest conditions, including, but to limited to (i) a commitment that no South African employee could be retrenched involuntarily as a consequence of the merger; (ii) for a period of five years, the merged entity will ensure that it will retain the aggregate employment levels; (iii) a ZAR 1 billion SDF would be established to support small businesses and emerging farmers; and (iv) a commitment to maximising local procurement of inputs including through a programme to support local farmers (with a target of creating at least 2,600 new jobs and 800 new farmers) that will maximise exports from South Africa and minimise imports into South Africa.[14]

The Walmart case and, to a greater extent in the Coca-Cola ad AB InBev mergers, demonstrate the increase in intervention by various ministries who seek to play an increasingly significant role in merger control proceedings in order to achieve certain government objectives.[15] What is evident from the AB InBev case is that the nature of intervention has evolved such that there is no standardised public-interest test. Instead, there appears to be a greater discretion in the hands of the minister, as to the extent and nature of the 'conditions' to be imposed. In fact meetings were held by the AB InBev parties and the Minister for Economic Development, Ebrahim Patel, behind closed doors prior to the Commission's recommendations.[16] However, the thrust of these negotiations took place within the framework set out by the Court in its Walmart decision.

Subsequent to these developments, the Competition Commission tried to give greater content and hence guidance to the case law principles. It has published a set of

---

12. Mandirza et al. at 15.
13. *The Coca-Cola Company v. Coca-Cola Beverages (Pty) Ltd Competition Tribunal* LM02/April 17.
14. *Anheuser-Busch InBev SANN v. SAB Miller plc Competition Tribunal* LM21/January 2016.
15. John Oxenham, Andreas Stargard, Michael James Currie, *Developments in South African Merger Control – Ministerial Interventionism and the Impact on Timing and Certainty*. Unpublished paper, March 2016. The minister responsible for the Competition Commission opposed the latter's decision to approve the Walmart merger before the Competition Appeal Court. In Coca-Cola and AB InBev, the minister negotiated the condition which were then approved by the Tribunal.
16. Oxenham, Stargard, Currie *supra*.

draft guidelines in respect of the public interest component of the merger enquiry, which indicates a determination to vindicate the Act's ambition.[17]

In terms of these guidelines, the Commission will adopt the following steps in undertaking the public interest inquiry:

(1) determine the likely effect on the public interest;
(2) determine whether the alleged effect on a specific public interest is a result of that merger or is merger specific. In other words, is there a sufficient causal nexus between the merger and the alleged effect;
(3) determine whether these effects are substantial;
(4) consider whether the merging parties can justify the likely effect on the particular public interest; and
(5) consider possible remedies to address any likely negative effect on the public interest.

In the application of these principles, the Commission states that, in the first line of public interest enquiry following from a negative competition finding, the Commission will consider the effects of a proposed merger. If there are positive, public interest effects, the Commission will assess whether the claimed positive effects are merger specific and substantial such that these claimed positive effects could outweigh the negative competition effects. In this case, the merging parties will have to justify the substantial positive effects on public interest. This will be followed by a balancing of the negative competition effects and the positive public interest effects.

In the event that the competition finding is negative and the public interest effect is negative, the Commission will consider whether these are merger specific and substantial. In this case, the Commission would consider a prohibition of the merger.

However, if the public interest effects are negative, then the Commission will proceed to determine whether these are merger specific, substantial and justifiable. Where the public interest effect is neutral, the Commission will consider what the negative and positive effects are and balance these. The Commission will also determine whether these are merger specific and substantial.

The guidelines reveal a clear commitment on the part of the Commission to incorporate the public interest factors specified in section 12A (3) into a holistic enquiry concerning the effect upon competition in the relevant market, should the merger be permitted to proceed.

§11.04 CONCLUSION

In assessing the challenges posed by the public interest provisions contained in the merger dispensation Hodge, Goga and Moahlali observed, that economic evidence may

17. Competition Commission of South Africa: Guidelines on the assessment of public interest provisions in merger regulation under the Competition Act: 23 January 2015.

well be helpful in the determination of the weight to be given to the public interest considerations:

> While other public-interest considerations have units of analysis (like jobs) that may be difficult to compare with potential price and output changes, economists' ability to both quantify and determine the incidence of different effects may still prove useful in reaching a decision. For instance, if faced with a substantial employment gain from a potentially anticompetitive transaction, it would be useful to understand both the magnitude of the price effect and the incidence on different groups of consumers who may themselves hold different weightings in public interest. Indeed, the incidence of public-interest costs as against potential beneficiaries was a feature of the economic debate in both the Metropolitan/Momentum and Wal-Mart/Massmart mergers.[18]

The problem for competition authorities focusses on the mechanism by which to weigh these competing concerns; in other words if, as in Walmart prices may decrease pursuant to the merger but, pursuant to the merger, there may also be an adverse effect on small domestic suppliers, how does the adjudicator weight these consideration and determine whether the merger should still be permitted or refused?

The decision in *Walmart* was criticised for nodding too vigorously in the direction of the public interest factors. Staples, Holland and Rossouw[19] argue that the 'labour condition' imposed upon Walmart represented the construction of 'a competition bridge too far.' The core of their criticism is captured in the following paragraph:

> By imposing a condition that extends beyond their public interest mandate, the competition authorities have created the potential for a number of negative consequences to arise from the Walmart condition.
>
> An economic analysis of the impact of the Walmart condition indicates that, to the end that SACCAWU's entrenched position affords it additional bargaining power, the net effect could be detriment to employment when the merged entity grows, or when employees are lost through natural attrition. In these circumstances, the objectives of the Competition Act would not be supported (in so far as these include the promotion of employment),
>
> In addition, the Walmart condition raises significant concern in that it does not provide for the possibility of a change in SACCAWU's position within the emerged entity or for altering the merged entity's obligations in these circumstances. This could prejudice both the interest of the employees and the merged entity's business.

There is some merit in this observation in that the decisions required of the Tribunal and/or Court are difficult to determine with any certainty, in that they hold uncertain polycentric consequences. In addition, the assumption upon which the decision in Walmart was based proved *ex post facto* to be faulty. Contrary to the predictions placed before the Court, Massmart has not become a dominant player in the relevant market. Its competitors, particularly the powerful national chains, Shoprite

18. In Moodaliyar and Roberts at 13.
19. 2013 *South African Journal of Mercantile Law* 94 at 106.

Checkers and Pick 'n Pay continue to maintain market share and are not subject to similar restrictive conditions.

Given the history of South Africa, the drafters of the Act considered it to be a important section of the Act. Challenges concerning a false positive or negative were considered to be extreme in these cases, given the open textured nature of the mandated proportionality enquiry. However, as the theoretical paradigm for competition law and policy has shifted over the past decade, South Africa is no longer an outlier. The role of public interest issues, particularly in merger inquiries, has been embraced by other jurisdictions. The OECD has noted that pubic interest issues are considered in a number of countries, with important qualification: there is no universally accepted list of public interest issues. Second, sector regulators are often employed to deal with public interest issues as defined.[20] It has also cautioned that:

> Merger control involves a forward-looking analysis, meaning that agencies must assess the likely impact of the merger on competition in the medium to long-term. Including public interest considerations in such assessment may force agencies to balance what appear to be valid short-term solutions based on current public policy considerations, against what might be more uncertain longer-term consequences for competition and consumer welfare. The balance between short-term gains and the long-term benefits of sustaining competitive markets is not easy.

The socio economic arguments in favour of the system set out in section 12 of the South African Act have become more compelling in; that their rejection may cause the competition enterprise to have some deficit of legitimacy. Admittedly, writing in a broader context, Baker and Salop[21] have drawn attention to the relationship between competition policy and inequality. Manifestly in a country with an adverse gini-coefficient such as South Africa, this issue is of pressing importance. As Baker and Salop note:

> We recognize that implementing this approach in practice for mergers, which we will use as an example, would require undertaking a detailed distributional analysis. The difficulty of determining the downstream effects of price increases on intermediate inputs often would make this type of distributional analysis challenging. Thus, in application, the approach likely would focus primarily on mergers in markets for consumer products. Even in dealing with mergers in markets for final goods, moreover, it would be necessary to formulate rules for making tradeoffs among groups of buyers. Should harms to the poor count more than harms to the middle class? Can gains to the wealthy ever outweigh losses to those less wealthy-for example, if the gains are large and the losses small? If inequality is adopted as an antitrust goal, these will be important issues to debate.[22]

Baker and Salop, of course, have written within the context of US anti-trust law. But, given the implications of public interest, as set out expressly in the South African Act, the challenge they pose is one which raises a significant possibility for a

20. OECD Executive summary of the Roundtable on Public Interest Considerations in Merger Control: 14 June 2016 at 4.
21. Jonathan Baker and Steven Salop "*Anti-trust Competition Law and Inequality*" 2015 104 Geo LJ 1 at 15.
22. *See also* Ioannis Lianos *Polycentric Competition Law*: Inaugural lecture at UCT: 19 October 2017.

developing jurisprudence within a country which has disturbing levels of inequality, together with state policy which manifestly has not done sufficient to deal with this problem.

§11.05 POSTSCRIPT

Twenty years after the introduction of the South African Act, it appears that the Act has enjoyed extremely modest success in respect of changing the concentrated structure of the South African economy inherited from Apartheid. A recent study conducted by the Competition Commission analysed more than 2,150 mergers to identify the dominant firm in a defined product markets for the period 2009–2016, using the statutory presumptive threshold of 45% market share.[23] The study found that there were 294 dominant firms in defined markets in the thirty-one sectors it considered.[24] At least 70 % of South Africa's economic sectors have defined product markets dominated by three to four large firms who command an average market share of between 46% and 67%.[25] The study used the Heirfindahl-Hirschmann index to assess the concentration levels in those sectors and found nine sectors to be highly concentrated.

Further, studies on the South African economy conducted by the World Bank and the OECD have also found high levels of concentration, especially in the manufacturing and export sectors.[26] The World Bank study reveals that in the manufacturing and export markets just a few firms account for the majority of the market, including non-mineral exports in which the top 5% of firms account for 93 % of the total non-mineral exports.[27] The OECD Report found that most industries are highly concentrated, with state-owned enterprises dominating the network industries, and the weakness of competitive pressures contributing to below par innovation.[28] South Africa's remote location and its relatively small-size economy suggest that single firm dominance is a major problem.[29] An additional problem concerns dominant firms, which developed under the umbrella of state regulation, protection and support associated with apartheid economic policies.

Unsurprisingly in the light of these developments in 2017, the Minister of Economic Development Mr Patel sought to expand the ambition of the South African Act. To an extent the animating normative idea behind his attempt is not all too removed from some of the arguments which Lina Khan articulated in her 2017

23. Memorandum on Competition Bill of 2018. A dominant firm is one which enjoys either at least a 35% share in the defined market or if less, is shown to exercise material power.
24. *Ibid.*
25. *See* the unpublished paper presented by Dr Liberty Mncube 11th Annual Competition Law Economics & Policy Conference, September 2017.
26. World Bank (2016) *South Africa Economic Update: Promoting Faster Economic Growth and Poverty Alleviation Through Competition*. Washington, World Bank; OECD (2013) OECD Economic Surveys: South Africa, Paris: OECD.
27. The World Bank, (2016) *South Africa Economic Update: Promoting faster Growth and Poverty Alleviation Through Competition*, February 2016, Ed. 8, at 5.
28. OECD *OECD Economic Surveys, South Africa*, Paris: OECD (2013).
29. World Bank (2016).

'Amazon's Antitrust Paradox',[30] namely the Bill wishes to push back even further against a consensus which focussed on consumer welfare to the detriment of the structure of the economy in general and a broader examination of market power. Like Khan, the minister considers that the consumer welfare standard is ill equipped to deal with the architecture of market power. In short, exclusive concerns about price and output are insufficient to deal with the skewed structure of a modern economy which perpetuates inequality and exclusion.[31]

This Bill is now before Parliament. Once the bill is introduced, it will provide the Competition Commission with significant powers pursuant to the mandated market enquiries including the remedy of divestiture and the introduction of a range of provisions to deal with monopsony power and an emphasis on the effect of dominant buyers upon SMEs which supply goods or services.

Merger provisions have also been strengthened in respect of public interest considerations, with the addition of a further consideration in respect of public interest 'the promotion of a greater spread of ownership, in particular to increase the levels of ownership by historically disadvantaged persons and workers in firms in the market'.

A new regime is about to be introduced. It will certainly test the ability of competition authorities to balance a series of competing objectives; in particular the relationship between consumer welfare and the structural considerations of which the minister is concerned. It will also require a balancing between the needs of a middle-income country to have firms that can compete in global value chains in particular and global markets in general and structural questions which give rise to an undue concentration of the economy. This, in turn, gives rise to a considerable challenge: to what extent will there be a clash between social and political objectives and economic rationality in the realm of competition law? South Africa promises to be a significant case study in order to answer these questions, way beyond the limited confines of existing public interest considerations.

30. Lina Khan "*Amazon Antitrust Paradox*" 2017 126 Yale Law J 564.
31. For the sake of accuracy, Khan has focused her attention on online platforms, in particular Amazon. Mr Patel is concerned with market power of the few firms that control the South African economy. In the explanatory memorandum to the 2018 Competition Amendment Bill it is stated:The main objective of these amendments is to address two persistent structural constraints on the South African economy, namely, the high levels of economic concentration in the economy and the skewed ownership profile of the economy.This is done through – (a) strengthening or clarifying the provisions of the Act relating to prohibited practices, restricted horizontal and vertical practices, abuse of dominance and price discrimination and mergers; (b) requiring special attention to be given to the impact of anti-competitive conduct on small and medium businesses and firms owned or controlled by historically disadvantaged person; (c) strengthening the provisions relating to market inquiries so that – (i) the outcomes of these inquiries result in action that promotes competitions; (ii) there is guidance on how to evaluate the adverse features of a market; and (iii) requiring special attention on small and medium businesses and firms owned by historically disadvantaged persons; (d) providing the national executive with effective means of participating in competition related proceedings and the power to initiate market inquiries into a sector and to intervene in mergers that affect the national security interest of the Republic; and (e) promoting the administrative efficacy of the Competition Commission ('Commission'), market inquiries and the Competition Tribunal.

CHAPTER 12

Competition Law and State-Owned Enterprises: A South African Perspective

Tembinkosi Bonakele[*]

§12.01 INTRODUCTION

The BRICS countries are all emerging economies with very strong state-owned entities (SOEs). In many developing countries SOEs are the backbone of their economic infrastructure and in economies such as China, they are at the very centre of commercial enterprise. Because of this central role, they tend to be viewed as national champions that are crucial for growth and development. SOEs are often also big employers with significant political capital. Understanding the role of these companies and their interface with competition law and regulators is crucial in assessing competition enforcement in these countries. This chapter explores the nexus among SOEs, competitiveness and competition enforcement in South Africa.

Economic theory tells us that absent any market failures, free and competitive markets optimise overall social welfare by efficiently driving prices for goods down to the level of the long-run average costs of firms (productive efficiency), and ensuring that the optimal amount of those goods is produced as determined by the consumer's willingness to pay (allocative efficiency). However, market failures are pervasive. In the face of these failures, the ability of the market to achieve socially optimal outcomes is diminished and governments will intervene to ensure socially beneficial outcomes.[1]

These interventions take various forms, including setting pro-competitive regulatory and policy frameworks within which firms operate or, in some cases, by establishing enterprises that intervene directly in commercial activity. Commercial

* The views expressed in this chapter are my own and may not necessarily reflect the views of the Competition Commission.

1. Black, P., Calitz, E. and Steenekamp, T. 'Public Economics for South African students', 2nd edition. (Oxford: Oxford University Press, 2003).

state-owned enterprises (SOEs) usually operate in markets with natural monopoly characteristics such as large sunk costs relative to market size, significant economies of scale and network effects that entrench first-mover advantage and make entry by subsequent firms unprofitable.[2] Examples of sectors with these characteristics include electricity, telecommunications and transport infrastructure.

But, the structure of these sectors is often such that while one level of the value chain may not be able to sustain competition (hence the need for government intervention), competition from private firms may well be possible at other levels of the industry.[3] In these cases, vertically integrated SOEs may have the incentive and ability to leverage their monopoly power at one level of the value chain into the segment where competition is possible.

The challenge facing competition authorities is thus to ensure that notionally competitive market segments are left open to entry and rivalry. This can be done in several ways including through the regulation of access to the non-competitive components of an integrated firm, ownership separation of the competitive and non-competitive components (structural separation), joint ownership of the non-competitive component by competing firms in the competitive component and limitations on the ability of the integrated firm to compete in the competitive component.[4]

This chapter uses three case studies to assess the South African experience with attempts to introduce competition in markets monopolised by SOEs. The case studies focus on vertically integrated SOEs with monopoly power in at least one market that face entry, or potential entry, from private firms in one of the markets in which they are active. We assess the response of the SOEs and government at large, as well as the successes and limits of competition law in opening markets to greater competition. The case studies cover telecommunications, electricity and long-distance petroleum pipelines.

In the telecommunications sector, the former state-owned fixed-line monopoly, Telkom, used its market power in upstream infrastructure to raise rivals' costs in the downstream market for internet and other telecommunications services. After resolving jurisdictional challenges, the competition authority reached a settlement with Telkom in which they agreed to functional separation of its (upstream) wholesale and (downstream) services businesses, achieving notable success in stimulating services-based competition.[5]

In the electricity sector, the intervention of the competition authority was less impactful and the benefits of potential competition were overtaken by short-term challenges to the sustainability and profitability of the state-owned utility. South Africa's electricity sector is dominated by Eskom, the vertically integrated state-owned electricity utility with a monopoly in generation and transmission, and a dominant position in distribution. As far back as 1998, the South African government resolved to

2. Kaserman, D. and Mayo, J. 'Government and Business: The Economics of Antitrust and Regulation', (New York: The Dryden Press, 1995), p. 9.
3. OECD. 'Restructuring Public Utilities for Competition', (Paris: OECD, 2001).
4. *Ibid.*
5. *Competition Commission v. Telkom* (623/2008) [2009] ZASCA 155 (27 November 2009).

open the sector to greater competition, putting forward that Eskom should be restructured into separate generation and transmission companies, that competition in generation should be encouraged and that there should be open and non-discriminatory access to the transmission system.[6] However, for inexplicable reasons, this policy position was never pursued. Since then, Eskom's performance and financial position have deteriorated significantly, and new entry and dynamism have been suppressed with deleterious effects on economic growth.

In petroleum pipelines, the competition authority was rendered ineffective by legislative constraints. The state-owned pipeline operator, Transnet, faced potential competition from a private sector entrant who intended to construct a long-distance petroleum pipeline competing with a planned Transnet pipeline. However, by virtue of its public status, Transnet received funding from the fiscus and beneficial tariffs from the sector regulator. This gave it an unassailable competitive advantage over the private sector entrant, whose business model became unprofitable relative to Transnet's subsidised price. The private sector provider was forced to exit. Despite the patently anticompetitive effect of the support afforded Transnet, the competition authority was unable to intervene as its jurisdiction does not extend to the exercise of public power by a state functionary.

The Transnet case highlights questions around competitive neutrality in markets where SOEs compete with private firms, and leads to one of the main conclusion of this chapter, which is that South Africa requires a comprehensive competition policy that commits all state functionaries to the principles of competition. The case studies also highlight the need to regulate for rivalry, particularly in the reform of SOEs, to ensure that we not simply entrench and transfer monopoly power from public to private hands.

This chapter proceeds in three parts. In the first part, we provide the economic rationale for SOEs which have in the past, and continue today, to play an important strategic role in the industrial development of many economies. In §1.02, we provide the historical context to the establishment of the SOEs and the competition concerns that have arisen involving these SOEs, highlighting the challenges faced by the competition authority in regulating these markets. The following cases cover a range of outcomes. The first is an example where competition enforcement against an SOE resulted in a good outcome (Telkom), the second reflects a failure to regulate *for* competition despite known benefits of doing so (Eskom), and the third reflects a case where intervention did not occur and the effects have been particularly ugly (Transnet). Finally, in §12.03, we draw general conclusions from the case studies and provide policy considerations for the promotion of competition in markets with state-owned monopolies.

6. Department of Minerals and Energy. *White Paper on the Energy Policy of the Republic of South Africa*. (1998). pp. 12 and 41.

§12.02 THE ROLE OF SOEs IN THE ECONOMY: ECONOMIC RATIONAL AND HISTORICAL CONTEXT

[A] Economic Rationale for SOEs

SOEs are usually justified in markets where market structure and incentives will lead to socially suboptimal outcomes if left to private firms. SOEs are commonly found when the following conditions are present: (1) natural monopoly, (2) capital market failure, (3) externalities and (4) equity or strategic considerations.[7] These are discussed further in the following texts.

Natural monopoly: a natural monopoly is a sector that can only profitably sustain one incumbent. Costs of entry, such as sunk infrastructure costs, are so high relative to the size of the market that potential competitors will be discouraged from entering regardless of the potential profit of the incumbent firm. The incumbent experiences significant economies of scale and has an unassailable cost advantage relative to any potential entrant who would have to incur the same significant cost of entry but would have access to a smaller residual market share over which to recover its costs. The result is that no other firms would enter, leaving the first entrant as a monopoly.[8]

An example of this is an electricity grid. The fixed cost of establishing a transmission grid across the country is significant and, once established, the variable cost of transmitting electricity is quite low. The cost of replicating the grid would be prohibitive (and socially wasteful) and would not be justified by the returns available. Under these conditions, the monopoly incumbent would be able to extract monopoly rents without the threat of competitive entry. In such a market, there is a strong argument to establish an SOE that is not solely reliant on profit rather than a private sector firm that may have an incentive to produce below the socially optimal level and extract monopoly profits.

Capital market failure: private capital markets are unlikely to support projects that have high returns in the long term but are very risky in the short term. In these cases, government has the benefit of cheap, patient capital that is not subject to short-term demands for returns.

An example of this is development of the strategic synthetic fuels industry in South Africa and the establishment of former SOE, the South African Coal and Gas Corporation (Sasol).[9] Sasol was established in 1950 and developed its own coal-to-liquid synthetic fuels technology. The company was considered a strategic national resource as South Africa has no significant gas or petroleum reserves and faced increasing international isolation as economic sanctions were imposed on the racist Apartheid regime declared a crime against humanity in a 1973 United Nations

7. Chang, H-J. 'State-Owned Enterprise Reform', (New York: UN Department of Economic and Social Affairs, 2007).
8. *Ibid.*
9. The acronym, Sasol is taken from the Afrikaans name for the firm, the 'Suid-Afrikaanse Steenkool, Olie and Gasmaatskappy'.

Convention.[10] Sasol made losses from the time it was commissioned in 1955 until the 1970s when global oil prices boomed. When oil prices dropped again in the 1980s and 1990s, Sasol again relied on state subsidies. Private creditors would not have been able, or willing, to sustain these losses.

Externalities: externalities occur when social returns diverge from private returns. In these cases, the market will either over- or under-produce goods or service relative to the socially optimal level. In short, market signals (prices) become unreliable.[11] The provision of basic sanitation and healthcare is a common example of services with significant positive externalities. These services have society-wide benefits that cannot be captured solely by the provider and, for this reason, a private firm would choose to supply less than the socially optimal level. Supplying the goods through public firms, or SOEs, would resolve the externality constraint.[12]

Finally, SOEs also emerge when there are important equity considerations in the provision of certain goods. This includes, for example, providing postal services to people in remote areas who may not be able to pay and certainly cannot pay a price that covers the costs of providing the service. Because government places a premium on certain services, these will be provided through public firms.

A common criticism of these justifications for SOEs is that all of these objectives can be achieved through other means. For example, a subsidy or tax could resolve the externality concern. However, these alternative measures have inherent transaction costs in terms of design, implementation and monitoring. Economic theory suggests that firms emerge to minimise transaction costs, and by the same logic, SOEs emerge to minimise these monitoring costs, among others. Similarly, though SOEs are generally said to be less efficient than private firms, the industrial organisation literature does not take such as stark position.

Instead, the industrial organisation literature presents a case for hierarchical arrangements (firms) rather than contracts (markets), and caution that all firms, regardless of ownership, suffer from agency and principal-agent problems.[13] The design problem that should be solved is how to set up conditions and incentives for SOEs that encourage efficiency and create consequences for inefficiency. One way of doing this is to force SOEs to meet export quotas which expose them to competition in export markets.

The value of SOEs in many countries' economic success lends further support to their importance in development. Throughout most of the twentieth century, countries like France, Norway and West Germany had large SOE sectors and performed well. In France, SOEs like Renault were at the forefront of industrialisation.[14]

10. United Nations. 'International Convention on the Suppression and Punishment of the Crime of Apartheid. Adopted by the General Assembly of the United Nations on 30 November 1973.' (1973).
11. Chang (2007), *supra*.
12. Kowalski,P. et al., 'State-Owned Enterprises: Trade Effects and Policy Implications', OECD Trade Policy Papers, No. 147 (Paris: OECD Publishing, 2013).
13. Chang (2007), *supra*.
14. *Ibid.*

[B] Application of Competition Law to SOEs

South Africa has a wide range of SOEs, from constitutional organisations such as the SA Human Rights Commission, through government entities (museums, research institutions, regulators), to commercially run companies. In 2013, the Presidential Review Committee on SOEs estimated that South Africa had more than 700 SOEs.[15]

The Commission's jurisdiction extends only to economic activity, thus limiting the application of the Act only to SOEs engaged in commercial activity. When the Competition Act first came into effect in 1998, section 3(1)(d) further limited the application of the Act, indicating that the competition authorities had no jurisdiction over 'acts subject to or authorised by public regulation' which meant that the competition authorities did not have jurisdiction over regulated entities, including SOEs. The Act was amended in 2000 to repeal this provision and introduce a new section which makes provision for concurrent jurisdiction with regulatory entities on competition matters.

The Act mandates that concurrent jurisdiction must be managed in terms of negotiated agreements to coordinate and harmonise the actions of the regulatory authority and the competition authorities. It is on this basis that the Commission has concluded a number of memorandums of agreements ('MOAs') with industry regulators. The main purpose of the MOAs is to clarify how the concurrent jurisdiction will operate where competition concerns overlap with regulatory responsibilities.[16]

The jurisdiction of the Commission is also limited to complaints where an SOE participates in a market as a competitor. This stems from the judgment in *AEC Electronics (Pty) Ltd v. The Department of Minerals and Energy,*[17] in which the Competition Tribunal ('the Tribunal') held that the objective of the Act's prohibited practice regime is to prevent anticompetitive practices by firms that *participate in markets* and not the review of the exercise of state power by state functionaries, whether or not this state power affects who may participate in markets (e.g., through licencing) or the conditions of participation (as may be set out in regulatory obligations).[18] A national department setting the rules for participation in certain markets cannot be characterised as participating in these markets, and its actions are not subject to review by the competition authorities. As discussed later, this restricts the Commission's ability to intervene in markets where SOEs benefit from market-distorting decisions made by government or regulatory bodies.

It is worth noting that the Commission has been quite active in investigating competition complaints against SOEs and that the majority (67%) of the abuse of

15. Presidential Review Committee on State-Owned Entities. (Pretoria: The Presidency, 2009).
16. The Commission has so far concluded memorandums of understandings with the following South African regulators: National Liquor Authority (2008), National Consumer Commission (2011), National Gambling Board (2011), Council for Medical Schemes (2012), Auditor General of South Africa (2014), North West Gambling Board (2014), ITAC (2015), Ports Regulator of South Africa (2015), Department of Agriculture, Forestry and Fisheries (2016), Construction Industry Development Board (2016), Broad Based Black Economic Empowerment Commission (2016), and the South African Bureau of Standards (2017).
17. *AEC Electronics (Pty) Ltd v. Department of Minerals and Energy* 48/CR/Jun09.
18. *AEC Electronics, supra,* Paragraph 18.

dominance cases successfully prosecuted in South Africa to date have related to conduct by SOEs or former SOEs.

[C] The Development of SOEs in South Africa and Competition Concerns That Have Arisen

This section provides a brief historical overview of the SOEs and their role in the South African economy. It also presents case studies of the competition concerns that have arisen involving these SOEs and highlights the challenges of competition enforcement in each case.

[1] Telkom

At the advent of constitutional democracy in 1994, South Africa's telecommunications services were vastly unequal with high tele-density and world-class services in urban and wealthier white areas and nearly no coverage in rural and low-income urban areas.[19] Historically, South Africa's economic landscape was shaped by the discovery of diamonds in Kimberley in 1867 and gold in the Witwatersrand in 1886 which led to the agglomeration of services in certain nodes. This was worsened by the racialised allocation of state resources under formal apartheid. In 1994, the first democratic government inherited an unequal telecommunications sector with a teledensity of 25.1% in historically white areas and as low as 0.1% in predominantly rural black areas.[20] Similar disparities were evident in the electricity and transport sectors which we discuss below.

The transformation of the South African telecommunications sector began in 1991 when the state department responsible for telecommunications services was corporatised to form the SOE Telkom Ltd. Comprehensive sector reform started in 1995 with the release of a policy paper for the development and transformation of the telecommunications sector which aimed to create a regulatory framework that would encourage investment, innovation and high quality services, and to extend the telecommunications network to millions of unserved South Africans.

Partly to meet these universal service obligations, Telkom was granted a monopoly on the provision of basic fixed telephone services and the development and maintenance of the public switched telephone network until 2001.[21] In 1997, Telkom reached an agreement to acquire a 30% strategic equity partner, SBC telecommunications international (18%) and Telkom Malaysia Berhad (12%). The partnership came with a commitment to instal an additional 2.8 million lines and replace 1.25 million analogue lines. Telkom's monopoly was set to end in 2002 when a second national operator was meant to be licensed, but this process faced several delays and the second

19. Cogburn, D. 'Globalization and State Autonomy in the Information Age: Telecommunications Sector Restructuring in South Africa'. Journal of International Affairs, Vol 52, No 2 (1998), pp 583–604.
20. Teledensity is measured as the number of telephone lines per 100 people.
21. Cogburn, *supra*.

national operator (SNO), Neotel, only entered the market in 2005. Some have argued that Telkom's conduct in undermining downstream competition, which we explore below, was linked to the imminent end to its upstream monopoly and strategic decision to extend its market power downstream.[22]

With the benefit of hindsight, it is clear that the Telkom privatisation was not handled well. It entrenched Telkom's dominance as a private monopoly (albeit with significant government shareholding), with a negative effect on its own performance and the competitiveness of the sector more broadly. Telkom's monopoly position was further enhanced by government's reversal of a previous decision to strengthen the competitive position of the SNO by transferring the telecommunications infrastructure of Eskom and Transnet to the SNO in exchange for an equity stake in the SNO.[23] Instead, this infrastructure was vested in another SOE, Broadband Infraco, which has performed particularly poorly since establishment. The SNO (Neotel) thus has to roll out a network from scratch and could not place any competitive constraint on Telkom.

Unsurprisingly, Telkom's ability to extract high profits from its fixed line business reduced its incentive to innovate. Meanwhile, market conditions were changing. Mobile providers grew significantly and their market capitalisation now dwarfs that of Telkom.[24] Telkom's slow response to the changing telecommunications landscape and to the growth of mobile telecommunications was partly because government took a strategic decision that Telkom would hold a 50% share in the first mobile operator to start operating in South Africa, Vodacom. In 2008, Telkom sold this share and realised too late that it was poorly positioned to compete against the larger operators.

Even in internet services, which form the basis of the complaint we discuss below, Telkom has lost ground. Competition from wireless technologies increased and a number of public and private providers are rolling out fixed fibre networks across the country.[25] Overall, Telkom is now a follower rather than a leader in the telecommunications sector. The settlement reached between Telkom and the Commission fundamentally changed its approach to competition and encouraged it to open its network to customers. This was not only beneficial to customers but also increased Telkom's profitability and efficiency. Its position as a challenger firm in the mobile sector has also changed its view of the benefits of competition. It has become a critic of the incumbency advantages and potential for exclusion by large mobile operators and an advocate for pro-competitive regulation.

22. Hawthorne, R. et al., 'Competition, Barriers to Entry and Inclusive Growth: Telecommunications Sector Study', (Johannesburg: University of Johannesburg, 2016).
23. Telecommunications Amendment Act, No 64 of 2001(2001).
24. As on 1 March 2019, Vodacom's market capitalisation was around USD 15 billion; MTN's about USD 12 billion and Telkom's about USD 2 billion.
25. A 2008 court judgment paved the way for all telecommunications service providers to roll out infrastructure, increasing the number of competitors to Telkom in telecommunications infrastructure. *See* Altech *Autopage Cellular (Pty) Ltd v. Chairperson of the Council of the Independent Communications Authority of South Africa and Others* (20002/08) [2008] ZAGPHC 268.

A Case Study of Effective Intervention: the case of Telkom

In 2002 the Commission received a complaint against Telkom from the South African Vans Association and twenty other internet service providers ('ISPs') alleging that it was abusing its dominance to exclude existing and potential competitors in the downstream market for internet services.[26] The Commission conducted an investigation into the allegations and referred the case to the Tribunal in February 2004. The Commission found that Telkom had:

(a) refused to supply access to essential facilities (its infrastructure) to independent Value Added Network Service ('VANS') providers;
(b) induced Telkom customers not to deal with the independent VANS providers;
(c) charged their customers excessive prices for access services; and
(d) discriminated in favour of its own customers by giving them a discount on distance-related charges which it did not advance to customers of the independent VANS providers.

Telkom challenged this referral in the High Court on various grounds, including the jurisdiction of the Tribunal to hear the case, arguing that the relevant jurisdiction to investigate the complaint lay with the Independent Communications Authority of South Africa, the regulator, and not the competition authorities. Following legal proceedings lasting several years, the Supreme Court of Appeal eventually rejected Telkom's argument and referred the matter back to the Tribunal to be heard, finding that the competition authorities had the requisite jurisdiction and were the appropriate authorities to deal with the complaint.[27]

The Tribunal found that Telkom had abused its dominance by refusing to grant competitors access to an essential facility (in contravention of section 8(b) of the Act) and that it had induced customers not to deal with competitors (contravening 8(d)(i) of the Act). The Tribunal imposed an administrative penalty of USD 51,600,000[28] on Telkom for this conduct.[29]

Around the same time, between 2005 and 2007, the Commission had been investigating a second complaint against Telkom alleging similar conduct. The Commission found that Telkom had again abused its dominance, engaging in several exploitative and exclusionary acts including excessive pricing, refusal to grant access to an essential facility, margin squeeze as well as tying and bundling.[30] The Commission negotiated a settlement with Telkom which included an admission of guilt, a further penalty and, most importantly, structural and behavioural remedies to prevent Telkom from pursuing similar conduct in future.

26. *Competition Commission v. Telkom SA Ltd*, Case No. Case 11/CR/Feb04 and *Competition Commission v. Telkom SA SOC Ltd* (016865) [2013] ZACT 62 (18 July 2013).
27. *Competition Commission v. Telkom* (623/2008) [2009] ZASCA 155 (27 November 2009).
28. Using a 2012 USD/ZAR exchange rate of 8.6965.
29. Tribunal Case number 11/CR/Feb04.
30. Section 8(a) prohibits excessive pricing, section 8(b) deals with essential facilities, section 8(c) prohibits general exclusionary acts such as engaging in a margin squeeze, and section 8(d)(iii) prohibits tying and bundling.

These remedies included the implementation of functional separation between Telkom's retail and wholesale divisions along with the implementation of a transparent transfer pricing programme to ensure non-discriminatory service provision by Telkom to its retail business and rival ISPs. The settlement was confirmed by the Tribunal in July 2013.[31]

The decisions against Telkom provided the Commission with the appropriate case law to have certainty around jurisdictional questions when investigating firms are subject to oversight by other regulatory bodies. It also provides an example of effective behavioural and structural remedies that unlocked competition throughout the value chain in an otherwise highly concentrated market, dominated by a single SOE. By separating Telkom's wholesale and retail divisions and operating them as distinct business units, the settlement improved the terms upon which independent service providers could access a non-replicable and essential facility owned by an SOE which supported entry and encouraged downstream services competition.

An impact assessment conducted by the Commission confirmed that the remedies had several positive effects. These included estimated cost-savings to customers of USD 24.7 million, increased levels of entry in both the upstream and downstream market, and lowered prices for key connectivity products utilised by Telkom's customers to deliver network services. This spurred market share growth by Telkom's competitors.

From a near monopoly with 90% market share in national fixed lines in the period preceding the settlement, Telkom's market share in national fixed lines reduced to 75% in 2016. Its market share in downstream internet access, which was stable at 25% prior to the settlement declined to 19% as competitors steadily increased their market shares. The structural remedy successfully changed the dynamics of the market, promoting competition and prompting lower prices.

[2] Eskom

Eskom, South Africa's state-owned electricity utility, was established in 1923.[32] Prior to its establishment, electricity was produced by municipalities and private companies. The city of Kimberley (where, as stated earlier, diamonds were discovered in the late nineteenth century) was the first African city to instal electric streetlights in 1882. In about 1891, an electricity reticulation system was established in Johannesburg, where gold was discovered in 1886, and private provision of electricity continued to grow to meet the demands of the mines.

In 1920 the South African government commissioned a report on the electrification of the country. This report led to the passing of the Electricity Act of 1922 which laid the basis for a regulated electricity industry and the emergence of an SOE, Eskom, tasked with the provision of cheap and abundant electricity.

31. Tribunal case number: 016865.
32. 'ESCOM 1923-1929 – The Years of Establishment – "Electrifying our beloved country".' (Johannesburg: Eskom, 2018). Available online at http://www.eskom.co.za/sites/heritage/Pages/1923.aspx.

At present, Eskom produces 96% of South Africa's electricity use. In the early 1990s following the transition to non-racial democracy, Eskom embarked on a massive electrification drive. In partnership with municipalities, it connected 1.75 million households by 1999 and 7.8 million households by 2004. It also brought the real price of electricity down; in early 2000, South Africa had some of the cheapest electricity in the world, a feature that would be reversed in later years as the utility came under increasing financial pressure and lower output.

Since the mid-2000s, Eskom's performance started to decline. From late 2007, South Africa started experiencing rolling blackouts that had a negative effect on economic growth. Eskom has also embarked on a programme to build new power stations but these have been delayed and have experienced significant cost-overruns. Today, Eskom finds itself in a dire financial position.[33]

Against this difficult backdrop, the government has again revisited its policy position on the unbundling of Eskom into separate generation and transmission firms to encourage competition in generation and ensure open access to the transmission grid. This represents a return, under challenging circumstances, to government's longstanding view that competitive restructuring would improve Eskom's performance and improve sustainable, efficient generation. However, even with the talks of reform underway, it is not clear to what extent competition and competitiveness are at the centre of the reform process.

Competing priorities – the case of Eskom

Eskom is the state-owned power utility, responsible for generating 96% of the country's electricity requirements. Eskom faces limited competition in generation from Independent Power Producers (IPPs) and some municipalities, who collectively generate less than 4% of South Africa's electricity requirements. As well as enjoying a near monopoly in generation, Eskom is vertically integrated throughout the value-chain, from generation to distribution, and owns the transmission network. Eskom accounts for approximately 60% of distribution; the rest is distributed by municipalities. Its sole ownership of the transmission network is protected by regulation.[34]

Although the transmission network has characteristics of a natural monopoly, electricity generation can be (and in several countries is) subject to competition. As the system operator, and designated 'Single Purchaser' of power, IPPs are mandated to sell all generated electricity to Eskom. Eskom transmits both its own and its competitors' electricity, making it both player and referee in the market. As a result, and despite a government decision as far back as 2003 that power generation capacity would be divided between Eskom (70%) and IPPs (30%),[35] little progress has been made in this regard.

33. Financial Mail. *South Africa's Energy Crisis: Eskom 2008–2015.* (2015). Online: http://cdn.bdlive.co.za/ebooks/Eskom%20and%20the%20SA%20energy%20crisis.pdf.
34. Eberhard, A. 'The Political Economy of Power Sector Reform in South Africa', (Cape Town: UCT Graduate School of Business, 2004).
35. Department of Energy. 'Independent Power Producers'. 2018.

The lack of competition in this market has likely contributed to South Africa's continued electricity shortages, black-outs and escalating electricity prices. In 2016 and 2017, the Commission received complaints relating to Eskom's outright refusal to sign purchasing agreements with IPPs.[36] The complainants alleged that this exclusionary conduct by Eskom results in the foreclosure of competing electricity producers. Moreover, the complainants alleged that the refusal to sign Power Purchase Agreements with IPPs means that they are effectively denied access to the national electricity grid, an essential facility.

Before the Commission was able to finalise its investigation, intervention by newly appointed Ministers of Public Enterprises and Energy resulted in the Power Purchase Agreements being signed. The basis for the complaints thus ceased.

Short of intervention by the Commission and government, IPPs had limited recourse.

As indicated earlier, government has a longstanding commitment to a more competitive electricity sector dating back to 1998. In 2001, Cabinet took a formal decision to restructure the electricity sector by, among other things; unbundling Eskom, selling a stake (approximately 30%) in generation, and gradually increasing private sector participation in generation.[37] The framework for private participation in the electricity sector was only set out in Electricity Regulation Act of 2006.

In recognition of the potential conflict of interest associated with Eskom's vertically integrated monopoly in both generation and transmission, government introduced the concept of an 'Independent Systems Operator' (ISO) in 2004. The ISO would manage the transmission network and set terms of access to the grid. It would have no interest in generation, thus eliminating potential conflict of interest in access to the grid.

The concept of the ISO remained part of energy policy, culminating in the introduction of the 'Independent Systems and Market Operator (ISMO) Bill' in parliament in 2012.[38] The draft legislation proposed the establishment of an independent entity along the lines defined before. ISMO would manage transmission and set non-discriminatory terms for access to the grid. The legislation envisaged that ISMO's pricing would be done in a transparent manner and that access to the grid would be regulated in the interest of more competitive prices to consumers. The Competition Commission was broadly in favour of this proposal, with the caveat that further information would be required to assess efficacy and cost savings at each level. The ISMO Bill has not progressed beyond the comments stage since its introduction in 2012.

Interestingly, Eskom established a 'System Market Operator Division' in 2007, subsequently arguing that this unit should play the role of the envisaged ISMO.[39] This points to the strategic advantages that important SOEs have to lobby government, particularly when faced with the prospect of greater competition.

---

36. Case Numbers: 2016OCT0544 and 2017FEB0037.
37. Department of Energy. *Energy Security Master Plan – Electricity 2007–2025* (2007).
38. Steyn, E. 'Dawn of a Competitive Electricity Sector for South Africa: The Independent System and Market Operator Bill B9-2012 – Context, Content and Comment'. *De Jure*, Vol 23 (2013) pp. 539–556.
39. *Ibid*.

Recently, the government has again announced its intention to review the structure and performance of Eskom which has faced severe financial constraints and a marked reduction in generation performance, leading to frequent blackouts throughout 2018. Government seems to be reverting to the 1998 position – again considering splitting the utility into three entities that would split generation from transmission and from distribution as part of a broader attempt to improve the efficiency, performance and sustainability of the utility. This would follow the general principle of isolating segments of the value chain where competition is limited (in this case, transmission and distribution) from those in which competition can contribute to lower cost, improved efficiency and increased choice, such as in generation.

Though functional or operational separation has not been effected in the electricity sector, the principles of opening generation to competition are accepted across government, acknowledging that a vertically integrated electricity utility would have the interest and incentive to exclude competitors, as seems to have been the case. These delay in implementing these changes have been detrimental to South Africa's economy at large.

[3] Transnet

Transnet was established in 1989 from its predecessor, 'South African Transport Services', a government-run entity which was established in 1910.[40] Transnet SOC Ltd is a public company with government as its sole shareholder. It is a holding company with five subsidiaries: freight rail, rail engineering, ports (a National Ports Authority and an entity managing port and cargo operations) and pipelines. These services are operated separately, with each unit responsible for their own budgets and financial performance. Economic regulation of Transnet's subsidiaries is inconsistent – the transport sector is not subject to sector regulation while ports and pipelines are subject to economic regulation under the Ports Regulator of South Africa and the National Energy Regulator of South Africa (NERSA) respectively.

Similar to Eskom and Telkom, Transnet's establishment was shaped by the needs of the mining sector in the late nineteenth century. The railways were seen as an important strategic asset to unify the British-controlled southern part of the country and Afrikaner-controlled north after the discovery of gold and the formation of the Union of South Africa in 1910.

Transnet's pipelines division was first established in 1965. It services the fuel and gas sectors and operates a network of 3,800 km of pipelines and associated pump stations, storage and tank farms and related infrastructure. At present, Transnet has no competitors in the long-distance pipelines for petroleum products, thus holding a complete monopoly. In 2007 Transnet was granted a license to build a second national multi-product pipeline which is the subject of this paper.[41]

40. Transnet. 'Overview and Our History'. 2018. Online: https://www.transnet.net/AboutUs/Pages/History.aspx..
41. Transnet Pipelines. 'Transnet Pipelines Profile and Capability Statement'. 201–207.

Undermining competition: the case of Transnet Limited

In 2007, the NERSA granted Petroline RSA Proprietary Limited ('Petroline'), a private energy company, a license to build a petroleum pipeline from Mozambique to South Africa (the Maputo-to-Gauteng pipeline).[42] The proposed pipeline would have been in direct competition with the existing coast-to-inland liquid fuels transmission pipeline owned by SOE, Transnet Limited ('Transnet'), which runs from Durban to Gauteng. In the same year, Transnet was also granted a license to build a new multi-product pipeline ('NMPP') from Durban to Gauteng.

To understand the significance of long-distance petroleum pipelines in South Africa, it is important to explain an unusual feature of South Africa's economic landscape. South Africa's economic geography was influenced by the discovery of gold in the inland region around present-day Johannesburg. The economic heartland of South Africa still lies inland, in the Gauteng Province, which contributes 35% of South Africa's gross domestic product (GDP) despite accounting for less than 2% of the country's landmass.[43] The inland demand for petroleum constitutes a significant proportion of total demand, and it is commonly held that long-distance pipelines are the most efficient mode of conveying petroleum products over long distances, making them crucial to South Africa's economy.[44]

In 2011 the Commission received a complaint from Petroline regarding the conduct of the National Treasury and NERSA. Petroline alleged that its pipeline project was rendered unviable by the fact that Transnet received a subsidy from the National Treasury and an allegedly unusual and highly favourable tariff decision from NERSA. In Petroline's view, the two events rendered tariffs on the NMPP too low for Petroline to be able to operate an alternative pipeline profitably. More formally, Petroline alleged that Transnet is dominant in the liquid fuel pipeline market that Transnet's conduct (aided by National Treasury and NERSA) amounted to predatory pricing and/or exclusionary behaviour.[45]

Had Petroline entered, it would have been the first competitor in the South African liquid fuels pipeline sector. It had invested approximately USD 12.3 million by the time it abandoned its project in 2011.[46] To make matters worse, Petroline also seemed to have a slight natural (geographic) advantage over the NMPP in that the distance from the port of Maputo to Johannesburg is shorter than from Durban and the terrain more favourable to construction of a pipeline.

The events leading to Petroline's exit are directly related to the National Treasury's decision to grant a subsidy to Transnet for the completion of the pipeline and NERSA's decision to alter the methodology it uses to calculate pipeline tariffs. Transnet lobbied heavily for both of these decisions.

42. Case Number: 2011May0059.
43. Provincial GDP figure is provided by Statistics South Africa for 2016. Available at http://www.statssa.gov.za/.
44. Competition Tribunal. *Sasol-Engen merger decision.* (2006) Case Number: 101/LM/Dec04.
45. The complainant alleged that the conduct amounted to a contravention of either section 8(c) which prohibits general exclusionary acts and, in the alternate, section 8(d)(iv) which prohibits predatory pricing.
46. Using a 2011 USD/ZAR exchange rate of 8.1285.

During construction, the cost of the Transnet pipeline rose substantially above projections and the NMPP was subject to numerous delays. At inception, the anticipated cost of the pipeline was approximately USD 670 million. By 2007, Transnet indicated that costs would be closer to USD 880 million, but by 2012 costs had escalated to USD 1.6 billion.

In 2010, faced with escalating costs of the pipeline and after extensive engagements with Transnet, National Treasury implemented a levy of 7.5c/l on fuel to contribute to the funding of the NMPP up to a maximum of USD 320 million. Transnet then lobbied NERSA to change the manner in which it values assets for the purpose of imposing tariffs by excluding grants such as the one it received from Treasury. This reduced the value of the Regulatory Asset Base that NERSA uses to determine the tariff, artificially reducing the Transnet tariff. Further changes were made to the tariff methodology in 2011/2012 that allowed Transnet to cross-subsidise the NMPP tariffs with other (older) pipeline infrastructure, further reducing the NMPP tariff. It is against this subsidised tariff that Petroline had to compete, rather than a tariff that reflected the true cost of the pipeline. This rendered Petroline's project unviable.

This case presents one of the ugliest examples of political manoeuvring by an SOE 'behind the scenes' to achieve an outcome that was clearly not in the interest of users. With no rival and limited incentive for efficiency, cost overruns and delays continued. The NMPP was completed five years behind schedule and the final cost ballooned to USD 2.47 billion in 2017. Despite the negative effect on competition, the authorities could not intervene. In line with the decision in *AEC Electronics* mentioned earlier, the competition authorities did not have the jurisdiction to enforce competition law in this instance as Treasury's decision to grant the subsidy and NERSA's regulatory decision amounted to the exercise of public power by state functionaries, and these decisions were not subject to review by the competition authorities.

This case provides an example of the political influence of incumbents and the limited room to change course once investment decisions by SOEs commit the state to a particular path. The lack of competitive pressure on Transnet likely contributed to the cost overruns and project delays. The unconditional support from National Treasury may also signal to potential competitors that the state will support and even favour SOEs, thus acting as a powerful and lasting disincentive for entry by private-sector firms.

§12.03 CONCLUSION

In the course of enforcing competition law, the Commission generally treats SOEs in the same manner as normal corporate entities. The complaints that the authority has investigated mostly relate to conduct by vertically integrated monopolists leveraging monopoly power from a market in which competition is unlikely into another market that could be, or is, open to competition from private firms. This is reflected in the Telkom and Eskom examples discussed earlier.

In both cases, vertical integration created incentives for these SOEs to extend their market dominance into the more competitive levels of the value chain, often through anticompetitive means. Both SOEs did this in the face of the threat of competitive entry. Importantly, these industries (telecommunications and electricity) form the basis of South Africa's infrastructure backbone, and effective competition in these sectors will have substantial positive externalities across a multitude of other industries.

Though less common, the Commission has also received complaints about state support that grants an undue advantage to SOEs relative to private firms in the form of cheap credit and advantageous tariffs. This conduct raises barriers to entry and limits the alternatives available to consumers.

The ability of the competition authorities to intervene in such cases to ensure competitive neutrality in the interest of effective competition is hampered by the current legal framework that does not allow the Commission to evaluate the decision of regulators of SOEs, despite substantial inefficiencies arising as a result, as highlighted in the Petroline case. Competition is not always the primary motivating factor, or even a strong consideration, of state functionaries which means that potential private sector rivals do not always compete on a level playing field.

Overall, absent a government-backed competition policy which could include measures on competitive neutrality, the Commission can only investigate complaints after the activity has occurred. In terms of forward looking enforcement, the Commission is limited to engaging in advocacy and conducting market inquiries.

The development and acceptance of a broader competition policy that emphasises the benefits of competition in policymaking across government is thus required to sensitise all state functionaries to the benefits of pro-competitive public policy and to place competition at the forefront of industrial and development policies.

At present, competition law operates in the absence of a broader commitment to competition principles which creates the perception that opening markets to competition is primarily the role of competition authorities. Developing a competition policy that covers all economic sectors and promotes competitiveness through trade policy, industrial policy, public procurement, development finance institutions and through the functions of SOEs, would encourage all social and economic decision makers to consider the benefits of competition in designing and implement policy. It would signal an economy-wide commitment to favouring entry and dynamism over the status quo and incumbency and would contribute to the development of a more competitive and inclusive economy.

It is also important that the overall policy for competition should be determined and administered outside the line departments responsible for SOEs. In the current debates about SOE reform, as is being contemplated with Eskom, careful thought should be given to the design of markets and future competitive effects to ensure that reform does not simply create a private monopoly able to extract monopoly rents with no incentive for efficiency or competition.

Part IV Challenges with Convergence, Regionalization and Future Perspectives

CHAPTER 13

Promoting Convergence in ASEAN Competition Laws and Practice*

Ruben Lapa Maximiano, Rachel Burgess & Wouter Meester

§13.01 INTRODUCTION

In 2010, only four of the Association of Southeast Asian Nations (ASEAN) Member States (AMSs) (Indonesia, Singapore, Thailand and Viet Nam) had enacted competition laws, and of these only Singapore and Indonesia were actively enforcing their laws. By December 2015, when the ASEAN Economic Community (AEC) came into effect, all AMSs (with the exception of Cambodia),[1] had introduced legislation addressing competition law and policy.[2] In addition, competition law enforcement across the ASEAN jurisdictions had dramatically increased.

The impetus to introduce competition law may largely be attributed to the increased political commitment in ASEAN thereto, linked to the initial AEC Blueprint 2008–2015. This Blueprint included a goal for all AMSs to have adopted a competition law and policy in preparation for the commencement of the AEC.[3] Subsequently, regional guidelines on competition policy were published in 2010 and the ASEAN Experts Group on Competition (AEGC) – set up in 2007 – was made responsible for

* The opinions expressed in this chapter are personal. This chapter in no way reflects the views or opinions of the OECD, its Committees or its Members.
1. This chapter therefore does not further consider Cambodia.
2. When referencing competition laws in the AMSs, the authors are referring to the following laws, current at the date of writing: Brunei: *Competition Order 2014;* Lao PDR: *Law on Business Competition 2015*; Indonesia: *No.5/1999 Regarding Prohibition of Monopolistic Practices and Unfair Business Competition*; Malaysia: *Competition Act (2010)*; Myanmar: *The Pyidaungsu Hluttaw Law No. 9/2015*; The Philippines: *Competition Act (2015)*; Singapore: *Competition Act 2004*; Thailand: *Trade Competition Act (2017)*; Viet Nam: *Competition Law, No. 23/2018/QH14.*
3. ASEAN Secretariat, *ASEAN Economic Community Blueprint (2008–2015)*, Jakarta: ASEAN Secretariat, 2008, paragraph B41, p. 18. Available at https://www.asean.org/wp-content/uploads/images/archive/5187-10.pdf (accessed 30 July 2019).

guiding the implementation of competition law and policy in ASEAN.[4] Finally, in 2016, an ASEAN Competition Action Plan 2016–2025 (ACAP) identifies 'moving towards greater harmonization of competition policy and law in ASEAN'[5] as one of its five strategic goals and sets the AEGC the task of developing 'a strategy for regional convergence'.[6]

The introduction and development of competition law and policy in the region has also resulted in strengthened enforcement. In the past few years, the various competition authorities in the AMSs have worked hard to increase their capacity as well as their knowledge and understanding of competition law and policy with a view to strengthening the competition culture in the respective AMS and gaining the respect of governments and business communities, both locally and internationally.

The reason for ASEAN's focus on competition law and policy and the consequent desired convergence seems apparent. The intended regional economic integration and subsequent free(er) flow of goods, services and capital between AMSs can foster cross-border trade and interactions and enhance economic growth in the different AMSs. However, competition law and policy plays an important role in this process as opening domestic markets goes hand in hand with the necessity to protect the competitive process and avoid cross-border anti-competitive practices.[7] The regional benefits of the creation of a common economic community will be affected by the varying stages of economic development and the extent to, and ways in which, AMSs have implemented competition laws and policy.

ASEAN and its Member States have made the choice not to have one regional competition framework, enforced by one supranational authority, but instead to have national competition laws enforced by national authorities. This raises the inevitable question of whether convergence of competition law and policy in ASEAN is achievable. The extent to which laws are drafted using similar language and substantive tests will be an important element in achieving a high degree of convergence (we call this 'hard' convergence). As competition law is highly dependent on complex legal and economic analysis and interpretation, the approach taken by the AMSs to interpreting those laws will also have a significant effect on the potential for convergent outcomes (we call this 'soft' convergence). With diverse historical backgrounds and a mix of civil and common law legal systems, there is a risk that the AMSs will take diverse approaches to competition law and policy implementation.

In October 2018, a Regional Cooperation Framework ('RCF') was established to guide cooperation between the AMSs in competition cases. The RCF, which has been endorsed by the ASEAN Economic Ministers, sets out the general objectives, principles

4. The AEGC has four priority areas: (1) Strengthening the regulatory environment in ASEAN, (2) Institutional capacity building and law enforcement of CPL in ASEAN, (3) Developing a strategy and tools for regional competition advocacy, and (4) Building cross-cutting regional initiatives. *See* https://www.asean-competition.org/aegc (accessed 30 July 2019).
5. ASEAN Secretariat, *ASEAN Competition Action Plan (ACAP) 2016–2025*, Jakarta: ASEAN Secretariat, 30 December 2017, p. 2.
6. ACAP, p. 8.
7. *See also* OECD (2018). Regional Competition Agreements: Benefits and Challenges, OECD, a background note for Session III at the seventeenth Global Forum on Competition on 29–30 November 2018.

and possible areas of cooperation in relation to the development, application and enforcement of competition laws.[8]

Against this background, this chapter argues that continuing efforts are needed in relation to both hard and soft convergence if convergence is to be achieved. Convergence is mostly likely to occur if there is coordination and cooperation between the ASEAN competition authorities. To support this discussion, the chapter focuses on the text of the AMSs' competition laws and policies as well as the available published guidance. Insofar as is possible, the chapter also considers decided cases to determine where reliance on established jurisprudence exists in the interpretation of the law and policies. The institutional structures of the ASEAN competition authorities are considered as they will greatly influence the likelihood of convergence. If interpretation of the law and the powers and priorities of the regulators and competition authorities differ too greatly, convergence will be more difficult.

§13.02 POLICY OBJECTIVES OF COMPETITION LAW IN ASEAN

The policy objectives behind the introduction of competition law in the AMSs need to be considered from two perspectives. First, on a regional level, there are a range of policy statements incorporated into ASEAN documents that are instructive. Second, from the national perspective, the laws and policy statements of each AMS give an insight into the likelihood of consistency in approach between the AMSs as they interpret and apply their laws.

[A] ASEAN Policy Objectives

The AMSs first committed to endeavour to introduce competition law and policy by 2015 in Singapore in 2007. One of the tasks set out in the AEC Blueprint 2008–2015 was the development of regional guidelines on competition policy, which were completed by 2010.[9] The Regional Guidelines were intended to:

> serve as a general framework for the AMS as they endeavour to introduce, implement and develop competition policy in accordance with the specific legal and economic context of each AMS.[10]

Although the Guidelines are not binding on the AMSs,[11] the document makes important statements about the policy objectives that can be achieved with the introduction of competition law:

---

8. https://www.cccs.gov.sg/media-and-consultation/newsroom/media-releases/22nd-aegc-meeting-asean-establishes-competition-enforcers (accessed 30 July 2019).
9. ASEAN Secretariat, *ASEAN Regional Guidelines on Competition Policy*, Jakarta: ASEAN Secretariat, 2010. Available at https://www.asean.org/storage/images/2012/publications/ASEAN%20Regional%20Guidelines%20on%20Competition%20Policy.pdf (accessed 15 February 2019).
10. Regional Guidelines, paragraph 1.2.1.
11. Regional Guidelines, paragraph 1.2.2. and indeed are not expressly referenced by the AMSs in any of the guidelines, to date.

> The most commonly stated objective of competition policy is the promotion and the protection of the competitive process. Competition policy introduces a 'level-playing field' for all market players that will help markets to be competitive. The introduction of a competition law will provide the market with a set of 'rules of the game' that protects the competition process itself, rather than competitors in the market. In this way, the pursuit of fair or effective competition can contribute to improvements in economic efficiency, economic growth and development and consumer welfare.[12]

The Guidelines then go on to explain the concepts of economic efficiency, economic growth and development, and consumer welfare. Other possible policy objectives that can be achieved by competition policy are noted to include:

> the integration of national markets and promotion of regional integration, the promotion or protection of small businesses, the promotion of technological advancement, the promotion of product and process innovation, the promotion of industrial diversification, environment protection, fighting inflation, job creation, equal treatment of workers according to race and gender or the promotion of welfare of particular consumer groups.[13]

Many of these policy objectives have been incorporated by the AMSs into their own competition laws.

The AEC Blueprint 2016–2025, which came into effect in 2015, emphasises the need for operational and effective competition policy and law (CPL). To achieve this, the Blueprint sets out strategic measures which include:

(a) effectively implementing CPL in all AMS based on international best practices and agreed upon ASEAN guidelines;
(b) achieving greater harmonisation of CPL in ASEAN by developing a regional strategy on convergence; and
(c) continuing to enhance CPL in ASEAN taking into account international best practices.[14]

Following on from the AEC Blueprint 2016–2025, the ACAP 2025 was adopted. While Strategic Goal 5 is 'moving towards greater harmonization of competition policy and law in ASEAN',[15] the ACAP recognises that convergence can only be achieved after introduction of, and enforcement of, those laws.[16] Although recognising that the laws across the AMSs are different (and may remain different for many valid reasons), the ACAP nevertheless notes a commitment to promoting 'the similarities and convergence and eliminating contradictions'.[17]

12. Regional Guidelines, paragraph 2.2.1.
13. Regional Guidelines, paragraph 2.2.3.
14. ASEAN Secretariat, *ASEAN Economic Community Blueprint (2015–2025)*, Jakarta: ASEAN Secretariat, 2015, paragraph B1, pp. 12–13. Available at https://asean.org/?static_post=asean-economic-community-blueprint-2025 (accessed 15 February 2019).
15. ACAP, p. 8.
16. ACAP, p. 8.
17. ACAP, p. 8.

Many important benefits of harmonisation[18] are then noted:

- A seamless policy environment for goods, services and capital to move around freely and without barriers;
- Companies can operate and allocate their resources in the most efficient ways possible;
- Enhancing transparency and predictability of the investment climate;
- Facilitating regional cooperation with regard to competition law enforcement (under Strategic Goal 3).[19]

[B] Policy Objectives at a National Level

At a national level, the policy objectives to be achieved in each AMS' competition law will be relevant to the manner in which the laws are interpreted on a daily basis. Most of the AMSs state the policy objective of their competition law to be the promotion of competition and consumer welfare (with the limited exception of Thailand), consistent with recommendations made in the Regional Guidelines. Many AMSs have also included additional policy objectives, such as economic efficiency and development (Brunei, Lao PDR, Malaysia, Viet Nam) and economic growth (Indonesia, Myanmar, the Philippines). These additional policy objectives are also consistent with those suggested in the Regional Guidelines.

Hence, at least at a policy level, there is broad consistency in what is hoped to be achieved through the adoption of a CPL in ASEAN.

However, the scope of the laws and the exemptions provided for will also be relevant to hard and soft convergence. Some jurisdictions exclude (or provide for potential exemption for) agreements entered into by small- and medium-sized enterprises;[20] agreements that results in an improvement of business success;[21] farmers and cooperatives;[22] and agreements relating to intellectual property rights.[23] As noted below, vertical agreements are exempt from competition law in Singapore and Brunei.

Another relevant element for convergence, in particular in ASEAN, given how important a role state-owned enterprises (SOEs) play in the region, is whether enforcement actions are legally exempted and/or whether the Competition Authorities are unwilling or unable to pursue such actions in practice. The fact that SOEs can be exempted (de jure or de facto) from the competition laws means there is preferential treatment which is not compatible with the promotion of market competition, in particular with harmonised markets across ASEAN. In effect, AMS exempting or not

18. Please note that for the purposes of this article the terms harmonization and convergence are used interchangeably.
19. ACAP, p. 8.
20. Section 50 Indonesian Competition Law; Article 45 Lao Competition Law; Article 8(b) Myanmar Competition Law.
21. Article 14 and 33 Myanmar Competition Law; Article 14 Viet Nam Competition Law.
22. Section 4 Thailand Competition Law.
23. Section 50 Indonesian Competition Law.

applying their competition laws to SOEs, gives SOEs that directly or indirectly compete with private firms in the provision of goods and services possible undue advantages.[24]

The vast majority of AMS laws do not exempt SOEs from their competition laws, with two exceptions where this is unclear: in Myanmar and Brunei. Two further countries have limited exemptions, both for reasons of public interest (Thailand and Indonesia). In the case of Thailand, its recent change to the law has removed the blanket exemption of SOEs that existed until 2017.[25]

What is less evident is whether there is active enforcement of the competition laws against SOEs. To date, there are a limited number of examples of enforcement of competition law against SOEs. In Malaysia, penalties were imposed against Malaysian Airlines for market sharing arrangements (recently upheld by the High Court). In Singapore, a government-owned ticketing service operator was found to have abused its dominant position through exclusive contracts. To date, there has been only one infringement decision in Viet Nam (*see* below section on Unilateral Conduct), the case against Vinapco, a SOE. In Indonesia, seems to be an exception as there have been numerous cases reported involving state-owned operators.

Exchanging case studies and examining how best to approach these sensitive cases may lead to increased enforcement against SOEs where appropriate and necessary to safeguard a level playing field, not only in each AMS but also across ASEAN[26].

§13.03 THE THREE PILLARS OF ASEAN COMPETITION LAWS

Effective competition laws prohibit anti-competitive agreements, unilateral conduct and mergers (commonly referred to as the three pillars of competition law). The competition laws enacted across ASEAN address all three pillars, with the exception of Malaysia, which does not currently have merger provisions.

To assess the likelihood of convergence as a result of consistent laws and interpretation, this section reviews the wording of the laws enacted in the AMSs and its interpretation, based on the available guidance and case law.

[A] Anti-competitive Agreements

Commonly, competition law provisions addressing anti-competitive agreements prohibit hard-core cartels and other anti-competitive agreements (both horizontal and vertical) that adversely affect the markets in question. Different tests may be applied to

24. OECD (2012). "Competitive neutrality; Maintaining a level playing field between public and private business, OECD Publishing, Paris, and OECD (2011). Competitive Neutrality and State-Owned Enterprises: Challenges and Policy Options, OECD Corporate Governance Working Papers, No. 1.
25. Section 4 of the Trade Competition Act, B.E. 2560 (2017) ("2017 Trade Competition Act"). However, it sets out some exceptions, including under Section 4(4) "businesses that are specifically regulated under other sectoral laws having jurisdiction over competition matters".
26. This sort of exchange was conducted for instance in the 2nd Meeting of High-Level Representatives of Asia-Pacific Competition Authorities in Paris on November 28, 2018, where the issue of competitive neutrality was the main topic of debate.

assess this adverse effect. In some ASEAN jurisdictions, vertical agreements are exempt from competition law.

[1] Hard-Core Cartels

The Regional Guidelines suggest that:

> AMSs may consider identifying 'hardcore restrictions', which will always be considered as having an appreciable adverse effect on competition (e.g. price fixing, bid-rigging, market sharing, limiting or controlling production or investment).[27]

The Guidelines then define each of those hard-core restrictions.[28] This approach is consistent with international best practice. The OECD Recommendation concerning Effective Action against Hard-Core Cartels defines 'hard core' cartels to be:

> an anticompetitive agreement, anticompetitive concerted practice, or anticompetitive arrangement by competitors to fix prices, make rigged bids (collusive tenders), establish output restrictions or quotas, or share or divide markets by allocating customers, suppliers, territories, or lines of commerce.[29]

Of great significance to the question of potential convergence is the fact that all ASEAN competition laws prohibit hard-core cartels. In many cases, the terminology follows that used in the European Union (EU).

Sanctions for hard-core cartels across the ASEAN regimes are most commonly civil, but the potential for criminal sanctions also exists in a number of jurisdictions (Philippines, Indonesia, Thailand, Lao PDR and Myanmar[30]). This may raise issues regarding the standard of proof which is higher for criminal offences than for civil or administrative sanctions as well as the interface between the competition authority and the public prosecutor or similar office that normally is in charge of prosecuting criminal charges.

Although the above analysis suggests consistency in relation to hard-core cartels, consideration needs to be given to the tests that will apply to determine the existence of the cartel.

In some jurisdictions around the world, hard-core cartels are considered so harmful to competition that they are per se prohibited. This means that the competition authority does not need to prove that the agreement had an adverse effect on competition in the market. Instead, the authority needs only to establish the existence of the cartel agreement. This is the case in the United States where horizontal price-fixing and market sharing (unrelated to a combination of business effort that

27. Regional Guidelines, paragraph 3.2.2.
28. Regional Guidelines, paragraph 3.2.2.1–3.2.2.4.
29. Recommendation of the OECD Council concerning Effective Action against Hard Core Cartels, as approved by Council on 25 March 1998 C(98)35/FINAL – C/M(98)7/PROV. Available at http://www.oecd.org/daf/competition/2350130.pdf (accessed 11 February 2019).
30. Section 30 Philippines Competition Law; Article 48 Indonesian Competition Law; section 72 Thailand Competition Law; sections 39–42 Myanmar Competition Law and Article 92 Lao PDR Competition Law (although it is not clear which provisions are subject to the criminal offence).

offers efficiencies) are per se condemned.[31] Under European Law, Article 101 of the Treaty on the Functioning of the EU applies an object test.[32] In practice, this means that an agreement is presumed to be anti-competitive unless the cartelists can demonstrate efficiencies. This burden is extremely high, so the object test can be argued to be in effect similar to a per se test.

In the Regional Guidelines, the intention appears to have been that all the AMSs treat price fixing, market sharing, bid rigging and limiting production or supply as hard-core offences subject to the per se test[33] although it leaves room for each AMS to determine what is appropriate in its jurisdiction:

> AMSs *may* consider identifying specific 'hard core restrictions', which will always be considered as having an appreciable adverse effect on competition (e.g., price fixing, bid-rigging, market sharing, limiting or controlling production or investment), which need to be treated as per se illegal [emphasis added].[34]

The approach taken by the AMS to this issue is potentially inconsistent. The words 'per se' are expressly used in the Philippines legislation (in relation to price fixing and bid rigging only)[35]. A number of other jurisdictions use the 'objects or effects' terminology (Singapore, Brunei, Malaysia[36] and the Philippines in relation to market sharing and limiting production). It is not clear whether the 'object' component is intended to apply as equivalent to a 'per se' (as in the US) or more akin to the European standard. In the remaining jurisdictions, neither the words 'per se' nor 'object or effect' are used, leaving the question entirely open as to which standard will be applied. This is therefore an area where further convergence could be achieved.

Leniency

Leniency is an important tool used by competition authorities to uncover cartels. Generally, a leniency regime operates to provide complete or partial immunity from fines to the leniency applicant, which can be those that come forward to a competition authority with information about a cartel.

The scope of this chapter prevents a detailed discussion of the leniency provisions in the AMSs' competition laws. However, in the context of convergence, leniency should not be overlooked. A consistent approach to leniency across ASEAN will be

31. Jones, Alison and Kovacic, William E., *Identifying Anticompetitive Agreements in the United States and the European Union: Developing a Coherent Antitrust Analytical Framework* (17 February 2017). Antitrust Bulletin, Forthcoming; GWU Law School Public Law Research Paper No. 2017-12; GWU Legal Studies Research Paper No. 2017-12. Available at SSRN: https://ssrn.com/abstract=2919312, p. 20.
32. By object restrictions have 'net negative effects', that is they have 'high potential to create negative effects but, more importantly, these are restrictions which are (highly) unlikely to create efficiencies'. *See* Pepperkorn, L. *Defining 'by object' restrictions,* Concurrences No. 3, 2015, pp. 40–50, p. 41–42. Available at http://concorrencia.pt/lisbonconference2015/assets/05.concurrences_3-2015_doctrines_peeperkorn.pdf (accessed 9 February 2019).
33. Regional Guidelines, paragraph 3.2.3.
34. Regional Guidelines, paragraph 3.2.2.
35. Section 14(a) Philippine Competition Act 2015.
36. Note Section 4(2) Malaysia Competition Act **deems** cartels to have the object of significantly preventing, restricting or distorting competition

important if cross-border cartels are to be prosecuted and if competition authorities are to be able to cooperate effectively and efficiently. For this they need to avoid conflicting requirements.[37] An inconsistent approach will risk convergence as cartelists may forum shop for the most favourable leniency regimes. Singapore,[38] The Philippines[39] and Malaysia[40] each have a leniency regime currently in operation. The laws of Brunei,[41] Thailand[42] and Viet Nam[43] make provision for a leniency regime but they are not yet in operation, while Indonesia is proposing to amend its law to allow leniency. The position in Lao PDR is unclear[44] while the leniency provision in Myanmar appears to be limited.[45] Given the number of new leniency programmes that have yet to be developed (and this lies at least to a certain extent at the discretion of the competition authorities), this is an area where convergence can be advanced in the coming years. When developing their leniency programmes, the AMSs' competition authorities should try to ensure consistency in their approaches and follow international best practices.

Case Law

As the introduction of competition law into AMSs is relatively new in many jurisdictions, at the time of writing, only Singapore, Indonesia, Malaysia and Viet Nam had prosecuted cartels. As only Singapore and Malaysia have made their decisions publicly available in English, the ability to assess similarities and differences in case law is limited. In this regard, it is interesting to note that both of these jurisdictions have relied on EU jurisprudence.

In Singapore, the regard for European jurisprudence has been express. In the first decision of the Competition Commission of Singapore (CCS, now the Competition and Consumer Commission of Singapore (CCCS)) finding a bid-rigging cartel,[46] the [then] CCS stated:

> As competition law is a new area of law in Singapore, cases from these jurisdictions may be persuasive or useful in assisting the Commission in reaching its decision. (para 37)

37. OECD (2018) *Challenges and Co-Ordination of Leniency Programmes*. Available at http://www.oecd.org/competition/challenges-and-coordination-of-leniency-programmes.htm (accessed 18 February 2019).
38. *See CCCS Guidelines on Lenient Treatment for Undertakings Coming Forward with Information on Cartel Activity 2016*. Available at https://www.cccs.gov.sg/approach-cccs/applying-for-leniency/submit-a-leniency-application (accessed 15 February 2019).
39. Section 35 Philippines Competition Law.
40. Section 41 Malaysia Competition Law.
41. Section 44 Brunei Competition Law.
42. Section 79 allows for a settlement procedure but it is not yet clear how this will work.
43. Called 'clemency' under section 112 Viet Nam Competition Law.
44. *See* Article 86 Lao PDR Competition Law.
45. Section 52 Myanmar Competition Law.
46. *Collusive Tendering (Bid-Rigging) for Termite Treatment/Control Services by Certain Pest Control Operators in Singapore* (9 January 2008). Available at https://www.cccs.gov.sg/public-register-and-consultation/public-consultation-items/collusive-tendering-bidrigging-for-termite-treatmentcontrol-services-by-certain-pest-control-operators-in-singapore?type=public_register (accessed 15 February 2019).

The same decision then makes regular references to EU jurisprudence.[47] Subsequent decisions of the CCCS continue to refer to EU jurisprudence,[48] as has the Competition Appeal Board in its decisions on appeals from the CCCS.[49]

In Malaysia, in the high-profile case against Malaysian Airlines and AirAsia, the Malaysia Competition Commission (MyCC) indicated a desire to interpret Malaysia's law consistently with those in the EU:

> This position [that it is not necessary to prove effect once object is shown] is consistent with the judgements in the EU as held in the case of *Competition Authority v Beef Industry Development Society Ltd and Barry Brothers (Carrigmore) Meals Ltd (BIDS)* and the case of *European Night Services v Commission* where in the EU position has similar deeming provision in respect of agreement between competitors.[50] (para 64).

However, subsequent decisions of the MyCC have not expressly referred to European case law.[51]

[2] *Other Anti-competitive Horizontal Agreements*

All of the AMSs' competition laws contain a general prohibition on anti-competitive horizontal agreements (other than hard-core cartels).[52]

The Regional Guidelines suggest that AMSs should evaluate an anti-competitive agreement 'by reference to its object and/or its effects where possible'.[53] In the case of Brunei, Malaysia, the Philippines and Singapore, this terminology is expressly adopted. The new Vietnamese law applies a 'causing impacts or likely to cause significant

47. *See* for example paragraph 44.
48. The most recent decision of the CCCS, *Infringement Decision against the Exchange of Commercially Sensitive Information between Competing Hotels*, Case CCCS 700/002/14, 30 January 2019 refers extensively to European jurisprudence. Available at https://www.cccs.gov.sg/public-register-and-consultation/public-consultation-items/id-against-hotels?type=public_register (accessed 12 February 2019).
49. *See* for example, *Price Fixing of Coach Bus Services for Travelling Between Singapore and Destinations in Malaysia from 2006 to 2008* (28 December 2009). Available at https://www.cccs.gov.sg/public-register-and-consultation/public-consultation-items/price-fixing-of-coach-bus-services-for-travelling-between-singapore-and-destinations-in-malaysia-from-2006-to-2008?type=public_register (accessed 15 February 2019).
50. *Finding of Infringement under Section 40 of the Competition Act 2010 – Infringement of Section 4(2)(b) of the Competition Act 2010 by Malaysian Airline System Berhad, AirAsia Berhad and AirAsia X Sdn.Bhd*, paragraph 64. Available at http://www.mycc.gov.my/sites/default/files/MAS%20AIRASIA.pdf (accessed 12 February 2019).
51. The Malaysian law contains other references to EU concepts. For example, in section 2, the concept of a 'single economic entity' is adopted: 'a parent and subsidiary company shall be regarded as a single enterprise if, despite their separate legal entity, they form a single economic unit within which the subsidiaries do not enjoy real autonomy in determining their actions on the market'.
52. Section 11(1) Brunei Competition Law; Articles 23 and 24 Indonesian Competition Act; Articles 20, 21(4), (5), (6), (7), (9), 25, 26, 27, 28 Lao PDR Competition Law; section 4(1) Malaysian Competition Law; section 13 Myanmar Competition Law; section 14(c) Philippines Competition Law; section 34(1) Singapore Competition Law; sections 55, 56 and 58 Thailand Competition Law; Article 11 Viet Nam.
53. Regional Guidelines, paragraph 3.2.2.

impacts on restraint of competition in the market' test. Lao PDR, Myanmar and Thailand use terminology referring to reductions or restrictions of competition.[54]

In Indonesia, the Guidelines on Cartels[55] sets out indicators that help the Business Competition Supervisory Commission (KPPU) assess the effect on competition. Guidelines published in Singapore and Malaysia do not explain how 'effect' will be determined but do reference factors that will be relevant in the assessment[56] or examples of scenarios where anti-competitive effect is likely.[57]

The Regional Guidelines suggest that the AMSs prohibit horizontal and vertical agreements between undertakings that 'prevent, distort or restrict competition'. The AMSs have adopted this (or similar) terminology in their laws. The Regional Guidelines explain the words 'prevent, distort or restrict' as referring:

> respectively, to the elimination of existing or potential competitive activities, the artificial alteration of competitive conditions in favour of the parties of the agreement, and the reduction of competitive activities. They are meant to include all situations where competitive conditions are adversely affected by the existence of the anti-competitive agreement.[58]

The Regional Guidelines recognise that not all agreements that prevent, distort or restrict competition should be prohibited, alluding to the role that safe harbours may play:[59]

> AMSs may decide that an agreement infringes the law only if it has as its object or effect the appreciable prevention, distortion or restriction of competition.[60]

In the ASEAN competition laws, some jurisdictions have chosen to include an 'appreciability test' in the text of the law itself although different terminology is used: 'substantially' (Philippines), significantly (Malaysia). To assist in identifying what 'significantly' means, the MyCC applies a threshold of 20% combined market share for agreements between competitors and 25% market share each where the agreement is between parties that are non-competitors.[61]

In Singapore, the 'appreciability' threshold is set out in Guidelines. The CCCS *Guidelines on the Section 34 Prohibition* state that agreements will not have an appreciable effect on competition where the combined market share of the parties to the agreement is less than 20%. In the case of non-competitors, the market share

---

54. Section 18 Lao PDR Competition Law; Article 2(g) Myanmar Competition Law; section 54 Thailand Competition Law.
55. 4/2010. Available at http://eng.kppu.go.id/newkppu/wp-content/uploads/Pasal-11-KARTEL.pdf (accessed 18 February 2019).
56. *See* paragraphs 2.25–2.27 CCCS *Guidelines on Section 34 Prohibition.*
57. MyCC *Guidelines on Chapter 2 Prohibition.*
58. Regional Guidelines, paragraph 3.2.1.5.
59. Safe harbours are commonly used in competition law and policy to indicate the market circumstances where anti-competitive agreements are unlikely to have an effect on competition. Usually, a safe harbour is linked to the size of the players in the relevant market.
60. Regional Guidelines, paragraph 3.2.2.
61. *See* paragraph 3.4 MyCC *Guidelines on Chapter 1 Prohibition.*

threshold for each party is 25%, lower than which there will be presumed to have no appreciable effect on competition.[62]

At the time of writing, no other ASEAN competition regulator has indicated whether a safe harbour will apply.

As with the cartel cases, it is to be noted that the CCCS has relied heavily on European jurisprudence in decisions prohibiting anti-competitive agreements, most recently evidenced in *Infringement Decision against the Exchange of Commercially Sensitive Information between Competing Hotels.*[63]

[3] Vertical Agreements

The scope of this chapter prohibits a detailed analysis of the vertical agreement provisions in ASEAN competition law.[64] However, it is an area that must not be overlooked in the context of convergence as divergence already exists. Of particular importance is the express exclusion of vertical agreements from the application of competition law in Singapore and Brunei.[65] This has the effect that resale price maintenance agreements are not prohibited (or sanctioned in any way) in these jurisdictions but would be subject to civil sanctions in Indonesia, Malaysia, Myanmar, the Philippines, Thailand and Viet Nam.[66] It is not clear whether the provisions in the Lao PDR competition law are also intended to apply to vertical agreements. This is an area where further hard convergence can be achieved.

[4] Conclusion on Anti-competitive Agreements and Convergence

It has been shown that, in many jurisdictions, the ASEAN competition laws have adopted similar provisions prohibiting anti-competitive agreements, particularly in relation to cartels. It is not clear whether the 'object' standard applied in some jurisdictions is intended to operate as equivalent to a 'per se' or whether it will apply in a manner similar to the EU. Nor is it clear what standard will be applied in the jurisdictions that are silent on the issue. Going forward, the competition authorities need to provide clear guidance on which standard ('per se' or 'object or effect') will be applied in respect to cartels. This is an area where convergence of the policy approach would be highly beneficial.

62. Paragraph 2.25 CCCS *Guidelines on the Section 34 Prohibition.*
63. Case CCCS 700/002/14, 30 January 2019 refers extensively to European jurisprudence. Available at https://www.cccs.gov.sg/public-register-and-consultation/public-consultation-items/id-against-hotels?type=public_register (accessed 12 February 2019).
64. For an excellent discussion of this issue, *see* Jones, Alison. *Antitrust Appraisal of Vertical Agreements in the ASEAN Economic Community: Proposals for a More Harmonised Approach* in B. Ong (ed.), *The Regionalisation of Competition Law and Policy in ASEAN* (Cambridge University Press). Available at https://ssrn.com/abstract=2867005.
65. Singapore: Clause 8, Third Schedule to Competition Act 2004; Brunei: Clause 8, Third Schedule to Competition Order 2014.
66. Articles 6, 8, 15 Indonesian Competition Law; section 4(1) Malaysian Competition Law; section 13 Myanmar Competition Law; section 14(c) Philippines Competition Law; section 55 Thailand Competition Law; Article 12(4) Viet Nam Competition Law.

The consistency in competition policy in this area should permit a large degree of convergence to be achieved, particularly where laws are interpreted to reflect international competition law concepts. It will be vital that a consistent approach is taken to cartels in particular if international cartels are to be captured in ASEAN. Cooperation and coordination between the competition authorities will be of great benefit in achieving this required consistent approach.

[B] Unilateral Behaviour

The second pillar of competition law is that which prohibits anti-competitive unilateral conduct, also referred to as 'abuse of dominance'.

In ASEAN, all AMSs have prohibitions against abuse of dominance which apply to entities that hold a dominant position in the relevant market.[67] In most cases, collective dominance (where more than one entity together holds the dominant position) is also explicitly provided for in the law.[68]

More than half of the jurisdictions have (or will have) a presumption of dominance above a stated market share threshold, which is as low as 30% in Viet Nam but as high as 60% in Malaysia and Singapore.[69] In some cases, this presumption is rebuttable (Philippines,[70] Singapore (indicative)[71] and Malaysia (indicative)[72]), in others it is a prerequisite for a finding of dominance (Indonesia,[73] Viet Nam[74]), while in the remaining jurisdictions, the position is not yet clear.

Sanctions for abuse of dominance across the ASEAN regimes are most commonly civil but criminal sanctions also apply in a few jurisdictions (Indonesia, Myanmar and Thailand).[75]

The Regional Guidelines on Competition Policy state that the AMSs 'may provide an *illustrative* list of [abusive] conduct'[76] [emphasis added]. Although the terminology differs, the types of conduct covered by the abuse of dominance provisions across ASEAN appear to be relatively consistent.

67. Brunei, section 21; Indonesia, Article 25(1); Lao PDR, Article 30; Malaysia, section 10; Myanmar, section 13(c), Philippines, section 15; Singapore, section 47; Thailand, section 50; Viet Nam, Article 27. Note that Viet Nam also contains a prohibition against abuse of a monopoly position (Article 27).
68. Only Myanmar and Thailand do not appear to recognise collective dominance. The Regional Guidelines on Competition Policy define a dominant position to include 'where an undertaking, either individually or together with other undertakings', thus expressly contemplating collective dominance (*see* paragraph 3.3.1.1).
69. Indonesian Competition Law, Article 25(2); Lao PDR, to be determined by BCC; Malaysia, *Guidelines on Chapter 2 Prohibition;* Article 30; Philippines, section 27 *PCA* and Rule 8, section 3, *Implementing Rules and Regulations*; Singapore, *Guidelines on section 47 Prohibition*; Thailand, to be determined by OTCC; Viet Nam, Article 24.
70. Section 27 Philippine Competition Law.
71. Paragraph 3.8 CCCS *Guidelines on Section 47 Prohibition.*
72. Paragraph 2.14 MyCC *Guidelines on Chapter 2 Prohibition.*
73. Article 25 Indonesian Competition Law.
74. Section 24 Viet Nam Competition Law.
75. It is not clear which offences result in a criminal sanction in Lao PDR.
76. Regional Guidelines, paragraph 3.3.2.

Almost all jurisdictions prohibit both exclusionary and exploitative practices.[77] Exclusionary practices are those which exclude competitors (actual or potential) from the market, to the detriment of consumers. Exploitative practices are those where consumers are exploited directly (usually through high prices). Indonesia expressly refers to exploitative and exclusionary practices in its *Guidelines on Article 25*,[78] as does Malaysia.[79] Singapore only refers to exclusionary practices.

With the exception of Myanmar and Thailand, all ASEAN jurisdictions prohibit predatory pricing.[80] Most jurisdictions prohibit bundling and tying (Brunei, Indonesia, Lao PDR, Malaysia, the Philippines, Singapore and Viet Nam),[81] while many also prohibit refusals to supply (Indonesia, Lao PDR, Malaysia and the Philippines).[82] Many AMSs' jurisdictions also cover a range of other exclusionary practices including exclusive purchasing (Indonesia, the Philippines and Viet Nam),[83] however it can be difficult to reconcile the prohibitions without further guidance on what is intended to be covered due to the terminology used.

In terms of exploitative practices, some jurisdictions prohibit unfair purchasing or selling prices,[84] and all jurisdictions apart from Myanmar and Thailand prohibit the imposition of discriminatory conditions.[85]

Case Law

According to the CCCS website, Singapore has finalised six cases finding an abuse of dominance. All but one of those cases has been closed following the receipt of commitments from the party in question. This makes it harder to comment on the likely approach to be taken by the CCCS and the Competition Appeal Board in applying the abuse of dominance prohibition in Singapore. In the only case subject to a final decision by the CCCS, *Sistic Pte Ltd*, the CCCS referred extensively to European

77. The Regional Guidelines on Competition Policy refer to conduct as being exclusionary, exploitative, discriminatory or limiting production, markets or technical development to the prejudice of consumers (paragraph 3.3.2.4).
78. Available at http://eng.kppu.go.id/newkppu/wp-content/uploads/Pasal-25-POSISI-DOMINAN.pdf (accessed 12 February 2019).
79. Paragraph 3.1 *Guidelines on Chapter 2 Prohibition*.
80. Brunei, section 21(2)(a); Indonesia Competition Law, Article 20; Lao PDR Competition Law, Articles 31(2), (33); Malaysian Competition Law, section 10(2)(f); Philippines Competition Law, section 15(a); Singapore Competition Law, section 47(2)(a); Viet Nam Competition Law, Article 27(1)(a)).
81. Brunei Competition Law, section 21(2)(d); Indonesia Competition Law, Article 15(3); Lao PDR Competition Law, Articles 31(4), 35; Malaysian Competition Law, section 10(2)(e); Philippines Competition Law, section 15(c),(f); Singapore Competition Law, section 47(2)(d); Viet Nam Competition Law, Article 27(1)(dd).
82. Indonesian Competition Law, Article 25(1); Lao PDR Competition Law, Articles 31(3), 34; Malaysia Competition Law, section 10(2)(c); Philippines Competition Law, section 15(e).
83. Indonesia, section 25(1); Philippines, section 15(b),(j); Viet Nam, Article 27(1)(c) and (e).
84. Lao PDR Competition Law, Article 31(1), 32; Malaysian Competition Law, section 10(2)(a); Philippines Competition Law, section 15(g),(h); Thailand Competition Law, section 50(2); Viet Nam Competition Law, Article 27(1)(b).
85. Brunei Competition Law, Article 21(2)(c); Indonesia Competition Law, Article 19(d); Lao PDR Competition Law, Articles 31(5), 36; Malaysia Competition Law, section 10(2)(d); Philippines Competition Law, section 15(d); Singapore Competition Law, section 47(2)(c); Viet Nam Competition Law, Article 27(1)(d).

jurisprudence (with some reference to US jurisprudence) in relation to the single economic entity doctrine,[86] market definition,[87] the concept of dominance[88] and the factors for assessing dominance.[89] The factors for assessing dominance reflect at least a partial reliance on European jurisprudence.

Malaysia has reached only one decision finding an abuse of dominant position[90] which was upheld by both the Competition Appeal Tribunal and the High Court on appeal.[91] This case involved the supply of insurance services by the dominant player (who held the government concession) in a discriminatory manner to its competitors which prevented competition in the downstream market.

To date, there has been only one infringement decision for abuse of monopoly (not dominance) in Viet Nam,[92] the case against Vinapco (a SOE) in which Vinapco abused its position by charging a higher price for fuel than it charged its parent company Viet Nam airlines.[93] The decision is not available publicly.

Guidelines

To date, only Indonesia, Singapore and Malaysia have issued guidelines on their abuse of dominance prohibitions.

In Indonesia, the KPPU has published *Guidelines on Implementation of the Provisions of Article 25 concerning Abuse of Dominant Position.*[94] Although the guidelines assess dominance by reference to factors including market power and barriers to entry (interpreted to cover constraints from actual or potential competitors and countervailing buyer/seller power), a finding of dominance under section 25 will not be found unless the relevant market share thresholds are met (50% for one entity, or 75% for two or more entities).[95]

In its Guidelines, the KPPU sets out an explanation of 'trading terms' as used in Article 25(a) which seems to be intended to cover refusals to deal. In addition, the

86. *Abuse of a Dominant Position by SISTIC.com Pte Ltd, Case CCS/600/008/07*, paragraphs 4.3.6–4.3.14. Available at https://www.cccs.gov.sg/public-register-and-consultation/public-consultation-items/abuse-of-dominant-position-by-sisticcom-pte-ltd?type=public_register (accessed 15 February 2019).
87. *Abuse of a Dominant Position by SISTIC.com Pte Ltd*, paragraph 5.2.
88. *Abuse of a Dominant Position by SISTIC.com Pte Ltd*, paragraphs 6.1.2–6.1.6.
89. *Abuse of a Dominant Position by SISTIC.com Pte Ltd*, Ability to eliminate a competitor – paragraph 6.3.2; market share – paragraph 6.4.3; barriers to entry – paragraph 6.5; countervailing buyer power 6.6.
90. MyCC, *Finding of Infringement of Section 10 of the Competition Act 2010 by My E.G. Services Berhad.* Available at http://www.mycc.gov.my/sites/default/files/Section-40-Notice-of-Finding-of-an-Infringement-by-My-Services-Berhad.pdf (accessed 15 February 2019).
91. *See My EG Services Bhd and My EG Commerce Sdn Bhd v Malaysia Competition Commission*, Appeal No. TRP 3-2016. Available at http://www.mycc.gov.my/sites/default/files/CAT%27s%20Decision%20dated%2028%20December%202017.pdf (accessed 20 June 2018).
92. The other abuse of dominance complaint was withdrawn after the party ceased its conduct. A settlement fee was imposed.
93. OECD, *Competition Review of Viet Nam*, 2018, p. 14, Available at http://www.oecd.org/daf/competition/VietNam-OECD-Competition-Review-2018-ENG.pdf (accessed 14 February 2019).
94. Available at http://eng.kppu.go.id/newkppu/wp-content/uploads/Pasal-25-POSISI-DOMINAN.pdf (accessed 20 June 2018).
95. Article 25(2) Indonesian Competition Law.

Guidelines make it clear that exclusive supply or purchase, refusing access to an essential facility, predatory pricing, price discrimination and exclusive distribution agreements are included in the types of conduct that could amount to an abuse of a dominant position. These concepts reflect European case law.[96]

In Singapore, the CCCS has published *Guidelines on the Section 47 prohibition*, which make it clear that dominance will be assessed based on 'the extent to which there are constraints on an undertaking's ability to profitably sustain prices above competitive levels'. These constraints include existing competitors (with market share being only one measure), potential competitors (affected by barriers to entry) and other factors such as powerful buyers and economic regulation.[97] In making a determination of dominance, the CCCS states:

> Market shares, by themselves, may not necessarily be a reliable guide to market power. Other determinants of competition, such as entry barriers, the degree of innovation, product differentiation, the responsiveness of buyers to price increases, and the price responsiveness of competitors, may need to be considered as well.[98]

The Guidelines list the types of conduct that may be considered abusive to include predatory pricing, discount schemes, price discrimination, margin squeezes, vertical restraints, refusals to supply and essential facilities, once again, concepts familiar in Europe.[99]

Malaysia takes a very similar approach to Singapore. In assessing dominance, the MyCC states in its *Guidelines on the Chapter 2 Prohibition* that in addition to market share, the constraints faced by an enterprise will be relevant. These constraints may come from existing or potential competitors or countervailing buyer power. In addition, like Singapore, the MyCC recognises the role that government regulation may play.[100] In making the determination of dominance, the MyCC will consider factors such as the degree of product differentiation, likely response by buyers to price increases, the degree of innovation in the market and barriers to entry. The Guidelines expand on section 10(2) to describe the types of conduct that may be considered abusive: predatory pricing, price discrimination, exclusive dealing, loyalty rebates and discounts, refusal to supply and sharing of essential facilities, buying up scarce or intermediate resources and bundling and tying.[101]

The Philippine Competition Commission (PCC) has not issued Guidelines on its abuse of dominance prohibition to date, but it has published *Implementing Rules and Regulations* which deal, in part, with abuse of dominance. In Rule 8 (Determination of Dominance), section 2 (Assessment of Dominance), it is made clear that market share is only one factor to be considered. Other factors include existence of barriers to entry,

96. In its predatory pricing guidelines, the KPPU refers to the EU trend towards using the Avoidable Total Cost test to assess predatory pricing cases.
97. *Guidelines on the Section 47 prohibition*, paragraph 3.2.
98. *Guidelines on the Section 47* prohibition, paragraph 3.7.
99. *Guidelines on the Section 47* prohibition, paragraph 11.2 onwards.
100. *Guidelines on the Chapter 2 Prohibition*, paragraph 2.9.
101. *Guidelines on the Chapter 2 Prohibition*, paragraphs 3.11-3.31.

existence of competitors, expansion by competitors or new entry by potential competitors, countervailing power, access to inputs by competitors, switching power, ownership, possession or control of infrastructure, vertical integration and economies of scale and scope. These factors expand on section 27 *Philippine Competition Act* (Market Dominant Position) which sets out the factors the PCC will consider when determining dominance.

In Thailand, the Office of Trade Competition Commission (OTCC) has also not published any guidelines on abuse of dominance, however, the OECD Report on Asia Pacific jurisdictions states:

> When determining dominance, the [OTCC] takes into account market share factors as well as non-market-share factors, such as number of competitors, amount of capital, access to key production factors, distribution channels, business networks, etc ...[102]

Conclusion on Anti-competitive Unilateral Conduct and Convergence

All of the AMSs have adopted an abuse of dominance regime that reflects international best practice. Commonly recognised abuse concepts such as predatory pricing, refusals to supply and bundling/tying appear to be covered in most jurisdictions, indicating a significant degree of hard convergence. Challenges to hard convergence will arise where legislative requirements differ, for example, in those jurisdictions where a minimum market threshold levels is required before the unilateral conduct prohibitions are applied (Indonesia and Viet Nam).

The approach taken in the (albeit limited) published guidelines also appears to be relatively consistent with international jurisprudence and provides promise for continuing soft convergence. For example, stated reliance on a range of factors to determine dominance (not just market shares) and consistency in the types of behaviour that may constitute an abuse reinforce the potential for convergence.

In a practical sense, convergence is more likely to arise if the competition authorities cooperate and coordinate in relation to their abuse cases. One area where a consistent approach should be encouraged is in relation to SOEs. SOEs commonly hold a dominant market position and can significantly affect competitiveness if not subject to the competition rules. Too diverse an approach to applying abuse provisions to SOEs across ASEAN would pose a significant risk to convergence.

[C] Anti-competitive Mergers

The third pillar of competition law is the review of mergers and acquisitions in order to avoid anti-competitive concentrations of economic power.

102. OECD, *Competition Law in Asia-Pacific: A Guide to Selected Jurisdictions*, p. 212. Available at http://www.oecd.org/countries/fiji/competition-law-in-asia-pacific-guide.htm (accessed 15 February 2019).

With the exception of Malaysia,[103] all AMSs with competition laws in force have chosen to provide for a merger control regime. However, substantial differences exist. This section discusses these differences by looking at merger notification procedures, the scope of the merger regimes and the substantive assessments.

Notification Thresholds and Process

A first indication of the differences between the AMSs, and hence the potential for convergence, are the notification thresholds and processes. The Regional Guidelines indicate that:

> a specific procedure may be established by which the competition regulatory body is tasked to assess mergers, following a (voluntary or mandatory[104]) notification by the merging undertakings [...].[105]

Most of the AMSs provide for mandatory notification of transactions, some of which have a suspensory clause, i.e., the transaction cannot be implemented before clearance. Figure 13.1 provides an overview of the different regimes in the AMSs.

Figure 13.1 Merger Notification Regimes in ASEAN

Mandatory regimes	
Ex-ante	Philippines Viet Nam
Ex-ante or ex-post	Brunei Thailand
Ex-post	Lao PDR
Ex-post with voluntary ex-ante option	Indonesia

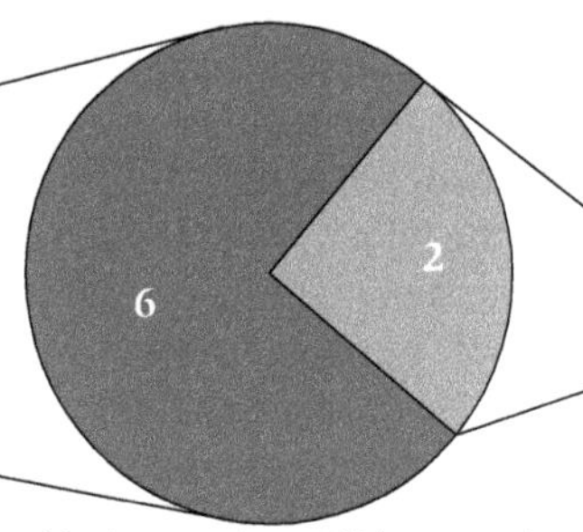

Voluntary regimes	
Ex-ante	Myanmar
Ex-ante or ex-post	Singapore

Source: Authors' analysis.

A compulsory notification regime can be found in six out of eight countries, and within these, some require ex-ante reviews, some ex-post, and others have both ex-ante and ex-post notification systems. In Thailand, the timing of the merger

103. The Competition Act 2010 does not provide for merger control. However, there are sector-specific laws and guidelines in certain sectors of the economy that regulate the antitrust aspects of mergers. This pertains to the aviation services sector and the communications and multimedia sectors, where the laws and guidelines are enforced by the Malaysian Aviation Commission, and the Malaysian Communications and Multimedia Commission (MCMC) respectively.

104. Mandatory notification prevents the undertakings from implementing the transaction until they have received merger clearance from the competition regulatory body, while voluntary notification allows businesses to do their own merger self-assessment, to decide if they should notify the competition regulatory body to clear the merger. *See* Regional Guidelines, Article 3.4.2.

105. ASEAN Regional Guidelines on Competition Policy, Article 3.4.2.

notification depends on whether a merger can cause a monopoly or dominant position, in which case the merger needs to be notified ex-ante (and require clearance), while mergers with a minimum amount of market share, sales revenue, capital amount, number of stocks or assets can be notified ex-post (and no clearance is required). In Indonesia, mergers can be voluntarily notified pre-completion, but it is compulsory to notify the merger post-completion. Brunei includes in its competition law a notification requirement for both anticipated mergers (ex-ante) and completed mergers (ex-post).

Whether a given merger transaction needs to be notified or not, depends on (i) the definition of a merger transaction and (ii) whether certain notification thresholds are met.[106] When looking at ASEAN, we see that these two jurisdictional thresholds for merger transactions can be somewhat different across the AMSs.[107]

When defining a merger transaction, two types of criteria are used: 'objective' numerical criteria, and 'economic' criteria, which are more aligned with the mechanism through which a merger transaction might harm competition.[108] These two criteria are not mutually exclusive; some jurisdictions combine objective and economic criteria. Six out of the eight AMSs with a merger control regime have chosen for economic criteria (Brunei, Indonesia, Singapore, the Philippines, Thailand and Viet Nam)[109]. Obtaining 'control' is the key criterion, but the exact interpretation of what constitutes 'control', or the level of intensity of the influence, is different in some AMSs. Both Brunei[110] and Singapore[111] use the acquisition of 'decisive influence over the activities of the undertaking'. The Philippines refers to the ability to 'substantially

106. *See* OECD Policy Roundtable on "Definition of Transaction for the Purpose of Merger Control Review" (2013), p. 12.
107. AMSs use different terminology when classifying merger transactions in their respective competition laws. Brunei, Singapore and Thailand classify merger transactions as 'Mergers', Indonesia as 'Mergers, Consolidations and Acquisitions', Lao PDR as 'Combinations', Myanmar as 'Collaboration among Businesses', The Philippines as 'Mergers and Acquisitions' and Viet Nam as 'Economic concentrations'. Notwithstanding this difference in classification, AMSs include often similar types of transactions. Six out of the eight AMSs with a merger control regime include mergers, acquisitions and joint-ventures in their merger provisions (only Indonesia and Thailand have not included a legal definition of a joint-venture).
108. *See* OECD Policy Roundtable on "Definition of Transaction for the Purpose of Merger Control Review" (2013), p. 14. An example of the 'objective' approach is the percentage thresholds for share acquisition (e.g., 25% or 50%). 'Economic' criteria used in the definition of a merger transaction are more directly aligned with the mechanism through which a transaction might harm competition, by focusing on whether a transaction will enable a firm to acquire the ability to exercise some form of control over a previously independent firm. An example is EU's merger review regime that uses an acquisition of 'control/decisive influence' standard (EC Merger Regulation, at 3(1) and (2)).
109. Lao PDR and the Myanmar Competition Law are less explicit in what they consider a merger transaction. Lao PDR only defines a merger as a transfer of assets, rights, obligations and interests (Article 3 Lao PDR Competition Law), while the Myanmar Competition Law only lists the types of transactions (section 30 Myanmar Competition Law): 'In collaboration among businesses the following acts are included: (a) merger of businesses, (b) consolidation of businesses, (c) purchasing or acquisition of other business by a business, (d) joint-venture of businesses, (e) performing other means of collaboration among businesses specified by the Commission'.
110. Art. 23 Brunei Competition Law.
111. CCCS Guidelines on the Substantive Assessment of Mergers 2016, Para. 3.6.

influence or direct the actions or decisions of an entity'[112] Indonesia, Thailand and Viet Nam seem to adopt slightly different wording and assess the ability to determine or influence the 'enterprise's management and policies' (Indonesia[113]), 'enterprise's policy, business administration, direction, or management' (Thailand[114]), or 'enterprise or a business line' (Viet Nam[115]). Three of the aforementioned six AMSs with economic criteria (Indonesia, The Philippines and Singapore) have chosen to add also an objective criterion (in all cases the ownership of more than 50% of the voting rights).

The second element that determines the requirement for notification, the notification thresholds, most commonly refers to the size of the transaction or of the parties and seeks to eliminate transactions that most likely have no material impact in a given jurisdiction. The Regional Guidelines allow for AMSs to 'filter out mergers with no significant impact', for instance by using turnover or market shares.[116] For notification thresholds, the Recommendation of the OECD Council on Merger Review mentions that clear and objective criteria should be used.[117]

So far, only four of the AMSs (Indonesia, Philippines, Thailand and Viet Nam) have created specific notification thresholds for mergers in their legislation. The first two use solely objective criteria, as Indonesia has defined minimum asset values and/or sales values[118] and the Philippines minimum revenues, asset values or value of the transaction.[119] Thailand and Viet Nam use both objective and subjective criteria. Thailand[120] uses both market share (subjective) and sales turnover (objective), while Viet Nam considers market share (subjective) combined with asset values, turnover

112. Rule 2(a) and (f) and Rule 6, Section 1 of Act no. 10667 (Rules And Regulations to implement the provisions of the Philippines Competition Act).
113. Art. 1 and the explanation of art. 5(4) in the Government Regulation No. 57 of 2010 (Concerning Merger or Consolidation of Business Entities and Acquisition of Shares of Companies Which May Cause Monopolistic Practices And Unfair Business Competition).
114. Section 51 Thailand Competition Law.
115. Art. 29(4) of Viet Nam Competition Law.
116. *See* Regional Guidelines, Art. 3.4.3.
117. *See* OECD (2005). Recommendation of the OECD Council on Merger Review, p.2.
118. In Indonesia, the combined value of the assets should exceed IDR 2.5 trillion (or IDR 20 trillion for banks); and/or the combined value of the sales turnover should exceed IDR 5 trillion. Ar. 5, Government Regulation No. 57 of 2010.
119. In the Philippines, mergers need to be notified when (i) the aggregate annual gross revenues or value of the assets of at least one of the ultimate parent entities exceeds PHP 5.6 billion, or (ii) the value of the transaction exceeds PHP 2.2 billion. The merger thresholds have been adjusted twice since the Philippine Competition Act was passed in 2015: the first adjustment took place in 2018 through the PCC Memorandum Circular 18-001 (Amendment of Rule 4, Section 3 of the Implementing Rules and Regulations and Republic Act. No. 10667 (Threshold Adjustment)). This Circular established the automatic annual adjustment of the thresholds based on the nominal gross domestic product (GDP) growth of the previous year rounded up to the nearest hundred millions. As of 1 March 2019, the thresholds are increased a second time, using the nominal GDP growth in 2018 (of 10.23 percent, based on official estimates from the Philippine Statistics Authority). See the PCC Advisory 2019-001: Adjustment of the Thresholds for Compulsory Notification of Mergers and Notifications.
120. Section 5 of Thailand Competition Law.

and transaction value (all objective).[121] None of the other countries have implemented notification thresholds.

Legal deadlines for the competition authority to review the merger are important when designing mergers and acquisitions regimes, given the effects this may have on stock prices and costs of financing, among other aspects. In ASEAN, these review timelines are different for every country. Many AMSs (Lao PDR, the Philippines, Singapore and Viet Nam) have a deadline for (first) review of thirty days after receipt of a complete notification, which corresponds to the more experienced merger control jurisdictions in the wider Asia region (China, Japan and Korea). However, potential extension periods differ and some have the possibility to go to a second phase (in-depth) investigation (The Philippines, Singapore and Viet Nam). For the latter countries, the total review time can respectively be 90 days,[122] 120 days[123] and 150 days[124] for the second phase). These varying deadlines in the AMSs may create difficulties for collaboration between competition authorities in cross-border merger cases.

The above indicates substantial differences regarding the notification thresholds and processes in ASEAN. Various thresholds, diverse timelines and differing concepts of what constitutes a merger can make convergence difficult, resulting in possible increased costs and uncertainty for parties pursuing a cross-border merger in ASEAN.

Substantive Assessment

Most competition authorities rely on one of two main tests to assess whether a merger has anti-competitive effects: (i) the dominance test and (ii) the significant lessening of competition (SLC) test.[125] The European Commission (EC), with the implementation of the new EC Merger Regulation in 2004, changed its legal test for assessing a merger from the SLC test to the SIEC test ('significant impediment of effective competition'). However, the SIEC is considered equivalent to the SLC and is interpreted as extending, beyond the concept of dominance, to the anticompetitive effects of a concentration

121. Art. 33(2) Viet Nam Competition Law. The exact values shall be stipulated by the Government "in accordance with the socio-economic conditions in each period". Currently, there are proposed thresholds, but further legislation needs to be issued: (i) either party's total assets in the Viet Nam market exceeds VND 500 billion; (ii) either party's total turnover exceeds VND 1,000 billion in the preceding fiscal year; (iii) the value of the transaction exceeds VND 500 billion; or (iv) the combined market share of the combining entities in the relevant market meets a threshold to be stipulated.
122. Rule 4 Section 5(h) and (i) of Act no. 10667 (Rules And Regulations to implement the provisions of the Philippines Competition Act)
123. Art. 2.8 of CCCS Guidelines of Merger Procedures 2012.
124. Art. 36(2) of Viet Nam Competition Law.
125. Under the dominance test, a merger is anticompetitive and can be prohibited if it strengthens or creates a dominant position in the market. Under the significant lessening of competition test, a merger has anti-competitive effects if it is likely to substantially lessen competition in the market. In comparison with the dominance test, the SLC test focuses on the effects of the merger on the market and on the loss of competition among firms rather than on threshold structural issues such as market shares.

resulting from the non-coordinated behaviour of undertakings which would not have a dominant position on the market concerned.[126]

The Regional Guidelines explicitly mention SLC and SIEC as reasons for prohibiting a merger: 'AMSs may consider prohibiting mergers that lead to a substantial lessening of competition or would significantly impede effective competition in the relevant market or in a substantial part of it, unless otherwise exempted'.[127]

Comparing the legal tests used in the different AMSs, there is a substantial amount of consistency. All AMSs with merger control provisions use a type of SLC test, albeit using different terminology.

Brunei and Singapore prohibit mergers that 'result in a substantial lessening of competition',[128] while the Philippines prohibits mergers that 'substantially prevent, restrict or lessen competition'[129] and Thailand prohibits mergers that result in a 'substantial reduction of competition'.[130] The other countries use terminology less close to the SLC, although the assessment focuses on the effects of the merger. In the case of Lao PDR, a merger ('combination') that restraints competition, i.e., aimed 'to reduce, distort and/or prevent competition', is prohibited.[131] Indonesia assesses whether a merger 'causes monopolistic practices and/or unfair business competition',[132] while Viet Nam prohibits a merger that has 'a significant competition-restrictive impact'.[133] Finally, the terminology in the Myanmar Competition Law emphasises the dominance as a result of a merger (it prohibits 'collaboration among businesses' that 'raise extremely the dominance over the market'),[134] but it seems to focus on effects of the merger as well.[135] Although the "spirit" in all countries seems similar, these differences in terminology could result in different interpretations and merger assessments, potentially leading to legal uncertainty and increasing transaction costs for merging parties.

The exemption for small and medium enterprises in Singapore is not mentioned in the Singapore Competition Act. Instead, it is mentioned in the CCCS Guidelines on Merger Procedures 2012 that 'CCCS is unlikely to investigate a merger situation that

126. *See also* OECD, Policy Roundtable on Standard for Merger Review, 2009.
127. *See* Regional Guidelines, Art. 3.4.1.
128. Art. 23(1) Brunei Competition Law and art. 54(1) Singapore Competition Law.
129. Section 20 Philippines Competition Law.
130. Section 51 Thailand Competition Law.
131. Articles 18, 19 Lao PDR Competition Law. Art. 38 dictates that a merger is aimed to restrain competition if it leads to restrained market access and technology development, and creates a negative impact on consumers, other business operators and the national socio-economic development. Hence, this seems also an SLC test.
132. Article 28(1) Indonesia Competition Law. Moreover, art. 3(2) of the Government Regulation No. 57 of 2010 prescribes that the merger assessment will include an analysis of market concentration, barriers to market entry, potential of anti-competitive behaviour, efficiency and/or bankruptcy).
133. Article 37(2) Viet Nam Competition Law.
134. See Myanmar Competition Law, art. 30 and 31(a).
135. It assesses whether a collaboration intends to 'decrease competition'. Art. 31(b).

only involves small companies [...]'.[136] To date, only Indonesia, the Philippines and Singapore have issued guidelines on their merger control regime.

Sanctions

Finally, some differences exist between the sanctions that can be imposed in the different competition laws of AMSs. All of the AMSs have adopted the possibility to impose a sanction on merging parties for substantive infringement of the merger provisions, with some of the AMSs having (at least theoretically) the possibility of criminal sanctions. Finally, Indonesia, the Philippines and Thailand have adopted fines for the failure to notify.

Case Law

Overall, merger control in half of the AMSs is not yet actively enforced. Brunei, Lao PDR, Myanmar and Thailand have yet to start applying merger control in their jurisdictions, while Indonesia, the Philippines, Singapore and Viet Nam have decided on cases.

The KPPU has had approximately 500 merger notifications since 2010, according to its website.[137] However, many of these merger notifications are still waiting for a decision.[138]

In the case of Singapore and the Philippines, merger decisions are publicly available (in English). The CCCS in Singapore has completed approximately 75 Phase 1 cases, while it is currently reviewing its 8th Phase 2 merger case.[139] In the Philippines, the PCC has reviewed more than 125 cases,[140] and it blocked a merger-to-monopoly deal early 2019 between URC and Don Pedro-RHI sugar millers.[141] In Viet Nam, the number of mergers that is notified with the Viet Nam Competition Authority (VCA) is quite small, despite the requirement to file proposed mergers. Between 2008 and 2016, thirty-two mergers were filed.[142]

136. Art. 3.5. Small companies are defined as companies where the turnover in Singapore in the financial year preceding the transaction of each of the parties is below S$5 million and the combined worldwide turnover in the financial year preceding the transaction of all of the parties is below S$50 million.
137. *See* http://www.kppu.go.id/id/merger-dan-akuisisi/. The number of merger notifications since 2010 have been 3 (2010), 43 (2011), 36 (2012), 69 (2013), 55 (2014), 51 (2015), 65 (2016), 90 (2017), 74 (2018), 17 (in the first month of 2019).
138. For instance, at the time of writing (according to the KPPU website), none of the (approximately 90) notifications received since the beginning of 2018 have been reviewed, because the KPPU is still verifying whether the submission is complete.
139. The CCCS Annual Report of FY 2017 reports that until 31 March 2017 it had completed 64 Phase 1 cases and 7 Phase 2 cases. The website of CCCS (at the time of writing) had another 11 cleared Phase 1 cases from 31 March and one pending Phase 2 case.
140. *See* OECD/KPC. (2018). Competition Law in Asia-Pacific: A guide to Selected Jurisdictions.
141. *See also* https://phcc.gov.ph/press-releases/pcc-blocks-merger-to-monopoly-deal-between-urc-don-pedro-rhi-sugar-millers/.
142. *See* OECD (2018), OECD Peer Reviews of Competition Law and Policy: Viet Nam, http://oe.cd/vtn. The Peer Review considers that this low number of notifications may indicate that a significant number of notifiable transactions are completed without notification.

Conclusion on Anti-competitive Mergers and Convergence

Convergence of merger control regimes in ASEAN is important given the increase in cross-border mergers which results in a need to notify in multiple jurisdictions. Very different regimes across ASEAN may lead to increasing costs and legal uncertainty for the businesses community, worsening the investment climate in the region.

The above analysis clearly indicates that there will be some risks in achieving convergence. More specifically, the notification thresholds and processes (mandatory/voluntary notification, ex-ante/ex-post, legal deadlines), the type of transactions that should or could be notified as well as the sanctions show large differences between the countries. The legal test in the countries is overall more consistent, but the different terminology can lead to variations when it comes to the actual assessment in the different AMSs.

[D] Institutional Structures and Approach to Enforcement

Now we have looked at the three pillars of competition in all AMSs, this section looks at the institutional set-up that AMSs use to enforce competition law provisions and how this can influence convergence of competition law and policy across ASEAN.

First, the degree of independence, the budget as well as the number and quality of the staff of each competition authority plays a role in how the competition law is interpreted, enforced and implemented. Institutions with a significant level of independence and specialised quality resources can ensure technical competition enforcement, based on the most recent widely accepted and modern economic theories.

A second institutional factor that can influence the application of competition provisions is whether there are one or several authorities with competition powers within each AMS. In some AMSs, there are multiple sector regulators with competition powers and if achieving convergence and uniformity of application within a country can be a challenge in itself, this multiplication of regulators can certainly multiply the challenges across the ASEAN region.

Third, the role of courts is crucial in the interpretation of the competition law, so the degree to which they are prepared to engage with competition economics and competition law more broadly is also of significant importance. These three institutional factors will be briefly discussed in the following texts.

[1] Independence of the Competition Authority

There is wide recognition in the international community that agency independence is a key element in a competition regime.[143] For a competition authority, it is particularly important to be able to undertake its analysis in an independent manner,[144] prioritising

143. OECD (2016), Independence of Competition Authorities – from designs to practice.

144. The OECD Best Practice Principles on the Governance of Regulators (OECD 2014) identifies four factors to consider in creating an independent and structurally separate regulatory body, namely the need for credibility, stability, impartiality and specialist regulator expertise. Since

its own cases and activities. The degree of independence conferred upon the competition authorities of ASEAN is therefore a relevant element to consider when analysing the application of competition law in practice.

Institutional Design

There is no one-size-fits-all regarding the institutional design in the AMSs as this design must fit into and reflect a country's specific legal and political culture and frameworks. Currently, AMSs have many different institutional set-ups with differing degrees of independence. In four of the AMSs, the competition authority is set up under a ministry (Brunei, Myanmar, Singapore and Viet Nam),[145] which could potentially undermine its independence. Furthermore, four of the agencies have board members appointed by other governmental bodies (Brunei, Malaysia, Myanmar and Viet Nam).[146] Even if completely objective decision-making can be achieved under a ministerial institutional framework, the fact that board members are drawn from sectoral ministries with ownership of SOEs may risk its independence. A conflict of interest may exist between the appointees' duties to their line ministries and their role adjudicating in relation to SOEs owned by their primary employers. It is well accepted that SOEs play a very important role in many AMSs' economies.

The example of Viet Nam is paradigmatic. The OECD Peer Review of Viet Nam in 2018 refers to stakeholders having a 'great deal of scepticism concerning whether decision is objective arising from the fact that VCC [Vietnam Competition Council] members are drawn from sectoral ministries with ownership of SOEs'. The Viet Nam Peer Review also found that 'there is not only a perceived conflict of interest between the appointees' duties to their line ministries and their role adjudicating in relation to SOEs owned by their primary employers, SOEs accused of wrongdoing have actually approached line ministries seeking assistance from the VCC members appointed'.[147]

Resourcing and Staffing

Another factor influencing the independence and effective enforcement of competition laws in AMSs is the resourcing available to the competition authority. Without sufficient resources, it will be challenging for the competition authority to make a sound technical legal and economic analysis which will help it deliver the desired efficiency benefits and productivity gains to the economy.

International comparisons on resource availability are complex as they can be highly influenced by the legal system,[148] the size of the economy in question, labour

for competition authorities the need for all these four factors is high, competition authorities meet the conditions to create a legally independent and structurally separate regulatory body.

145. This information does not include Cambodia and Lao PDR.
146. This information does not include Brunei, Cambodia and Lao PDR.
147. OECD (2018), OECD Peer Reviews of Competition Law and Policy: Viet Nam, http://oe.cd/vtn.
148. For example, there are significant cost implications of whether cases must be brought in court or can be handled administratively and, if they are taken to court, whether the country has a split bar or whether agency lawyers present the case.

costs and other important factors (all of which are beyond the scope of this chapter). However, they can be instructive as a broad indicator.

Table 13.1 Budget and Staff of Selected Competition Authorities for 2017 and GDP and Population Context

AMS	*Budget of Competition Authority (EUR Million)*	*GDP in USD Million*	*No. of Staff Members Working on Competition*	*Population (Million)*
Brunei	NA	12,128	NA	0.4
Cambodia	NA	22,158	NA	16
Indonesia	8.8	932,259	355	264
Lao PDR	NA	16,853	NA	6.9
Malaysia	2.6	296,359	58	31.6
Myanmar	NA	67,069	NA	53.4
The Philippines	7.1	313,595	159	104.9
Singapore	10.6	296,966	39	5.6
Thailand	NA	455,303	60–80	69
Viet Nam	0.6	202,616	27	95.5

Source: GDP figures World Bank Notes https://databank.worldbank.org/data/download/GDP.pdf. Indonesia's budget figure is for 2016, conversion rate as of 11 February 2019. For resource and staff numbers, the source was OECD/KPC. (2018). 'Competition Law in Asia-Pacific: A guide to Selected Jurisdictions'. Thailand is the expected number for the first year of operation (end of 2018).
Note: NA means that information is either not available or not applicable.

As can be observed from Table 13.1, budget and staff count differ significantly not only in absolute but also in relative terms. Singapore and the Philippines seem to have a relatively high budget compared with others (taking into account its GDP), while Singapore has by far the largest relative staff count (taking into account the population). A lower budget indicates a relatively marginal importance of competition matters on the national public policy agenda. Without the necessary investment from the public purse, there is a decreased likelihood that a competition authority can fulfil its duties under the competition law. A shortage of staff can lead to challenges in terms of the number and quality of investigations of competition law violations the authority can execute. Moreover, given the (growing) importance of economics in competition law, a competition authority requires a sufficient number of sufficiently qualified (economic and legal) staff.[149] Regarding the economics capabilities, most agencies

149. Given that competition law lies at the interface of law and economics, a sound competition enforcement of competition law requires a sufficient number of well-qualified staff with sophisticated skills.

neither have specialised economists in their staff roster, nor do they have dedicated economic teams. Exceptions are Indonesia, the Philippines and Singapore.

In summary, low budgets and staffing can pose a challenge for the independence of – and the sound technical decisions made by – competition agencies of the AMSs. This in turn can eventually deter further convergence of decision making across ASEAN based on well-accepted and well-tested competition law and economics.

[2] Sector Regulators with Competition Powers

The presence of sector regulators with competition powers may also be a further challenge for the convergence process. There may be different legal provisions in the sectoral laws, or the regulators may be implementing the same legal tests differently. They may not even be applying them at all, as they do not see it as their main responsibility and priority, among their competing tasks. Moreover, the risk of regulatory capture might be greater with regulators[150] that have a narrower focus of action. In ASEAN, many AMSs have not excluded the application of the general competition law to specific sectors, but some have, as can be observed from Table 13.2. Regulators with competition powers can vary from two in Thailand to more than thirty in Viet Nam. Some have concurrent powers, others exclusive competition powers.

Table 13.2 Comparison of Whether SOEs are Exempted, Whether There Are Excluded Sectors and of Regulators with Competition Powers

AMS	*Excluded Sectors*	*Regulators with Competition Powers*
Brunei	No	NA
Cambodia	NA	NA
Indonesia	No	No
Lao PDR	NA	NA
Malaysia	Yes	3
Myanmar	No	Yes*
The Philippines	No	No
Singapore	Yes	4
Thailand	Yes	2
Viet Nam	Yes	30+

Source: The OECD/KPC Competition Law in Asia-Pacific: A guide to Selected Jurisdictions (2018).
*Myanmar was contemplating competition powers for the telecoms regulator, but at the time of

150. *See* the discussion at section 5 of the 'Institutional Design of Competition Authorities' Note by Allan Fels and Henry Ergas. This Note was submitted as background material for the Roundtable on Changes in Institutional Design of Competition Authorities which took place at the 122nd meeting of the OECD Competition Committee on 17–18 December 2014.

writing this was not yet decided. Viet Nam Review of competition related regulations and regulated sectors, VCA and JICA, 2014.
Note: NA means that information is either not available or not applicable.

Some examples: In Malaysia, the Malaysia Communication and Multimedia Agency, the Energy Commission and the Malaysian Aviation Commission are responsible for the enforcement of competition related provisions under respectively Act 588, Act 610 and the Malaysian Aviation Commission Act 2015. Similarly, in Singapore, there are sector regulators that have exclusive authority in the enforcement of competition regulations in their specific sectors: Infocomm Development Authority (telecoms), Media Development Authority (media), Energy Market Authority (energy) and Civil Aviation Authority of Singapore (airport service). Where there are cross-sectoral competition issues, they will be dealt with by CCCS in consultation with the relevant sectoral regulators. In Thailand, there are other sector regulators that have competition powers beyond the OTCC: the National Broadcasting and Telecommunications Commission regulates competition issues relating to broadcasting and telecommunications sectors, while the Energy Regulatory Commission regulates competition issues relating to energy and gas industry operation. These two regulators have their own competition section under their laws. Neither covers all the anti-competitive conducts, so the Trade Competition Act will still apply to those. In Viet Nam, most sectoral regulations provide for a specific provision on competition, and the Viet Nam Competition and Consumer Authority (VCCA) and sector regulators operate based on a mechanism of cooperation.

Malaysia has attempted to mitigate the different interpretations of competition provisions by different regulators by forming a Special Committee on Competition (meeting twice a year) to share common issues on competition law and policy.[151] Similarly, the PCC has entered into Memoranda of Agreement with the National Telecommunications Commission and Energy Regulatory Commission.

The number of regulators with competition powers can make convergence more difficult in the application of competition laws or competition provisions. However, implementing mechanisms of cooperation between the regulators and the competition authority to ensure similar interpretations might serve to lessen such concerns.

[3] *The Role of the Courts*

Another factor that can affect the system of competition law enforcement is the application and interpretation by the courts. It is widely accepted in the international community that independent judicial review of decisions of a competition authority is

151. The Special Committee Meeting includes the: MyCC; Malaysian Aviation Commission; MCMC; Energy Commission; Securities Commission; National Water Services Commission; Central Bank of Malaysia; Land Public Transport Commission; and Intellectual Property Corporation of Malaysia. MyCC has also entered into a Memorandum of Understanding with the Central Bank of Malaysia to clarify areas of consultation and cooperation in competition issues affecting the financial sector.

desirable to ensure fairness and integrity of the decision-making process (e.g., OECD's Procedural Fairness and Transparency Report of 2012). Specifically, regarding competition policy, the judiciary has the important function of ensuring procedural due process and applying the substantive principles of the competition law in a correct and consistent manner. The latter requires that the courts be equipped and ready to engage with competition economics.

As mentioned earlier, the underlying economic nature of competition laws means that for an adequate adjudication of competition cases, economic facts and concepts must be brought into legal reasoning and be subject to the rule of law. Courts interpreting core economic concepts in competition law (such as 'market', 'market power', 'significant lessening of effective competition' or similar/equivalent concepts[152]) in a consistent manner will help the convergence in the application of competition laws across ASEAN.

All the AMSs follow the administrative system, meaning that the competition authority is the decision maker, and courts undertake judicial review. A number of AMSs have specialised tribunals that act as a first instance court, such as Malaysia and Singapore. In the remaining countries, the judicial review of competition cases is up to the generalised courts. In all instances there is either no or limited systematic training of judges on competition policy. One of the exceptions is the annual competition law seminar for Asia Pacific Judges organised by the OECD/KPC.

A more systematic education of judges on competition law and economics would help ensure a more consistent approach and therefore greater convergence across ASEAN as to how the competition laws are ultimately interpreted and enforced. In this case FCA/OECD Primers on Competition Law for ASEAN Judges can serve as a good starting point.[153]

Conclusions on Institutions and Scope of Application the Law

It is clear that in order to achieve greater soft convergence of ASEAN competition law and practice, the institutional structures pose some challenges that will need to be addressed. Sufficient independence of the agencies is required, while respecting the cultural and legal roots of each AMS. Establishing courts that are willing and capable to deal with competition policy and economics will need to be a priority when discussing the next steps for convergence. The number of national entities dealing with competition provisions also needs consideration and strong mechanisms need to be implemented to ensure consistency of coordinated application across sectors and across ASEAN.

152. The OECD has prepared together with the Federal Court of Australia the Primers on Competition Law for ASEAN Judges which provide more details here: http://www.oecd.org/daf/competition/asean-capacity-building-for-judges.htm.
153. http://www.oecd.org/daf/competition/asean-capacity-building-for-judges.htm.

[E] Conclusion

ASEAN has embarked on a route of regional economic integration, which should lead to free(er) flow of goods, services and capital between AMSs, foster cross-border trade and enhance economic growth in the different AMSs. Competition law and policy plays a key role in this process as these laws and policies can protect the competitive process and avoid cross-border anti-competitive practices.

The political commitment of AMSs has led to a rapid development of competition laws and policies in almost all jurisdictions. An explicit choice was made to have national competition laws instead of a regional competition framework (with supra-national enforcement body). However, in order to reap the full benefit of these often new and developing competition laws, it is important that they are applied and enforced in a similar fashion. This increases legal predictability and improves the investment climate in the region.

This chapter argues that, while there are many similarities already among AMSs, which is to be welcomed, to achieve further convergence, efforts still need to be made on both 'hard' (laws, legislation and guidelines) and 'soft' (competition law enforcement and interpretation) convergence. Neither can do without the other, but the foundation should be the adoption of similar competition laws and substantive provisions that ensure the desired level of convergence in ASEAN. The second step is the practical application of those laws in a consistent manner.

Regarding hard convergence, this chapter has identified a number of areas that would benefit from further convergence by the AMSs. For all three pillars of competition, the article has identified areas with divergent legal provisions. Examples are differing legal tests when it comes to restrictive agreements (different definition of a hard-core cartel), varying minimum market threshold levels when establishing abuse of dominance, and differences in merger notification thresholds and processes (mandatory/voluntary notification, ex-ante/ex-post, legal deadlines).

For soft convergence to take place, this chapter argues that institutions need to be independent and have sufficient financial and human resources that will allow them to deploy internationally accepted competition law and economic principles at a technical and not political level. Moreover, the number of regulators with competition powers in different AMSs should be reduced, and/or mechanisms should be introduced to ensure consistent application of substantive principles even in country.

Furthermore, this chapter argues that cooperation between the authorities is key to achieve greater soft convergence. Cooperation is required on the exchange of technical expertise best practices on cases, as well as how to best deal with the challenges of competition enforcement against SOEs. The recently created RCF is a great further step in the direction of soft convergence, creating a framework for cooperation on enforcement cases.

Finally, this chapter argues that training of judges is also fundamental, as the convergence work done between the agencies can be undone by courts if they lack the capacity to apply the often technical and economical framework of analysis used in competition law. This requires continuous training of judges on competition law and economics.

CHAPTER 14

Regional Competition Arrangements: The Case of Latin American and the Caribbean

Mario A. Umaña[*]

§14.01 INTRODUCTION

[A] Economic Integration in the Latin America and the Caribbean: The Spaghetti Bowl (Enhanced)

Latin American and Caribbean countries (LAC) have engaged in multiple economic integration efforts during the last sixty years.[1,2] These processes include: (i) four major initiatives aiming at the formation of deep economic blocs in the form of customs unions and common markets: the Central American Common Market (CACM), the Andean Community (CAN), the Caribbean Community (CARICOM) and the Southern Common Market (MERCOSUR); (ii) multiple RTAs, including: CAFTA-DR, Economic Partnership Agreements with CARIFORUM and Central America, the brand new trade agreement among the United States (US), Canada and Mexico (USMCA), and (iii) new generation agreements such as the Pacific Alliance (AP), among others. It is well documented that the proliferation of RTA's is a cause of trade diversion.[3] More importantly for the purposes of this chapter, in the case of the four deeper integration processes, the original single market and custom union goals are still unfulfilled. This reality complicates even more the functioning of modern regional competition agreements (*see* Figure 14.1).

* The opinions expressed, and arguments employed herein do not necessarily reflect the official views of the Inter-American Development Bank (IADB).

1. https://utopiayouarestandinginit.com/2014/06/17/jacob-viner-and-the-ambiguous-welfare-effects-of-preferential-trade-agreements/.
2. The region has more than 132 trade agreements. *See*: http://sice.oas.org/agreements_s.asp.
3. https://onlinelibrary.wiley.com/doi/full/10.1111/twec.12295.

Figure 14.1. The Spaghetti Bowl[4]

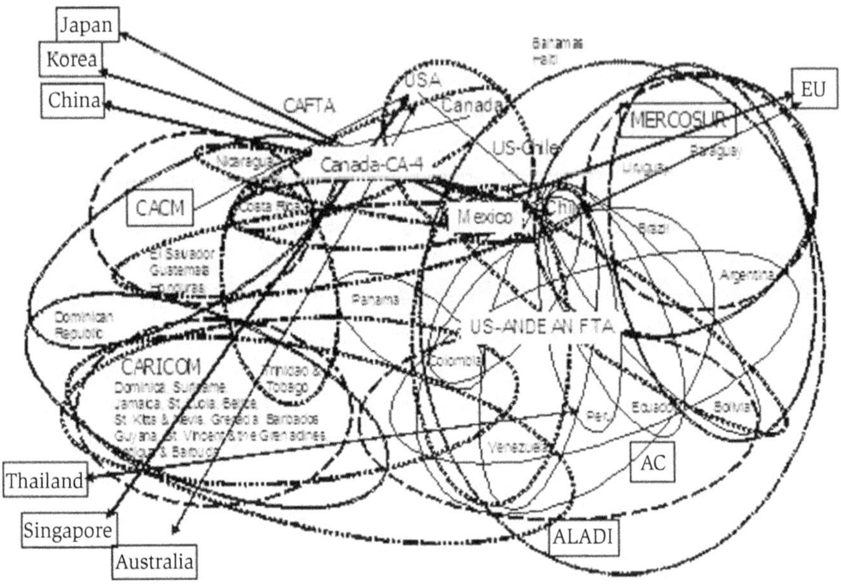

This chapter updates previous work on the developments in Regional Competition Policy Agreements in LAC,[5] but first let us look at some basic data:

CACM.[6] The CACM is the oldest integration process in the Americas, established in 1960 for the economic integration of Guatemala, El Salvador, Honduras, Nicaragua and Costa Rica. It covers a market of 45 million people, USD 210 billion gross domestic product (GDP) and more than USD 10 billion in intra-regional trade.

CAN.[7] The CAN (formerly the Andean Pact) was established in 1969 and includes an economic integration process for Bolivia, Colombia, Ecuador and Peru. There are five associate members: Argentina, Brazil, Paraguay, Chile[8] and Uruguay,[9] and one observer: Spain. It coves a market of more than 100 million people and a regional GDP purchasing power parity (PPP) of nearly USD 1 trillion.

4. https://www.researchgate.net/figure/Spaghetti-bowl-RTAs-in-the-Western-Hemisphere_fig1_228430490.
5. This is an updated of a previous paper presented in the 2013 Latin American Competition Forum. *See* http://www.oecd.org/officialdocuments/publicdisplaydocumentpdf/?cote=DAF/COMP/LACF(2013)5&docLanguage=En.
6. http://sice.oas.org/trade/camers.asp.
7. http://sice.oas.org/Andean/instmt_s.asp.
8. Chile was an original full member but left the bloc a few years after, returning as an observer in 1976 and later as an associate member in 2006.
9. Mercosur also granted similar associate membership to CAN members.

CARICOM.[10] The CARICOM was established in 1973 by the Chaguaramas Treaty signed in Trinidad and Tobago for the economic integration of fifteen full members: Antigua and Barbuda, The Bahamas, Barbados, Belize, Dominica, Grenada, Guyana, Haiti, Jamaica, Montserrat, St Lucia, St Kitts and Nevis, St Vincent and the Grenadines, Suriname, and Trinidad & Tobago, and five associate members: Anguilla, Bermuda, British Virgin Islands, Cayman Islands, and Turks and Caicos; and eight observers: Aruba, Colombia, Curacao, Dominican Republic, Mexico, Puerto Rico, St Martin and Venezuela. It covers a market of approximately twenty-three million[11] people and a GDP (PPP) of USD 135 billion.

MERCOSUR.[12] The Southern Common Market is the newest bloc, established by the Treaty of Asuncion in 1991 for the economic integration of Argentina, Brazil, Paraguay and Uruguay. Venezuela is a full member but has been suspended since 2016. It has seven associate members: Bolivia, Chile, Colombia, Ecuador, Guyana, Peru and Suriname, and two observers: New Zealand and Mexico. It covers a market of 264 million people and a GDP (PPP) of USD 4.47 trillion.

New developments: The sophistication of trade agreements is increasing, yet the attention on the need of regional competition rules is not.[13]

AP: Trade bloc formed in 2012 by Chile, Colombia, Mexico and Peru. It has four associate countries: Australia, Canada, New Zealand and Singapore, and fifty-four observer states.[14] It covers a market of 210 million people and a GDP (PPP) of USD 3.75 trillion (35% of LAC's GDP). It is considered to have the latest generation of trade agreements in the world, with common regulations and policies in seventeen areas, including consumer protection, services and capitals, and trade facilitation, but nothing specifically on Competition Policy, even though the four full original members are clear leaders on competition policy in LAC.

United States-Mexico-Canada FTA (USMCAN).[15] This is the recent revision to the 1994 North American Free Trade Agreement (NAFTA), considered for many years as one of the benchmarks in RTAs in the world. It covers a market of 490 million people and a GDP (PPP) of USD 24.8 trillion (21% of the world's GDP), and it is only second in size to the Regional Comprehensive Economic Partnership, a proposed agreement between ten-Member States of ASEAN and six trading partners: Australia, China, India, Japan, South Korea and New Zealand.

10. http://sice.oas.org/CARICOM/instmt_s.asp.
11. https://data.worldbank.org/indicator/SP.POP.TOTL.
12. http://sice.oas.org/Mercosur/instmt_s.asp.
13. Except for the EU Association Agreement with Central America, where the EU pursued a regional competition arrangement.
14. *See* https://en.wikipedia.org/wiki/Pacific_Alliance.
15. *See* https://ustr.gov/trade-agreements/free-trade-agreements/united-states-mexico-canada-agreement/.

European Union (EU)-Central America Association Agreement.[16] This partnership agreement is one of multiple similar agreements that the EU has negotiated and signed with LAC countries which also include the Economic Partnership Agreement with CARICOM, with Chile, Colombia, Mexico and Peru.

§14.02 CURRENT CHALLENGES FOR THE DEVELOPMENT OF MODERN REGIONAL COMPETITION SYSTEMS IN LAC

[A] Poor/Dated Normative Framework and Institutional Design

Out of the four major trade blocs, only CAN and CARICOM have current regional competition enforcement rules and supranational bodies, but only CAN has had few actual cases adjudicated, albeit in the form of pre-judicial opinions of the Justice Tribunal of the Andean Community (TJCA). MERCOSUR has a competition regional intergovernmental body. In every case, the normative framework is becoming dated, and perhaps sclerotic due to the limited use.

[1] CAN: A Working Progress Process

CAN has developed a basic, albeit functional regional framework based on Articles 93 and 94 of the Treaty of Cartagena and Decision 608 of the Commission. Articles 72–78 of the Treaty promote the free trade of goods and Articles 79 and 80 the liberalization of trade in services. As freer trade promotes economic efficiency in the regional market benefiting consumers, anticompetitive conduct may hinder these goals. Chapter X on "Commercial Competition" gives the authority to the Commission to adopt competition rules upon suggestion from the General Secretariat of the Andean Community (SGCA).

Decision 608 was the culmination of a long process of thirty-four years in the making. It started with Decision 45 of December 18, 1971, which put in place the first basic antitrust regulations. This norm was subsequently replaced by Decision 230, published on December 18, 1987, and later by Decision 285 published on April 4, 1991. Finally, on March 2005, Decision 608 (current antitrust regional framework) was approved. The scope of the system is layout in Article 5 of the Decision based on the "Effects Doctrine" for cross-border anticompetitive conducts conceptually developed in the US and the EU antitrust models.[17] It covers: (a) anticompetitive conducts practice originated in one or more members, with real effects in other(s) member(s); and (b) anticompetitive behavior originated in non-member countries but with real effects inside CAN jurisdictions. Decision 608 is applied using the Practical Guidelines of October 2007 elaborated by the SGCA.[18]

16. *See* http://www.sice.oas.org/Trade/CACM_EU/Text_Sept14/Index_s.asp.
17. http://www.ipglossary.com/glossary/effects-doctrine/#.W-M6uEtKhnI.
18. Working paper SG/dt 396 "Norms for the protection and promotion of free competition in the Andean Community.

CAN has a relatively large, yet thin, communitarian apparatus which cover nine areas and twenty-one topics[19] but lacks the adequate focus on Competition Policy enforcement. The institutional design of CAN includes the SGCA and the TJCA. The SGCA structure was updated in 2014 and includes three General Directions covering twenty-one topics. It has a very small unit for Competition and Trade Remedies (1 of 7 within General Direction 1). The TJCA oversees the legality in all regional matters.

Resources, both financial and human are very limited. The SGCA has a total annual budget of roughly USD 5.6 million, mostly used for salaries of seventy-one staff. General Direction 1 has a staff of only thirteen people for all seven units it is responsible for. The Competition and Trade Remedies Unit (actual supra-national competition agency) is too small, probably compromising the ability of the SGCA to investigate regional cases. Yet, so far this is the only regional system within the LAC with actual cases/pre-judicial opinions.

[2] CARICOM: When Institutional Design Does Not (Necessarily) Meet with Actual Enforcement

This integration process has a regional competition scheme that includes the enforcement of regional rules (Articles 173 and 174 of the Rev. Chaguaramas Treaty). As in the case of CAN, CARICOM rules were included in the foundational treaty itself to prevent that anticompetitive behavior could derail the completion of the single market. It is very telling that the framers of the integration treaty included strong regulations on competition since the beginning, perhaps influenced by the EU experience where specific rules[20] were adopted since the creation of the European Communities. In 2011, Rules of Procedure were adopted to make enforcement possible and fulfill the objectives of the policy. Moreover, in 2013 some guidelines for investigations have been prepared but remain as an internal document. These important efforts have not produced major results yet: no cases, few member countries (4 out of 15) with national competition laws, while markets show strong concentration and weak rivalry.[21]

The institutional design includes a specific, yet modest, regional competition agency CARICOM's Competition Commission (CCC) headquartered in Suriname with both investigative and adjudicative functions, and the Caribbean Court of Justice (CCJ) who reviews the decisions on appeal. There could be a concern for the lack of Chinese walls between investigation and adjudication.

Annual budget of the CCC is very limited but the agency is pursuing some alternative technical and financial resources such as the EU-EPA Capacity Building Project, US Federal Trade Commission and other extra regional sources.

19. http://www.comunidadandina.org/Prensa.aspx?id = 3529&accion = detalle&cat = NP.
20. Articles 81 and 82 of the EC Treaty, later revised and replaced by Articles 101 and 102 of the Treaty on the Functioning of the European Union. *See* https://www.slaughterandmay.com/media/64569/an-overview-of-the-eu-competition-rules.pdf.
21. On concentration and lack of competition in the Caribbean *see*: http://www.centralbank.cw/index.php?eid = 1734.

The CCC has six Commissioners (from various member countries) and a small staff in Paramaribo of five members (two of which are administrative officers and one accountant). After several years of being understaffed, the CCC is preparing the appointment of the Executive Director, the Senior Legal Counsel and the Registrar, all expected to start in January 2019. Given the agency's fragility, and despite being active for ten years, it is not surprising that the CCC has issued no enforcement decisions so far. This inactivity may be coming to an end as there is one case before the adjudication panel and another one being investigated.

[3] MERCOSUR: A Divorce with Best Practices

The Southern Common Market has a relative light regional competition policy scheme more oriented towards coordination of national competition authorities rather than regional enforcement/adjudication.[22] Initial Competition rules were adopted on December 1996 through the Protocol of Fortaleza of 1996 also based on the "Effects Doctrine."

This regulation has been updated by Decision CMC 43/2010 by the Common Market Council (highest authority of MERCOSUR), which include – as an Annex – the Agreement for the Defense of Competition of MERCOSUR.[23] The objectives of the Agreement are as follows: (i) promote coordination and cooperation among competition authorities, (ii) mutual assistance among authorities when necessary, (iii) identification of common interests in competition policy and (iv) elimination of anticompetitive practices through the enforcement of national laws.

On the institutional side, the Technical Committee for the Defense of Competition No 5 (CT5) is the entity responsible for applying the Decision. It is an intergovernmental group made up of a national coordinator from each member country's competition authority The committee is in charge of discussing: (i) consultations by a member country of competition-related issues and investigations conducted at national level, (ii) coordination of actions by each national authority in order to avoid possible contradictions (as possible), (iii) technical cooperation and exchange of information, (iv) notification of actions that may affect other member and (v) confidentiality of opinions and right of each member to refuse to share information in cases national law prohibits it or is contrary to national interests. After twenty-two years from the Fortaleza Protocol and eight years from the current Decision, there have not been cross-border investigations. CT5 met twice in 2017 and items of discussion included: (i) presentation of new Argentinean Competition Authorities, (ii) exchanges on the scope of Decision CMC 43/2010, (iii) 2017 work program, including exchanges of information in cases of anticompetitive practices, mergers, procedural and institutional issues, market studies, and (iv) a regional system of peer review; new Argentinean competition law, and presentation by Brazil of relevant cases and their leniency program.[24]

22. https://revistas-colaboracion.juridicas.unam.mx/index.php/latinoamericana-derecho/article/view/21304/18978.
23. http://www.loa.org.ar/legNormaDetalle.aspx?id = 14094.
24. Meetings of CT5 LXIII and LXIV of March and November 2017.

This institutional design aims more to cooperation and not enforcement of regional anti-competitive practices or regional merger control.

[B] Tensions Between the Regional and National Schemes, and Between Trade and Competition Authorities

Every integration process will produce some level of tensions derived from the need of national systems to transfer competencies to the regional apparatus. Below there is a description of some of the tensions in LAC major blocs when implementing competition policy.

[1] CACM: A Tale of Unfulfilled Commitments and Gridlock Regarding Competition Policy

Even though Central America does not have a regional competition arrangement in place, it is worth to explore the various unsuccessful intents towards this goal. As of today, all countries have national competition laws except for Guatemala.

The Protocol of the General Integration Treaty, known as Protocol of Guatemala, contains language where contracting parties agree to adopt common rules to avoid monopolistic conducts and the promotion of competition within the member countries. Similarly, in the agreement Establishing the Customs Union in 2012, Member States committed to adopt a regional regulation in Competition Policy and a regional competition authority.

The regional process was further reinforced in the EU-Central America Association Agreement, where signatory countries committed to adopt regional competition rules and the creation of a regional Competition Authority.

All these efforts have not materialized, and the regional regulation is not in place despite substantial efforts by Central American Competition Authorities and their regional network RECAC with the support of the IADB. The main reason for the lack of progress has to do with tensions between trade and competition authorities.[25]

Between June 2016 and February 2018, RECAC and the Council of Ministers of Trade and Economy COMIECO have been going back and forth with a draft text for a regional competition regulation. Part of the tension comes from the fact that COMIECO asked the Technical Group on Competition, composed of Trade (not competition) authorities, to review the draft text. An element of disagreement is the conformation to a supranational body to enforce the regional rules.

25. The integration process in CACM is led by the Ministers of Economy/Trade. Competition Authorities under RECAC have not been able to become part of SICA and their technical recommendations for the regional competition regulation have not been addressed fully.

[2] CAN: Tensions with National Competition Authorities Resulting from the Decisions of the TJCA

The best way to exemplify the tensions of regional and national authorities is the small set of competition cases reviewed by the TJCA:

(a) Case 78-IP-2018 of TJCA (September 2018). Interpretation on the scope of Decision 608. The issue was raised after the competition authority of Colombia (SIC)[26] sanctioned a group of firms for fixing prices in the baby diaper market. Subsequently, the competition authority of Ecuador requested CAN's SGCA to start an investigation for another cartel in the tissue and toilet paper markets. Some firms were members of both cartels. One of the executives of the firms in Colombia requested to annul the decision by the SIC and requested an interpretation by the TJCA of Decision 608, Article 5 based on the following arguments: (a) A National authority has jurisdiction only if the conduct is originated and produces effects in the territory, (b) the cartel had cross-border nature, thus the SIC had no jurisdiction, (c) the alleged illegal conduct had effects outside Colombia, thus the case should be tried before the SGCA, and (d) the documents related to the leniency process in Colombia contains evidence that the cartel had activities in two countries. The SIC denied the existence of cross-border effect in this cartel. The TJCA issue a pre-judicial opinion based on the principle of *non bis in idem*, according to which no one can be investigated nor sanctioned twice for the same conduct, provided there is a triple identity and no impunity is facilitated: (i) the economic agents should be identical; (ii) the illegal conduct should be the same. The conduct is not the same if the products are not the same; and (iii) the legally protected good should be the same, both at the national and at the regional level. This interpretation on the scope of Decision 608 and the conflict with national competition law is now on the hands of a local court in Colombia[27] for a final decision on the case. This case has implications for the ability of a national authority such as the SIC to implement leniency in the fight against local cartels. Even though it seems that the complete triple identity is apparently not plausible in this case as per TJCA decision, the potential for tension is real.

(b) Case 472-IP-2016 OF TJCA (September 2018). Interpretation on the scope of Article 49 of Decision 608. The issue raises after the Minister of Productive Development and Plural Economy of Bolivia confirmed a sanction to the national Bolivian brewing company by the Authority for the Supervision and Control of Firms (AEMP) because of abuse of dominant position and exclusionary conduct. Bolivia did not have a national competition law at that

26. http://www.sic.gov.co/.
27. Sección Primera del Juzgado Quinto Administrativo Oral del Circuito de Bogotá, Colombia.

time,[28] so it used the communitarian rules instead. The case is before Bolivia's Supreme Court where the plaintiff (the brewing company) states that Decision 608 is not applicable because there are not cross-border effects per Article 5 requirements. Upon request, the TJCA issued a pre-judicial opinion for the Bolivian Supreme Court. The Andean Justice Tribunal analyzed the scope of Decision 608 and its Article 5, noting also that Article 49 allows Bolivia and Ecuador to apply the Community rules on Competition (Decision 608) as their national laws since these two countries lack national rules. The opinion from the Tribunal was also an opportunity to confirm the concepts of direct applicability and direct effect as principles of CAN Law. The recent opinion will inform the case before the Court of Justice, mostly defending the primacy of the regional rules over the national laws. Further implications may appear when (if) Bolivia enacts a national competition law, something that the TJCA may have been indirectly pursuing in this decision.

(c) Case 05-AN-2015. Annulment petition by a local firm in Colombia (ANGELCOM SA) of a communication (not a formal Decision) by the SGCA rejecting to open an investigation for collusive behavior in public procurement against Transmilenio SA (Colombia). The SGCA considered that the request did not fulfill Article 5 of Decision 608 which requires cross-border (real) effects. ANGELCOM also alleged that the communication was not motivated, violating the rules of procedure in Article 12 of Decision 425. The TJCA concluded that there was no real cross-border effect and thus the community rules (Decision 608) could not be applied for this case. Moreover, it concluded that the communication was sufficiently motivated and did not constitute a violation of Decision 425. The TJCA also rejected an allegation by the SGCA that the case had prescribed per the statute of limitations. It also requested the SGCA to adopt formal decisions for similar future cases and not mere communications. Overall, the TJCA with these few decisions confirms it is now active on cases related to the scope of Decision 608, but the TJCA has yet to decide directly on a cross-border case of anticompetitive conduct.

§14.03 SOME IDEAS TO MOVE FORWARD: PREPARING FOR BETTER REGIONAL RULES AND STRONGER REGIONAL AGENCIES

With few exceptions, LAC region and sub-regions have shown the difficulties of effectively implementing regional competition schemes. Part of the problem may be explained by the economic deacceleration of major integration blocs and the relative weakness of regional rules. Nevertheless, markets are becoming regional and global, enhancing the need for regional rules.

---

28. Bolivia enacted an Executive Decree 29519 in 2008 but this is not considered a national competition law per international standards, but instead some regulation to control enterprises. https://www.lexivox.org/norms/BO-DS-29519.xhtml. In support of this view, the Bolivian AEMP was the one asking the TJCA to apply the regional rules instead.

At the institutional and regulatory level, CARICOM, CAN and MERCOSUR have put in place different models of regional systems, but only CAN shows some level of activity through few pre-judicial opinions.

Given these challenges, some ideas to move forward may include:

(a) *Preparation of technical work conducive to an update/overhaul of the Regional Competition rules* in CAN, CARICOM and MERCORSUR based on international best practices. In that regard, the region can benefit from its current partnership/association agreements with the EU and obtain more technical support from DG-COMP. Similarly, the IDB could continue the support to these efforts with technical cooperation programs. The fact is that it is time to review the regional normative framework designed many decades ago for most of the blocs, and include, among other things, regional merger review when cross-border mergers, and leniency for cross-border cartels investigations with permanent coordination with national authorities. MERCOSUR may also consider the benefits of adopting a supra-national body (similar to CAN or CARICOM) and improved regional substantive rules to complement the (good) recent developments of the national authorities of Brazil and Argentina, insufficient by themselves to tackle successfully cross-border anticompetitive activity. CARICOM's CCC may benefit from a clear separation of the investigation phase and the adjudication role. Given the fact that only four countries have adopted national competition laws, this bloc could also consider CAN's approach (Article 49 of Decision 608) of using the regional regulation as national law for those countries who have still to legislate in this matter. The bloc could also adopt a regional merger control system given the size of the regional market and that most mergers have cross-border implications.

(b) *More attention is required to the political economy.* Because integration blocs are typically led by trade and foreign affairs ministers, an adequate interaction of competition agencies (national and regional) with these authorities is crucial and, if not addressed properly, it may become a barrier as the process in Central America has shown. As in most turf battles, the issue can be resolved when finding the value of achieving common objectives and assessing the cost of gridlock and failure.

(c) *Smart advocacy for more resources is needed.* It is essential to increase the financial and human resources of the regional competition authorities. Even in the case of CARICOM and CAN, it is clear from the evidence that the allocation of resources is limited. Regional authorities should improve their strategy to obtain larger budgets. The key for success here is the ability of the agencies to show greater accountability and independent evaluation to assess the benefits of competition, including the impact on fiscal spending, poverty fight and productivity efforts.

(d) *Focus on bringing cases.* Without actual enforcement there is no meaningful progress. The recent jurisprudence by the TJCA can be a preliminary incentive to CARICOM (and subsequently to CACM and MERCOSUR) to move quicker towards the benefits of regional enforcement of competition law. This tribunal has also proven the value of regional advocacy, after issuing some guidelines on unfair competition and intellectual property.[29]

(e) *Other RTA schemes could also be helpful.* New RTAs could consider enhanced frameworks for the cooperation and joint action of national level authorities in actual cases, particularly in the implementation of leniency in international cartels as well as Merger control in cross border activity:

   (i) The Pacific Alliance (5th World's Economy in 2020) may be an opportunity. It is the more advanced integration platform with multiple coordination efforts in many areas. Its members have some of the strongest competition authorities in the whole region. Further work in regional competition arrangements could be explored to enhance the benefits of trade and cooperation in public policies.

   (ii) The USMCAN agreement includes a chapter on Competition Policy like the one NAFTA had, with the commitment to enforce national competition laws, but also with the possibility of cross-border enforcement when there is nexus to the local jurisdiction (Articles 21.1.2 and 21.1.5 (b) (c)).

(f) *Move to new generation of MOUs.* Many of the national authorities have moved to the signature of MOUs[30] but some of these may be symbolic or insufficient. There are new generation cooperation agreements, like the ones between FNE and INDECOPI of Peru, between FNE and COFECE of Mexico, and between the SIC of Colombia and INDECOPI with more substantive and useful content. Other agreements involve the CNDC of Argentina and various countries, and cooperation agreements within RAC in Central America.

29. *See* https://lalibrecompetencia.com/2015/10/05/propuestas-del-tribunal-de-justicia-de-la-can-de-una-agenda-normativa-para-la-integracion/.

30. The OECD has a large inventory of current MOUs between competition authorities in the world. http://www.oecd.org/competition/inventory-competition-agency-mous.htm.

CHAPTER 15

China's Merger Control Enforcement: Recent Developments and Trends

Cunzhen Huang & Yiming Sun

§15.01 INTRODUCTION

In July 2018, Qualcomm terminated a USD 44 billion acquisition of NXP Semiconductors after failing to secure Chinese merger control approval by its set deadline.[1] This is one recent example illustrating how significant effect Chinese merger control enforcement could exert on a global transaction. Indeed, China has become one of the most important jurisdictions of the global merger control enforcement.[2] Despite the great efforts to shorten the review timeline for cases under the simplified procedure, the Chinese merger review process for cases under the normal procedure continues to be lengthy and unpredictable. At the same time, China has appeared to be more deferential to Chinese stakeholders and does not shy away from taking a harsh stance towards some international mega-deals; even doing so may give rise to deviation from other jurisdictions.

This chapter summarizes the recent developments and characteristics of Chinese merger control enforcement, from unconventional substantive review, stakeholders' interventions, to complex review timeline, and to heightened enforcement on failure to notify.

1. *See*, "Qualcomm ends $44 billion NXP bid after failing to win China approval," Reuters, July 25, 2018, available at: https://www.reuters.com/article/us-nxp-semicondtrs-m-a-qualcomm/qualcomm-ends-44-billion-nxp-bid-after-failing-to-win-china-approval-idUSKBN1KF193.
2. *See*, Mergers in China: An Overview of Leading Case Law, George S. Cary, Cunzhen Huang, Yiming Sun, Concurrences, 2016.

§15.02 OVERVIEW OF CHINESE MERGER CONTROL REGIME

Since 2003, China has adopted a mandatory and suspensory merger control regime, which was reinforced by China's Anti-Monopoly Law ("AML") coming into force in 2008. The regime requires that any transaction that constitutes "concentrations of undertakings" under the AML and triggers the turnover-based thresholds be filed to and approved by the merger control authority in China before it can be consummated.[3]

Prior to May 2018, the authority in charge of the merger control enforcement was the Anti-Monopoly Bureau (AMB) within the Ministry of Commerce ("MOFCOM"). In May 2018, as the result of the integration of China's three antitrust agencies into a new agency, namely State Administration for Market Regulation (SAMR),[4] the AMB of MOFCOM was also integrated into the new AMB of SAMR.[5]

Based on its review, MOFCOM could decide to unconditionally approve a transaction, to approve a transaction subject to restrictive conditions, or to prohibit a transaction. The vast majority of filings that MOFCOM reviewed to date were cleared unconditionally—through the end of October 2018, the authority completed the review of 2,437 filings in total, of which 2,398 were cleared unconditionally, 37 were cleared with conditions, and 2 were prohibited.[6] As shown in Figure 15.1, the number of filings that MOFCOM received, accepted and reviewed each year has been steadily increased. MOFCOM's work load has increased about five times since 2008, while the number of case team staff has stagnated—approximately thirty over these years.

3. *See*, AML, Article 21.
4. More detail of this institutional reform will be introduced in the section 1.09.
5. For the purpose of consistency and convenience, we still refer to MOFCOM as China's merger control agency in this chapter.
6. *See*, the speech given by Ms. Lin Gan, the vice minister of SAMR in charge of antitrust work, at the AML Tenth Anniversary Press Conference. In addition to the thirty-seven conditionally approved cases, Praxair/Linde was approved with conditions on September 30, 2018, and UTC/Rockwell Collins was approved with conditions on November 23, 2018.

Figure 15.1 Number of Filings Received, Accepted, and Reviewed by MOFCOM (August 2008 August–November 9, 2018)

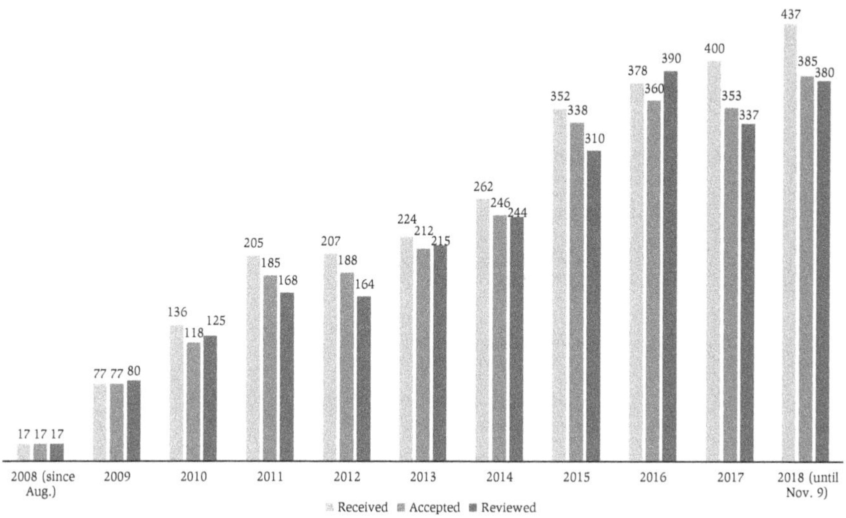

MOFCOM used to review all cases through a unified process. In February 2014, a simplified procedure was introduced which allows a fast-track review of "simple cases" that satisfy certain criteria (such as combined market share lower than 15% in horizontal mergers).[7]

§15.03 UNCONVENTIONAL THEORY OF HARM INCREASINGLY APPLIED IN CHINA: CONGLOMERATE EFFECT

Figure 15.2 shows the types of mergers where MOFCOM intervened (i.e., prohibited or imposed remedies).

7. *See,* MOFCOM's Interim Regulation on the Standards Applicable to Simple Cases of Concentrations Between Business Operators, available at: http://www.mofcom.gov.cn/article/b/c/201402/20140200487038.shtml. For more detailed guidelines on the simplified procedure, *see also* Guiding Opinion on the Notification of Simple Cases of Concentrations between Business Operators (Trial), http://fldj.mofcom.gov.cn/article/i/201404/20140400555353.shtml. This guiding opinion was updated by SAMR in September 2018. *See,* Guiding Opinion on the Notification of Simple Cases of Concentrations between Business Operators (as amended on September 29, 2018), available at: http://samr.saic.gov.cn/xw/yw/wjfb/201809/t20180929_276169.html.

Figure 15.2 Types of Mergers in Interventional Decisions (August 2008–November 2018)

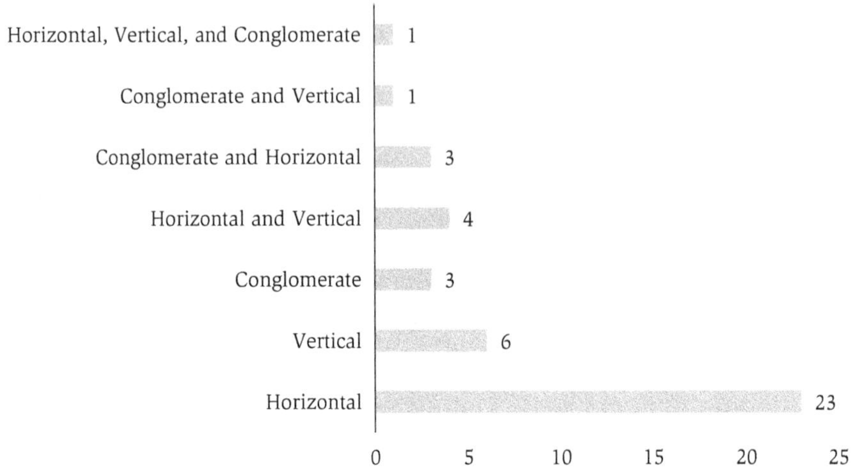

As shown in Figure 15.1, there is one specific type of merger that we notice was more frequently intervened in China than elsewhere, i.e., conglomerate merger. As shown by the Figure 15.1, conglomerate theory of harm was raised in eight out of forty-one MOFCOM's interventional decisions, accounting for approximately 17%. Such decisions include Coca Cola/Huiyuan (2009), which was the first transaction that was prohibited in China. However, after Coca Cola/Huiyuan, MOFCOM did not use conglomerate theory of harm very often in subsequent cases (only two cases during 2010–2016[8]) until more recently, when potential conglomerate effect has been routinely and heavily examined—conglomerate theory of harm was raised in five of eleven conditional clearance decisions issued by MOFCOM during 2017 and 2018.[9]

The typical conduct where MOFCOM raised conglomerate concerns is post-transaction tying and/or bundling. Except for the first two decisions,[10] tying and bundling was raised in all the remaining six conglomerate cases. Other conglomerate concerns that have been raised by MOFCOM include, for instance, interoperability among complementary products.[11]

While there have not been any official rules or guidelines on MOFCOM's approach to establish conglomerate theory of harm, based on its recent decisional practice, MOFCOM seems to have used the "ability-incentive-effect" framework that

8. These cases are Wal-Mart/Niuhai Holding (2012) and Merck/AZ Electronic Materials (2014).
9. These cases are Broadcom/Brocade (2017), HP/Samsung Electronics (2017), Bayer/Monsanto (2018), Essilor/Luxottica (2018), and UTC/Rockwell Collins (2018).
10. In these two early cases, SAMR only generally described conglomerate concern as caused by leveraging effect and did not specify the conduct that the parties would potentially engage in to realize the leveraging effect.
11. This was raised in Broadcom/Brocade (2017) and HP/Samsung Electronics (2017).

has been used by the the European Commission (EC).[12] However, in terms of outcome, MOFCOM diverged from the EC in all the five cases that were also filed to the EC for approval (and all happened to be approved between 2017 and 2018)—in these cases, the EC did not discuss conglomerate effects at all in HP/Samsung Electronics or United technologies (UTC)/Rockwell Collins, was convinced by the parties during in-depth review and did not impose remedies addressing conglomerate effect in Bayer/Monsanto and Essilor/Luxottica, and only required interoperability and confidentiality assurance in Broadcom/Brocade. On the contrary, SAMR took the view that Bayer/Monsanto has conglomerate concerns (though not imposing a specific remedy addressing that), required remedies in HP/Samsung Electronics, Essilor/Luxottica, Broadcom/Brocade, and UTC/Rockwell Collins. In other words, it is far more difficult to persuade MOFCOM to drop its conglomerate concerns.

Different geographies may not be able to fully explain this divergence, because three out of the five cases involved global markets. One possible reason is that even if the relevant geographic market is in global scope, MOFCOM's review still considers any special considerations characteristics of Chinese customers and competitors. For example, in Broadcom/Brocade (2017), both MOFCOM and EC defined global markets. The EC discussed three types of potential conglomerate concerns, i.e., interoperability among complementary products, misuse of third party's confidential information by the parties, and mix-bundling strategies.[13] The Commission eventually dismissed the concern on mix-bundling strategies on the ground that the parties lacked the ability and incentive to engage in mixed-bundling strategies in detrimental to competition mainly due to the asynchronicity of the sales of the complementary products, and unbundling strategies of downstream OEMs.[14] MOFCOM, on the other hand, upheld all the three conglomerate concerns, including the concern on mixed-bundling. MOFCOM explained that what discerned China from the global market is that Chinese end-users are small and fragmented and therefore lack the countervailing power to the parties. MOFCOM also mentioned that considering that the market demand is growing in China and that end-users are pursuing lower costs and increased profits, Chinese end-users are likely to purchase the parties' tied or bundled products. MOFCOM's decision was silent on whether asynchronicity of sales for example was also considered by MOFCOM, and if so, why it was not a credible defense.

The investigation of conglomerate effect often results in significantly prolonged review process and behavioral remedies. The average review time for these eight conglomerate decisions is around 320 days, whereas the average review time for the rest of MOFCOM's interventional cases, i.e., those where no conglomerate concerns were raised, is around 225 days.[15] In a lot of cases, third-party stakeholders may use

12. *See*, the European Commission's Guidelines on the assessment of non-horizontal mergers under the Council Regulation on the control of concentrations between undertakings (2008/C 265/07) ("EU Non-Horizontal Guidelines"), paragraph 94.
13. *See*, Case COMP/M.8314—Broadcom / Brocade, the European Commission decision of May 12, 2017, paragraphs 149.
14. *See*, *id.*, paragraphs 222–227.
15. To exclude the impact of extreme cases, the average time provided here does not count the shortest and the longest review times.

vague conglomerate effects, even unsubstantiated ones, to achieve their non-merger-specific purposes, given that MOFCOM takes industry stakeholders' views and conglomerate concerns seriously.

§15.04 MORE FREQUENT USE OF BEHAVIORAL REMEDIES

MOFCOM has shown more willingness than its counterparts to require behavioral remedies. As shown in Figure 15.3, MOFCOM imposed behavioral remedies in thirty-two out of a total of thirty-nine conditional approvals, and only seven transactions were approved with structural remedies only. To draw a general comparison with the European Union (EU) and United States (US) authorities, out of the thirty-two cases where MOFCOM imposed behavioral remedies, twenty-five cases were reviewed by the authorities in the EU, the US, or both. MOFCOM's behavioral remedy only converged with other's remedy in one case, i.e., ARM/Giesecke & Devrient/Gemalto/JV (2012) where both MOFCOM and EU imposed behavioral remedies to address a vertical concern. In nine cases, the transactions were unconditionally cleared in the EU and US, but remedies were imposed in China. In the rest eighteen cases, MOFCOM imposed remedies that were either broader than or different from those imposed in the EU and US. This comparison shows that MOFCOM has imposed behavioral remedies more often and in a broader scope than its counterparts in the EU and the US.

Figure 15.3 Types of Remedies Imposed by MOFCOM (August 2008–November 2018)

MOFCOM routinely uses behavioral remedies to address all types of concerns, including, notably, horizontal ones—out of the thirty-two cases where MOFCOM imposed behavioral remedies, sixteen involved horizontal concern only. This may sound counter-intuitive, since it is structural remedy that is widely believed to be the preferred solution to address horizontal concerns. Furthermore, MOFCOM also uses behavioral remedies to address non-competition concerns (such as industry policies, energy or resource safety, and Chinese companies' commercial interests).[16] In some cases, Chinese third parties complained to MOFCOM about the parties' past business practice, how irrelevant with the transaction under review, MOFCOM was also willing to consider behavioral remedies to appease third parties' concern.

Figure 15.4 shows the types of behavioral remedies that have been most frequently imposed by MOFCOM. In addition, MOFCOM has also imposed a variety of other types of behavioral remedies, such as restriction on shareholders' rights and termination of contracts of cooperation.

Figure 15.4 Frequently Used Types of Behavioral Remedies in China

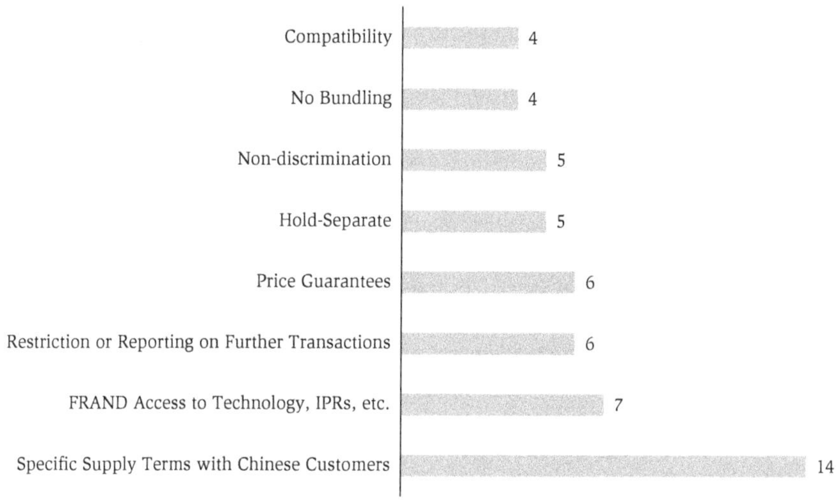

Many of these behavioral remedies are unconventional, compared with the international norm. Four examples are discussed below in detail:

- *Specific Supply Terms With Chinese Customers.* It is one of the most frequently used type of behavioral conditions in China. For example, in Linde/Praxair (2018), MOFCOM's conditions required the parties to steadily and timely supply the relevant industrial gas to Chinese customers at reasonable price and volume based on the existing contracts and the then market conditions. Similar conditions were imposed in Uralkali/Silvinit, Henkel Hong Kong/Tiande, Glencore/Xstrata, MediaTek/MStar, Dow/DuPont, HP/Samsung, ASE/SPIL, Agrium/Potash, Essilor/Luxottica, Bayer/Monstanto, and UTC/Rockwell Collins.
- *"FRAND" access to technology, IP Rights, and etc.* MOFCOM frequently imposed conditions to ensure that Chinese customers and players can get access

16. AML provides that SAMR can take into consideration a transaction's effect on national economic development. *See*, AML, Article 27.

to technology, IP rights and etc. In Alcatel/Nokia, Microsoft/Nokia, and Google/Motorola, MOFCOM imposed behavioral remedies which basically required the parties to restate their commitments to standard setting organizations ("SSOs") to license their standard essential patents ("SEPs") on a fair, reasonable, and non-discriminatory ("FRAND") terms. MOFCOM also used FRAND terms in non-SEP and non-patent related cases. For example, in Bayer/Monsanto, MOFCOM required the parties to provide Chinese app operators and users with access to their digital agriculture platform and products on FRAND terms. Some specific supply terms as abovementioned also include FRAND requirements—UTC/Rockwell Collins is an example.

- *Price Guarantee.* Another type of remedy that is uncommon elsewhere is a commitment to sell at certain price levels post-transaction. In Glencore/Xstrata, MOFCOM required detailed price commitments with regard to the prices to be charged by the parties for supply of copper concentrate to Chinese customers. In Thermo Fisher/Life Technologies, MOFCOM's remedy required a price decrease by 1% each year and maintenance of discount level for Chinese distributors. More recent price guarantee examples include Linde/Praxair and Dow/DuPont.
- *Hold-Separate.* Hold-separate remedy is probably the most unique and controversial behavioral remedy ever imposed by MOFCOM. While temporary hold-separate requirement is routinely used in divestiture remedies to ensure the competitiveness and marketability of the to be divested businesses, MOFCOM's hold-separate remedy was imposed in horizontal mergers for the merging parties to keep operating separately for a long period of time after the completion of the mergers. Such long-term hold-separate remedy has been imposed in Seagate/Samsung, Western Digital/Hitachi, Marubeni/Gavilon, MediaTek/MStar, and ASE/SPIL. Except for Western Digital/Hitachi, all the other transactions were either cleared without conditions or not notifiable, in the EU and the US. As for Western Digital/Hitachi, a divestiture remedy was imposed in the EU, US, and China, and China also imposed a long-term hold-separate remedy. The long-term hold-separate remedy is very controversial, because it would delay synergies, give rise to severe long-term disruption to business operations, unintended consequences, as well as burdensome and costly compliance.

The duration of behavioral remedies imposed by MOFCOM ranged from twenty-four months to indefinite, with five years and ten years being the most common. The majority does not have a sunset clause—the remedies will not terminate automatically at the end of the remedy term; rather, parties will need to apply for MOFCOM's approval of the removal or revision of the remedies. It has remained difficult to petition MOFCOM to remove or modify behavioral remedies. MOFCOM has substantial discretion during its review and there is no time limit on such review. In six out of seven behavioral remedy review cases so far, MOFCOM took seven to twenty-nine months to reach a decision after a full competitive re-assessment, as shown in Table 15.1.

Table 15.1

Case	*Time of Approval*	*Duration of Behavioral Remedies*	*Remedies Lifted or Modified*	*Time of Application*	*Time of Decision*
GE/Shenhua/JV	November 10, 2011	Indefinite	Lifted due decreased shares and new market entrants	November 2017	August 22, 2018
Media Tek/Msatr Cayman	August 26, 2013	3 years (termination upon review)	Lifted due to decreased shares and other material market changes	September 2016	February 9, 2018
Henkel HK/Tiande	February 9, 2012	Indefinite	Lifted as Henkel transferred JV shares to Tiande	July 2017	February 1, 2018
Wal-Mart/Yihaodian	August 13, 2012	Indefinite	Lifted after foreign investment policies in e-commerce sector loosened in June 2015	July 2015	May 30, 2016
Western Digital/Hitachi	March 2, 2012	2 years (termination upon review)	Modified after six rounds of implementation plans submissions	March 2014	October 19, 2015
Seagate/Samsung	December 12, 2011	1 year (termination upon review)	Modified after meetings with parties, stakeholder consultation, and economic analysis	May 2013	October 10, 2015
Google/ Motorola Mobility	May 19, 2012	5 years (early termination possible upon application)	Lifted one of the behavioral remedies after the sale of Motorola Mobility business to Lenovo	December 1, 2014	January 6, 2015

§15.05 COMPLEX PICTURE OF REVIEW TIMELINE

The review process of MOFCOM could be divided into the following periods: pre-acceptance period (where MOFCOM's review focuses on completeness of filing materials which could last weeks or even months), Phase I review period (up to thirty calendar days), Phase II review period (up to ninenty calendar days), and extended Phase II review period, i.e., Phase III review period (up to sixty calendar days).[17]

Although the China merger review process has always been considered lengthy since 2008, the speed of review has actually been improved in recent years. According to MOFCOM's official statistics, the number of cases that were concluded within Phase I (thirty days) period were increased by 85% compared to 2008, and the average review time in 2017 was shortened by more than 50% compared to in 2013.[18]

This significant acceleration of review process appears, to a very large extent, a result of the introduction of the simplified procedure in 2014—most cases under the simplified procedure were cleared within the Phase I after acceptance.[19] As shown by Figure 15.5,[20] simplified-procedure cases are on average cleared rather quickly after being accepted and as shown in Figure 15.6,[21] simplified-procedure case accounted for 75%–85% of the total cases concluded. It is worth nothing though that MOFCOM's review of whether the case qualifies for the simplified procedure has become very strict, data heavy, and time consuming.

Figure 15.5 Simplified-Procedure Case—Average Length of Review (Days)

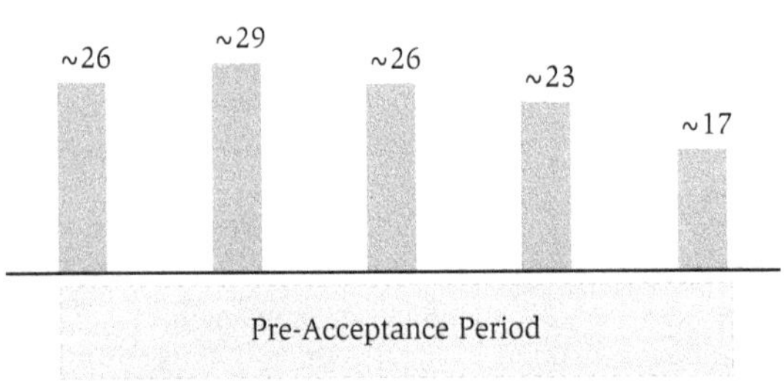

17. *See*, AML, Articles 25 and 26.
18. *See*, the speech given by Ms. Lin Gan, the vice minister of SAMR in charge of antitrust work, at the AML Tenth Anniversary Press Conference.
19. *Id.*
20. The statistics in Figure 15.5 are based on the basic information that published for public consultation on the website of MOFCOM's AMB: http://fldj.mofcom.gov.cn/article/jyzjzjyajgs/.
21. The statistics in Figure 15.6 are based on the quarterly merger filing statistics published by MOFCOM on its website: http://fldj.mofcom.gov.cn/article/zcfb/.

Figure 15.6 Percentages of Simplified-Procedure Cases in Total Merger Review Cases

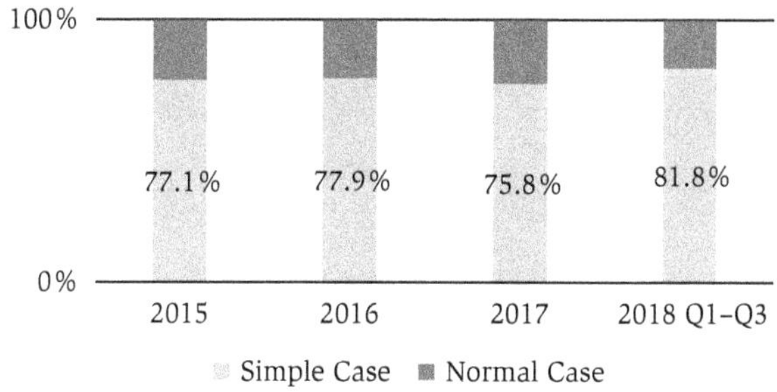

While the Figure 15.5 shows that the simplified procedure has significantly reduced the average review timeline, only the simple cases that are unlikely to give rise to any concerns and have limited exposure to third-party stakeholder during the review process. For normal cases, especially the complex ones, the review timeline has not been significantly shortened.

Since MOFCOM does not publish the notification or acceptance time for unconditionally cleared normal cases, only the review time of conditionally cleared cases are being examined here, which are the most complex cases handled by MOFCOM. Figure 15.7 shows the longest and shortest review timeline (from notification to clearance) of MOFCOM's conditional clearances between 2009 and 2018 Q3.[22] Figure 15.8 shows the number of conditionally approved cases where the parties pulled and refiled. Unfortunately neither figure shows a clear trend of shorter review time. In fact, both the longest and shortest review time in 2018 is the longest among the recent years, and all the four cases in 2018 were pulled and refiled.

22. The Figure 15.7 does not include the data for 2008 and 2010, for each of which MOFCOM only issued one conditional clearance decision.

Figure 15.7 Conditional Clearances—Longest and Shortest Review Time (Days) (2009–2018)

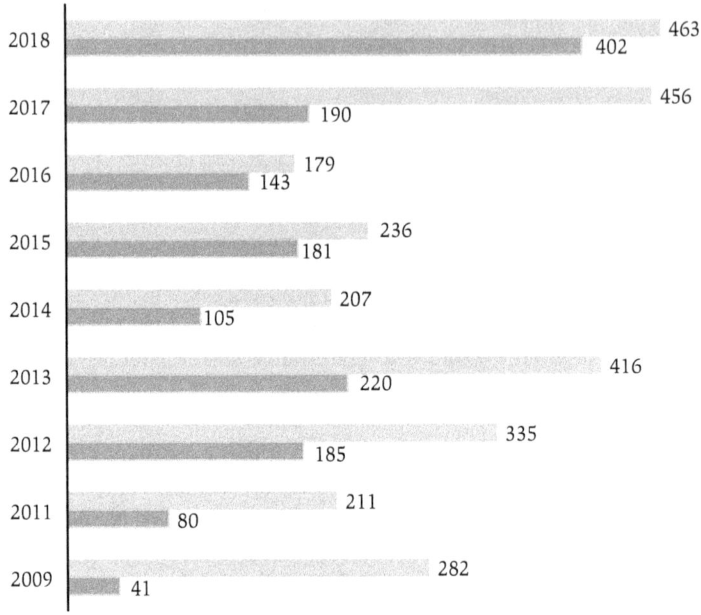

Figure 15.8 Conditional Clearances—Number of Pull-and-Refile Cases (2012–2018)

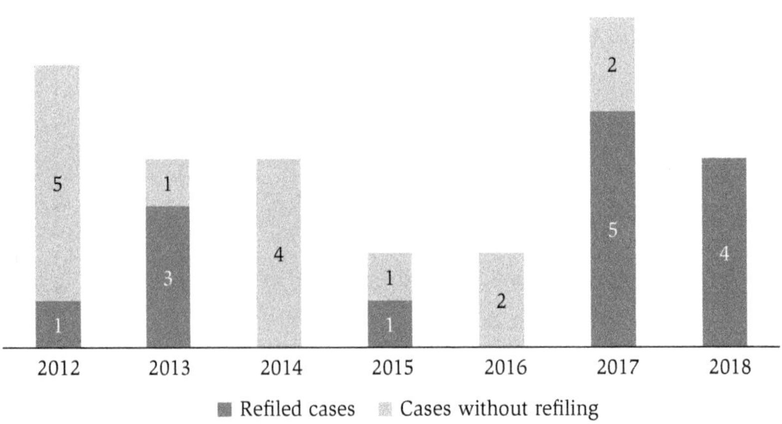

As discussed earlier, MOFCOM is actually not always the last agency to clear a global mega deal, as conventional wisdom holds.[23] Table 15.2 lists the conditional clearances where China was not the last jurisdiction to clear, which represents almost 30% of MOFCOM's conditional clearances. Among these cases, the US was always the last jurisdiction to approve the transaction, and for more than 80% of these cases,[24] the delay was due to the fact that the US required an upfront buyer (i.e., buyer identified and approved by the US authority before the main transaction was cleared).

Table 15.2 Conditional Clearance Cases Where China Was Not the Last One to Clear

Case Name	*EU*	*US*	*China*
Linde/Praxair	08/20/2018	10/22/2018	09/30/2018
Bayer/Monsanto	03/21/2018	05/29/2018	03/13/2018
Becton, Dickinson and Co./C.R. Bard	10/18/2017	01/26/2018	12/27/2017
Dow/DuPont	03/27/2017	06/15/2017	04/29/2017
NXP/Freescale	09/17/2015	11/ 25/2015	11/25/2015
Thermo Fisher/Life Technologies	11/26/2013	01/ 31/2014	01/14/2014
UTC/Goodrich	07/26/2012	07/26/2012	06/15/2012
Western Digital/Hitachi	11/23/2011	03/05/2012	03/02/2012
Novartis/Alcon	08/09/2010	08/16/2010	08/13/2010
Panasonic/Sanyo	09/29/2009	11/24/2009	10/30/2009
Pfizer/Wyeth	07/17/2009	10/14/2009	09/29/2009

Moreover, the following factors add further complications and unpredictability to MOFCOM's review time:

- Unpredictable and usually long pre-acceptance phase. MOFCOM's pre-acceptance period could take several weeks, or even up to several months in extreme cases. There is no statutory time limit on pre-acceptance review.
- Exceptional simplified-procedure cases. Although most simplified-procedure cases were cleared within Phase I, there have been some exceptions. In extreme cases, the review time was prolonged to nearly nine months. Figure 15.9 summarizes the simplified-procedure cases which were cleared more than thirty days from 2016 until 2018 Q3.[25] It shows that the cases involving horizontal overlaps are more likely to receive lengthy review. It is also found

23. *See*, e.g., U.S. Chamber of Commerce, Competing Interests in China's Competition Law Enforcement: China's Anti-Monopoly Law Application and the Role of Industrial Policy 50 (September 8, 2014), available at: https://www.uschamber.com/sites/default/files/aml_final_090814_final_locked.pdf.
24. The United States did not formally require an upfront buyer in Dow/DuPont and UTC/Goodrich.
25. The types of cases were based on the criteria which are applied to qualify the cases for the simplified procedure. For example, horizontal type refer to the cases that meet the horizontal

that the industries involved in these exceptional simplified-procedure cases vary, including real estate, home improvement, mining equipment, logistics, semi-conductor, lithium-ion battery, jewelry, food, natural resources, and port. Although such simplified-procedure cases are truly exceptional, accounting for a tiny portion of the total number of simplified-procedure cases, as mentioned earlier, it is observed that MOFCOM may have been increasingly stringent in reviewing whether a case qualifies for the simplified procedure.[26] Disqualifying from the simplified procedure may lead to possible refiling under the normal procedure, which, once happened, would significantly prolong the review.

Figure 15.9 Simplified-Procedure Cases—Cases Cleared Over 30 Days (2016–2018 Q3)

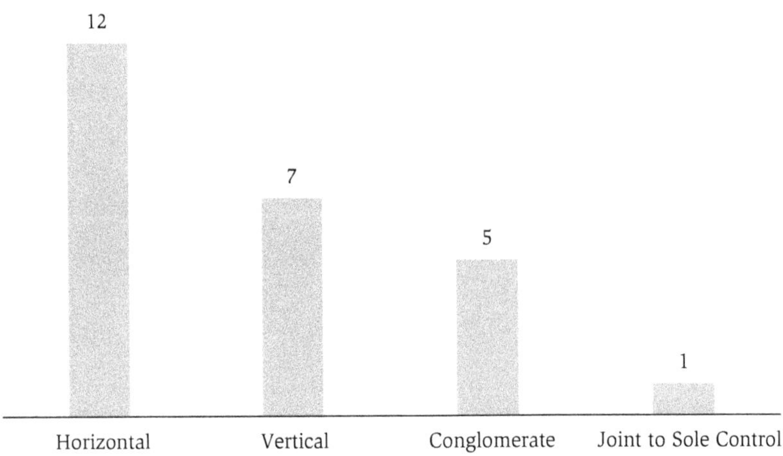

- Uncertainty arising from the political environment. In the second half of 2018, MOFCOM's review of some US-related deals have been allegedly affected by the trade tension between China and the US. For instance, the acquisition by Qualcomm of NXP, as we mentioned in the beginning of this chapter, is the largest US deal that has failed due to failure to obtain the merger control approval in China. Figure 15.10 shows major events of Qualcomm/NXP China review process. It was also noticed that MOFCOM may have slowed down or

overlap test, i.e., the combined share is less than 15% in each relevant overlapped market, to qualify for the simplified procedure.

26. *See*, e.g., Frederic Depoortere et al., The Hidden Risks of MOFCOM's Simplified Procedure, SKADDEN, ARPS, SLATE, MEAGHER & FLOM. LLP (November 21, 2017), https://www.skadden.com/insights/publications/2017/11/the-hidden-risks-of-mofcoms-simplified-procedure.

suspended its review of some US-related cases. Similar situations also happened a few years ago to Japanese companies when Sino-Japan relations materially deteriorated.

Figure 15.10 Timeline of Major Events of Qualcomm/NXP China Filing

- Third party intervention. As explained in section 1.06, concerns (often non-antitrust concerns) raised by third parties and to work out a solution to such concerns significantly complicates and prolongs MOFCOM's review.

§15.06 THIRD PARTY INTERVENTION

MOFCOM routinely seeks information and opinions from a wide range of third parties, including other relevant government agencies, trade associations, upstream and/or downstream Chinese companies, competitors, and other industrial players during its review. MOFCOM is also in general more deferential to local third parties' opinions than other authorities. Given the significant weight MOFCOM has given to third parties' views, a lot of Chinese trade associations and Chinese companies have tried to take advantage of such consultation process and play gamesmanship.

Third party intervention could significantly complicate and prolong the review by bringing into the review process non-antitrust and/or non-merger specific issues. To make it worse, both the procedure of the consultation process and the substantive issues raised during the consultation process are opaque to the filing parties. There is no access to file as such and thus filing parties' right of defense and ability to effectively and efficiently address any concerns are severely jeopardized.

The reluctance of MOFCOM to override third parties' non-competition, non-merger specific or unsubstantiated concerns, combined with the opaque consultation process, makes third party consultation process the most unpredictable part of MOFCOM's review. It often results in a prolonged review process and imposition of behavioral remedies that were not intended to address antitrust issues arising from the transaction.

§15.07 STEPPING UP ENFORCEMENT ON FAILURE TO NOTIFY

MOFCOM has stepped up its enforcement against companies that failed to fulfill their obligation to file in China. MOFCOM officials have on multiple occasions mentioned that cracking down failure to notify is among the agency's priorities.[27] In 2018, MOFCOM imposed fines in a record number of failure to file cases—as shown in Figure 15.11, according to MOFCOM's public decisions, the number of cases surged to fourteen (by mid-December) in 2018, more than the total number of cases penalized in 2016 and 2017.

Figure 15.11 Number of Failure to Notify Cases

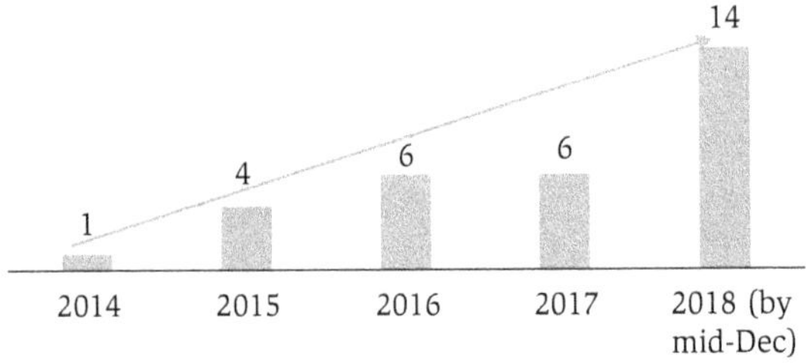

Failing to notify a transaction in accordance with the AML could lead to a fine up to RMB 500,000 and other non-monetary penalties, including suspension of the transaction or transfer of shares or assets to restore the market competition.[28] In reality, MOFCOM has never imposed non-monetary penalties on failure to file cases. Since May 2014, MOFCOM has started to publish its penalty decisions on failure to file, and by the end of 2018, forty-eight companies[29] have been publicly named, and fined, among which thirty-one are domestic, including twenty-one State Owned Enterprises (*see* Figure 15.12).

27. *See*, e.g., Mr. Lefu Xu, a deputy director general of SAMR's Anti-Monopoly Bureau mentioned in a competition forum held in September 2018 that: "enforcement of non-compliance with merger notification is among SAMR's priorities."
28. *See*, AML, Article 48.
29. When a company was fined for more than one time, we counted the times it was fined as proxy of numbers of companies. For example, if a company was fined twice, we counted it as two companies.

Figure 15.12 Types of Companies Penalized for Failure to Notify

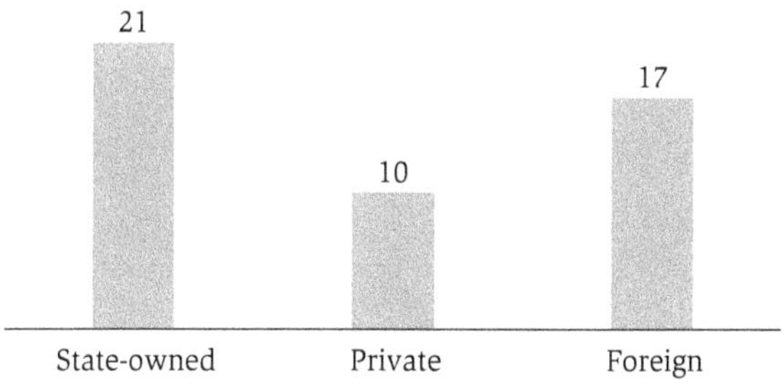

In terms of types of cases, as shown by Figure 15.13, the most frequently penalized type of case is establishment of joint ventures. All the rest of the cases involved share purchase, among which a frequently penalized type is the multi-step share purchase. In the decision on Canon's acquisition of Toshiba Medical, MOFCOM found that the multi-step deal structure that delayed the filing obligation could not protect Canon from failure-to-notify penalty. In that transaction, the deal was split into two steps: first, the target transferred all voting shares to a special purpose vehicle ("SPV"), and one non-voting share and warrants to Canon (the first step was completed immediately upon signing of the two sales and purchase agreements between Toshiba with the SPV and with Canon, respectively); second, Canon would exercise the warrants (involving payment of a nominal fee) and convert them into ordinary shares, while Toshiba would buy back and cancel the voting shares from the SPV and the non-voting share from Canon. Canon filed the transaction with MOFCOM after completing the first step. However, MOFCOM took the view that Canon should have filed before the completion the first step and imposed a fine of RMB 300,000 on Canon. Notably, the EC opened an investigation for the same transaction and the Japanese Fair Trade Commission also issued a public warning to Canon. This case demonstrates that MOFCOM has been taking a hard stance towards using multi-step deal structure to delay or avoid filing obligation.

Figure 15.13 Types of Failure to Notify Cases

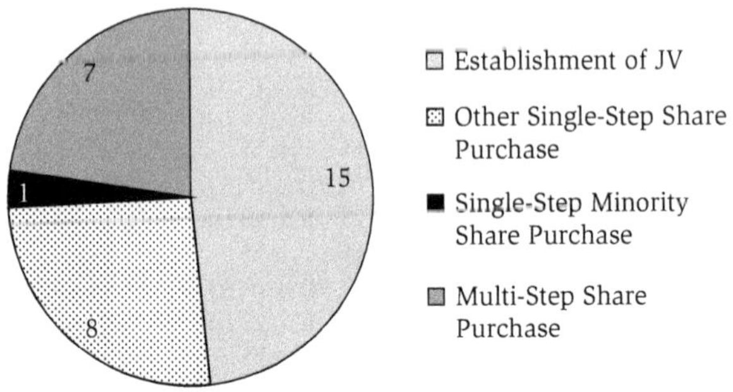

§15.08 EXPANDED INTERNATIONAL COOPERATION

MOFCOM has been actively promoting international cooperation. As shown in Figure 15.14, to date, MOFCOM has signed a memorandum of understanding (MoU) on antitrust cooperation with the antitrust authorities in the US, EU, United Kingdom, Spain, Japan, South Korea, India, Russia, Canada, South Africa, Australia, Brazil, and Kenya.

Figure 15.14 International Cooperation—Jurisdictions with Which China Has Sign a MoU

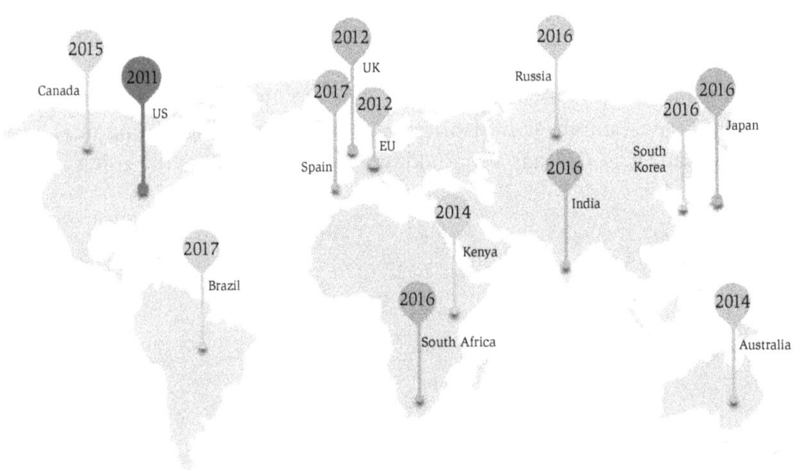

MOFCOM has increasingly cooperated with other antitrust authorities during case review. Confidentiality waiver has been routinely requested by MOFCOM to communicate with other authorities about global transactions. According to a MOFCOM official, from January to August 2017, MOFCOM cooperated with other antitrust authorities in more than eleven cases, including Broadcom/Brocade and Dow/DuPont, representing approximately 5% of the overall cases reviewed.[30] Apart from the EU and the US, MOFCOM also cooperated, during its case review, with antitrust authorities in other jurisdictions, such as South Africa and Russia. Furthermore, the scope of international cooperation in case review has also been broadened to include discussions from market definition and verification of data to substantive competitive analysis.[31]

In addition to cooperation on actual cases, MOFCOM also maintains antitrust related communications with international organizations, such as American Bar Association, Organization for Economic Co-operation and Development, United Nations Conference on Trade and Development, and Asia-Pacific Economic Cooperation, and continues participating in antitrust cooperation projects that aiming to foster convergence of competition policies (e.g., the EU-China Competition Week).

§15.09 AGENCY INTEGRATION

In May 2018, at the dawn of AML's tenth anniversary, China's merger control review department (within MOFCOM) was integrated with China's another two antitrust agencies, the antitrust branch of the National Development and Reform Commission ("NDRC") which was in charge of price-related investigations, and the antitrust branch of the State Administration for Industry and Commerce ("SAIC") which was in charge of non-price related investigations, into a newly-established agency, namely the SAMR. This integration is part of China's overall cabinet reshuffle.

Officially established in April 2018, SAMR consists of twenty-seven bureaus and departments, including the AMB in charge of antitrust enforcement, both merger and non-merger cases. In addition to antitrust, SAMR also assumes a wide range of other market supervision related functions, such as consumer protection, cooperate registration, quality supervision, food safety, and intellectual property protection.

The new authority is headed by Mr. Mao Zhang, the former minister of SAIC. Ms. Lin Gan, a former vice minister of SAIC, was appointed to be the vice minister of SAMR overseeing the AMB. Mr. Zhenguo Wu, the former head of merger control agency, was appointed as the Director General of AMB. AMB has four deputy director generals, three from previous antitrust positions in MOFCOM, SAIC, and NDRC respectively and one from a non-antitrust position in another agency integrated into SAMR. As shown in Figure 15.15, AMB has approximately forty-five staff and ten divisions, including, three merger review divisions, three investigation divisions, a supervision and enforcement division, and a competition policy and international cooperation division. Although the vast majority of the merger review staff were transferred from MOFCOM to SAMR, there are some staff who did not have merger control review experience but were appointed to the merger review divisions.

30. The speech given by Mr. Lefu Xu, a then director at MOFCOM, in the 2017 China competition policy forum held in Shanghai on August 30–31 2017. *See*, MOFCOM Expands Its Cooperation With Other International Antitrust Enforcers On Merger Cases, Mlex, August 30, 2017.
31. *Id.*

Figure 15.15 Organizational Structure of SAMR's AMB

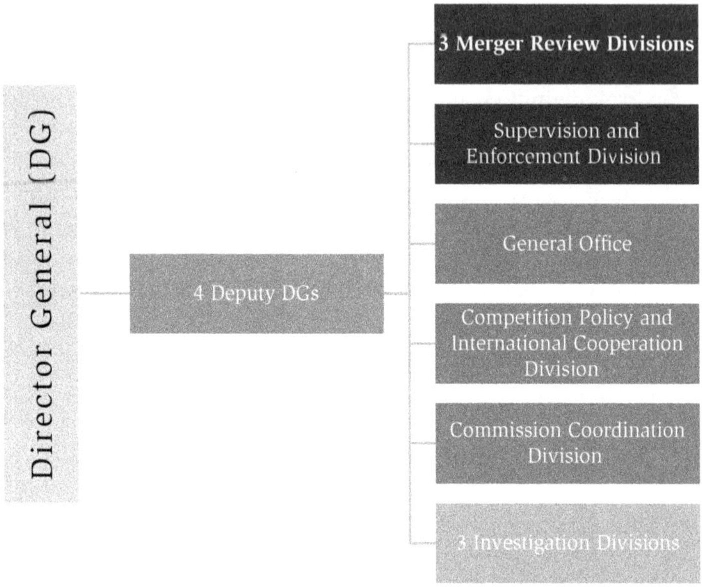

In November 2018, SAMR announced that the integration at central level is understood to have been complete, and the integration at local level is expected to complete by year end.[32]

The integration is expected to streamline and further bolster antitrust enforcement and to improve consistency in antitrust rule-making and enforcement practices. SAMR indicated that its antitrust enforcement priorities are administrative monopolies, infringements by public utilities, failure to notify, and remedy implementation.

§15.10 CONCLUSION

China's merger control enforcement has been evolving quickly in the recent years. Although many efforts have been made to improve its efficiency and transparency, China's merger control review still demonstrates its distinct characteristics. It remains to be seen whether the new antitrust authority SAMR will be able to make faster progress on the way to international antitrust enforcement convergence.

32. *See*, the speech given by Ms. Lin Gan, the vice minister of SAMR in charge of antitrust work, at the AML Tenth Anniversary Press Conference.

CHAPTER 16

Argentine Competition Law and Policy: To Be a Public Policy or Not to Be

Pablo Trevisán[*]

'It is preferable to be poor in a rich empire,

than to be rich in a poor empire.'

Valerius Maximus[1]

§16.01 INTRODUCTION

The Argentine Constitution deals with the fundamental organizational design of the state and government. It formulates the goals that are intended to be achieved and indicates what it considers the adequate means for this purpose; it also establishes the mechanisms of limitation, control, coordination and reciprocal cooperation of the governing bodies and recognizes the fundamental rights that are attributed to citizens and social groups.

From this perspective, there are many points of contact that can be established between the Constitution and the design, execution and evaluation of public policies, such as that of the defence of competition.

The defence of competition has constitutional status in Argentina, since section 42 of the Constitution establishes that the authorities will provide 'the defence of

* The opinions expressed herein are strictly personal and do not necessarily reflect those of the CNDC.

1. Cited in Saint Thomas of Aquinas' *Summa Theologiae*, in the reply to Objection 2, of Article 10, Question 47 'Of Prudence Considered in Itself', of the 'Treatise on Prudence and Justice', in the Second Part of the Second Part (QQ. 1-189), Benziger Bros. Ed., 1947.

competition against all forms of market distortion' and 'the control of natural and legal monopolies'.

Although our country has a long competition law tradition, it is also true that the execution of its norms and the application of its principles have fluctuated, in more or less, according to the times, and we still have not achieved a deep-rooted culture of genuine and consolidated competition law enforcement towards the interior of our society.

Argentina has had some kind of competition law for almost a century. In 1923, the first antitrust law was enacted following the model of the Sherman Act of the United States (US). That law was reformed in 1946. Neither of them had a significant application.

In 1980, the first comprehensive law on competition was introduced through Law 22,262, which created the National Commission for the Defence of Competition (CNDC) and established criminal sanctions.

An important reform took place in 1999, through the enactment of Law 25,156, which created an independent authority, the Competition Defence Tribunal (TDC) - which was never put into operation - and introduced a merger control system in Argentina.

An unfortunate reform took place in 2014, through Law 26,993, which abolished the TDC and introduced some inconvenient reforms to Law 25,156.

With the change of government in December 2015, the CNDC was given the responsibility of drafting a new competition bill. The CNDC published its final draft bill in August 2016. During the drafting sessions, comments and suggestions were provided by legislators, academics and professionals, both local and international. The bill had two main objectives in mind: (i) Argentina's return to international best practices; and (ii) to do so in the light of good and bad local experiences in the application of competition rules during the previous decade in Argentina.

In August 2016, the CNDC launched a public consultation, which received valuable comments and proposals that, once reviewed and analysed, allowed the CNDC to improve the bill.

On 27 September 2016, the bill was finally presented to Congress.[2] The Lower Chamber approved the bill on 22 November 2017. On 18 April 2018, the Senate approved the bill with some minor changes, for which it returned to the Lower Chamber, which finally approved the bill, promulgating the new Competition Law 27,442[3] (the 'LDC'), on 9 May 2018. On 23 May, the Executive Power regulated the LDC through Decree 480/2018.[4] The LDC entered into force on 25 May 2018.

2. In that act, the project of the CNDC was presented as the unification of two bills of antitrust law that had been presented to the Congress in May 2016 by Legislators Carrió and Negri (the latter had made a re-entry of a project that he had presented in 2014 together with Deputy Lousteau, a project that had lost parliamentary status). For this reason, when referring to the project - from then on - the media made reference to the 'Carrió-Negri Project'.
3. Law 27,442: http://servicios.infoleg.gob.ar/infolegInternet/anexos/310000-314999/310241/norma.htm.
4. Decree 480/2018: http://servicios.infoleg.gob.ar/infolegInternet/anexos/310000-314999/310663/norma.htm.

The authorities of the CNDC participated in several of these discussions, explaining the main changes proposed, both at the Lower Chamber[5] and at the Senate.[6]

It is important to note that the LDC addresses all the recommendations included in the conclusions of Organisation for Economic Co-operation and Development's (OCED's) peer review on Argentine competition law and policy of 2006[7] (as reviewed in 2012), as well as those of United Nations Conference on Trade and Development's (UNCTAD's) Voluntary Peer Review of 2016.[8]

The new LDC introduces important changes and, undoubtedly, constitutes the main reform to the Argentine antitrust system of the last almost twenty years. As a result of these changes, our country once again has a strong legislation on the subject and in line with the best international practices.

Among the most important changes, the following should be highlighted:

(i) Institutional revamp, through (a) the creation of a new authority, the National Competition Authority (the 'ANC'), more independent and with renewed powers, and (b) the creation of a Specialized Chamber on Competition Matters within the Civil and Commercial Federal Court of Appeals (the 'Chamber') for judicial review[9];
(ii) Greater deterrence to fight anticompetitive conducts, through (a) the updating and significant increase of applicable sanctions, with a more burdensome criteria for their determination than those established by its predecessor, Law 25,156, (b) the creation of a modern leniency programme and (c) the establishment of new rules for private damages enforcement; and
(iii) Better optimization of resources, through (a) the establishment of a real ex ante merger control, which corrects the incentives for this type of control; and (b) updating and improving the method for calculating notification thresholds for such economic concentrations, which will allow the ANC to concentrate its efforts only on those transactions that may actually have an effect on the general economic interest, allowing it to concentrate enough efforts in the fight against anticompetitive conducts.

5. Session of Deputies of 22 November, 2017: https://www4.hcdn.gob.ar/sesionesxml/provisorias/135-20.htm; *See also*: *Analizaron el proyecto de ley de Defensa de la Competencia*, ÁMBITO, 30 May 2017, http://www.ambito.com/884759-analizaron-el-proyecto-de-ley-de-defensa-de-la-competencia.
6. Comisión de Derechos y Garantías, Argentine Senate: https://www.youtube.com/watch?v=RIzZjObbvoU; http://www.senado.gov.ar/prensa/16137/noticias; Trevisán, Pablo (@pabstw), TWITTER (22 March 2018, 10:41 hrs.), https://twitter.com/pabstw/status/976876577299550210; Trevisán, Pablo (@pabstw), TWITTER (7 April 2018, 6:27 hrs.), https://twitter.com/pabstw/status/982610742452113408.
7. Country Studies, *Argentina – Peer Review of Competition Law and Policy*, 43–51 OCDE y BID (2006).
8. Berenguer, Luis, *Voluntary Peer Review of Competition Law and Policy – Argentina*, UNCTAD 28, 2017.
9. On 22 August 2018, the Commission for the Selection of Magistrates and the Judicial School of the Council of the Magistracy (Consejo de la Magistratura, in Spanish) published in the Official Gazette the call to Public Competition of Opposition and Antecedents, to cover the three positions of Vocal in the Specialized Chamber in Competition Matters of the Civil and Commercial Federal Court of Appeals.

The LDC is the product of great efforts and political consensus,[10] being the best possible law that our country could have in its current economic-political context and in the state of development in the matter.

For future discussions, questions will remain as to whether it would be advisable to reinstate in our country specific criminal sanctions of imprisonment for certain anticompetitive conducts[11]; or if the institutional design should enjoy greater independence from the central administration,[12] to name two issues that are likely to merit further treatment and analysis in the near future.

The purpose of this chapter is to analyse briefly the present and future challenges under Argentine competition law and policy enforcement, after the essential – but only initial – milestone that implies the entry into force of the new LDC. In this framework, we examine the present or immediate challenges, such as putting in operation the new ANC, the implementation of the leniency programme and dealing with a transitory ex post control. Then we briefly develop the future or long-term challenges, such as those related with greater institutionalism, transparency and due process that should be consolidated in the administrative and judicial procedures for the protection and defence of free competition; the importance of implementing a real ex ante merger control, the challenge of developing a private enforcement system for the reparation of damages caused by anticompetitive infringements under the LDC and the proposal for the incorporation of sanctions of imprisonment as part of the dissuasive arsenal that a competition law and policy system must contain. Finally, we make some final considerations as way of brief conclusions.

§16.02 PRESENT AND FUTURE CHALLENGES: POLICY, NOT POLITICS

The tree is measured by its fruits,[13] they say at the farm. Everything is yet to be seen.

It will be of little use to have a very good legal framework, if its application is far from reasonable. In other words, the LDC will be as good as the application, execution and fulfilment of its spirit, its objectives, its principles and its provisions in practice.

---

10. Trevisán, Pablo (2018-I), *Rebuilding the Argentine Antitrust House While Living in It: A View from the Trenches*, en *Douglas H. Ginsburg, An Antitrust Professor on the Bench – Liber Amicorum, Volume I*, pp. 561–586, Concurrences Review, 2018.
11. The favourable opinion to the incorporation of the same in the LDC is anticipated. In fact, the first draft of the LDC project, under the responsibility of the undersigned, included penalties of imprisonment for up to three years, for cartelization cases in public tenders (bid rigging). Finally, their inclusion in the LDC was not accepted.
12. There are different models of antitrust agencies around the world. Some of the models are more independent than others. Among the known models, we consider with special interest the Chilean model, where the investigating authority, the National Economic Prosecutor's Office, is located under the orbit of the Executive Power, and the body that resolves, the Tribunal (TDLC), is outside said Power, its resolutions being appealable before the Supreme Court of Justice of Chile.
13. Beveraggi de la Serna, Walter, *Bienvenida, Sala Especializada en Defensa de la Competencia*, en *Comentarios a la Ley de Defensa de la Competencia*, in Trevisán – Del Pino – Chamatropulos, Thomson Reuters La Ley, Buenos Aires, 2018.

In this regard, in our country we have experience, of the bad, about what we have already referred to in previous works.[14] In this sense, and without prejudice to consider that the new LDC is the most important and initial step for Argentina to return to a more reasonable, solid and predictable competition policy, the reality indicates that much of it depends on the consistent, coherent and systematic implementation of its rules.

In this context, it should be understood that the right to a free competition, among other things, reflects the state's willingness to intervene in economic activities, encouraging companies to shape their practices with a broader objective: the execution of a competitive market, where consumers may buy products of good quality and at reasonable prices.

[A] Present Challenges

Immediate Establishment of the New ANC and Due Respect of the Institutional Design Created by the LDC

During the entire duration of Law 25,156, as the TDC was never established and put into operation, a legal scandal took place - in the words of the different Courts of Appeals[15] and the Argentine Supreme Court of Justice (CSJN).

14. Trevisán, Pablo (2018-II), *Due Process and Competition Law: Global Principles, Local Challenges, An Argentine Perspective*, in *Frédéric Jenny Liber Amicorum, Standing Up for Convergence and Relevance in Antitrust*, Concurrences Review, 2018.
15. There have been several judicial cases that made reference to this situation. To name a few:

   - CNCont. Adm. Fed., Room III, 16 April 2007, in the *Multicanal* ruling, analyzing and ruling on whether the CNDC had the power to issue precautionary measures, said that this does not arise from section 35 or of section 58 LDC, concluding that 'until the TNDC is constituted, the issuance of precautionary measures finds coverage only in the memorandum art. 24 inc. m) LDC, according to which the competent judge may request the precautionary measures deemed appropriate ... can not be admitted that in the administrative procedure the administrative body - for lack of constitution of the TNDC - is at the same time party and judge within a same cause. Pretend that the administrative body has jurisdictional powers and can issue precautionary measures against the republican principle of separation of powers, and the entity that did incur excessive power.'
   - CNCiv. and COM. Fed., Room II, on 27 July 2009, in the case of *Telefónica/Telecom*, it maintained a similar criterion to that of Room II in *Multicanal*: that '... power ... of Section 35 LDC ... is attributed to an administrative tribunal that has not yet been constituted and that has certain guarantees of independence regarding its constitution and operation'.
   - CNAPE, Room A, on 21 October 2009, also within the framework of Telefónica/Telecom held that '... the exercise of a judicial function by a body of the EP, ... violates the provision of Section 109 of the CN (...) the delay incurred in the integration of the administrative court constitutes a legal scandal'.
   - CNCiv. and COM. Fed., Room II, on 19 February 2010, in Cablevisión case, stated that 'in accordance with the criteria established by the Chamber in other cases, the CNDC would not have powers to issue precautionary measures under the terms of Section 35 of the LDC (conf. "Telecom Italia SpA and other") (...). The CNDC has not received all the powers that Law 25,156 places at the head of the TNDC.' Adding that 'this House has recently highlighted the omission incurred by the Executive Power in constituting the TNDC - superior to ten years -, which is why it put this circumstance in the knowledge of the president of the Supreme Court of Justice of the Nation in order to consider

Undoubtedly, the enforcement authority of the old Law 22,262, dependent on the National Executive Power, lacked the powers and independence that the legislator of 1999 intended to grant to a body of the characteristics designed for the TDC of Law 25,156.[16] It should also be noted that the legislator of Law 25,156 had wanted to keep the enforcement authority of Law 22,262 - that is, the CNDC and the Secretary of Commerce - in an exclusively transitory nature[17] and until the TDC was put into operation,[18] situation that became permanent,[19] until the disappearance of all traces of the TDC after the enactment of Law 26,993[20] in 2014. It is hoped that this will not happen again under the new LDC, and that the new ANC will settle and start up sooner rather than later.

These and other factors clearly indicate that the mere existence of a good antitrust legal regime does not guarantee the effective application of the antitrust policy.[21] This is one of the main immediate competition enforcement challenges, after the recent enactment of the LDC.

measures or procedures that may be deemed appropriate, aimed at favoring the constitution of the aforementioned court' (Cfr. Acordada N° 16/09, of 2.12.09). In a similar way, Room A of the CNAPE sent a similar communication to the Supreme Court of a similar tenor (conf. 'Telefónica de España, Olimpia and others.').
- Cám. Nac. Civ. And Com. Fed., Room 2, 25 February 2010, in Direct TV, insists on emphasizing the obligation to establish the TNDC.

16. The autarky of the TDC was one of the issues that had greater approval in the National Congress when the sanction of the LDC was discussed. Similarly, one of the most criticized points during said debate was, incidentally, the lack of independence of the previous body constituted under the predecessor Law 22,262. Beyond the abundant parliamentary precedents that are fruitful to fully interpret the intention of the legislator, it is enough to analyse carefully the terms of section 18 of the LDC to conclude that there are no doubts regarding the intention to provide the TDC with an independence of criteria of the National Executive Power which, for natural reasons, lacked and will lack the CNDC/SCI. Said section 18 states: 'The National Competition Defense Tribunal shall be composed of seven (7) members with sufficient background and suitability to hold office, of which at least two shall be lawyers and two other professionals in economic sciences, all of them with more than five (5) years in the exercise of the profession. The members of the court will have exclusive dedication during their mandate, with the exception of the teaching activity'.
17. LDC, section 58: 'Law 22,262 is repealed. Notwithstanding the foregoing, the cases in process at the date of entry into force of this law shall continue to be processed in accordance with its provisions before the enforcement body of said law, which shall remain in force until the establishment and operation of the National Tribunal for the Defense of Competition. Likewise, it will understand in all the causes promoted from the entry into force of this law. Once the Tribunal is constituted, the causes shall be referred to it for the purpose of continuing with the substantiation thereof.'
18. Trevisán, Pablo, *La Creación y Puesta en Funcionamiento del Tribunal Nacional de Defensa de la Competencia No Permite Mayores Dilaciones*, El Cronista, 23 March 2010, Buenos Aires.
19. Trevisán, Pablo (2014-I), *Política de Defensa de la Competencia: Un Debate Pendiente*, El Cronista, 1 September 2014, Buenos Aires.
20. Trevisán, Pablo (2014-II), *Competencia: Otra Oportunidad Perdida*, El Cronista, 1 October 2014, Buenos Aires.
21. Gal, Michal, *The Ecology of Antitrust – Preconditions for Competition Law Enforcement in Developing Countries*, in COMPETITION, COMPETITIVENESS AND DEVELOPMENT 20–58, 21 (UNCTAD, 2004).

In the first place, it is not unreasonable to clarify that the jurisdictional activity of the administration, as established by the CSJN,[22] is one in which the organs or officials of the Administration exercise jurisdictional functions[23] that, in the normal order of the institutions, correspond to the judges of the Judicial Power.

In this sense, regarding the jurisdictional content of the administrative act, it must be remembered that the CSJN admitted the performance of administrative bodies with jurisdiction, after establishing with particular emphasis that the validity of the procedures of said bodies was subject to the pertinent laws allowing an expeditious subsequent judicial instance, thus avoiding the objection that may arise from section 109 of the Constitution. The appropriate means to get the respective judicial body to review the decision of the administrative jurisdiction is the appeal.

The institutional design of Argentina's competition policy required total re-engineering, since the ANC has historically lacked certain basic attributes.

As mentioned earlier, Argentina has a long tradition of antitrust legislation, although it has a huge debt related to the vigorous compliance with its policies and the correct execution of its written regulations. One of the main causes of this situation is due to the permanent lack of impartiality and independence of its enforcement authority.

Integrated institutions, such as the Argentine case, raise the concern that the integration of investigative, execution and adjudication functions may create bias or lack of objectivity, or the appearance thereof, in the performance of adjudicative or resolution functions granted to such agencies.

When we refer to an independent authority, we refer to an authority with greater autonomy of the central power, its own budget, stability of its members - who must be eminently technical and suitable for the position - and, definitely, with sufficient essential faculties and capacities that allow it to combat anticompetitive behaviours and promote the benefits of free competition.[24]

The proposed institutional system is one of the main innovations of the LDC, as confirmed by the recent UNCTAD Voluntary Peer Review,[25] commenting on the - by then - draft bill of the LDC. As mentioned previously, it is expected that the new NCA will soon replace the current transitory application authority (i.e., the CNDC and the Secretary of Commerce).

The ANC will be formed by two Secretariats, one for conducts and one for concentrations, which will investigate the cases, and the Tribunal for the Defence of Competition, as a collegiate body of decision making. Through this institutional design, a clear separation of the investigative and execution functions of the resolutive functions is guaranteed, also addressing one of the main criticisms presented by the current applicable framework.

22. Fallos, T. 248, pp. 516-518, in re '*Martín Aberg Cobo*', among others.
23. Fallos, T. 247, pp. 646 y ss., paragraph 17, in re '*Elena Fernández Arias y otros c/José Poggio*'.
24. Kovacic, William E. & Hyman, David A., *Competition Agency Design: What's on the Menu?*, GW Law Faculty Publications and Other Works, Paper 628 (2012).
25. Berenguer, Luis, *Voluntary Peer Review of Competition Law and Policy – Argentina*, UNCTAD 28, 2017.

The system by which the members of the ANC must be elected is transparent and contains the necessary elements to avoid the possibility of arbitrary appointments or appointments of members that can be considered as accommodating to the political power.

Once the ANC is put into operation in the administrative sphere, in parallel with the constitution and operation of the Chamber in the judicial orbit, a promissory integral institutional design will have been put into operation that, among other benefits, will allow the ANC and its authorities to gradually improve their resolutions, making them issue responsible and highly reasoned decisions that must be able to pass the control of the judicial review that the Chamber will make about it.[26]

Implementation of the Leniency Programme

Chapter VIII of the LDC establishes a modern leniency programme. From the mid-1990s, anti-cartel policy in the European Union ('EU') and the US owes part of its success to the existing leniency programmes in those two jurisdictions.

The companies participating in cartels are generally aware that their conduct is illegal and, through all kinds of manoeuvres, try to keep it secret and avoid being detected by the antitrust authorities. An important tool for competition authorities is the possibility of granting leniency to 'whistle-blowers'.

The leniency programme generates incentives for defection and therefore modifies the cost-benefit ratio of remaining in the anticompetitive arrangement, increasing the risk of being denounced. For that reason, in addition, risks increase and it becomes less attractive to be part of a cartel. The main reason to take refuge in a leniency programme, after all, is that the probability or the sanction or both are as sufficiently great so to induce to the denunciation and rupture of the cartel.[27]

When a company applies to the programme and provides information about a cartel, it increases the marginal or incremental cost of the other members of the cartel since it imposes the payment of the fine. Given this, of course, the leniency programme has or should have dissuasive effects.

Section 60 of the LDC establishes the essential conditions for the operation of the leniency programme, which to a large extent is in line with the similar programme in

26. OECD (2016), *The resolution of competition matters by specialized and general jurisdiction bodies: Balance of international experiences*: 'In this sense, a specialized jurisdictional body that correctly fulfills its role, which consists in monitoring that the authority's actions adheres to the current regulations, and revoke their decisions when there are flawed aspects in them, can also have an effect on the quality of the decisions of the competition authorities. That is, the cumulative effect of the number of findings made by the court may, in fact, affect the exercise of the functions of the authority and in that sense affect its operation and results. Therefore, the authority's learning curve can lead to good decisions, based on solid evidence and the rule of law, which will generally be less likely to be overturned by the specialized court.'
27. Theoretical studies are (with limits) conclusive in that leniency programmes generate incentives to destabilize cartels and that they are effective tools to discourage the formation of cartels. Motta and Polo (2003) and Spagnolo (2003), Aubert, Kovacic and Rey (2006), Chen and Harrington (2007), Harrington (2008) and Hinloopen and Soetevent (2008). *See also*, Hinloopen, J., and Soetevent, A.R. *Laboratory Evidence on the Effectiveness of Corporate Leniency Programs*, RAND Journal of Economics, (2008); 39 (2); 607–616.

force in the EU.[28] Likewise, such section 60 establishes the so-called leniency plus, a mechanism that does not exist in the EU, but does exist in the USA, and in the United Kingdom, whereby a company that was under investigation in relation to a certain cartel and reports on the existence of another different cartel, could obtain a reduction of up to one third of the fine it has to pay in relation to the first.

Section 61 of the LDC provides that human persons can benefit from leniency applications of a company, in cases where there may be personal liability under section 58 of the LDC. Something similar happens in the United Kingdom, where natural persons can be protected by the request for immunity from their employer.[29]

The introduction of the leniency programme is accompanied by a very necessary and high increase in sanctions, one of the conditions for its effectiveness. Also, other tools, such as greater independence and powers of the agency and other reforms that should increase the effectiveness of the agency, increasing the probability of detection, for which another important element highlighted by the literature is fulfilled. The cultural tradition and the quality of the institutions in general, can affect the effectiveness of the programme, but regarding the former it is auspicious, at least, the success of these programmes in most of these countries and in particular those that have similar traditions and close business cultural values, such as Mexico, Chile or Brazil.

The new leniency programme is an important step in the evolution of competition law enforcement in Argentina. The challenge for the ANC will be to make it work in practice, something whose difficulty has not been underestimated and the learning curve during this process will be important, both for the authority and for the business community.

Dealing with the Ex-Post Merger Control System

The rationale for merger control is to prevent mergers that may result, with high probability, in a detriment to the general economic interest, by decreasing the levels of rivalry in the markets.

In the US, there is a long tradition in the matter. Section 7 of the Clayton Act of 1914 prohibited mergers and acquisitions that affect or reduce competition. Then the Hart Scott Rodino Act was sanctioned in 1976 in that country so that agencies can carry out an ex-ante control, that is, prior to the completion of the operation. The central idea is that blocking or restoring competition once an anticompetitive concentration has been carried out is, like when trying to unscramble the eggs, too complex, if not impossible.

28. OJ (2006) C: 298/17. In the EU, the Commission adopted the '*Communication on leniency policy*' in 1996. Under this communication, full immunity is guaranteed to the first company of a cartel that provides information to the Commission allowing it to carry out an inspection or discover a violation of Section 101 of the TFEU. Conditions for access to the immunity guarantee must be met, including cooperation that is genuine, continuous and expeditious; abandonment of cartel activity, unless the Commission considers that continuing involvement is useful for preparing inspections; and there must be no destruction, falsification or concealment of relevant evidence. There is a system of indicators to determine who is entitled to immunity. Companies that provide the Commission with more relevant evidence may be entitled to reductions in their fines.
29. *Applications for leniency and no-action in cartel case*, OFT 1495, July 2013.

Although it consists of a preventive type procedure, the ideal of the merger control procedure would be that it operates prior to the consummation of the economic concentration and not a posteriori as, to a large extent, it happens under the conduct regime. The costs to be avoided, associated with an ex-post control, are too high for society when it is determined that a certain operation must be blocked or conditioned, after its consummation.

The problem with a control system that works ex-post, as in practice happened in Argentina, product of a misapplication of section 8 of Law 25,156 and other systemic failures, such as the direct and indirect consequences of never putting in place the independent tribunal, created in 1999, is that it introduces a large part of the costs and eliminate, to a large extent, the benefits of a preventive or ex-ante prospective procedure, making the procedure less attractive and inefficient, and in many cases useless.

Under a genuine ex-ante control system, the parties have important incentives to cooperate since the delay in providing the relevant information to the agency runs at their expense, since until the competition authority's approval is not issued, the transaction in question cannot close or consummate. That is, the delay resulting from the lack of information and full collaboration with the enforcement authority is paid by the companies involved.

In an ex-post control system, costs increase and delays in procedures are often frequent, largely because there are no necessary incentives for the procedure to conclude in a short time, thus increasing private costs and, worse, the public costs of an ex-post control procedure.

One of the main benefits, then, is to prevent anticompetitive concentrations by preserving the status prior to the concentration, a situation that is not verified with the possible high costs that adopting structural remedies would imply – after the consummation of the transaction under analysis –, which can be costly for the parties and society in general. After the firms are integrated, it would be highly costly, if not impossible, to impose a structural remedy, after, for example, the closure of a factory, the discontinuity of production of certain products, the joint use of distribution networks, or any other of these measures that might be impossible to roll back.

We believe that under the new LDC, prior to the establishment of a full ex-ante merger control, two serious avoidable errors have been committed:

> The first, in our opinion, consists of the introduction of a transitory scheme of subsistence of the previous merger control system of the Law 25,156, until one year after the start of operations of the new ANC.[30]
>
> In this regard, we consider that there were no sufficient or well-founded reasons to incorporate such a scheme in the new LDC. During the discussion of the LDC project, some voices argued that the inclusion of said transitory regime was necessary, due to the long resolution times of merger control cases

30. Section 81, LDC: 'The regulation of this law shall establish the conditions under which the processing of the files initiated shall continue under the terms established in chapter III of law 25,156.'

of the enforcement authority under the previous Law 25,156. On the contrary, we have sustained that it was important to make an immediate change, leaving aside the harmful ex-post control, and turn to a real ex-ante control, considering that the conditions were absolutely given for it.

In sustaining this, we indicated two factual arguments that are absolutely verifiable: one, what happened in Brazil, whose economy is significantly larger than that of Argentina, and that, at the time of the reform of its merger control system in 2012 towards an ex-ante one, counted with statistics and experiences very similar to those of Argentina in 2015; and, mainly, what happened in Argentina between the end of 2015 and May 2018, when the new law was passed.

In Brazil, despite the bad omens of the Brazilian business sector at that time, from 2012 onwards the competition authority of that country managed to significantly reduce the times of its merger control processes, to the point that – to date – Brazil has a review average from beginning to end of this type of cases of no more than twenty-five days, being up to the best international practices.

On the other hand, in our country, and even under the application of Law 25,156 whose thresholds were absolutely out of date, the enforcement authority managed to reduce very significantly the review periods for these procedures; specifically, from an average of more than three and a half years, to December 2015, at an average of just over three months, to May 2018.

That is, like Brazil in 2012 but with the advantage that our country had already significantly improved the indicators before sanctioning the new LDC, Argentina was already prepared to go directly to an ex-ante control, without the need for a transitional ex-post regime.

Second, and unnecessarily complicating matters even more, Decree 480/2018 introduces through the last sentence of its section 84 a change that may have gone unnoticed by some, but that further deepens the issue, by suspending the application of the third paragraph of section 9 of Law 27,442.[31] Beyond considering that in this point Decree 480/2018 may have exceeded its scope by modifying a law promulgated by the National Congress, in practice, it means that in Argentina – and until a year after the new ANC is put in place – we will have an ex-post merger control system as never seen in our country, with all the previously mentioned '*contraindications*'. Based on the provisions of section 84 of said Decree, the notifying parties, without doubt, may – from then on, not only close transactions, but also consummate them, previously and independently of the intervention of the competition authority. This is an unnecessary absurdity, in our opinion.

31. Section 9, Third Paragraph, LDC: 'The acts of economic concentration that are concluded in breach of the provisions of this section, as well as the consummation of the takeover without the prior approval of the Competition Tribunal, shall be sanctioned by said Tribunal as an infraction, under the terms of Section 55, paragraph d) of this law, without prejudice to the obligation to reverse them and remove all its effects in the case in which it is determined that it has been reached by the prohibition of Section 8 of this law.'

Under the previous legislation, Law 25,156, it was provided that the notification could be filed after (up to a week) the takeover of the company in question. *A contrario sensu* of the recurrent interpretation made by the enforcement authority in this point, we have always sustained[32] that the wording of the first paragraph of section 8 of Law 25,156 was procedural in nature, and indicated when the procedural formality should be complied with to notify a concentration transaction. However, the second sentence of section 8, which was of a substantial nature, provided that the operation brought to the attention of the enforcement authority could not have effects between the parties and with respect to third parties until the authority resolves in this regard. That is, although under an unhappy wording, former Law 25,156 allowed closing the operation prior to notification, but – in light of the second sentence of section 8 – it did not allow the consummation of such operation, until the authority's resolution.

Regrettably, even though the intention of the LDC is clearly to go towards an ex-ante concentration control, during the transition phase an ex-post control will be applied that is extremely more ex-post than that which existed during the validity of Law 25,156. Undoubtedly, we consider that this will be one of the main immediate challenges that will have to be dealt with under the new LDC, until the ANC is put into operation and the ex-ante control is fully operational.

Interpretation of the Scope of Section 2 of the LDC

Section 2[33] of the LDC establishes the presumption of illegality of certain horizontal agreements. Strictly speaking, this had already been clearly established through case law,[34] which is why some consider that the incorporation of this presumption of section 2 was unnecessary. However, we consider that the inclusion is positive, especially in regard to placing special emphasis on the spirit of the new LDC, that aims to give a clear message to the whole society, regarding the extreme seriousness of these types of behaviours and, in particular, regarding the priorities set by the legislator for the enforcement authority of the LDC with respect to horizontal agreements between competitors.

Basically, according to the wording of LDC's novel section 2, it is presumed that the agreements for the fixing of prices, limiting of production, division of markets or collusion in bids cause a serious damage to the general economic interest.

32. Trevisán, Pablo (2018-I), *supra*, p. 583, Concurrences Review, 2018.
33. Section 2, LDC: 'It shall constitute absolutely restrictive practices of competition and are presumed to cause harm to the general economic interest, agreements between two or more competitors, consisting of contracts, agreements or arrangements whose object or effect is: a) Agree on directly or indirectly, the sale or purchase price of goods or services that are offered or demanded in the market; b) Establish obligations to (i) produce, process, distribute, buy or market only a limited or limited amount of goods, and/or (ii) provide a restricted or limited number, volume or frequency of services; c) Distribute, divide, assign or impose horizontally zones, portions or segments of markets, customers or sources of supply; d) Establish, arrange or coordinate positions or abstention in tenders, contests or auctions. These agreements will be null and void and, consequently, will not produce any legal effect.'
34. This, both through various Opinions (513/2005, 510/2005, 986/2015, etc.) of the CNDC (confirmed by the respective Resolutions of the Secretary of Commerce), as well as by related rulings of the different Courts of Appeals (CNACyCF and CNPE).

The result of this presumption is that it will not be necessary for the Antitrust Tribunal to demonstrate that such agreements harm competition: the law presumes such harm. The intention is that by reducing the burden of proof, it will be easier for the Tribunal to arrive at convictions in cartel cases.

The presumption contained in section 2 of the LDC is not *iure et de iure*, but is of a *iuris tantum* nature, that is, admits evidence to the contrary or, in other words, allows the parties to the presumptive cartel agreement to refute it, producing proof that there is no harm to the general economic interest[35]; however, the burden of doing so weighs on them and not on the Tribunal.

Consequently, and contrary to what some authors have said when commenting on the new LDC, we consider that section 2 of the LDC does not introduce a per se rule as the term is used, for example, in the US. In that country, a horizontal agreement whose hard core is price fixing is per se illegal according to section 1 of the Sherman Act in the sense that, if it is proven to exist, it is illegal regardless of whether it could cause economic harm (e.g., price increases) or whether it could be compensated by economic efficiency.[36] To put it another way, some agreements are automatically illegal under US law, without the need to carry out an economic analysis of its effects. Most agreements under US law do not fall into the category of per se illegality, but they must instead be subject to the 'rule of reason', which does require an economic analysis. The agreements in section 2 of the LDC are those that in the US would be per se illegal.

Thus, we could conclude that the wording of section 2 of the LDC responds more to the spirit of section 101 of the Treaty of Rome (TFEU), according to which there would be no per se illegality similar to that of the US.[37] Section 101(1) of the TFEU prohibits agreements that have as their 'object or effect' the prevention, restriction or distortion of competition; section 101(3) of the TFEU provides for the validity of agreements (both those that restrict competition by their purpose and their effect) if the parties can meet the four requirements of that provision, which essentially requires the demonstration of economic efficiencies that will produce a benefit to consumers. Within section 101(1) there are certain agreements that restrict competition 'by its object': in this case an analysis of the effects of the agreement is not required. In other words, there is a presumption that they are caught[38]: this would be analogous to the presumption established in section 2 of the LDC. If an agreement does not restrict competition for its purpose, a full analysis of its effects is required in order to declare it illegal. Any agreement, whether restrictive by object or effect, can be defended

35. Section 29 of the LDC contains a provision that allows the Competition Tribunal to authorize an agreement, including the type established in section 2, if it is not detrimental to the general economic interest.
36. Whish, Richard (2018), *Comment and General Assessment of Law 27,442 of 2018 from a European Competition Law Perspective*, in *Comentarios a la Ley de Defensa de la Competencia*, Trevisán - Del Pino - Chamatropulos, Thomson Reuters La Ley, Buenos Aires, 2018.
37. Whish, Richard (2018), *supra*.
38. Italianer, Alexander, *Competitor Agreements under EU Competition Law* (2013) Fordham Corporate Law Institute (Ed. Hawk), Chapter 2, is emphatic about the possibility of justifying these agreements under section 101 (3) of the TFEU.

according to section 101(3) provided that the parties to the agreement can demonstrate that efficiencies will be obtained.[39]

To the extent that a particular agreement falls within the terms of section 2 of the LDC, the ANC will have the presumption of illegality and will not have to show how the agreement harms competition. If the parties to the agreement are able to demonstrate that the agreement will not harm the general economic interest, it will then be the ANC's responsibility to evaluate the evidence and either estimate it and dismiss the case, or rebut it and issue a decision declaring the violation.

The evolution of this issue will have to be closely monitored in the jurisprudence of both the ANC and the Chamber, in order to determine how the presumption of section 2 of the LDC ends in practice. While some of this has already happened with cases resolved prior to the new LDC, this reaffirmation of the legislator under section 2 of the LDC will determine more clearly that some cartels are so obviously harmful, that it would be reasonable to assume that the parties that conform it will not try to refute the presumption by proving that they are beneficial for the general economic interest, which consequently may lead to the application of other new institutes of the new LDC, such as being eligible for the leniency programme, among others.

[B] Future Challenges

Institutionality and Transparency in the Operation of the ANC to Increase Due Process Guarantees

In addition to strict compliance with the legal framework granted by the LDC, as well as the substantive and procedural rules, it will be essential that the new ANC, as soon as it is put into operation, has its clear internal rules of proceedings that, ultimately, shall allow a more transparent and orderly operation, as well as full respect for the guarantee of due process.

For a process to satisfy the guarantee of due process, it is necessary that it complies with the unavoidable requirement of granting individuals the sufficient opportunity to participate with utility and sufficiency in said process.

We believe that there are some general or minimum guarantees, such as the right to an impartial process[40] and to a speedy process,[41] as well as some more specific

39. *Matra Hachette v. Commission*, Case T-17/93 EU T: 1994: 89, paragraph 85; *see* similarly *Pierre Fabre Dermo-Cosmétique S.A.*, Case C-439/09 EU: C.201: 649, paragraphs 49 and 57; *Beef Industry Development Society*, Case C-209/07 EU: C: 2008: 643; *Glaxo Smith Kline v. Commission*, Cases C-501/06 P etc. EU: C: 2009: 610; and *Pierre Fabre*, Case C-439 *Pierre Fabre Dermo-Cosmétique* EU: C: 2011: 649; *Ski Taxi S.A. v. Government of Norway*, Case E-3/16.
40. The right to an impartial process is one of the main guarantees of due process. This imposes on the authority the scrupulous respect of contradiction in the investigation activity, and the strict observance of the duty to motivate its decisions, through a careful analysis of the evidence produced and the indication of the reasons for its conviction on the facts. Various treaties and international conventions indicate the importance of the process as a guarantee to support and argue rights. This process must meet at least two essential principles: to promote the effectiveness of the jurisdictional service through an unrestricted process and to guarantee that the sentence arrives in due time.

guarantees, like the right of standing,[42] to prove[43] and to appeal,[44] that can help ensure due process under the LDC.

Implement an Ex-Ante Merger Control System

The ex-ante merger control system requires from the enforcement authority greater speed of approval, at the risk of constituting a real limit to the speed of trade.

Successful cases from neighbouring countries with similar backgrounds, such as the one in Brazil mentioned above, show that it is possible to efficiently and timely manage an ex-ante merger control system, in particular by establishing special simplified procedures, without stopping the running of businesses for cases of concentrations that, given certain objective characteristics, do not present competition problems and other additional modifications.

41. The right to a fast process refers to establishing a reasonable time, appropriate to the circumstances of each conflict, but always associated with the principle of procedural economy and effectiveness of the institution. Consequently, the obligation of celerity is assumed as a duty of the jurisdiction, as well as a power of the justiciable. In summary, the result of a process must be pronounced within a period of time compatible with the nature of the litigious object; otherwise, the judicial protection would be illusory, making a certain aphorism that says 'unjust the sentence that judges when it should no longer judge'.
42. The right of access implies both the right of access without restrictions and the right to a useful process, therefore, we think of resolving the dispute in a fair process, not based on sterile rejections supported by ritual provisions, or that the procedural rules act on purely formal operations. There is also a new right here: that the action initiated not only has the effects of the initial movement, but moves and is projected to all instances that lead to the sentence: this is the sense of the right of due process, or judicial protection effective that proclaim other fundamental norms. Argentina, after the reform of its Constitution in 1994, adopted the same philosophy, based on the rights and guarantees established in sections 36–43 of the Constitution; especially, through the right of protection. What distinguishes our right to defenc through this guarantee, the right to an 'effective judicial protection' recognized by Spanish law (section 24, Spanish Constitution), the Italian constitutional law (section 24, Italian Constitution) or the Law Basic of Bonn (section 19.4, German Constitution), arises from a natural fact like the absence of a specific organ of constitutional control as they have in these countries, in such a way that the Argentine norm is more about guaranteeing a kind of rapid response and secure to the rights crisis, instead of safeguarding the internal supremacy of the fundamental construction. After a minimum accreditation of the interest to protect, this right (or procedural guarantee) allows the interested party to open a process that facilitates the discussion of the conflict, avoiding any possibility of making decisions without the possibility of having heard said process.
43. In addition to the proof in its mission to verify and clarify to arrive at the truth, there is a constitutional right to prove. Because of its essential nature, based on the right to due process (since it is a vital part of the exercise of the right of defence), it raises its premises on the solemnities of the procedure to consecrate a 'right to evidence'. The right to evidence is part of due process, as underlined by the jurisprudence of the CSJN. It is important to abandon the idea of proof as an act of the process, to include it within the guarantees of the right of defence and, as such, as a guarantee of adjective due process.
44. The right to appeal implies access to an instance review that opens a new stage in the process, through which the sentence can be modified or revoked. The aggrieved party (that is, the party that has received substantially less sentence than it claimed) can challenge it and reopen the contradictory, to the extent permitted by the procedural order. Since the Pact of San Jose of Costa Rica, and more specifically since the reform of the Constitution of 1994, the right to appeal a resolution or ruling before a judge or a higher court has been reinforced in Argentina.

In this sense, the LDC seeks to increase the efficiency of the procedure, for which it significantly increased the notification thresholds of the previous law,[45] which had been totally out of date and had forced the agency to examine unimportant concentrations, charging costs to the agency and the economy in general.

The LDC establishes a threshold that, in order to avoid becoming obsolete due to inflation, is not set in current national currency, but refers to a unit of account, the so-called Mobile Unit ('UM'). Thus, only those concentrations whose turnover exceeds 100 million UM in Argentina should be notified. This type of threshold is in accordance with international guidelines on the subject in order to focus efforts on operations that, because of their magnitude, may present problems to the general economic interest, avoiding allocating resources to operations that would not have an effect on the general economic interest.

The UM is initially set under the LDC in twenty pesos (ARS 20, which at the time of the enactment of the LDC was the equivalent of almost one US Dollar) and will be updated annually by the enforcement authority, taking as an indicator the consumer price index (CPI) prepared by the National Institute of Statistics and Census. The LDC, therefore, introduces a threshold of ARS 2,000 million (i.e., significantly greater than the ARS 150 million of Law 25,156, effective until May 2018).

Another important measure to gain in efficiency was to adopt a procedure that allows shortening the time to approve simple mergers, something that in fact had begun to be done in practice by the current CNDC, even prior to the enactment of the new LDC.

This happens, for example, when a company that engages in activity B buys another that is engaged in activity C, and when B also does not need C for its production and vice versa. In these cases, known as 'conglomerate', there are rarely competition problems. Same applies when the companies that merge are engaged in the same activity and hold, even jointly, a low market share that indicates that there will be no dominant position in the relevant market.

The LDC also formally introduces previously existing advisory opinions, by which the parties to an operation, when they have doubts about whether to notify a certain operation, may formally consult the ANC as to whether they are required to notify.

The bill also sets out in legal hierarchy the procedures to determine whether uninformed transactions should have been notified. Thus, as was the case with the preliminary proceedings ('diligencias preliminaries', in Spanish) not foreseen but applied under the previous Law 25,156, ex officio or by complaint, the enforcement authority would be allowed to initiate an investigation with the purpose of establishing if certain transaction should have been notified.

It will be interesting to follow the development of this subject, while we anticipate that – by virtue of the reforms introduced to the LDC – the panorama is auspicious, since the authority will have greater resources to concentrate on the most

45. At the time of the promulgation of Law 25,156, the threshold by volume was, in Argentine pesos, equivalent to USD 150 million and, by the mere effect of inflation, at the time of the sanction of the new LDC – i.e., May 2018 – it represented something around USD 7.5 million.

relevant operations and, in addition, it will be able to free up resources that may allow – in parallel – that it concentrate greater efforts in the analysis of the most serious anticompetitive behaviours.

Damages: Develop a Solid System of Private Enforcement

The corrective measures applied by a competition authority – which respond mainly to the general interest of society – provide a certain degree of deterrence against current and potential offenders, although clearly they are not sufficient – by themselves – to achieve, at the same time, the protection of private interests.

In this context, and without losing sight of the fact that the main objective of damages actions in competition matters is mainly a private interest to repair the damages suffered as a consequence of an anticompetitive conduct, it is important to take into account the important dissuasive effect that these actions also present.[46]

This is one of the most important contributions of the new LDC, through the establishment of new guidelines and tools,[47] which, undoubtedly, shall contribute to the reparation of damages produced as a result of anticompetitive acts to stop being a chimera and become a reality.[48]

Thus, the combination and interaction of a renewed implementation of the LDC -both public and private – will also contribute to maintain and restore the integrity of the market, to prevent artificial forces from influencing prices, in the optimal provision of goods and services, in the elimination of entry barriers to markets, in the innovation of competitive products and in the best general welfare of consumers.[49]

46. There is vast comparative doctrine that comments and discusses widely on the real extent of the dissuasive effect of damages actions in competition law, whose analysis exceeds the object of the present work. However, we consider that beyond this discussion, there are no doubts that damages actions present an important additional factor of deterrence in those jurisdictions in which they have presented an important development. For further illustration, please *see*: Rosochowicz, Patricia H., *Deterrence and the Relationship Between Public and Private Enforcement of Competition Law*, International Bar Association, EU Private Litigation Working Group, February 2005; Wils, Wouter P.J., *The Relationship between Public Antitrust Enforcement and Private Actions for Damages*, World Competition, (March 2009); 32 (1).
47. The LDC introduces a whole new chapter in the area of Reparation for Damages, Chapter IX, which goes from sections 62–65.
48. For an in-depth analysis of the subject and the modifications recently introduced in the subject matter in the new LDC, *see* Trevisán, Pablo (2018-III), *Reparación de Daños por Conductas Anticompetitivas a la Luz de la Nueva Ley de Defensa de la Competencia*, in *Comentarios a la Ley de Defensa de la Competencia*, Trevisán – Del Pino – Chamatropulos, Thomson Reuters La Ley, Buenos Aires, 2018.
49. Frederic Jenny, *Optimal Antitrust Enforcement: From Theory to Policy Options*, in I. Lianos and I. Kokkoris, *The Reform of European Competition Law: New Chalenges*, The Hague: Kluwer, 2009. On this point, Frederic Jenny correctly observes the intimate relationship that appears between the sanction of the authority and the compensation of damages, from the dissuasive point of view, even though the beneficiaries of the compensation are different in both cases: 'It does not make a difference if the payments are made to the state budget or to the consumers. Therefore, the current discussion of EU damages actions should take into account the fact that, even if the purpose of private damages actions is to compensate victims rather than punish those who violate the law, the possibility of adding compensatory damages to administrative (or criminal) penalties increases the total cost to violators of being discovered and, consequently, increases the deterrent effect of the execution system'.

The principle of civil liability for which the one who causes an injury must repair it, is fully applicable in the matter of compensation and reparation for anticompetitive acts. The latest reform of the Argentine Civil and Commercial Code extends this principle even more, as case law has previously ruled, establishing that not only is there a duty to repair, but there is also an obligation to avoid causing harm. In previous works we have referred to the prevention of damages in the context of competition law and enforcement, to which we refer the reader, since the subject exceeds the theme of this work.[50]

In practice, it will be the parties and the judges who must carry out a process of adapting the principles and general rules of civil liability to specific situations that may arise as a result of anticompetitive behaviour. In this process, the principles and objectives of competition and antitrust regulations must be respected. Consequently, the scenario is generally presented with the structural elements of civil liability, and from the most particular, sifting this responsibility by the guiding principles and specific rules of competition.[51]

New section 62 of the LDC provides that: 'Human or legal persons damaged by the acts prohibited by this law, may exercise the action of reparation of damages according to the rules of general law, before the competent judge in that matter'. That is, the right of those affected by acts prohibited by the LDC, will be governed by the general civil liability regime of the Argentine Civil and Commercial Code (sections 1708–1780).

Having said that, it will be necessary to clarify in the first place which is the nature of this responsibility resulting from anticompetitive illicit acts. Some consider that the responsibility in these cases is contractual, be it in situations of restrictive agreements or abuses of dominant position. That is, a pre-existing bargaining relationship would be affected by the anticompetitive illicit, by default of one or both parties.

In our opinion, the responsibility for anticompetitive illicit acts is mainly non-contractual. Any agreement, in whole or in part, written or unwritten, that is held in violation of the antitrust rules is null and void and, consequently, does not generate any contractual relationship between the parties. We consider this is also applicable to those cases in which a breach of contract is generated as a result of an anticompetitive, collusive, exploitative or exclusive illicit, since in these cases it will not be the anticompetitive conduct itself that grounds the action of liability, but the consequences or effects of that conduct on contractual obligations.

Also, as we stated at the beginning of this work, it should be taken into consideration that competition principles have received constitutional status in our

50. Trevisán, Pablo (2016), *Acción Preventiva de Daños y Defensa de la Competencia,* RCCyC, 4 April 2016, pp. 63 & ss., Ed. La Ley, Buenos Aires, 2016.
51. De la Vega, Fernando, *Responsabilidad Civil Derivada del Ilícito Concurrencial, Resarcimiento del Daño Causado al Competidor*, Civitas, Madrid, 2001, p. 56. This author argues that '(...) civil liability for damages caused by unlawful acts of concurrence should not be considered, therefore, as a sanction proper to Competition Law, is a legal consequence that derives from a behavior performed in a market scope with concurrent purpose and that has as a normative element of an essential and primary nature the rules of civil liability, leaving in the background the legal arrangement of the concurrential activity (...)'.

country in the last reform of 1994, being then a right and obligation that is imposed on all contracting parties. That is, this principle accepted by our National Constitution (section 42[52]), constitutes a clear limit to the autonomy of will of the contracting parties and, therefore, is an obligation that does not require an express contractual agreement.[53]

On the other hand, and although the LDC only includes express provisions referring to the nullity of the legal acts prohibited by it under the new section 2, we consider that the terms of the LDC (section 1) are sufficient grounds to cause the nullities provided in the Civil and Commercial Code in relation to said acts.[54]

Among other important reforms that the LDC introduces in this topic, the so-called 'follow-on actions' stand out, that is, those actions that derive from those cases in which the ANC had previously resolved, as provided in section 63[55] of the new LDC.

Notwithstanding the aforesaid, having special consideration of the essentially economic nature of antitrust issues, we also consider that in those cases in which there was no prior resolution of the ANC, the judges intervening in the cases for reparation of damages for anticompetitive conducts may request that the enforcement authority issue an opinion.

---

52. CN, section 42: 'Consumers and users of goods and services have the right, in the consumer relationship, to the protection of their health, safety and economic interests; to adequate and truthful information; to freedom of choice, and to conditions of equitable and dignified treatment. The authorities will provide the protection of these rights, education for consumption, the defense of competition against all forms of market distortion, the control of natural and legal monopolies, the quality and efficiency of services public, and the establishment of associations of consumers and users. The legislation will establish effective procedures for the prevention and resolution of conflicts, and the regulatory frameworks of public services of national competence, providing for the necessary participation of consumer and user associations and the interested provinces, in the control bodies.'
53. Martinez Medrano, Gabriel, *Control de los Monopolios y Defensa de la Competencia*, 1st Ed. Buenos Aires, Depalma, 2002, p. 25, this author maintains that: 'In the 1994 Constitution, third generation rights are enshrined, among which is the right to effective competition. Section 42 of the CN establishes three pillars of the system of effective competition: the freedom of choice of the consumer, the defense of competition against all forms of distortion of the markets and the control of legal or natural monopolies. The free choice of the consumer implies the possibility of choosing among the existing offers in the market, which presupposes that the greatest number of possible offers will be promoted, that is, the participation of the largest number of competitors in the given market.'
54. Cabanellas de las Cuevas, Guillermo (h), *Derecho Antimonopólico y de Defensa de la Competencia*, Ed. Heliasta, Buenos Aires, T. II, p. 393. In the same sense, and even when referring to Velez Sarfield's old Civil Code, this author considers that '(...) the terms of the prohibition included in Section 1 of the LDC are sufficiently broad to give rise to the nullity provided for in Sections 953 and 1,044 of the Civil Code, in a manner consistent with the provisions of Section 18 of the same Code.'
55. Section 63, LDC: 'The decision of the Competition Tribunal on the violation of this law, once it is final, will be res judicata on this matter. The action for reparation of damages that takes place on the occasion of the final decision issued by the Competition Tribunal, will proceed according to the summary procedure established in chapter II of title III, of the second book of the National Code of Civil and Commercial Procedure. The competent judge, when deciding on the repair of damages, will base its ruling on the conducts, facts and legal qualification of the same, established in the resolution of the Competition Tribunal, dictated by reason of the application of the present law.'

In such cases, it will be important to coordinate the judicial actions with the administrative ones. In this sense, the provisions of sections 1774–1780 of the Civil and Commercial Code are fully applicable. Consequently, if the administrative action has been initiated, a judicial civil decision may not be issued until there is no administrative resolution.[56] On the other hand, if there is an administrative conviction, the existence of the infraction or the fault of the defendant should not be discussed in the civil process.[57] On the other hand, if there is an administrative acquittal, it cannot be argued about the existence of the main act on which the acquittal had fallen.[58]

As we anticipated in previous papers,[59] we consider that the wording of Law 25,156 with regard to this issue left aside the requirement for the need of a prior administrative pronouncement. Should the legislator's intention had been to maintain such requirement, the legislator would have established it expressly, as other similar legislations have done,[60] especially taking into account that its predecessor, Law 22,262, expressly required it. We agree with the interpretation given by the dissenting vote in '*Equipos y Controles*',[61] which held that the subtle practices aimed at seeking a dominant position in a market by eliminating significant competition, cannot be left out of the evaluation that the judge must do.

On the other hand, and in line with the concepts previously expressed on the nature of the rules of the LDC, we add with regard to this particular issue that the transgressions to the provisions of the LDC entail the nullity of said acts, agreements or conducts and, therefore, could be articulated directly before the ordinary jurisdiction. This interpretation is a necessary consequence of the general precept of civil law that provides for the nullity of acts and legal business contrary to peremptory norms.[62]

The new LDC has taken a significant step in the right direction, by establishing that the rulings of the Tribunal of the ANC that provide for the violation of the LDC will

56. Cfr. CCyC, Article 1775.
57. Cfr. CCyC, Article 1776.
58. Cfr. CCyC, Article 1777.
59. Trevisán, Pablo (2013), *Indemnización de Daños y Perjuicios por Infracciones a las Normas de Defensa de la Competencia*, JA 2013-IV, Nbr. 4, Ed. La Ley, Buenos Aires, 2013.
60. It is worth mentioning here the case of Chile, which by means of a modification to its legal regime, similar to the new LDC in this matter, incorporated the requirement that the civil judge who knows in cases of damages for anticompetitive illicit acts, must resolve on the basis of the judgment issued by the TDLC. Paradoxically, as of the date of such modification, only one conviction had been made in Chile for damages caused by attacks on free competition (a situation similar to that of our country at the time of writing this chapter). This indicates that until then, there was a clear disincentive in that country to demand compensation for this type of damage, with evident procedural complications. For further information on this particular subject, *see* Lewin Muñoz, Nicolás (2010), *supra*, pp. 44 et seq.
61. National Chamber of Appeals in the Commercial, Room C, Buenos Aires, *Equipos y Controles S.A. s/Concurso Preventivo s/Incidente de Apelación*, of 27 December 2002, El Derecho, 1 December 2003, pp. 9 and ss.
62. Uría Fernández, Francisco, *Las Consecuencias Jurídico-Privadas de las Conductas Contrarias a la Ley de Defensa de la Competencia. Aportaciones de la Ley 52/1999*, Yearbook of Competition 1999, Madrid-Barcelona, 2000, pp. 171 et seq. This author provides valuable concepts and comes to the same conclusion, applied to the case of Spain, which in this sense has a legal configuration similar to that of our country.

be res judicata on the matter, in order that these can then serve as basis to the judges[63] and the parties to the process (i.e., the aforementioned 'follow-on actions').[64] This, as we have been claiming for some time,[65] in addition to lightening the burden of proof of the victims, will also allow the procedures to be processed not by the ordinary route – as it happened until the sanction of the new LDC –, but through a more expeditious judicial procedure. Something similar is available to the European Commission in analogous issues to those mentioned here, through the scope established by the Damages Directive of 2014.[66]

Another important change, on section 64 of the new LDC, introduces the possibility that the victim of an anticompetitive conduct may expressly request before the judge that the offender be imposed a civil penalty of a punitive nature[67] in favour of the injured party.

The punitive damage is a kind of accessory civil penalty,[68] which is added to the compensation for damages – being of a compensatory nature –, applied for the benefit

63. It should be noted here what happened in the case of *AutoGas*, long before the entry into force of the new LDC, in which the Judge, in Recital II, Point 1 of his sentence, ruled: 'For which it is necessary to remember that with regard to the abuse of a dominant position, this aspect has been definitively decided. This in response to the opinion of the National Commission for the Defense of Competition that concluded with the sanction imposed on YPF SA by the Ministry of Industry, Commerce and Mining through resolution no. 189/99 (Annex V of the application). Who deserved full reception by Room B of the National Chamber of Appeals in Economic Criminal in the ruling of 24.11.2000 (Annex VI of the complaint) confirmed by the Supreme Court of Justice of the Nation.'
64. Komninos, Assimakis, *Private Enforcement: An Overview of EU and National Case Law*, Prologue to the Special Issue of e-Competitions, No. 44442, www.concurrences.com. This author, on the subject of follow-on-action, mentions that in general, in Europe, 'a comparative analysis of national competition laws shows that although a prior decision of the administrative authority could be used by courts and litigants to establish and prove certain facts, in civil actions follow-on, said prior administrative decision does not normally acquire the status of binding authority, although it could be considered persuasive authority. However, some Member States have introduced the rule whereby civil courts are bound by the final decisions of the national competition authorities in follow-on actions of damages determination.'
65. Trevisán, Pablo (2013), *supra*.
66. The direct precedent of the Antitrust Directive of Europe, the 'Communication from the Commission on the quantification of damages in claims for damages for breach of Articles 101 or 102 of the Treaty on the Functioning of the European Union', (2013 / C 167/07), published in the Official Journal of the European Union, C. 167/19, Strasbourg, on June 11, 2013, when it maintained that: 'In accordance with Article 16, paragraph 1, of Regulation No 1/2003, decisions of the Commission relating to proceedings under Sections 101 or 102 of the Treaty have probative effect in subsequent claims for damages, since a national court can not adopt resolutions likely to enter into conflict with such decisions of the Commission. It is appropriate to grant a similar effect to the final decisions of infringement adopted by the national competition authorities (or by a national court for review). If an infringement decision has already been adopted and has become final, the possibility that the offending company would raise the same issues in subsequent claims for damages would be inefficient, would generate legal uncertainty and would lead to unnecessary costs for all parties involved and the judicial power.'
67. Lorenzetti, Ricardo L., *La responsabilidad civil*, LLP, 2002-1302. In this work, Lorenzetti argues that one of the main functions of civil liability is the preventive function, which is fulfilled through inhibitory protection and which includes, among other institutes, punitive damages.
68. For a broad and comparative development of civil fines or punitive damages, *see* Chamatropulos, Alejandro D., *Los Daños Punitivos en las Normas de Protección a la Competencia y al*

of the victim, with the purpose of punishing the person who incurs serious misconduct and the ultimate objective of creating more deterrence for those who cause or may cause harm.[69] These are granted to the victim of damages beyond the actual damages suffered, that are granted in addition to the patrimonial and the non-pecuniary damage.[70]

Without intending to delve into the analysis of this institute, since this would by far exceed the object of this work, we must mention briefly that this institute is under development in Argentina and at the centre of the debate.[71] In this sense, some have argued their unconstitutionality,[72] on the basis that it would violate certain constitutional guarantees (e.g., the right of *non bis in idem*) and that strictly speaking – in the case of a retributive sanction – it should be framed within the guarantees and principles of criminal law for crimes and penalties. We anticipate our opinion that the institute is absolutely constitutional (following the previous example, the right of *non bis in idem* would not be violated, since the punitive damage would be an accessory condemnation of the principal), in addition to considering that our legislator has previously admitted other similar institutes that have the objective of preventing the person who causes damage from taking advantage of its illegality.[73]

That said, we consider that for the purposes of this chapter, this institute is presented as a tool of undoubted value to reinforce deterrence of potential offenders to the LDC, limit the abuses of certain companies and, especially, avoid situations in which it would seem cheaper to carry out the damage and then compensate it, rather than avoid it directly.

The Discussion on Criminalization

It is widely accepted that cartelization reduces competition in markets to the detriment of consumers and, therefore, is prohibited in all jurisdictions that have antitrust legislation.

Consumidor: Análisis Comparativo, in *Comentarios a la Ley de Defensa de la Competencia*, Trevisán - Del Pino - Chamatropulos, Thomson Reuters La Ley, 2018.

69. Vítolo, Daniel Roque, *Sanciones Pecuniarias Disuasivas*, Diario La Ley, 4 September 2013, p. 2. In his work, this author presents a similar definition of the institute, makes a valuable introductory analysis of punitive damages, analyses in detail the current text of Section 52 bis of Law 24,140 of Consumer Protection and makes a criticism based on the virtues and defects of the new proposals presented in this matter in the Civil and Commercial Code.
70. Sanchez Costa, Pablo F., *Los daños punitivos y su inclusión en la ley de defensa del consumidor*, Diario La Ley, 20 July 2009, p. 2.
71. For an in-depth analysis of this institute, *see*: López Herrera, Edgardo, *Los Daños Punitivos*, Abeledo Perrot, 2nd Ed. 2011; Pizarro, Ramón D., *Daños Punitivos*, in *Derecho de Daños*, 2nd part. Tribute to Professor Félix Alberto Trigo Represas, Buenos Aires, La Rocca, 1993.
72. Picasso, Sebastián, *Sobre los denominados daños punitivos*, La Ley, 2007-F, p. 1154.
73. To name a few examples, we have in our legislation the possibility of signing criminal clauses (section 656, former Civil Code), the astreintes (section 666 bis, former Civil Code), punitive or sanctioning interests (section 45, National Civil and Commercial Procedural Code).

Recent experience indicates that administrative fines may not be sufficiently dissuasive among certain employers. Some authors even suggest that corporate collusion often remains profitable, net of fines and damages.[74]

Thus, we propose that it is necessary to focus on the persons who participate in cartels, on behalf of their employers. Although in general it is the companies that are declared responsible, strictly speaking, it is the people who carry out the crime or those who carry out the 'dirty' work. Executives who carry out anticompetitive acts on behalf of the companies they represent, will be effectively discouraged from carrying out those acts when they consider that there is a reasonable risk of being personally affected by the sanction. This could be achieved mainly through sanctions of imprisonment.

These sanctions also attempt to address the problems such as: (i) that the imposition of fines on companies – including those that are very substantial – may not have a sufficient deterrent effect, especially when the cost of fines is simply transferred to customers through higher prices; and (ii) when a fine is so large that it may result in the insolvency and subsequent liquidation of a company, constituting an unintended consequence, which will result in the loss of a market competitor, a perverse achievement for a system of competition.[75]

As we know, prison sanctions are an important feature of US antitrust law, where many high-profile cases have taken place in recent years in which top executives of the major companies served some time in prison. Some EU Member States also have some form of criminal sanctions in their respective antitrust frameworks.

This trend has also reached countries in Latin America, such as Brazil or Chile, for example, which recently reformed its competition law, including prison sanctions.[76]

While the draft bill of the LDC was being prepared, the inclusion of imprisonment for the most serious cases (i.e., the intrinsically harmful cartels) was seriously considered. Finally, it was decided not to include prison sanctions in the LDC, following a gradualism criterion, and considering that Argentina has gone through more than a decade of poor enforcement of competition law and policy.

However, we seriously consider that colluding among competitors to establish anticompetitive prices is nothing other than stealing. Consequently, it could be reasonable to conclude that collusion between competitors constitutes a crime.

In this sense, there would be no conceptual difference between the artificial fixing of prices between competitors and stealing. The difference lies in the degree of social effect of cartelization practices among competitors, these being more onerous, since cartelization among competitors presents a much more serious and much more extensive economic damage.

---

74. Foer, Albert, Ginsburg, Douglas H., Lande, Robert H. & Wright, Joshua, *DOJ Has the Power to Crush Price-Fixers: Column*, USA Today Weekend, 29-31 May 2015, at 11A.
75. Whish, Richard & Bailey, David, 452 Competition Law (8th Ed. 2015).
76. They established – after a long discussion, the result of which led to the inclusion of prison sentences when certain incidents came to light regarding how parties to a cartel had thrown computers into a river to destroy evidence – prison sanctions for up to ten years, with a minimum period of effective imprisonment.

Those who argue that it would have been imprudent to incorporate sanctions of imprisonment to Argentine competition law and policy, base their arguments on the potential risk of abuses that could result from such sanctions, or that few would be convicted. Under this reasoning, similar arguments could be considered to avoid penalizing crimes such as money laundering.

However, if the real goal is to promote a deep cultural change to emphasize the values of competition, the system should establish serious and individual punishments for those who violate those values. On the other hand, attention should not be focused on achieving the highest number of convicts, but on avoiding or preventing anticompetitive collusive acts.

The discussion is open.

§16.03 CONCLUSION

The biggest challenge in the medium and long term is to ensure that in Argentina, definitively, competition law and policy are consolidated as a public policy.

The political and social reality of our country has reflected a serious lack of institutionalism in the field of competition, while a significant degree of general disinformation and ignorance in the matter is perceived, both among consumers and between businessmen and public officials. The efforts made in recent years by the enforcement authority and the recent sanction of the new LDC allow us to be very optimistic about the future of antitrust enforcement in our country.

In the immediate term, as we have said, the greatest challenge will be the institutional one, since much of all the good efforts done up to now, together with the intrinsic benefits presented by the new LDC, will depend to a large extent on the institutional context that contains them. Repeating the mistakes of the past would be unforgivable. Sooner rather than later, the institutional design devised and created by the legislator should be fully operational. When this happens, it will be very interesting to observe in practice how the ANC will work, from the orbit of the administration, together with the Specialized Chamber on Competition Matters, with an axis in the Judicial Branch.

Within this context of greater institutionalism, and immersing competition law and policy in a wider legal-economic context in which it must increase and maintain a permanent dialogue with other branches of law, the scenario for the successful implementation of the new tools and institutes created under the new LDC, such as, among others, the ex-ante merger control system, the private enforcement through damages actions for anticompetitive conducts and a solid and modern leniency programme, take real force and contribute to achieve the common objective, which is to protect and promote the general economic interest, the legal right protected by the LDC.

Everything is yet to be seen, but the moment of the great challenges is now.

Part V Final Remarks

CHAPTER 17

Global Competition Enforcement: What's Ahead?

William Evan Kovacic & Paulo Burnier da Silveira

The contributions in the book "Global Competition Enforcement: New Players, New Challenges" shared a great number of enforcement experiences ranging from those of leading emerging economies (i.e., BRICS countries) to smaller economies (i.e., Mauritius and Colombia) and mature economies (i.e., Japan and Australia).

The main idea of the book was to give voice to jurisdictions that are often less heard in the international fora. This allows us to learn from their rich experiences and to offer a better view of the state of art in competition enforcement around the globe. The study of case law has a great value to the understanding of competition law in practice.

With this in mind, the last essay of the book highlights three key aspects that arise from the chapters and may likely guide global competition enforcement in the next few years:

(1) digital economy as a great global competition challenge;
(2) domestic cooperation as an extra tool to fight cartels and corruption; and
(3) international cooperation as a necessary instrument to foster convergence.

A better assessment of these aspects follows below. At the end, this contribution will conclude with final remarks on future perspectives for global competition enforcement.

§17.01 DIGITAL ECONOMY AS A GREAT GLOBAL COMPETITION CHALLENGE

Over the past years, a great number of competition authorities expressed concerns about digital economy issues. In addition to exploring the precise scope of its competition issues, enforcers sought to understand the best place of competition enforcement considering the multidisciplinary features of digital economy. A second stage is the enforcement of competition laws itself, which requires dealing with the challenges in practice. In many jurisdictions, digital issues are being reviewed through merger control and fight against cartels and abuse of dominance cases.

In merger review, one challenge concerns the criteria for merger notifications. The business in digital economy may have particularities including the absence of turnover in several countries due to its offers of "free" services (Facebook, WhatsApp, Waze, etc.). Considering that most jurisdictions require a minimum turnover of both acquiring and acquired companies to trigger a mandatory notification, enforcers have been discussing new ways of reviewing these transactions. The idea of adopting additional criteria based on the transaction value has emerged and a couple of countries have already adopted this strategy. In addition to the criteria for notification, there are also other challenges such as the definition of markets as well as the concept of market-power which is often related to the first.

As for anticompetitive practices, the main concern is related to cases of abuse of dominance. It seems clear today that tech companies may abuse their dominant positions. The Google Shopping case is an interesting example as it has been analyzed in several jurisdictions including the U.S., the European Union and Brazil. In Europe, the case led to a severe conviction, while in the U.S. it was filed as the FTC choose not to challenge the case before the Judiciary. In Brazil, the decision was split in half by CADE's board members (3 x 3), which forced CADE's president to use his casting vote to break the deadlock and untie the final decision. It was nevertheless stressed that Google was understood to have a dominant position, as well as the capacity and the incentives to abuse of its market-power; thus elements that enabled the exercise of its dominance and potentially market abuses.

The main message is that competition authorities are paying careful attention to competition issues in the digital economy. The particularities of digital economy, including its network effects and data management, justify a fresh look at traditional tools used for antitrust analysis of abuse of dominance cases. In this sense, exclusionary behaviors in the digital economy should be monitored by competition authorities, in order to assure the presence of proper incentives for innovation. One should always remember that competition drives quality even in "free" markets.

§17.02 DOMESTIC COOPERATION AS AN EXTRA TOOL TO FIGHT CARTELS AND CORRUPTION

Recent enforcement experiences suggest that competition policy will likely benefit from its interface with other related areas including anti-corruption efforts. The strongest example was in Brazil where the "Car Wash" investigations lead to a significant impact in the fight against cartels. Besides highlighting the importance of leniency programs as a means to detect wrongdoing, the case is widely recognized as a success story of cooperation among competition and anti-corruption enforcers.

One should also note that the "Car Wash" operation had a regional impact as other Latin American countries began similar investigations. The cases combine collusion in public procurements and corruption at political levels, which are aggravated by cultural issues that have prevailed in certain countries for decades. Domestic cooperation among national enforcers will likely play an equally important role in these jurisdictions.

Another effect of "Car Wash" cases is the proliferation of compliance programs. It seems that companies have decided to invest in a compliance strategy, which has been seen as a real competitive advantage in business. It takes less to prevent than to cure antitrust wrongdoings. As for competition authorities, they have also noticed that is often better to prevent than to punish anticompetitive practices, so many have encouraged compliance efforts through advocacy strategies and other incentives such as fine discounts.

In sum, bid-rigging investigations have increased at national levels in developing countries, which is great news for global competition. At the same time, civil actions will likely increase worldwide in the following years. This trend will require careful legal treatment of documents in order to preserve the proper incentives for future leniency applications. The full impact of these investigations is yet to be determined but certain benefits are already widely observed.

§17.03 INTERNATIONAL COOPERATION AS A NECESSARY INSTRUMENT TO FOSTER CONVERGENCE

International cooperation will continue to play a relevant role in global competition enforcement.

Looking back, international cooperation played a special role in transnational merger control. Since the GE/Honeywell transaction in 2001, when the European Commission decided to block a global merger in spite of its clearance in the U.S., huge efforts in international cooperation were taken to reduce the chances of inconsistent decisions in merger control around the world. The International Competition Network (ICN) emerged as its finest example, with dozens of documents build by consensus such as guidelines and recommendations to competition authorities.

Looking ahead, it seems that international cooperation will have a greater role in other enforcement areas including cartel investigations and abuse of dominance cases. Some concrete examples are the toilet paper cartel case in Latin America as well as the frequent exchanges concerning big tech investigations among key competition authorities around the globe. In addition, non-enforcement activities, such as advocacy strategies, are also likely to play a greater role. Examples include the recent joint statement released by the so-called Latin American Alliance which gathers competition authorities from Argentina, Brazil, Chile, Peru and Mexico.

Last but not least, training programs are now a current practice around the world. Many institutions are supporting initiatives in this sense (OECD, ICN, UNCTAD, Universities, etc.). They are also a dimension of international cooperation and they have certainly helped to train enforcers and judges around the world. It is indeed important to level the playing field considering that companies often hire the best competition lawyers and economists to defend their interests. The training programs also create a competition culture, which is important for many developing countries as it was seen in the contribution related to State-Owned-Enterprises (SOEs).

§17.04 FINAL REMARKS

It is no secret that competition enforcement has become global. Today more than 100 countries have a competition law, most with similar provisions to tackle cartels, fight abuses of dominant firms and review mergers. At the same time, countries have different histories and may disagree about legitimately different priorities, which partially explains some nuances in the application of competition laws around the globe. In this sense, the efforts of convergence in global antitrust should serve both a general and a specific purpose: more broadly, it should aim to increase the general consumer welfare in the world; more specifically, it should help to achieve better lives for people in each jurisdiction concerned. This will enable competition authorities to gain local legitimacy in order to invest more time and energy in addressing global competition issues.

INTERNATIONAL COMPETITION LAW SERIES

1. Ignacio De Leon, *Latin American Competition Law and Policy: A Policy in Search of Identity*, 2001 (ISBN 90-411-1542-0).
2. Wim Dejonghe & Wouter Van de Voorde (eds), *M & A in Belgium*, 2001 (ISBN 90-411-1594-3).
3. Yang-Ching Chao, Gee San, Changfa Lo & Jiming Ho (eds), *International and Comparative Competition Law and Policies*, 2001 (ISBN 90-411-1643-5).
4. Martin Mendelsohn & Stephen Rose, *Guide to the EC Block Exemption for Vertical Agreements*, 2002 (ISBN 90-411-9813-X).
5. Clifford A. Jones & Mitsuo Matsushita (eds), *Competition Policy in the Global Trading System: Perspectives from the EU, Japan and the USA*, 2002 (ISBN 90-411-1758-X).
6. Christian Koenig, Andreas Bartosch, Jens-Daniel Braun & Marion Romes (eds), *EC Competition and Telecommunications Law*. Second Edition, 2009 (ISBN 978-90-411-2564-4).
7. Jürgen Basedow (ed.), *Limits and Control of Competition with a View to International Harmonization*, 2002 (ISBN 90-411-1967-1).
8. Maureen Brunt, Economic Essays on Australian and New Zealand Competition Law, 2003 (ISBN 90-411-1991-4).
9. Ky P. Ewing, Jr., *Competition Rules for the 21st Century: Principles from America's Experience*, Second Edition, 2006 (ISBN 90-411-2477-2).
10. Joseph Wilson, *Globalization and the Limits of National Merger Control Laws*, 2003 (ISBN 90-411-1996-5).
11. Peter Verloop & Valérie Landes (eds), *Merger Control in Europe: EU, Member States and Accession States*, Fourth Edition, 2003 (ISBN 90-411-2056-4).
12. Themistoklis K. Giannakopoulos, *Safeguarding Companies' Rights in Competition and Anti-dumping/Anti-subsidies Proceedings*, Second Edition, 2011 (ISBN 978-90-411-3404-2).
13. Marjorie Holmes & Lesley Davey (eds), *A Practical Guide to National Competition Rules across Europe*, Second Edition, 2007 (ISBN 978-90- 411-2607-8).
14. Sigrid Stroux, *US and EU Oligopoly Control*, 2004 (ISBN 90-411-2296-6).
15. Tzong-Leh Hwang and Chiyuan Chen (eds), *The Future Development of Competition Framework*, 2004 (ISBN 90-411-2305-9).

16. Phedon Nicolaides, Mihalis Kekelekis and Maria Kleis, *State Aid Policy in the European Community: Principles and Practice,* Second Edition, 2008 (ISBN 978-90-411-2754-9).
17. Doris Hildebrand, *Economic Analyses of Vertical Agreements: A Self- Assessment,* 2005 (ISBN 90-411-2328-8).
18. Frauke Henning-Bodewig, *Unfair Competition Law: European Union and Member States*, 2005 (ISBN 90-411-2329-6).
19. Duarte Brito & Margarida Catalão-Lopes, *Mergers and Acquisitions: The Industrial Organization Perspective,* 2006 (ISBN 90-411-2451-9).
20. Nikos Th. Nikolinakos, *EU Competition Law and Regulation in the Converging Telecommunications, Media and IT Sectors*, 2006 (ISBN 90-411- 2469-1).
21. Mihalis Kekelekis, *The EC Merger Control Regulation: Rights of Defence. A Critical Analysis of DG COMP Practice and Community Courts' Jurisprudence*, 2006 (ISBN 90-411-2553-1).
22. Mark R. Joelson, *An International Antitrust Primer: A Guide to the Operation of United States, European Union and Other Key Competition Laws in the Global Economy*, Third Edition, 2006 (ISBN 90-411-2468-3).
23. Themistoklis K. Giannakopoulos, *A Concise Guide to the EU Anti-dumping/ Anti-subsidies Procedures*, 2006 (ISBN 90-411-2464-0).
24. George Cumming, Brad Spitz & Ruth Janal, *Civil Procedure Used for Enforcement of EC Competition Law by the English, French and German Civil Courts*, 2007 (ISBN 978-90-411-2471-5).
25. Jürgen Basedow (ed.), *Private Enforcement of EC Competition Law,* 2007 (ISBN 978-90-411-2613-9).
26. Jung Wook Cho, *Innovation and Competition in the Digital Network Economy: A Legal and Economic Assessment on Multi-tying Practices and Network Effects*, 2007 (ISBN 978-90-411-2574-3).
27. Akira Inoue, *Japanese Antitrust Law Manual: Law, Cases and Interpretation of the Japanese Antimonopoly Act*, 2007 (ISBN 978-90-411-2627-6).
28. René Barents, *Directory of EC Case Law on Competition,* 2007 (ISBN 978-90-411-2656-6).
29. Paul F. Nemitz (ed.), *The Effective Application of EU State Aid Procedures: The Role of National Law and Practice*, 2007 (ISBN 978-90-411-2657-3).
30. Jurian Langer, *Tying and Bundling as a Leveraging Concern under EC Competition Law,* 2007 (ISBN 978-90-411-2575-0).
31. Abel M. Mateus & Teresa Moreira (eds), *Competition Law and Economics – Advances in Competition Policy and Antitrust Enforcement*, 2007 (ISBN 978-90-411-2632-0).
32. Alberto Santa Maria, *Competition and State Aid: An Analysis of the EC Practice*, 2007 (ISBN 978-90-411-2617-7).
33. Barry J. Rodger (ed.), *Article 234 and Competition Law: An Analysis,* 2007 (ISBN 978-90-411-2605-4).

34. Alla Pozdnakova, *Liner Shipping and EU Competition Law*, 2008 (ISBN 978-90-411-2717-4).
35. Milena Stoyanova, *Competition Problems in Liberalized Telecommunications: Regulatory Solutions to Promote Effective Competition*, 2008 (ISBN 978-90-411-2736-5).
36. *EC State Aid Law/Le Droit des Aides d'Etat dans la CE. Liber Amicorum Francisco Santaolalla Gadea*, 2008 (ISBN 978-90-411-2774-7).
37. René Barents, *Directory of EC Case Law on State Aids*, 2008 (ISBN 978- 90-411-2732-7).
38. Ignacio De Leon, *An Institutional Assessment of Antitrust Policy: The Latin American Experience*, 2009 (ISBN 978-90-411-2478-4).
39. Doris Hildebrand, *The Role of Economic Analysis in EU Competition Law: The European School*, Fourth Edition, 2016 (ISBN 978-90-411-6245-8).
40. Eugène Buttigieg, *Competition Law: Safeguarding the Consumer Interest. A Comparative Analysis of US Antitrust Law and EC Competition Law*, 2009 (ISBN 978-90-411-3119-5).
41. Ioannis Lianos & Ioannis Kokkoris (eds), *The Reform of EC Competition Law: New Challenges*, 2010 (ISBN 978-90-411-2692-4).
42. George Cumming & Mirjam Freudenthal, *Civil Procedure in EU Competition Cases before the English and Dutch Courts*, 2010 (ISBN 978-90-411-3192-8).
43. A.E. Rodriguez & Ashok Menon, *The Limits of Competition Policy: The Shortcomings of Antitrust in Developing and Reforming Economies*, 2010 (ISBN 978-90-411-3177-5).
44. Mika Oinonen, *Does EU Merger Control Discriminate against Small Market Companies? Diagnosing the Argument with Conclusions*, 2010 (ISBN 978-90-411-3261-1).
45. Eirik Østerud, *Identifying Exclusionary Abuses by Dominant Undertakings under EU Competition Law: The Spectrum of Tests*, 2010 (ISBN 978-90-411-3271-0).
46. Marco Botta, *Merger Control Regimes in Emerging Economies: A Case Study on Brazil and Argentina*, 2011 (ISBN 978-90-411-3402-8).
47. Jürgen Basedow & Wolfgang Wurmnest (eds), *Structure and Effects in EU Competition Law: Studies on Exclusionary Conduct and State Aid*, 2011 (ISBN 978-90-411-3174-4).
48. George Cumming (ed.), *Merger Decisions and the Rules of Procedure of the European Community Courts*, 2012 (ISBN 978-90-411-3671-8).
49. Eduardo Molan Gaban & Juliana Oliveira Domingues (eds), *Antitrust Law in Brazil: Fighting Cartels*, 2012 (ISBN 978-90-411-3670-1).
50. Giandonato Caggiano, Gabriella Muscolo & Marina Tavassi (eds), *Competition Law and Intellectual Property: A European Perspective*, 2012 (ISBN 978-90-411-3447-9).
51. Ben Van Rompuy, *Economic Efficiency: The Sole Concern of Modern Antitrust Policy? Non-efficiency Considerations under Article 101 TFEU*, 2012 (ISBN 978-90-411-3870-5).

52. Liyang Hou, *Competition Law and Regulation of the EU Electronic Communications Sector: A Comparative Legal Approach*, 2012 (ISBN 978-90-411-4047-0).
53. Barry Rodger, *Landmark Cases in Competition Law: Around the World in Fourteen Stories*, 2012 (ISBN 978-90-411-3843-9).
54. Andreas Scordamaglia-Tousis, *EU Cartel Enforcement: Reconciling Effective Public Enforcement with Fundamental Rights*, 2013 (ISBN 978-90-411-4758-5).
55. Bernardo Cortese (ed.), *EU Competition Law: Between Public and Private Enforcement*, 2014 (ISBN 978-90-411-4677-9).
56. Barry Rodger (ed.), *Competition Law: Comparative Private Enforcement and Collective Redress across the EU*, 2014 (ISBN 978-90-411-4559-8).
57. Nada Ina Pauer, *The Single Economic Entity Doctrine and Corporate Group Responsibility in European Antitrust Law*, 2014 (ISBN 978-90-411-5262-6).
58. Urška Petrovčič, *Competition Law and Standard Essential Patents: A Transatlantic Perspective*, 2014 (ISBN 978-90-411-4960-2).
59. David Telyas, *The Interface between Competition Law, Patents and Technical Standards*, 2014 (ISBN 978-90-411-5418-7).
60. Katerina Maniadaki, *EU Competition Law, Regulation and the Internet: The Case of Net Neutrality*, 2014 (ISBN 978-90-411-4140-8).
61. Horacio Vedia Jerez, *Competition Law Enforcement and Compliance across the World: A Comparative Review*, 2015 (ISBN 978-90-411-5815-4).
62. Kadir Ba, *The Substantive Appraisal of Joint Ventures under the EU Merger Control Regime*, 2015 (ISBN 978-90-411-5816-1).
63. Alberto Santa Maria, *Competition and State Aid: An Analysis of the EU Practice*, Second Edition, 2015 (ISBN 978-90-411-5818-5).
64. Lúcio Tomé Feteira, *The Interplay between European and National Competition Law after Regulation 1/2003: "United (Should) We Stand?"*, 2016 (ISBN 978-90-411-5663-1).
65. Giovanni Pitruzzella & Gabriella Muscolo (eds), *Competition and Patent Law in the Pharmaceutical Sector: An International Perspective*, 2016 (ISBN 978-90-411-5927-4).
66. Małgorzata Cyndecka, *The Market Economy Investor Test in EU State Aid Law: Applicability and Application*, 2016 (ISBN 978-90-411-6102-4).
67. Damiano Canapa, *Trademarks and Brands in Merger Control: An Analysis of the European and Swiss Legal Orders*, 2016 (ISBN 978-90-411-6717-0).
68. Inge Graef, *EU Competition Law, Data Protection and Online Platforms: Data as Essential Facility*, 2016 (ISBN 978-90-411-8324-8).
69. Anders Jessen, *Exclusionary Abuse after the* Post Danmark I *Case: The Role of the Effects-Based Approach under Article 102 TFEU*, 2017 (ISBN 978-90-411-8996-7).
70. Baskaran Balasingham, *The EU Leniency Policy: Reconciling Effectiveness and Fairness*, 2017 (ISBN 978-90-411-8479-5).
71. Eugene Stuart & Iana Roginska-Green, *Sixty Years of EU State Aid Law and Policy: Analysis and Assessment*, 2018 (ISBN 978-90-411-8869-4).

72. Anna Renata Pisarkiewicz, *Margin Squeeze in the Electronic Communications Sector: Critical Analysis of the Decisional Practice and Case Law,* 2018 (ISBN 978-90-411-6246-5).
73. Ploykaew Porananond, *Competition Law in the ASEAN Countries: Regional Law and National Systems,* 2018 (ISBN 978-90-411-9102-1).
74. Corinne Ruechardt, *EU State Aid Control of Infrastructure Funding,* 2018 (ISBN 978-90-411-9099-4).
75. Amalia Athanasiadou, *Patent Settlements in the Pharmaceutical Industry under US Antitrust and EU Competition Law,* 2018 (ISBN 978-94-035-0113-0).
76. Miroslava Marinova, *Fidelity Rebates in Competition Law: Application of the 'As Efficient Competitor' Test,* 2018 (ISBN 978-94-035-0570-1).
77. Gabriella Muscolo & Marina Tavassi, *The Interplay Between Competition Law and Intellectual Property: An International Perspective,* 2019 (ISBN 978-90-411-8687-4).
78. Fevzi Toksoy, Bahadir Balki & Hanna Stakheyeva, *Merger Control in the EU and Turkey: A Comparative Guide*, 2019 (ISBN 978-94-035-0934-1).
79. Paulo Burnier da Silveira & William Evan Kovacic (eds), *Global Competition Enforcement: New Players, New Challenges*, 2019 (ISBN 978-94-035-0283-0).

www.ingramcontent.com/pod-product-compliance
Lightning Source LLC
Chambersburg PA
CBHW071239230926
51849CB00001B/153